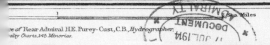

The Power
and the Glory

The Power and the Glory

Royal Navy Fleet Reviews from Earliest Times to 2005

STEVE R DUNN

Seaforth PUBLISHING

Title pages: The royal yacht passing through the lines of warships during the Coronation Review of 1911. An admiral's barge is in the foreground and a battleship to the left with decks manned and yards dressed. *(Alamy KRD1JT)*

By the same author

Battle in the Baltic: The Royal Navy and the Fight to Save Estonia and Latvia, 1918-1920
Southern Thunder: The Royal Navy and the Scandinavian Trade in World War One
Bayly's War: The Battle for the Western Approaches in World War One
Securing the Narrow Sea: The Dover Patrol 1914-1918
Blockade: Cruiser Warfare and the Starvation of Germany
Formidable: A true story of disaster and courage
The Coward? The Rise and Fall of the Silver King
The Scapegoat: The Life and Tragedy of a Fighting Admiral and Churchill's role in his death

www.steverdunn.com

Copyright © Steve R Dunn 2021
First published in Great Britain in 2021 by
Seaforth Publishing,
A division of Pen & Sword Books Ltd,
47 Church Street,
Barnsley S70 2AS
www.seaforthpublishing.com
British Library Cataloguing in Publication Data
A catalogue record for this book is available from the British Library

ISBN 978 1 5267 6902 2 (HARDBACK)
ISBN 978 1 5267 6903 9 (EPUB)
ISBN 978 1 5267 6904 6 (KINDLE)

Pen & Sword Books Limited incorporates the imprints of Atlas, Archaeology, Aviation, Discovery, Family History, Fiction, History, Maritime, Military, Military Classics, Politics, Select, Transport, True Crime, Air World, Frontline Publishing, Leo Cooper, Remember When, Seaforth Publishing, The Praetorian Press, Wharncliffe Local History, Wharncliffe Transport, Wharncliffe True Crime and White Owl

Typeset and designed by Stephen Dent
Printed and bound in India by Replika Press Pvt Ltd

Contents

Preface   8

Part One: Beginnings
1. The Sea and Britain   12
2. What is a Royal Fleet Review?   20
3. Frightening the French, 1346–1415   24
4. The Stuarts and the Glorious Revolution, 1662–1714   31
5. The House of Hanover, 1714–1837   41

Part Two: Victorian and Edwardian Pomp
6. Emperors, Kings and Princes, 1842–1845   58
7. Crimean Imbroglio, 1853–1856   73
8. France and Eastern Concerns, 1865–1878   89
9. Golden Years, 1887–1896   108
10. Diamond Jubilee, 1897–1901   129
11. Edwardian Splendour, 1902–1910   145

Part Three: Georgian Apotheosis and Decline
12. Countdown to War, 1911–1914   176
13. Finance and Silver Jubilee, 1919–1935   191
14. German *Revanche*, 1936–1944   210

Part Four: The Ebb Tide
15. Decline …, 1945–1977   228
16. … and Fall, 1993–2005   253
17. The Royal Yacht   272
18. Conclusions   281

Envoi   289

List of Royal Fleet Reviews from 1346 to 2005   290

Appendices
1. Ships' Rates, Seventeenth to Nineteenth Century   292
2. Queen Victoria's Navy, 1837   293
3. The Royal Navy Fleet in 1897   294

4. Foreign Navy Ships at the 1897 Diamond Jubilee Review   295
5. Foreign Navy Ships at the 1911 Coronation Review   295
6. Foreign Navy Ships at the 1953 Coronation Review   296
7. Comparison of Royal Navy Fleets, 1953 vs 1977   297
8. Allied Merchant Shipping Losses (All Causes) in the North Atlantic,
     1939–1945   297
9. Main Warships at the BA50 1993 Commemoration   298
10. The Decline of the Royal Navy in the 1990s   299
11. Numbers of Vessels at the 2005 'Trafalgar 200' Fleet Review   300
12. 21 October 2005 Trafalgar Night Dinner Menu   301
13. Ratio of Naval Expenditure to Foreign Trade in the United
     Kingdom Self-governing Dominions and India 1907–1908   302

Author's Note   303

Notes   305

Bibliography   310

Index   314

Dedication

This book is dedicated to the men, women and boys of the Royal Navy, past, present and future.

Others may use the Ocean as their road
Only the English make it their abode.
    Edmund Waller (1606–87), *Of a War with Spain and a Fight at Sea.*

—————

Admirals all, they said their say
(The echoes are ringing still).
Admirals all, they went their way
To the haven under the hill.
But they left us a kingdom none can take –
The realm of the circling sea –
To be ruled by the rightful sons of Blake,
And the Rodneys yet to be.
    Henry Newbolt, *Admirals All, A Song of Sea Kings* (1897).

—————

The liberties of the people and the integrity of the Empire are deeply rooted in constitutional monarchy, and the ancient usages and traditions centring upon the crown have become … a bulwark against dictatorship and the symbol of the union of all the members of the British Commonwealth of nations.
    Resolution of the Select Committee on the Civil List, 26 April 1937.

—————

Last summer green things were greener
Brambles fewer, the blue sky bluer.
    Christina Rossetti, *A Bird Song* (1873).

Preface

———✦———

AS AN ISLAND surrounded by sea, Britain (or more correctly England up until the Act of Union of 1707) has been perforce a maritime nation. Trade, fisheries, communication, defence and conquest abroad all played their role in the making of Britain. And all of these factors led ineluctably to the need for a navy to protect or project such drivers of national wealth and defence.

The navy that came into being was initially a very *ad hoc* affair, men and ships called to serve at their king's command from fishing and trading resources and dissolved and dispensed with by similar caprice. But slowly the navy, the so-called 'Navy-Royal' from the time of Henry VIII, took a more formal shape and became increasingly part of the fabric of British society, war-making and eventual empire. The Stuart rulers, Charles II and James II, did much to create a structured and professional navy. And by the end of the reign of Queen Victoria, the Royal Navy was the most powerful fleet in the world, providing a career path for the gentry and aristocracy and occupying an important part in British life, self-belief and self-image, employment and wealth, and power projection.

With this naval pride came the Royal Fleet Review, which reached its zenith under Queen Victoria, King Edward VII and King George V. The review by British monarchs of their fleet had been an opportunity for pomp and ceremony since mediaeval times. It is difficult to put a precise date to the earliest formal review; but the assembly of ships before Edward III sailed for France and Crécy in 1346, and a similar massing of ships under Henry V in 1415 ahead of the campaign that led to Agincourt, can perhaps be accepted as the first reliably documented instances of English kings presiding over navies arrayed for their inspection and self-glory.

From then on, whether to impress or deter a foreign power, provide reassurance for domestic consumption or celebrate a sovereign's accession, British Royal Fleet Reviews were a regular and integral part of political posturing and national pride.

Rulers of potential (or actual) allies and enemies were invited to marvel at British prowess, and shudder at the risk of incurring the country's wrath. The British public could revel in their nation's naval superiority; advances in technology and ship design were showcased; and due homage paid to kings and queens at the head of their fleets.

The intention of this book is to tell the story of the Royal Fleet Review. Starting with an examination of the reasons for Britain's need for, and close association with, a navy, the book goes on to explain the historical, political and technological context for British fleet reviews from the times of Edward III onwards. Edward was probably the first English ruler to aggressively assert his sovereignty of the seas and from his time onwards successive rulers (with a few exceptions) claimed this privilege for themselves and their fleet.

The Royal Navy reached its apogee of size and importance in the extended nineteenth century and *The Power and the Glory* examines this period in particular detail, taking an extensive look at the aims and ambitions of the twenty-one reviews in Queen Victoria's and King Edward VII's reigns and the subsequent eleven under George V, Edward VIII and George VI. Surely this was the era of 'Our Wonderful Navy … the sure shield in peace and war'.[1]

As with any major national story, it is necessary to examine political manoeuvring, technological change and the personal accounts of many of the naval characters participating in or planning the reviews, together with the histories of some of the ships involved and their often precipitous decline from prominence to scrapyard as naval strategy and scientific expertise changed around them.

From the end of the Great War, the story turns to one of a long-term regression, interrupted only by the resurgence of the Royal Navy in the Second World War, where the lessons of the first global conflict had to be relearned.

And after the Second World War and the Coronation Review of Queen Elizabeth II in 1953, the Royal Navy entered a long period of almost terminal decline which has perhaps been mirrored in the lack of any Royal Review since 2005, and the country's decline as a seapower. The narrative examines the reasons for this loss of what had been for centuries the main pillar of British power.

Finally, the book surveys the royal yachts, used for conveying the sovereigns around their fleet, and in which some monarchs took an extremely personal interest.

This volume is not intended to be a work of reference or textbook. Rather it is a celebration of the great contribution that the Royal Navy has made to British life, told through the medium of a monarch's review of, and relationship with, his or her fleet. The author hopes that there is sufficient history in the book to set the Royal Reviews in context but it is not intended as a history book or primer. Instead, it is the author's fervent hope that *The Power and the Glory* gives pleasure to the reader and reminds them of glories past and pitfalls present.

The book is divided into four main sections. The first looks at the beginnings of the navy and the naval review tradition. The second is an examination of the Victorian and Edwardian naval and imperial pomp and splendour; the third describes the First World War naval apotheosis, triumph and subsequent decline. And finally there is a review of the Georgian and Elizabethan drift into relative insignificance.

All timings are given according to the 24-hour clock and where the original documents used ante and post meridian the time has been converted.

In many respects the narrative of the Royal Navy over the centuries is the story of the country and its people. *Sic transit gloria mundi*, some might say.

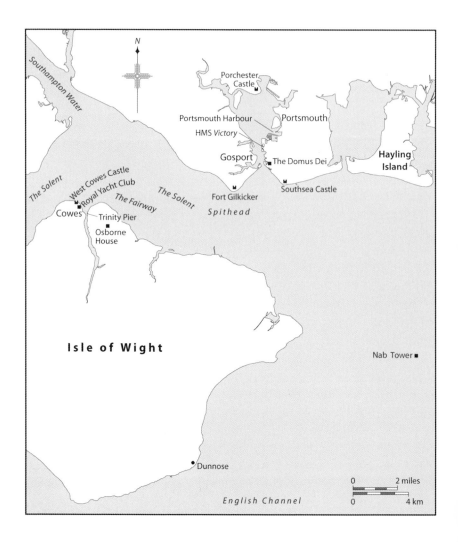

Map of Portsmouth Harbour, Spithead and its environs. *(Peter Wilkinson)*

Part One:

———◦———

BEGINNINGS

This precious stone set in the silver sea,
Which serves it in the office of a wall,
Or as a moat defensive to a house,
Against the envy of less happier lands.

Shakespeare: *King Richard II*, Act 2 Scene 1 (1595).

Chapter 1

The Sea and Britain

ON 1 MAY 1876, Queen Victoria assumed the additional title of Empress of India. She had been Britain's monarch for 39 years, and would continue to be so for another 25. Her new title, a piece of artful flattery by Prime Minster Benjamin Disraeli, reflected the importance of India to the British Empire, over which she reigned, and which was approaching its apogee. It was the largest empire in the world, encompassing Canada, Australasia, approximately 40 per cent of Africa, all of India, the Caribbean and some Pacific Islands. This domain was built on, and for, trade; and to protect that trade, keep the seaways free for British and Imperial commerce and enforce Britain's rights where necessary, the country required a strong navy. By tradition and by need the Royal Navy, the largest and the most powerful navy in the world, was the senior service, Britain's saviour at Trafalgar, against the Spanish Armada and elsewhere. Admirals such as Hood, Rodney, Jervis and Nelson, or Drake, Raleigh and Frobisher from an earlier age, were names familiar to every Victorian child and adult. To be a Royal Navy man had a cachet; to be a naval officer was to be in the front rank of empire.

Britain and her empire were reliant on trade. And the economic purpose of empire was to provide a ready market for British-made goods and a source of raw materials for their manufacture. Successive Navigation Acts from 1651 onwards dictated that all colonial merchant traffic be shipped via British ports in British ships. So-called enumerated products – tobacco, sugar, cotton, rice – had first to be shipped to either England or Scotland before onward freight to their final destination, thus denying the Dutch or French any bilateral commerce with British possessions. Overall, the Acts formed the basis for English and later British overseas trade for nearly 200 years. They were not repealed in their entirety until 1849, following the gradual acceptance of free trade as an economic doctrine.

During the eighteenth and nineteenth centuries, a growing industrial-isation, the repeal of the Corn Laws (1846), allowing cheaper wheat to enter the country and reducing the incentives for home-grown grain, and the drift of population from the countryside to the cities caused a dependence on seaborne commerce for both earnings through export and feeding the population through imports. A powerful navy thus became a necessary aid to national survival. As historian Glen O'Hara has remarked, 'Britain became a great bellows sucking in raw materials and exotic consumer goods and blowing out manufactures to pay for them … the power of the Royal Navy … helped her avoid entanglements which might have allowed other European powers to throttle her economy'.[1]

By the twentieth century, Britain had become highly dependent on imported food supplies. During the five years between 1909 and 1913 imports accounted for 78.7 per cent of wheat and flour consumed, and 56.2 per cent of cereals and pulses overall. British agriculture had responded to the Corn Laws' repeal by specialising in meat and dairy produce, but even here imports still accounted for 35.7 per cent of meat, 43.4 per cent of butter and 74.2 per cent of cheese consumption. By 1913 Britain imported 18.1 million tons of foodstuffs and 64 per cent of the calories consumed came by sea.

The sea was the highway for such imports and exports and British ships dominated the methods of transportation. Shipyards in Belfast, on the Tyne, Wear, Clyde and the Thames produced all kinds of cargo vessels to carry the trade. Even in 1914, Britain – with over 20 million tons – owned more steam and motor ship tonnage than Germany (by a factor of four), the USA (by a factor of ten) or France (also by ten). Indeed, British cargo tonnage was greater than the aggregate of Germany, America, France, Norway, Sweden and Denmark in total.[2]

But Britain was not self-sufficient and, as an island nation, was vulner-able to interdiction of its export and import traffic. More than 400 years ago this universal truth was recognised by Sir Walter Raleigh when he wrote 'there are two ways in which England may be afflicted. The one is by invasion … the other by impeachment of our trades'. And in 1734 Thomas Lediard wrote in his two-volume *Naval History of England in all its Branches* 'our trade is the mother and nurse of the security of our seamen; our seamen the life of our fleet; and our fleet is the security and protection of our trade … both together are the WEALTH, STRENGH AND GLORY OF GREAT BRITAIN'.[3]

The protection of trade to and from Britain was not a new problem. Parliament addressed the issue of the fragile nature of the supply chain to the British Isles at least five times during the Dutch, French Revolutionary and Napoleonic Wars of the seventeenth, eighteenth and nineteenth centuries. As but one instance, the Compulsory Convoy Act of 1798 compelled all British merchant ships to and from the nation's ports in time of war to sail in convoy, protected by Royal Navy ships. Merchants paid a fee for the protection provided. This Act was not repealed until 1872, pressure from the shipowners being the driving force. This repeal was in fact a major change in war strategy for the Royal Navy, although this was little recognised at the time. The navy's role was now defined by phrases such as 'securing the sea communications', 'protecting the ocean highways' and 'preserving the sea routes'; all phrases that hid the fact that merchant ships would no longer receive direct protection. Here lay the roots of a huge problem in the twentieth-century time of war.

It was an appropriate act of war to bring about the interdiction of an enemy's trade on the high seas. Whether it be Drake and Raleigh, licensed privateers plundering Spanish ships for the Virgin Queen in the sixteenth century, or Joseph Barss in the *Liverpool Packet* capturing fifty American vessels in the War of 1812, the disruption of an opponent's trade was seen as a legitimate (and often profitable) activity. So too was blockade of an enemy's coastline. In the eighteenth and nineteenth centuries such a strategy proved successful, particularly against France. As one example from many, during the Seven Years War of 1754–63 Louis XV's plan for the invasion of Britain was ruined and his fleet destroyed by the close blockade of Admiral Edward Hawke and others. In September 1759, Hawke himself was deployed off Brest, Captain Robert Duff off Morbihan, Rear-Admiral George Brydges Rodney off the Normandy coast, and Commodore William Boys positioned off Dunkirk while frigates watched the coast of Flanders and Le Havre to the west. The French fleet was bottled up, its invasion barges eventually destroyed and its ships put to the sword by Hawke at Quiberon Bay. It was the navy that saved Britain then, as it was in the First World War, when the blockade of Germany broke that country's morale.

Britain lived by and from the sea. From prehistory, the sea provided a rich source of food for the inhabitants of the British Isles. Oyster shells are found in Stone Age middens. They were a commonplace food in taverns and markets throughout the eighteenth and nineteenth century, so much so that apprentices complained about the quantity of oysters they were forced to eat. Salmon was a food for the masses from mediaeval times until modern times, as was cod and herring, often preserved by salting. Days on which only fish could be eaten were prescribed not just by canon law but also by royal decree; for keeping a healthy fishing fleet in work and profit was good not just for landing fees and taxes but also to ensure that a pool of experienced seafaring men was available for naval duties, as required. This was an important facet of seaborne commerce, for there was no real standing navy until the seventeenth century. Before then, men were summoned from their nets or ships to form a naval force and then sent away again when the danger was over.

Fishing was also a major source of employment and of food. During the fifteenth century, Bristol was the second biggest port in the kingdom. Bristol's fishermen caught cod in Newfoundland and from there, John Cabot* sailed in 1479 and made landfall in North America. Ports such as Grimsby, Hull, Aberdeen and Great Yarmouth depended on the herring trade and waxed fat on it. Of Yarmouth, Daniel Defoe wrote as early as 1724 that 'the ships ride here so close, and as it were, keeping up one another, with their head-fasts on shore, that for half a mile together, they go cross the stream with their bowsprits over the land, their bowes, or heads, touching the very wharf; so that one may walk from ship to ship as on a floating bridge, all along by the shore-side'.[4] Whaling was important to the growth of Hull. By the eve of the First World War, there were 125,000 British fishermen across the country catching 1.25 million tons of fish a year in 3,000 large steamboats and an assorted mix of 10,000 other lesser but dedicated fishing boats. Even in 1950, Grimsby was the largest fishing port in the world.

The slave trade made Bristol and Liverpool merchants rich in the eighteenth century. When slavery was ended by statute, it was the Royal Navy that was sent to patrol the coast of Africa to cut off the commerce at source. London was the largest port in the world during the eighteenth and nineteenth centuries.

Nineteenth-century Britain was built on a foundation of coal, and the need to ship it for export or domestic use created the port of Cardiff. At one time Cardiff docks, essential for the movement of the best Welsh steam coal, so prized by the Royal Navy and others, was one of the largest dock systems in the world with a total quayside of almost seven miles. Coal had been exported from Newcastle since at least 1250; by 1615, 200 ships carried coal to London and another 200 supplied other parts of the country. Methil, a coal port on the Firth of Forth in Scotland, boasted three docks, ten coal hoists and eight cranes by 1914. Movement from the pitheads to the docks was by rail. There were over 25 miles of sidings and this network could hold up to 50,000 tonnes of coal, some 3,000 wagons, at any one time.

An Island Fortress

The accident of tectonic plate movement, successive ice ages and the flooding effect of glacial meltwater had gifted Britain with a superb defensive wall. As Shakespeare had John of Gaunt proclaim in *King Richard II*, it was 'a moat defensive'. Once joined to Europe by a land bridge that linked the Weald in Kent to the Boulonnais in the Pas de Calais, Britain exited the Pleistocene as a group of islands surrounded on all sides by water.

* Real name Zuan Caboto, a Venetian.

These seas first provided a route for invasion and settlement. First Romans, then Saxons, Jutes and Vikings all sailed over the North Sea or down the English Channel to settle Albion's pleasant shores. Then Normans crossed it to create a new dominion. But from that time on, with the single exception of the invited landing of William of Orange, Britain remained safe from foreign invasion, although the polyglot racial mix, and creole language, left behind by these incursions is surely one of Britain's distinguishing strengths, the 'envy of less happier lands'.

And Shakespeare knew that the sea was close to English hearts and experience; four of his plays begin with violent storms at sea – *Merchant of Venice*, *Twelfth Night*, *Othello* and *The Tempest*. Perdita is lost on a sea voyage in *The Winter's Tale* and King Lear is 'as mad as the vex'd sea'.[5]

One of the first monarchs to recognise the benefit of a fighting sea force was King Edgar (ruled 959–75). At his coronation he allegedly summoned six client kings to Chester, including the King of the Scots and the King of Strathclyde, and made them pledge their word that they would be his liege-men on sea and land. Later chroniclers made the number of kings into eight and have them all plying the oars of Edgar's state barge on the River Dee as an act of obeisance. With Edgar, the union of England under one dynasty became more firmly established. Highly conscious of the importance of sea power, the king was said to have built up a navy of 3,600 ships by the time of his death, which were deployed to guard England's coasts from the incursions of the Danes. There will, of course, be an element of exaggeration in this account, but even if halved the number of ships he could call upon if necessary was formidable.

Before Edgar, Alfred 'the Great' (King of Wessex from 871–*c*886 and King of the Anglo-Saxons from *c*886–99) had also seen the benefit of a fighting navy to protect against or repel the invasions of the Norsemen. Around 896 he had ordered the construction of a flotilla of longships to his own design, having sixty oars which made them twice the size of the Viking longships and thus able to carry double the number of fighting men.[6] He appreciated the doctrine of sea power and command of the sea. If enemy fleets could be intercepted before they landed, he might save his kingdom from despoliation. In practice his ships proved difficult to manoeuvre, but the tactical intent was important and served for future naval thought. Notwithstanding the unwieldiness of his ships, Alfred won important naval victories, perforce close to the littoral or in river estuaries, such as that of 896 when his nine new ships intercepted six Viking vessels and inflicted 120 casualties, at a loss of only half that number among his own forces. Unable to put out to sea through lack of manpower, the Norse ships were wrecked on the coast (possibly at Selsey Bill) and the survivors hanged at Winchester.

From the Plantagenet age on, the cost of this *ad-hoc* naval protection was met (at least in theory) by the levy of 'Ship Money', a tax on the inhabitants of coastal areas of England and one of several taxes that English monarchs could raise by royal prerogative, without the approval of Parliament. Under the Plantagenets (ruled 1154–1485), littoral towns and cities could commute the demand to supply ships and men in time of war or danger through the payment of a cash sum. Over time and in different reigns, this payment became an established tax, Ship Money, and an important source of income for the Crown, whether or not it was spent on naval protection. As late as 1619, James I was able to extract £40,000 of Ship Money from London and £8,550 from other maritime towns. It was the attempt by Charles I, desperately short of money and reluctant to ask for more from Parliament, to levy Ship Money during peacetime from 1634 onwards, and to extend it to the inland counties of England without Parliamentary approval, which provoked a backlash from the monied middle class and became one of the key issues which fomented the Civil War. Only when his son Charles II came to the throne was the navy established on a proper and more general taxation basis of funding.

Britannia Rules the Waves

The figure of Britannia – helmed, shield and trident carrying, female – became a universal emblem for the relationship between Britain and the sea, and indeed British dominion over the oceans. Of Roman origins, Britannia first came to symbolise English power during the reign of Elizabeth I. By 1672 she appeared on the reverse of Charles II's farthings. But Britannia really sprang to prominence after James Thomson used her in his poem *Rule Britannia*, set to music by Thomas Arne in 1740.

It was first sung as part of the masque *Alfred* performed at Cliveden, country home of Frederick, Prince of Wales, on 1 August 1740, and was inspired – at least in part – by Admiral Edward Vernon's capture of Porto Bello in Panama from the Spanish in November 1739. In 1799 the sculptor John Flaxman proposed erecting a 230ft high statue atop Greenwich Hill celebrating Britannia 'by divine providence triumphant' in recognition of recent British naval victories at Cape St Vincent, Camperdown and Aboukir Bay.[7]

By the time of Queen Victoria's accession to the throne, Britannia had come to be the epitome of Britain and her puissance, and was consistently stylised as a young woman with brown or golden hair, wearing a Corinthian helmet and white robes and holding Poseidon's trident. Often, she sat or stood before the ocean and ships representing British naval power, holding or standing beside a Greek hoplite shield, which depicted the British Union Flag, and at her feet the British Lion.

In 1847, Victoria and Albert commissioned William Dyce to paint the

fresco *Neptune Resigning to Britannia the Empire of the Sea*, emblematic of British naval power, and which was sited at the top of the pavilion staircase of their newly-built royal retreat, Osborne House on the Isle of Wight.

Kings at Sea

There has long been an association between British monarchs and the sea, a relationship which includes serving and fighting in sea defence of the British Isles. Apart from Kings Alfred and Edgar noted above, in mediaeval times Edward III and Henry V commanded fleets at sea (or at least in the English Channel). Henry VII selected Portsmouth as a Royal Dockyard in June 1495 and that port has held a pre-eminent position in the Royal Navy ever since. Henry VIII was responsible for the creation of a permanent proto-navy, with the supporting anchorages and dockyards. James II, while Duke of York, served as Lord High Admiral of England (until forced to resign owing to his Catholic leanings) and commanded the British fleet during the Second and Third Dutch Wars. William IV, as Duke of Clarence, was also Lord High Admiral for twelve months from 1827, having been an officer in the Royal Navy between 1778 and 1790 where he saw fighting at the battle of Cape St Vincent as a midshipman* and during the American War of Independence. He also sailed under Nelson before retiring with the rank of Rear-Admiral and was popularly known as 'The Sailor King'.

* The future king was not universally appreciated; 'everyone thought that William was a royal pain in the arse. He went on to have a dangerously disruptive career in the Royal Navy' (Willis, *The Struggle for Sea Power*, p 365),

King William IV, the sailor king, in an admiral's uniform, as painted by Sir Martin Archer Shee. His active naval service ceased in 1790. However, in 1793, anxious to serve in the Napoleonic Wars, he expected a command but broke his arm falling down stairs. William was made an admiral in 1798 and Admiral of the Fleet in 1811 but these were purely honorary positions. *(Author's collection)*

Of Queen Victoria's sons, the eldest, King Edward VII, did not serve at sea but took a keen interest in matters naval and was friends with Admiral 'Jackie' Fisher, supporting him in his attempts to reform and modernise the navy. Her second son, Prince Alfred, joined the navy aged 13 and retired in the rank of Admiral of the Fleet after a distinguished naval career of some 35 years.* Kings George V and his son George VI were both Royal Navy officers (the former between 1877 and 1892, the latter Mentioned in Despatches for his actions in the First World War). George V's fourth son George, Duke of Kent, was in the RN on active service between 1915 and 1929.† In more recent times, the navy was home to Prince Philip, Duke of Edinburgh (Mentioned in Despatches in the Second World War), Prince Charles, Prince of Wales, and his brother Prince Andrew, Duke of York.

Royal Fleet Reviews were thus generally a pleasure for royalty rather than a chore; as they were for those who did not serve, including Charles II, who loved sailing, and Queen Victoria, immensely proud of her navy and her sailors. But what was the purpose of these reviews?

* Admiral Percy Scott said of him that 'as a Commander-in-Chief, [he] had, in my humble opinion, no equal. He handled a fleet magnificently, and introduced many improvements in signals and manoeuvring' (Scott, *Fifty Years in the Royal Navy*, p 61).

† He died on active service with the RAF in 1942 when a Short Sunderland in which he was a passenger crashed into a Scottish hillside.

Chapter 2

What is a Royal Fleet Review?

T HE EXISTENCE OF THE INSTITUTION now known as a Royal Fleet Review did not come about by accident. As the sea became vital for the nation's sustenance and its livelihood, so a force to maintain access to the waters, or control over them, developed in lockstep. The interests of reigning monarchs, or in later times governments, lay in both providing safety on, and peaceable use of, the seas; for the enrichment of the merchants benefited the rulers too through taxation. Thus, as Britain became wealthier through trade, the desire for a sea-fighting force under national command became pressing, to defend what was held and to acquire what offered potential for further status or prosperity. The symbiosis of benefit between king, government and navy emerged. The national interest required that a powerful navy protect the realm, one which could be given standing and kudos by strong royal associations. From these sorts of converging forces came the Royal Fleet Review.

So what is a Royal Fleet Review? A possible description might be that it is a gathering of ships of the Royal Navy in honour of, and to be observed by, the reigning monarch or his or her representative. Such a review has certain essential characteristics, especially: the British monarch or delegated royal personage is present; the assembly of ships represents a sizeable portion of the Royal Navy's resources; and it is a public spectacle. On the basis of these characterisations, there have been some fifty-four Royal Fleet Reviews in recorded history.

But there is more to it than that, because Royal Fleet Reviews have been driven by a range of different requirements or aims: – to impress a potential enemy or ally; to celebrate a victory in war; for reasons of populist glorification; on mobilisation for war; to commemorate the coronation of the monarch and on the presentation of new Colours* to the Royal Navy.

* Colours were for carrying ashore in the same way as army Colours. They were only granted to the Royal Navy after the First World War.

Types of Royal Review

The assembly of the fleet in time of war is an obvious moment for royal benison to be bestowed upon the ships assembled. In 1346 and 1415, Edward III and Henry V inspected their naval forces before sailing to France to give battle. Likewise, Queen Victoria waved off Admiral Napier's Baltic Sea fleet in 1854.

But better than war is to persuade an enemy or reluctant friend of the benefit of being in Britannia's good books. A wolf or dog will bare its teeth and raise its hackles without wishing to get into a fight if that can be avoided by snarling frighteningly. In the wars between the city states which so disfigured life in Italy in the Middle Ages, each side would hire mercenaries who would demonstrate fiercely on the intended battlefield. But often the battles were bloodless because a mercenary force which considered itself out-demonstrated would simply leave the field.

In the same way, a spectacular display of naval might would serve to impress or deter potential allies and enemies. The multiple foreign rulers taken to see the fleet in 1844, including those of Russia, France and Prussia, would fit this category.

Bread and circuses have long been a panacea for a restive populace and fleet reviews have sometimes filled that role too. Charles II in 1662 greeting his new bride or the Silver Jubilee of George V in 1935 are examples of the type.

The growth of pomp and circumstance in the late nineteenth century was a reaction to both the growing economic might and global power of the country as well as the rise of modern mass society. The less monarchs and governments could rely on traditional forms of legitimacy, the more they invented public ritual to display their relevance and power. Thus, coronations became reasons for a parade of naval might from 1902. Celebration of victories in war gave rise to reviews in, *inter alia*, 1693 and 1814. And the presentation of new Colours to the navy occasioned naval festivities in 1969 and 2003.

Additionally, there were irregular fleet demonstrations specifically for members of the Houses of Parliament, such as in 1912, presumably so that legislators could see at first-hand what had happened to the funds they voted to the navy.

Royal Fleet Reviews usually took place at Spithead, a roadstead in the Solent off Gilkicker Point in Hampshire and close to the long-time naval base of Portsmouth. Spithead is a sheltered but deep-water anchorage, protected from all winds except those from the southeast and ideal for the massing of ships.

Reviews encompassed more than a simple inspection of the fleet. There were mock battles and landings, such as the attacks by gunboats on Southsea Castle before Queen Victoria in 1856. Massive illuminations of

the fleet took place in, for example, 1935 and 1937. Ships sailed on exercises, sometimes with the monarch on board, such as George VI in 1938.
Gunnery demonstrations took place at nearly all of the reviews in the
nineteenth and twentieth centuries. Rigorous drills were conducted with
ships sailing in precise formations for the monarch's delectation. And
crowds of people gathered on the seashore with picnics and spyglasses to
watch the whole spectacle unfold and revel in their pride in their navy.
Newspapers were filled with descriptions of the events and no doubt the
local traders and hostelries delighted in the sudden step change in footfall
and cash flow.

Finally, it should be noted that there was also an overt commercial aspect
to some fleet reviews. As well as putting the British naval forces on display,
they served as a shop window for British shipbuilding; historically, the
Royal Navy primarily used British-designed and built ships. Export orders
were commercially beneficial to the economy and much sought after,
particularly in the later part of the nineteenth and early twentieth
centuries. Amongst others, Japan, Turkey and assorted South American
states all placed orders on British shipyards.

Royal Yachts

Generally, the monarch inspected his or her fleet in a designated royal
yacht. From the time of Charles II, this was usually a specifically designed
and built vessel, set aside for the ruler's use. Charles, an enthusiastic sailor,
had some twenty-five of them in use during his reign and that of his
brother. In 1831 there were five simultaneously in service, and Queen
Victoria had three successive yachts named *Victoria and Albert*. Following
the Restoration in 1660, British monarchs have used a total of eighty-

A postcard depicting
a stylised represent-
ation of the fleet as
drawn up at
Spithead for the
1912 'Parliament-
arians' review'.
(Author's collection)

three royal yachts, the last being *Britannia*, which was retired in 1997. Since that time, Queen Elizabeth II has had to charter civilian vessels when necessary. Warships have occasionally filled in at reviews, as at the 1953 Coronation Review while *Britannia* was under construction.

Fleet Reviews in Other Countries

Naval reviews – necessarily generally non-royal – have become an institution in other countries too, and not just those of the Commonwealth. The Australian navy has organised seven reviews in total since 1921 including an International Fleet Review on 4 October 2013 to commemorate the 100th anniversary of the entry of the first Royal Australian Navy fleet into Sydney Harbour, which was attended by the Royal Navy and, *inter alia*, the Nigerian Navy. Canada has held five, one in front of Queen Elizabeth II in 1959, and New Zealand two, in 1991 and 2016.

In the United States of America, Navy Day was celebrated on 27 October as a quasi-holiday, although it has not been formally observed since 1949 (the navy being subsumed into Armed Forces Day). On this day, the US Navy used to send its ships to various port cities for the public to visit and admire; since its official abolition, the holiday has been maintained and celebrated through veterans' organisations and the Navy League of the United States.

In Russia, Navy Day is a national holiday which now normally takes place on the last Sunday of July. The holiday was originally introduced in 1939 and the date chosen was that of the battle of Gangut,* where the Imperial Russian Navy defeated Swedish forces in 1714. In China, the People's Liberation Army celebrates the founding of its naval arm on 23 April.

And in South Korea, an International Fleet Review was held at Jeju Island on 11 October 2018. A total of thirteen countries including the US, Russia and India sent forty-one warships – with the aircraft carrier USS *Ronald Reagan* as the centrepiece.

Public fleet reviews, or at least public celebrations of naval strength, are thus established around the world, although sometimes only recently. But they have been a fixture in Britain for many centuries and especially in the 'long nineteenth century', and the next chapter goes back in time to examine the first such royal reviews, when this very British tradition started.

* 27 July (Julian calendar), 7 August (Gregorian).

Chapter 3

———✦———

Frightening the French, 1346–1415

FOR MORE THAN 500 YEARS, France was England's (and then Britain's) natural enemy. The early kings of England were themselves of French descent and held that they had, with a greater or lesser legal force, a right to the French throne. One who made such a claim was Edward III (ruled 1327–77), who claimed the throne of France after the death of his uncle Charles IV of France. At the time of Charles' death in 1328, Edward was his nearest male relative through Edward's mother Isabella of France.

On the demise of Charles, Edward asserted his title to the throne through the right of his mother. However, he was not a popular choice among the French aristocracy and the French court decreed that, as a result of France having recently reaffirmed succession through the male line only (the Salic Law), Isabella could not have inherited the throne and therefore neither could Edward.

Instead, it was considered that Charles' closest relative through the male-only line was his first cousin, Philip, Count of Valois, who thus was crowned as Philip VI of France. Through no doubt gritted teeth, Edward paid homage to Philip as holder of the Dukedom of Aquitaine, a title and lands that Edward had inherited in 1329. Popularly known in England as Gascony, this was an area with a culture and language distinct from the French and the inhabitants of Aquitaine preferred to be associated to the English crown. However, Philip himself held ambitions over the territory and attempted to meddle in the affairs of the Gascons prior to confiscating Aquitaine from Edward in 1337, igniting war between England and France. In retaliation Edward declared himself King of France in 1340 and set about enforcing his right through war and invasion.

Edward's forces quickly gave the French a lesson in command of the sea, annihilating the French navy at the battle of Sluys on 24 June 1340. Here

Edward, sailing in his flagship *Cog Thomas*, personally led some 160 ships against 230 French vessels which he found in the harbour of Sluys. The French lashed their ships together into three lines, forming a large floating platform; but having manoeuvred to gain the advantage of wind and tide, the English fleet destroyed its opponents, who lost 16,000–20,000 men with only small English casualties in return. It was from this triumph that Edward arrogated to himself the title of 'Sovereign of the Seas'. He also had made five golden model ships as permanent memorials of the victory and presented them to Walsingham Priory, St Paul's Cathedral, Gloucester Abbey, and two to Canterbury Cathedral, together with the issue of a new commemorative gold coin. Such propaganda went down well in England and fed a new legend of England's naval superiority; the first inkling of 'Britannia rules the waves'.

The victory gave Edward unhindered access across the English Channel, although it did not stop continued raids by the French on both English ports and ships. But with the seaway under his control, the king was able to launch an invasion of France. Landing with 12,000 men, cutting through the Low Countries and plundering the countryside, he first attempted an (eventually abortive) siege of Cambrai and then led his army on a destructive *chevauchée* through Picardy, despoiling the land and destroying many villages, all the while shadowed by a French army. However, with funds running low, problems with the Scots on his northern border in England and the French army seemingly unwilling to give battle, Edward withdrew from France and his campaign came to a rather unsuccessful and limp end. Edward went back to England to settle the Scots and raise more money for another campaign. But he was determined to return.

The Sea Road to Crécy, 28 June 1346;

At the Great Council Meeting in February 1346, Edward made clear that he intended to invade France and claim his rightful crown that year. He started to gather the necessary ships immediately but adverse weather in March meant they could not be concentrated. The muster date was put back to 1 May but once again had to be deferred. Finally, at the end of May, the King had amassed 15,000 fighting men, including knights and mercenaries from the Holy Roman Empire and his 16-year-old son, Edward the Black Prince, together with a staggering 750 ships (a figure which included thirty-eight hired foreign vessels), all gathered at or around Portsmouth. Edward arrived at Porchester Castle, at the head of Portsmouth Harbour, on 1 June. And waited. All of Europe waited with him, for all knew that invasion would happen – but nobody except the king knew where. Gascony? Flanders? Brittainy? The rumours were rife.

Many were upset at the delay and the cost. The ships assembled were not owned by the King. They and their crews belonged to merchants or fishing masters. They had been 'arrested' for the King's service as early as February and their owners wanted them back. As Susan Rose has written, 'all this time soldiers and sailors had to be fed at royal expense while merchants chafed as a whole season wasted away with trading voyages impossible'.[1]

Edward issued sealed instructions to his captains as to their destination in case of separation of the fleet; and he ordered that no ship should leave England for a week after he had sailed, except for a small diversionary expedition to Flanders.

Then on 28 June, Edward boarded *Cog Thomas* and set sail. As he passed through the fleet, the soldiers and sailors crammed into the other ships of his invasion fleet cheered or knelt in reverence. His banners fluttered from his flagship's mast; more standards broke out on the other English vessels. The great fleet put to sea, 'flying their magnificent streamers',[2] heading westwards and hugging the coastline.

All present had just witnessed the first Royal Fleet Review. The sovereign passing through his armada preparatory to battle. And it took place, like so many that were to follow, at Portsmouth and Spithead.

A miniature of the battle of Sluys by Jean Froissart. The English ship flying Edward's flags can be seen on the left. Froissart depicts the way in which sea battles of the time were fought, broadside to broadside with archers and swordsmen fighting in the attempt to board, while men in the fighting tops hurl missiles down upon their enemies. *(Author's collection)*

A modern replica of a cog, similar to Edward III's flagship *Cog Thomas*. *(Author's collection)*

On 11 July, two weeks after setting out, their destination was finally made known. That morning, in clear sunshine, the trumpets on Edward's cog blared out, ships unfurled their sails, rowers bent their backs at their oars and all started sailing south. Just as some 600 years later, they were headed for the Normandy beaches.

To Agincourt, 1415

Almost 70 years later, another English king determined to claim the French throne prepared for war by assembling an invasion fleet, this time at Southampton.

Edward III had continued to style himself King of France until the Treaty of Brétigny on 8 May 1360, when he abandoned his claim in return for substantial grants of land in France. However, hostilities soon resumed between the two countries and in 1369 Edward again raised his right to the title of King of France. Eight years later he died with his demand unfulfilled.

When Henry V (ruled 1413–22) came to the English throne in 1413, he immediately reasserted his right to the French throne. Old commercial disputes and the support the French had lent to Owain Glyndŵr in his revolt against Henry's father, together with the disordered state of France under the mad King Charles VI which offered no security for peace, were all cited as reasons for war but the old dynastic claim to the French throne made conflict inevitable.

On coming to power, Henry found his kingdom's southern coast beset by French raids. In February 1415 he ordered that a small royal squadron, ships paid for by, and under, royal command, be detailed to guard the seas from Plymouth to the Isle of Wight, from Wight to Orford Ness and from Orford to Berwick whist he prepared to depart for France. Two ships, two barges and one balinger* were allocated to the first station, two barges and two balingers to the second, and one barge and two balingers to the third.

And on 19 March Thomas Earl of Dorset, Admiral of England, was ordered 'to cause all ships, barges, balingers and other vessels of England to be at the port of Southampton by 8 May'. Then on 27 July, two officers were commissioned 'to seize all ships and other vessels of the realm and foreign parts of the portage of twenty tuns and more in the port of London and take them to the port of Southampton with all possible speed to serve the king on his present voyage'.[3]

Meanwhile, in order to victual his fleet, Henry had directed the Sheriff of Hampshire to instruct the populace to 'bake and brew' for the next three months to provide food for the invasion force 'on pain of the king's grievous wrath'.[4]

Contemporary chroniclers reported that Henry had assembled 1,500 ships. This is undoubtedly an exaggerated figure but nevertheless, the fleet must have been of considerable size. The vast majority of these ships were quotidian transports, hired (or commandeered) for the occasion. Several hundred were probably chartered in Holland and Zealand. But at the core of the fleet were Henry's own ships, including his flagship, *Trinity Royal*, paid for out of his own funds, the first proto-navy, and this royal squadron was intended to protect against the possibility of attack by Castilian galleys or Genoese carracks, mercenaries in the service of the French Crown.

Pausing only to arraign and execute the ringleaders of a plot against his rule, Henry left Porchester Castle, like Edward before him, and on 7 August came to Southampton harbour. Here he took a barge to his flagship. The *Trinity Royal* was one of the two largest ships in the Henrician navy, of 540 tuns capacity and with a crew of 300 sailors. It had a huge purple sail and a long banner of the Trinity steaming from its main mast. Other standards, dozens of yards long, bore the arms of St George and of Henry himself. The fighting top was adorned with a large gilt copper crown, a golden leopard decorated the prow and on the capstan was a sceptre and a fleur-de-lys.

As he stepped on board, Henry ordered the main sail to be partially raised, a signal to the rest of the accompanying ships to ready themselves and close on his own vessel. To do so they had first to load their passengers, stores and some 12,000 horses to be transported for the expedition. This took time and the flagship did not move for some days; while anchored she served as the King's Chamber and another vessel, *Holigost*, was named the King's Hall. On these two ships Henry was attended by

* A balinger was an oared and masted vessel, of low tonnage, fast and manoeuvrable under sail or when rowed.

101 men of his household, with the members of his council coming and going from three smaller ships moored nearby, purposed as the King's Larder, Kitchen and Wardrobe respectively.

On 11 August, Henry had most of his fleet gathered around him. He could look out on them, and they could see him and his magnificently ornate ship; he had ruled in majesty over his armada from his flagship for five days. Now it was time to depart. He handed over formal custody of England to his brother, John Duke of Bedford. Then, at 1500, the great purple sail of *Trinity Royal* was raised to its fullest extent and Henry led his fleet out of harbour, passing through the smaller vessels like the swans which settled in his wake; they were considered to be a good omen. Less propitious was the smoke observed in some quarters. Three of his ships had caught fire and burned to the waterline without even leaving English waters.

Again, an English king had observed his fleet around him, and the sailors and soldiers had seen and acknowledged him. Two days later the fleet dropped anchor in the mouth of the River Seine. As Ian Mortimer has noted 'it was the largest army to leave England since the siege of Calais in 1347 … and at the time it was probably the largest fleet to have set out from England'.[5]

The fleet saw no action in 1415 because the French did not put to sea, or even try to prevent the English from landing in Normandy. Two sea battles were fought the following year and between 1416 and 1420 the royal squadron became a fleet of around thirty-six vessels which was used for patrolling and supporting the King's campaigns in northern France. And as a result of Henry V's conquest of Normandy between 1417 and 1419 he was able to achieve the much sought-after concept of command of the sea in the English Channel. And this allowed for a welcome peace for the towns and merchants of the south of England and relief from both piracy and French raids.

⸺◆⸺

So Edward III achieved eternal fame at Crécy and Henry V at Agincourt. And these battles were further commemorated in the names of Royal Navy ships down the ages too. Both victories owed their success to the kings' ability to sail a major fleet across the English Channel and to retain command of the sea, in order to land troops in France and to resupply and eventually to return their forces to England. And both monarchs showed themselves to their fleets, and surveyed their immense forces, with pride. Surely these were the very first, the prototypes, of the Royal Fleet Review.

Over 150 years would pass before the next recorded 'review'. There was a royal naval assembly on 2 August 1512 when King Henry VIII, 'desiring to see his Navie together', rode to Portsmouth. There 'he appointed captains to the *Regent* and the *Sovereign* and with them sixty of the tallest men in the king's guard'. Henry held a great banquet at the port with all his ship commanders and 'everyone sware to another to defend and comfort one another without failying and this they promised before the king which committed them to God'.[6]

The King does not appear to have sailed around or boarded his ships, which were reported to be some twenty-five in number. But the sailors were dressed in white gaberdine with a Tudor rose on the breast and the ships all flew flags at mast head and yard arm, which must have made a pleasing spectacle for him.

Sixty years later, in early February 1582, Queen Elizabeth I visited Rochester, together with her whole court, and in the company of the Duke of Anjou (the youngest son of King Henry II of France and a suitor for the Queen's hand) and his suite. There she showed the duke 'all her great ships which were in that place, most whereof his highness and the prince and lords of his train entered, not without great admiration of the French lords and gentlemen, who confessed that of good right the Queen of England was reported to be lady of the seas'. Anjou apparently commentated 'how all these ships were ready furnished and well appointed'. It is possible that there was a royal salute by the ships' guns for the *Holinshed Chronicles* record that 'so after all the great ordnance had been shot off, they returned for that day again to Rochester'.[7] But it was not until the restoration of the Stuarts that the ritual of royal reviews became more established.

Chapter 4

The Stuarts and the Glorious Revolution, 1662–1714

O N 14 MAY 1662, Infanta Catherine of Braganza, daughter of the King of Portugal, stepped ashore at Portsmouth and was taken to the Governor's House (the *Domus Dei*) to await the arrival of her husband to be, King Charles II. She had been brought from Lisbon in HMS *Henry*, a 64-gun Second Rate, accompanied by a Royal Navy squadron, all under the command of Vice-Admiral and Commander-in-Chief in the Narrow Seas Sir John Mennes, together with Edward Montagu, 1st Earl of Sandwich and Ambassador Extraordinary to Portugal.*

The *Henry* was met in the English Channel by a flotilla of the Royal Navy led by the Lord High Admiral and brother of the King, James Duke of York, and then escorted into port. On her landing, Catherine had her first taste of English beer which she disliked greatly, sending to her ship for tea, then little drunk in England. From then onwards the Queen was to be a great popularist for what became the national passion for tea drinking and afternoon tea.†

The indefatigable and salacious diarist and naval administrator, Samuel Pepys, confided to his diary that 'at night, all the bells of the town rung, and bonfires made for the joy of the Queen's arrival, who came and landed at Portsmouth last night. But I do not see much thorough joy, but only an indifferent one, in the hearts of people, who are much discontented at the pride and luxury of the Court, and running in debt.'[1]

Charles arrived on 20 May; he was perhaps not exactly thrilled by the wife he had never met but tried hard to like her.

I arrived here yesterday about two in the afternoon, and as soon as I had shifted myself I went to my wife's chamber. Her face is not so exact as to be called a beauty, though her eyes are excellent good, and not

* Montagu had commanded the fleet that brought Charles II back from exile in May 1660.

† She also brought the gift of Bombay as part of her dowry (together with Tangier and £350,000), laying the basis for Britain's obsession with what became the jewel in the imperial crown, India.

31

anything in her face that in the least degree can [shock] one; on the contrary, she hath much agreeableness in her looks altogether as ever I saw; and if I have any skill in physiognomy, which I think I have, she must be as good a woman as ever was born.[2]

Catherine refused any but a Catholic wedding and so on 22 May she was first married privately in the presence of half a dozen people in her bedroom, according to the Catholic rites. There then followed a formal Protestant ceremony a little later in the day in the chamber of Government House.

Charles also reviewed his fleet whilst in Portsmouth where the fleet assembled at Spithead. The instructions to ships' captains for this event decreed that as soon as the royal barge came near, the 'decks tops and yards are to be manned as if it were hung with men'.[3] As the barge came closer, trumpets were to sound until, when it was within musket-shot, they were to be replaced by the blowing of whistles three times and 'in every interim the ship's company are to hail him with joynt [sic] shout after the custom of the sea'.[4] The ships' sides and ladder were to be manned with the 'primest [sic] and best fashioned men' and 'the captain to receive the king upon his knee'.[5] Charles was to be entertained with music and as he went over the side to depart the trumpets were to sound *A Loath to Depart.**

Having arrived in England with naval splendour, Catherine was next presented to London as part of a royal fleet progress. Charles and his new bride sailed in procession from Hampton Court to Whitehall on 23 August. Pepys noted that

all the show consisted chiefly in the number of boats and barges; and two pageants, one of a King, and another of a Queen, with her Maydes of Honour sitting at her feet very prettily … Anon come the [actual] King and Queen in a barge under a canopy with 10,000 barges and boats, I think, for we could see no water for them, nor discern the King

* A 'loath to depart' was a common term for a song or a tune played when saying farewell to friends.

nor Queen. And so they landed at Whitehall Bridge, and the great guns
on the other side went off.[6]

If not a Royal Fleet Review in the strict sense this was certainly a monarch
in his glory, an ongoing major public spectacle involving the royal fleet and
many private vessels, which had commenced with Catherine's arrival
in May.

Both Charles and his brother James (later King James II) were keen and
accomplished sailors and great proponents of a strong navy. On his restoration in 1660, Charles had visited Portsmouth with his mother, Henrietta.
The navy he saw there was a sad inheritance, comprising 154 ships and
lesser craft totalling 57,463 tons, all of which were in a shocking state of
disrepair. During their two reigns they significantly upgraded the forces at
their disposal, focusing on large line-of-battle vessels to deliver the biggest
broadside possible.

In 1660 the brothers had inherited thirty First to Third Rate ships (line
of battle ships, or ships of the line*) and one hundred smaller Fourth to
Sixth Rates. By 1688, when James II was deposed, there were fifty-nine of
the former and sixty-three smaller ships.[7]

Under Charles, and with James as Lord High Admiral (until 1673) and
the talented Pepys as Chief Secretary to the Admiralty, the Royal Navy was
established on a much more permanent and professional basis. A navy
board was formed, including the treasurer, controller and clerk of the navy
plus three other commissioners and a major programme of ship refitting
instigated. The royal brothers' cousin, Prince Rupert of the Rhine, was
recruited as First Commissioner of the Admiralty in the 1670s, extending
royal patronage within the navy. Corruption, which had been rife
throughout the service, was slowly weeded out, although by no means
fully. A qualifying exam which had to be passed before a lieutenancy could
be awarded was introduced in 1677; it included for the first time a course
in navigation, conducted by Trinity House. Pepys was responsible, in his
nearly 30 years of administration, for replacing *ad hoc* processes with
regular programmes of supply, construction, pay, etc. He introduced the
Navy List which fixed the order of promotion and in 1683 established the
Victualling Board, which decided the ration scales. Slowly a permanent
group of effective (and loyal) commanders was established, serving a more
professional and organised Admiralty.

Charles himself was a regular visitor to the Royal Dockyards, took great
interest in building techniques and could discourse knowledgably on naval
subjects. Whilst in exile in Holland, the King had become enamoured of
the Dutch *jachts*, small and manoeuvrable sailing vessels that provided
transport in the ports of the United Provinces. Presented with one upon
his restoration, and type and the term 'yacht' were introduced to England.

* For the definition
of rates, see
Appendix 1.

Charles's early experience of Dutch *jachts* led him to build more for himself and these eventually became 'a navy within a navy'.[8] The King's yachts were not automatically units of the Royal Navy; they were initially the King's private property, only to be taken up 'into the list and charge' of the navy when the King willed it. The first English-built yacht was the *Katherine*, 49ft with a beam of 19ft. By 1685 there were twenty yachts (there would be twenty-five over the two reigns), including one specially built and launched in 1670 for the Queen, named *Saudadoes* ('Greetings to You' in Portuguese), although only seven were truly royal and assigned to the immediate service of the King and royal family. But Charles was perpetually short of money and increasingly the yachts were hired out to anyone who could afford them. Pepys complained that yacht voyages were even traded on the Royal Exchange.

The Stuart period was increasingly troubled by wars with the Dutch, particularly the Second and Third Anglo-Dutch wars of 1664–7 (when in 1667 the Dutch sailed up the Medway and towed away the English flag-ship, *Royal Charles*)* and 1672–4. The origins of the conflict were based around trade rivalry. There was competition for fish in the North Sea, antipathy to the Dutch near-monopoly of European trade, commercial

* For reasons of economy, Charles II and his minsters had laid up the British fleet and sent away the seamen, thus encouraging Dutch Admiral de Ruyter to sail up the Medway and burn some of the navy's best ships at Chatham. One might compare this false economy with that of the government immediately before the invasion of the Falkland Islands by Argentina, see Chapter 16.

Royal Visit to the Fleet on the Thames, 6 June 1672, in a painting by William van de Velde the Younger. The yacht in the left foreground is probably the *Anne* which was used by James, Duke of York. She flies the Red Ensign and is decorated with the figure of a woman holding a crown in her right hand on her stern, together with putti holding a garland above her head. Further away on her starboard bow is the *Cleveland* with her mainsail brailed up and a man aloft hauling down the royal standard. This indicates that King Charles has transferred from her to hold a council-of-war on board the *Prince*, the main ship in the painting. (© *National Maritime Museum BHC0299*)

conflict in the East Indies and dispute regarding the Dutch claim to the freedom of the seas. All of these issues conflicted with the British notion, propagated by Edward III, that Britain was the 'sovereign of the seas' and claimed all rights to the seas around the island and as far as Cape Finisterre.

Additionally, the Navigation Act of 1651 had cut out Dutch shippers

The *Cleveland* yacht in a painting by the Dutch painter Jacob Knyff. The presence of the royal standard, union flag and Admiralty standard indicate that the king is on board. She was at one time Charles II's favourite yacht and after his death was given to the Ordnance office. *Cleveland* is depicted here approaching a flagship at the Nore. (*Author's collection*)

from English trade. This legislation (and its successors of 1660 and 1662) decreed that all goods should be brought directly from the country where they were produced and had to be moved either in English ships or in vessels registered in the colony where they were coming from.

Charles saw the need to protect seaborne commerce as a paramount mission for the navy. From early on in the restored monarchy the brothers publicly declared their determination to support and protect trade. Convoy was introduced in time of war, with merchant ships escorted by the navy and ships were stationed out in what came to be called the Western Approaches to meet and escort in-coming merchantmen from the Mediterranean or the Atlantic. This is exactly the same problem and solution found by Admirals Lewis Bayly and Max Horton in the Western Approaches during the First and Second World Wars respectively.*

Charles frequently reviewed his fleet, formally or informally, and especially when he took personal control of the Admiralty following his brother's defenestration. After the battle of Solebay of 28 May (old style) 1672 where the Duke of York, in partnership with French allies, had fought an inconclusive battle which both sides claimed as a victory, the King stayed aboard with his fleet, then refitting on the Thames, for two nights from 6 June. And he again returned on 18 June with the Queen and all her court. This was a naval review in all but name and the royal attendance on the fleet of 6 June was sufficiently prestigious for it to be painted by William van de Velde the Younger at the King's commission.†

If the Royal Navy needs to be credited with a date of origin, then somewhere around 1660 would be it. Deeply flawed and alienating though they were, Charles II and James II undoubtedly transformed the navy into a powerful and permanent fighting force, and their love for it was shown in the way they made it part of their lives.

William III and the Glorious Revolution

James II's Catholicism and the birth of a male child to his wife Mary of Modena, a son who displaced his Protestant daughter from the succession and raised the spectre of an ongoing Catholic monarchy, led to his downfall. A group of prominent Protestants (the 'Immortal Seven'), including Rear-Admiral of England‡ Arthur Herbert, invited William of Orange, to invade England and claim the throne for himself and his wife Mary, eldest child of King James.

England's throne had limited attraction for William but the prospect of combining her navy (and finances) with that of Holland to fight against the French, with whom the Dutch had an ongoing conflict, held appeal.

Consequently, William assembled a large invasion fleet in the Maas. It consisted of fifty ships of the line,§ fifty smaller warships and fireships and about 400 transports. The ships all flew the Dutch flag but Admiral

* For a study of the Royal Navy in the Western Approaches in the First World War, see S R Dunn, *Bayly's War* (Barnsley: Seaforth Publishing, 2018).

† Although the painting may in fact depict a royal review of 10 September, the title refers to 6 June.

‡ From 1683 to 1688, when he was dismissed for refusing to support James II in the repeal of the Test Acts. Herbert carried the invitation to William from the 'Immortal Seven', disguised as a simple sailor.

§ During the second part of the seventeenth century, the term 'ship of the line' first came into use as sea warfare changed from a confused melee of individual ship duels to line tactics, rows of warships sailing on parallel courses and pounding each other with artillery. The 'line' imposed standards of manoeuvring and of design; line ships had to be strong and powerful enough to give and receive punishment.

Herbert was given overall command with *Leyden*, 62 guns, as his flagship. The fleet sailed on 20 October 1688, but strong northwest winds forced the fleet to return to its anchorage and it did not finally get away again until 1 November.

Four days later William landed at Brixham on 5 November, coming ashore from the *Brielle*, a newly-launched 53-gun Third Rate, and backed by a fleet vastly larger than that of the attempted invasion by the Spanish Armada, some 100 years earlier. Approximately 250 transport ships and sixty fishing boats transported 35,000 men, including 11,000 foot and 4,000 horse. James's support began to dissolve almost immediately upon William's arrival. Protestant officers defected from the English army and noblemen across the country declared their support for the invader.

As William's army advanced towards London, rather incongruously marching to the strains of *Lillibullero*,[*] James offered limited opposition and eventually fled the country to France on 11 December, throwing the Great Seal of England into the Thames as he went. Recaptured off Sheerness, he was imprisoned in Faversham but eventually allowed to resume his flight.

William and Mary were crowned together as joint sovereigns at Westminster Abbey on 11 April 1689, adopting the titles William and Mary, by the Grace of God, King and Queen of England, France and Ireland, Defenders of the Faith, etc.

One of William's first tasks was the pacification of Catholic Ireland where forces loyal to James were contesting William and Mary's accession. Here the ability of the combined navy to blockade towns and swiftly move land forces around Ireland's coast proved invaluable, as it would again after the Easter Rising of 1916.[†]

In March 1689, Irish Jacobites arrived from France with French troops in support to contest Protestant resistance at the siege of Derry. Naval forces were in the thick of the action and in May, at the battle of Bantry Bay, the navy under Admiral Herbert prevented a French squadron from landing soldiers on the southern Irish coast. After progress in expelling the Jacobites stalled, William himself landed at Carrickfergus on 14 June 1690 with a squadron of ships under the command of Sir Cloudesley Shovell in *Monck*, a 60-gun Third Rate. The King sailed in the yacht *Mary*.

William then personally led his armies to victory over James at the battle of the Boyne on 1 July 1690, after which James fled back to France. Leaving command of the military in Ireland to Dutch General Godert de Ginkell, William returned to England. After several further battles, de Ginkell succeeded in capturing both Galway and Limerick, thereby effectively suppressing the Jacobite forces in Ireland. A capitulation was signed on 3 October 1691, the Treaty of Limerick, and the Williamite pacification of Ireland was complete.

William recognised the service performed by the navy with his first

[*] A popular quick-step march composed by Henry Purcell in 1687, once regularly heard on the BBC World Service.

[†] See Dunn, *Bayly's War*.

Royal Fleet Review as King of England, which took place on the occasion of the taking of Limerick in 1691. The Dutch painter Everhardus
Koster recorded the event as a companion piece to a painting of William
departing from Hellevoetsluis for England in 1688.*

Two years later, in 1693, the King had reason once more to bestow
honours on the fleet. The English (and the Dutch) were once more at war
with France (the Nine Years War of 1688–97) whose king, Louis XIV, had
decided it would be expedient to support the Jacobite cause. Early in
1692, James II was at Cherbourg, preparing to re-invade England with
French help. The French fleet sailed from Brest in late May but was
attacked on 29 May off Cape Barfleur by a superior Anglo-Dutch force
under Admiral Sir Edward Russell, one of the original Immortal Seven
and flying his flag in the 100-gun First Rate HMS *Britannia*. The French
escaped after an engagement which lasted for 12 hours and, pursuing
them, the allied fleet burnt three of their ships including their flagship the
Soleil Royal, 104 guns, in Cherbourg Bay. Then on 3 June, James witnessed
twelve more French ships and most of his transports burnt in the Bay of
La Hogue by a squadron under Admiral Sir George Rooke with his flag
in the 70-gun Third Rate HMS *Eagle*. The threat of invasion was lifted and
thus ended all real hope of James regaining his throne.

Again, William recognised the contribution that the navy had made to
his cause. In February 1693, King William III and Queen Mary II
reviewed the fleet at Spithead, Portsmouth, commemorating the success at
the Battles of Barfleur and La Hogue.[†] Personal tragedy was to follow,
however; in December of the following year, Mary died of smallpox aged
only 32 and William reigned as sole monarch.

Tsar Peter the Great comes to England

A number of authoritative sources give William III conducting a fleet
review in honour of Tsar Peter ('the Great') in March 1700.[9] An anonymous article in the 1977 Silver Jubilee Fleet Review commemorative
brochure, for instance, states that 'mock naval battles were to become
popular at reviews and possibly the first one in British waters marked the
visit of Peter the Great, Tsar of Muscovy, to Portsmouth in March 1700'.[10]

But these sources are in error for one simple reason – Peter was in
Russia and then waging war with Sweden at that time. But although there
was no Royal Fleet Review for Peter in 1700, he did visit England at an
earlier date and the truth is in some ways stranger than the fiction.

Peter the Great arrived in England on 11 January 1698. He was travelling through Europe incognito as part of a Russian 'Great Embassy' under
the name Peter Mikhailov (not as an intentional disguise but rather to
avoid the limitations and ceremony of state visits). In Holland, where he
had spent the previous five months, he had laboured in the dockyards of

* Both paintings are now at the Victoria and Albert Museum.

† Queen Mary ordered that a new hospital for former seamen be built in celebration of the victory at La Hogue; this became the Royal Hospital at Greenwich (now the Old Royal Naval College).

A painting by Isaac Sailmaker of the First Rate HMS *Britannia*, flagship of Admiral Sir Edward Russell at the battle of Barfleur in 1692. She is shown side-on and stern-on and is flying the Royal Standard of William III. *(Author's collection)*

the Dutch East India Company's workshops in Amsterdam; he was keen to learn modern ship construction techniques first-hand in order to further his ambition to build a credible Russian navy. Whilst in Amsterdam, Peter personally worked on the construction of a warship which, on his departure, was presented to him. He named her *Amsterdam* and sent her to Archangel. The Tsar also engaged many skilled workers such as builders of locks, fortresses, shipwrights and seamen, up to and including Cornelis Cruys, a Dutch vice-admiral who became his advisor in maritime affairs.

Peter then travelled to England. William, keen to draw Russia into his system of alliances against the French, sent Vice-Admiral Sir David Mitchell with his flag in *Yorke*, together with the *Romney* and three smaller vessels, to escort the Tsar to England. Off the coast of Suffolk, coastal forts saluted them with gunfire and in the mouth of the Thames, Peter and Admiral Mitchell transferred to the yacht *Mary* which, in the morning of 11 January, anchored near London Bridge.

Here again Peter became deeply involved in naval matters, taking lodgings near Deptford, informally joining in with the work at the Deptford dockyard and studying ships' plans. Apart from alliances, William III and his government, the Whig Junto of 1694–9 (under Sir Charles Montague as First Lord of the Treasury), were keen to assist Peter and build a relationship with him, for there was an opportunity to increase commerce with Russia, which had plenty of pitch, potash, tallow, leather, grain and furs to trade. And by gaining rights to pass through Russia, English merchants might better join in the lucrative eastern luxury trade in silk and spices as well.*

On 2 March, King William went as far as to give Peter a yacht, *Royal Transport*, as a gift. Designed by Peregrine Osborne, Marquis of Carmarthen, it represented modern thinking, with an experimental plan and rig. The ship was altered and refitted for Peter, and given extra carved

* Later Peter also granted a lucrative tobacco monopoly to an English consortium; the colonies of Virginia and North Carolina were filled with tobacco-growing plantations.

and gilded decorations. Additionally, the Tsar was permitted access to naval and military bases, including the arsenal and gun foundry at Woolwich; visited the Royal Observatory at Greenwich, observing Venus with the first Astronomer Royal, John Flamsteed; and attended the Royal Society and the Tower of London to view the Royal Mint.

At Portsmouth, Peter was given the rare privilege of his own personal fleet review. A squadron comprising *Royal William*, *Victory* and *Association* took Peter and his suite on board and carried them into the Solent where they transferred to the flagship of Admiral Mitchell, *Humber*. Off the Isle of Wight, there were displays of tactics for his benefit and he assiduously noted down the details; seamen dressing the sails, the orders to helmsmen, the number, calibre and serving of the guns. Ships manoeuvred in unison and a mock battle took place: 'Peter was jubilant … it was a momentous day for a young man who scarcely ten years before had first seen a sail-boat.'[11] When the ships returned to their anchorage, a 21-gun salute boomed out in Peter's honour.

On 2 May 1698 the Tsar had finally to leave England for Vienna. He had intended to stay for two weeks but had remained for four months. He sailed in *Royal Transport* and was escorted to Europe by a Royal Navy squadron. He left behind a mistress, acquired at short notice in England on his arrival, the teenaged Laetitia Cross;* Peter gave her £500† as thanks for her 'hospitality'. She said it was not enough; he, that it was too much. Even now, Peter put his time to good use, visiting the port of Chatham as he departed and inspecting a naval stores depot.

On his return to Russia a large shipbuilding programme was put in hand and a fleet founded in the Baltic Sea. By the end of his reign 28,000 men were serving there, on 49 ships and 800 smaller vessels and in the nascent years of the Russian navy, many of the ships were English-built and maintained, yet another commercial benefit from the visit.

But given that Russia would become an adversary, particularly in the nineteenth century, William's hospitality may have come to be regretted by later generations. So, was 1698 a Royal Fleet Review? In strict terms no – but royalty was present in the form of the Tsar; and the result of it would impact upon future British naval history, especially in the Crimean conflict of the mid-nineteenth century, which itself would occasion no less than three Royal Fleet Reviews.

William III died in 1702, and was succeeded by a Stuart, Queen Anne. From 1707, under the acts of Union, she became sovereign of Great Britain. No fleet reviews embellished her reign, although the War of the Spanish Succession (which pitched Britain and her allies against France and hers) taxed the navy and at one point Anne took the office of Lord High Admiral herself. With her death in 1714, the Stuart monarchy came to an end.

* Laetitia Cross (1681 or 1682–4 April 1737) was a British singer and actress.

† £82,000 in today's money, according to the Bank of England's inflation calculator.

Chapter 5

The House of Hanover, 1714–1837

O N COMING TO THE THRONE, the Hanoverians broadly accepted the principle they were offered – a legally circumscribed Protestant kingdom with a powerful parliament. The early Hanoverians witnessed the transformation of Britain's naval power and by *c*1730, the Royal Navy was able to project global reach. The Treaty of Utrecht of 1713 ushered in a period of *détente* with France, which lasted until 1731, and the Royal Navy proved victorious in war with Spain in 1739–41 (the 'War of Jenkins' Ear') during which Admiral Edward Vernon ('Old Grog') defeated the Spanish fleet at Porto Bello. There followed the Seven Years War with Spain and France in which the threat of an invasion of Britain was comprehensively shattered by Admiral Edward Hawke at the battle of Quiberon Bay, 20 November 1759, when he demolished a French fleet off the coast of France at St Nazaire, and which had consequences for Britain that surely compares favourably with all that Nelson would achieve in the seas off Cadiz. Hawke destroyed six and captured one of the twenty-one ships that he faced. There was no invasion and no fleet review to celebrate his seamanship and bravery; but surely it merited one. At least William Boyce and David Garrick wrote *Heart of Oak* for him!*

Neither George I or George II conducted a Royal Fleet Review, although in September 1716, George, Prince of Wales (the future King George II) visited Portsmouth where he inspected several regiments and boarded some of the ships in the Dockyard. On arrival and departure, he was saluted by gunfire from the fortress and from the Royal Navy ships present. And in 1722, Prince George and his father, King George I, made a royal progress through Hampshire which also included a visit to Portsmouth. Here the King reviewed several naval vessels and was cheered as he stood on the quarterdeck of the newly relaunched 60-gun Fourth Rate, HMS *Canterbury*.

George III, who came to the throne in 1760, is now largely remembered

* Hawke was given an annual pension of £2,000 by Parliament, but not the immediate peerage such exploits usually attracted. He disdained to ask for the honour and it was not conferred on him until just before his death.

41

for being the monarch who tried to reassert his kingly 'rights', lost
America and suffered frequent (and eventually lasting) bouts of madness.
But he was also the monarch who, during his long reign, set the template
for a recognisably modern version of the Royal Fleet Review.

In June 1773, King George III departed for Portsmouth from his palace
at Kew by royal coach, flanked by outriders dressed in scarlet. June was his
birth month; it was also the month of his 'official birthday'. This was a
tradition started by George II, who was born in November, a month not
known in Britain for good weather. George wanted a big public celebration for his birthday and clearly November wasn't the time do it. So he
decided to combine such celebrations with an annual military parade in
the summer, originally the second Thursday in June. The review of the
fleet now planned was thus part of that pageantry.

On arrival at Portsmouth, George III was saluted by a 'triple discharge
of cannon' from 132 guns and at the Landport Gate was presented with the
keys to the fortress and greeted by John Montagu, 4th Earl of Sandwich,
First Lord of the Admiralty, and others of rank. Amongst the invited guests
for the occasion was the French ambassador. After driving through the
town, the King was escorted to the Dockyard by ropemakers carrying
green boughs in their hats and wearing purple scarves across their shoulders. Here, George held a reception at the Commissioner's House, where
his admirals and captains had assembled with their barges to escort the
King's barge to the fleet at Spithead, and knighted the mayor, John Carter.

There was no prescribed naval uniform at that date and captains often
dressed their men for special occasions. They themselves were resplendent
in the full-dress uniform first issued in regulations by Lord Anson in 1748.
Gold-braided tricorne hats over tie wigs, a brocaded kerseymere* waistcoat,
edged with lace, a gold-frogged dark blue coat, white knee breeches, white
silk stockings and silver-buckled shoes. Officers and men together must
have resembled nothing less than a bevy of tropical parrots in their gaudy.

On 22 June, the fleet assembled to greet the King comprised twenty
ships of the line, led by HMS *Barfleur*,† a 90-gun Second Rate, two frigates
and three sloops, most of them being vessels which had fought the French
and Spanish navies in the Seven Years War.

The King was rowed out to *Barfleur*, inspected the officers' quarters and
at 1530 sat down to a meal in the admiral's cabin with twenty-nine officers of the fleet. After this repast, yards were manned and he was rowed
around the lines of ships with an escort of captains' barges, receiving a
21-gun-salute from each vessel as he passed, before finally boarding the
royal yacht *Augusta*,‡ renamed as *Princess Augusta* by George in honour of
the occasion on 21 July. The painter John Cleveley captured the royal
progress in three watercolours. After dark, two strokes on *Barfleur*'s bell
prompted every gunport in the fleet to be opened to show a burst of light.

* Kerseymere is a fine twilled woollen cloth; frogging is ornamental braid or coat fastenings consisting of spindle-shaped buttons and loops.

† Later to make a name under Cuthbert Collingwood on the Glorious First of June.

‡ Ex-*Charlotte II* built in 1710, rebuilt with yacht rig in 1771 as *Augusta*.

George III reviewing the fleet on 22 June 1773, from a watercolour by J Clevely. The escort of captains' barges can be clearly seen. (© *National Maritime Museum D0439*)

For four days, this programme was repeated until on the 26th the royal yacht led the blue division of the fleet on a short cruise in Sandown Bay, on the southern side of the Isle of Wight. During the royal visit, twelve ladies of Portsmouth asked for the honour of rowing the King from the dockyard to a warship. George apparently enjoyed the experience. And at the conclusion of the royal visit, the King distributed more than £2,000 for the needy and ordered the release of all prisoners confined for debt.

Nothing like this had happened for over 70 years; the visit and review had been at Sandwich's suggestion and 'this demonstration of royal interest … advanced the king's own knowledge … provided a public demonstration of royal interest and support for the navy … and showed off the reality of British sea power and the speed with which it could be mobilised'.[1] Not least, one assumes, to the French ambassador.

1778 and the American Revolutionary War

Five years later, George conducted another review of his navy but in very different circumstances. Britain was at war with its American colonies; and France had allied herself with the colonists and was again at war with Britain.

Protests against 'taxation without representation' which followed the Stamp Act escalated into boycotts, culminating in the *soi-disant* 'Sons of Liberty' destroying a shipment of tea in Boston Harbour. When Britain responded by closing the port and passing a series of punitive measures against the Massachusetts Bay Colony (the 'Intolerable Acts'), the Massachusetts colonists established a shadow government which took control of the countryside from the Crown. Twelve colonies formed the Continental Congress to coordinate their resistance, establishing committees and conventions that effectively took over the governance of the colony. British attempts to disarm the Massachusetts militia in Concord led to open combat on 19 April 1775. From then on Britain and America were at war. But a great concern for minimising expenditure led Prime Minister Lord North to refuse to order a full naval mobilisation; in fact the Admiralty Board was instructed to decrease expenditure, which was achieved by reducing the dockyard workforce. As a result, 'orders for ships of the line had virtually ceased by 1777'.[2]

Seeing an opportunity to economically and militarily cripple her old enemy, Britain, together with the chance of regaining territories lost in the Seven Years War, France gave active support to the American cause. 'There was an explicit assumption in France that Britain would be gravely damaged if it no longer had a monopoly on American trade … France … would become the dominant trading partner.'[3]

Britain finally ordered a full naval mobilisation in January 1778; and France formally recognised the United States on 6 February 1778, through the signing of a Treaty of Alliance. Hostilities with Britain soon followed.* A French fleet was believed to be sailing or about to sail from Toulon for the North American Seaboard shortly thereafter and Admiral the Honourable Augustus Keppel, was ordered to organise a fleet and assemble it at Spithead. At this point George III, now interested in matters naval and seeking to assist his countrymen, decided that he should make a royal visit to Portsmouth to add some impetus to the fleet's preparations.

Keppel was a distinguished officer who had been present when Admiral George Anson took the Spanish treasure galleon *Nuestra Senora de Covadonga* in 1743, from which action he carried the scars of battle in missing teeth and shrapnel gashes. Quite what Admiral Keppel made of this sudden and probably unwelcome royal visit is not recorded. With his men busy preparing their ships for sea and a French fleet either out at sea or soon to be so, it must have caused some inconvenience. However, he was possibly placated when John Montagu, 4th Earl of Sandwich[†] and the First Lord of the Admiralty, wrote requesting that Keppel should arrange an entertaining and informative reception for the King but that he should not hesitate to put to sea if the need arose; such a spectacle would, in any case, no doubt entertain the monarch and his entourage.

George arrived at Portsmouth on 2 May with Queen Charlotte and Lord Sandwich in attendance. He was escorted to the Governor's House to the cheers of the populace and renditions of 'God Save the King'. On Sunday 3rd he attended divine service at the Royal Garrison Chapel and the following day boarded his favourite royal yacht, *Princess Augusta* for a Royal Fleet Review, which duly started at 1000.

As in 1773, the King sailed out of the anchorage with the fleet's captains' barges in close formation around his vessel and 21-gun salutes

* The Spanish (in 1779) and the Dutch (1780) would also join in on the American side. In the latter case Britain declared war first, in an attempt to cut off supplies to America from the Baltic, carried in Dutch merchantmen.

† Sandwich, tall, suave, driven, a lover of cricket and music was First Lord for the third time. His fondness for eating salt beef between two slices of bread led to the naming of the eponymous snack. He was notorious for living openly with his mistress, the opera singer Martha Ray, by whom he had a succession of children until she was murdered by a jealous would-be lover. In the matter of the King's interference, Sandwich was reaping what he had sown, for in 1773 he had invited the King to Portsmouth for the fleet review, and in 1774 he had commissioned a series of ship models and one of Chatham Dockyard as a gift to George III in an attempt to interest him in naval affairs.

blasted out from each warship as the royal party passed them by. At 1100 George raised his Royal Standard aboard Keppel's flagship, the Second Rate HMS *Prince George*, mounting 90 guns, to the accompaniment of a further 21-gun-salute from the fleet. For luncheon, the royal party dined under an awning aboard the flagship and then retired back to their yacht.

On 5 May, the uxorious King (for, unlike his forebears, he had no mistresses during his marriage and was devoted to his spouse) gave his wife the signal honour of her own fleet review; Queen Charlotte progressed around the fleet to cheers and cannon fire, no doubt enjoying the loyalty to her husband thereby demonstrated.

Keppel could be forgiven for thinking that this was the end of the royal intrusion on his preparations. But George now extended his stay, visiting *Centaur*, a 54-gun vessel which was in dry dock being sheathed, discussing naval tactics with Sandwich and the admiral and seemingly unaware (or uncaring) of the disruption his visit was causing, whilst at the same time urging the fleet's immediate despatch. The naval conversation must have been a particular trial for Keppel. He was a leading light in the 'Rockingham Whigs', a political grouping which saw themselves as fighting to restrain the King, possessed an acute fear of government and monarchical 'tyranny' and deeply distrusted any policy which might remove power from men such as themselves. Keppel was also a critic of the present government. Sandwich, although nominally also a Whig (albeit of a different faction), was a government minister in the party favoured by the King, primarily Tory, a political enemy of Keppel to the point that the admiral suspected that the First Lord would be happy to see him defeated. All the while, George was receiving letters from his prime minister, Lord North, who harboured strong reservations over his ability to conduct a new war with France and wanted to resign his office. The King ignored them and thus a man who was 'both weak and unwilling led the British war effort'.[4]

Finally, George departed on 9 May, to palpable relief. The fleet gained some small reward for their efforts, however. Several days later, each vessel received an additional ration of supplies from the King to thank them for their part in the review and there was a liberal sprinkling of honours and promotions for those officers present.

Keppel's fleet did engage the French, but not in the Atlantic, for a fear of invasion by forces based at Brest caused Sandwich to hold him back in British waters. On 27 July 1778, Keppel found the French Brest squadron off Ushant. In an inconclusive fight, both sides suffered heavy damage and, on his return, Keppel was court-martialled for his pains, accused of not following the official *Fighting Instructions* but attacking before forming line of battle and failing to do his utmost. He was exonerated, the court finding that the charges against him had been brought with malicious intent and were unfounded. Keppel became convinced that he had been betrayed by his second-in-command, Sir Hugh Palliser, who was politically and socially aligned with Sandwich (he had been Comptroller of the Navy at the Navy Board from 1770 to 1775, in which year he joined the Board of Admiralty as First Naval Lord to Sandwich's First Lord) and the government of Lord North. When the court's verdict was made public, ships in Spithead fired salutes and naval officers escorted Keppel to his house. Populist pro-Whig feeling ran high and a famous hotel on The Hard renamed itself 'The Keppel's Head' in his honour. Men marched through the streets of London and other cities wearing 'Keppel cockades' and demanding that windows be illuminated in celebration of the verdict. And Lord Sandwich had to flee the Admiralty building with his mistress when the mob broke down the gates.*

The war with America was not concluded until 1783. It had become a world war, encompassing Europe, India and the Caribbean. Indeed, the last shots of the war were fired between warships at the battle of Cuddalore in the Bay of Bengal on 20 June 1783. Despite the multiple demands on it, the Royal Navy had performed well overall, although Rear-Admiral Sir Thomas Graves failed in the major task of securing command of the sea in the battle of Chesapeake Bay on 5 September 1781. This was 'the pivot upon which everything turned'[5] according to George Washington, and forced the British army under Cornwallis to surrender. Nonetheless, in the West Indies, the British scored a major victory over the French navy in April 1782, when Admiral George Brydges Rodney defeated a French fleet and prevented an intended invasion of Jamaica. And later, the navy frustrated Spanish and French attempts to seize Gibraltar. On 3 September 1783, all the belligerent parties signed the Treaty of Paris, by which Great Britain agreed to recognise the sovereignty of the United States and formally end the war.

The need to fight on so many different fronts across the world and, from early 1778, to keep an army at home to deal with the threat of French invasion, meant that in the end Britain was defeated in detail in North America. The navy's strength could not be concentrated at the strategically vital points and the army was spread across too many operational spheres.

The American naval theoretician, Alfred Thayer Mahan, later noted that

* But the mob is always fickle. By 1782 Keppel was being accused of deliberate poor performance at the battle of Ushant to put Sandwich and the government in bad odour.

to be effective calls for superior numbers, because the different divisions are too far apart for mutual support. Each must therefore be equal to any probable combination against it, which implies superiority everywhere to the force of the enemy actually opposed, as the latter may be unexpectedly reinforced. How impossible and dangerous such a defensive strategy is, when not superior in force, is shown by the frequent inferiority of the English abroad, as well as in Europe, despite the effort to be everywhere equal.[6]

Over a hundred years later, this was a lesson not lost on First Sea Lord Sir John Fisher when he brought home British ships from across the empire to concentrate them in British waters, nor on Grand Fleet C-in-C Admiral Sir John Jellicoe who between 1914 and 1916 fought hard to keep his battleships together and concentrated in the North Sea and not frittered away in sideshows.

In the end, French involvement had proven decisive for the success of the American cause; but France made few gains and incurred crippling debts. Spain made some territorial additions but failed to recover Gibraltar. The Dutch were defeated and were compelled to cede territory to Great Britain. But the peace would be brief.

1789 and the King's Madness

The French Revolution can be said to have commenced on 5 May 1789. But of more immediate interest in Britain at that time was George III's recovery from so-called madness, which had afflicted him the previous year. In all probability, he was suffering from the disease now known as porphyria, in which substances called porphyrins build up, negatively affecting the skin or nervous system. By July he was recovering and it was decided that the King should take a holiday at Weymouth, together with his wife and daughters, on the first of what the press came to call his 'Aquatic Excursions'.[7]

To help celebrate the King's recovery, it was decided to stage a Royal Fleet Review at Plymouth and to that end, the King and his retinue departed Weymouth and travelled overland to Saltram House, a mansion designed by Robert Adam owned by the Parker family, arriving on 15 August. At Plymouth, instead of his beloved royal yacht *Princess Augusta*, the navy had placed the 32-gun frigate *Southampton* at the King's disposal, accompanied by the 74-gun Third Rate HMS *Magnificent*.

On 17 August at 1100 the royal party arrived at Plymouth Dockyard to the by-now usual salute of cannon fire, this time from the ramparts' and citadel's guns. They were received by the Dockyard commissioner, Captain John Laforey, the King's great friend the Earl of Chesterfield and the First Lord of the Admiralty Earl Chatham, together with members of the Admiralty Board and other local worthies. Philip Stanhope, 5th Earl of Chesterfield was a particular favourite of George III. In 1784 he had been sworn onto the Privy Council and appointed Ambassador to Spain, a post he held until 1787, without ever thinking that he might need to visit that country. John Pitt, 2nd Earl of Chatham, was the eldest son of William Pitt, the first earl, and two and a half years older than his more famous brother William Pitt the Younger who, as prime minister, had appointed him to the Admiralty in July 1788.

After taking refreshment the royal party went on board the brand new

Second Rate HMS *Impregnable*, which mounted 98 guns. She was flying the flag of the commander-in-chief at Plymouth, Rear-Admiral Sir Richard Bickerton, who had been knighted after steering the King's barge at the 1778 review. As George came aboard, all the other vessels in Plymouth Sound dressed ship and fired off salutes, answered by the artillery on shore. In a prefiguring of future fleet reviews, there was also a ship of a foreign navy present, the Dutch *Lynx*.

The royal party remained aboard for about an hour before returning ashore in their barge. They were escorted by a cutter 'rowed by six fine young women and steered by a seventh all habited in loose white gowns … and black bonnets'.[8] Each oarswoman had a sash across her shoulders of royal purple, emblazoned in gold with 'Long Live Their Majesties'.

On land once more, further time was spent inspecting the Dockyard until, at 1530, the royal party left by barge for Saltram, accompanied by 'an immense number of sloops, barges and boats'.[9] The guns of the citadel and the warships again sounded as the royal party passed them. There was an unfortunate incident when a sloop carrying spectators overturned and four women and a child were reported drowned. When the King was alerted to the mishap, he declared that any children orphaned by the disaster would be provided for.

The following day the fleet review took place. At 0800, the King was rowed out to *Southampton* and put to sea, together with *Lowestoft* (32 guns), *Magnificent* and the yacht of Charles Lennox, 3rd Duke of Richmond and Master General of the Ordnance, which carried a band playing away merrily. Shortly afterwards the sails of men-o-war could be seen from behind the Staddon Heights on the eastern side of the Sound and as the

George III in HMS *Southampton* reviewing the fleet off Plymouth, 18 August 1789, by Lieutenant William Elliott RN. Elliot was a naval officer as well as painter, who exhibited at the Royal Academy during the 1780s. This work is signed and dated 1790. HMS *Southampton* is centre left flying the Royal Standard. *(© National Maritime Museum B6883)*

Southampton rounded the Mewstone a further six ships of the line, two frigates and two cutters came into view. This was the squadron of Commodore Samuel Granston Goodall with his broad pennant in the 74-gun *Carnatic*, the so-called Observation Squadron, which had recently been stationed at the western end of the English Channel, unsettling the French. When the *Southampton* came within half a mile of Goodall's ships a royal salute of twenty-one guns was fired by every vessel, whereupon the larger ships, which were in line ahead and about two cable lengths apart, tacked out to sea and split into two divisions to commence the manoeuvres which allowed the fleet to stage a mock battle for the King's entertainment.

Another squadron under Captain John MacBride in HMS *Cumberland* took the part of the French and, after around an hour and a half of exercises, MacBride was compelled to haul down his colours and the 'French' were vanquished, no doubt to general rejoicing. Certainly, the King 'was highly pleased with his excursion'.[10] Goodall's ships then passed under *Southampton*'s stern, their rigging and masts fully manned. George expressed interest as *Cumberland* passed by, for her starboard gun ports were manned by a number of negroes dressed in white and wearing turbans.

One by one, the captains came to the royal ship's side and stood in their barges to kiss hands with the King and then followed *Southampton* back to the Sound. By 1900, George and his party were safely returned to Saltram House.

Thursday 20th saw the royal entourage visit the Victualling Office where the King sampled hardtack and a cask of salt beef, a portion of which he ordered be sent back to Saltram. The King then toured the lower parts of the citadel and later met with the mayor and corporation, invalids and the local militia, whose band serenaded him with *God Save the King*. Back on the water, George travelled to inspect the Gun Wharf and the ordnance before retiring to his temporary abode.

The King and Queen now enjoyed several days at leisure, including a visit to Mount Edgcumbe, home to Lord George Edgcumbe, himself a quondam commander-in-chief at Plymouth and who had fought at the battle of Quiberon Bay. Here, on the party's disembarkation, 'sixteen young maidens dressed in white preceded the royal pair, strewing roses, carnations and myrtles'. When they came to the steps up to the house 'each maiden on her knee, presented a curious flower to their majesties'.[11] Finally, on the 25th, the royal party left Saltram House to return overland to Weymouth, whilst Lord Chatham and others boarded *Southampton* to sail for the same port. George had enjoyed his visit and his family were delighted at his return to health. In gratitude for the hospitality shown, the king donated 1,000 guineas to the Dockyard workers, 250 guineas to the poor of Plymouth, Stonehouse and Plymouth Dock and 200 guineas to the barge crews who had attended him on his visit. Captain Byard of the

Impregnable, who had steered his barge on each day of the visit, was granted a knighthood and *Southampton*'s commander, Captain Douglas, was also made a knight for his hosting of the royal party aboard his ship. Additionally, there was a generous round of promotions for more junior officers and the hospitality at his home gained George Edgcumbe an elevation to the Earldom of Mount Edgcumbe. The fleet had demonstrated its splendour and fighting ability to its monarch. But it would soon face much greater tests.

1794 and the Glorious First of June

In early 1794 France was starving. Death stalked the land, both from hunger and from the reign of terror of the Jacobin Committee of Public Safety. One year previously, on 2 January 1793, French republican forts at Brest had fired on the British brig-sloop HMS *Childers* (14 guns), hitting her once and destroying one of her cannons. Weeks later, following the execution of King Louis XVI on 21 January, diplomatic ties between Britain and France were broken. On 1 February, France declared war on both Britain and the Dutch Republic. Britain was at war with France again.

During 1793 the harvest in France had failed and the winter had been harsh. Additionally, the British fleet was blockading France's harbours and preventing imports. Blockade of an enemy's ports, preventing any entry or exit, was a powerful weapon of war for Britain (and would work again 120 years later when Britain's distant blockade of Germany was a significant contributing factor to the German defeat in the First World War*). As a result of these two factors, the shortage of food in France was severe and starvation widespread.

France turned to her colonies in the Americas and to America itself, which owed a debt for French help during the revolutionary war. The French National Convention gave orders for the formation of a large convoy of sailing vessels to assemble at Hampton Roads in Chesapeake Bay, where French Admiral Pierre Jean Van Stabel would wait for them. Contemporary sources claim 350 ships gathered there, but more recent estimates give just over 100. This convoy had been assisted by the United States government with both supplies and ships and the primary foodstuff carried was 67,000 barrels of flour, together with 7,263 barrels of sugar; in total, the value of the shipment was estimated at £1.5 million.†

Britain had gained intelligence from a naval officer on the spot that the convoy was planned and during April and May the British fleet was deployed in the Atlantic Ocean, hoping to intercept the incoming supply ships. At the same time, the French Atlantic fleet, twenty-four ships of the line commanded by Rear-Admiral Louis Thomas Villaret-Joyeuse with his flag in the 120-gun First Rate *Montagne*, had sailed from Brest to escort the convoy into port.

* See S R Dunn, *Blockade* (Barnsley: Seaforth Publishing, 2016).

† Perhaps 130 times that amount at today's values.

On 28 May, in foggy conditions and 400 nautical miles west of the island of Ushant, the French battlefleet was found by Admiral Lord Howe commanding the Channel Fleet of thirty-four ships. Skirmishes and manoeuvring were followed the next day by more serious clashes. But on the morning of 1 June the weather was fine and clear and Howe's management of his ships in the preceding days had gained for the British fleet the weather gage, being windward of their opponents.

Like Keppel before him, Howe's plan was to ignore the *Fighting Instructions* and have his ships to run down onto the French fleet, break through all along their line and individually engage their opposite numbers. These intentions were difficult to transmit by signal and not all his captains fully understood or complied with the orders. In the end, only a few ships pierced the French line – Howe's flagship *Queen Charlotte*, together with *Defence, Marlborough, Royal George, Queen* and *Brunswick*.

All along the two lines of ships the fighting was severe. By the time the battle was over, eleven British and twelve French ships were wholly or partially dismasted. Some 7,000 French sailors were killed, wounded or captured and there were 1,000 British casualties. Six French ships were seized as prizes and another, the *Vengeur*, sunk by *Brunswick*. Many of the French fleet were badly damaged but most were able to effect an escape, for the British were too exhausted to pursue them. Tactically, the battle was a considerable Royal Navy success; but the main objective was not achieved, for the supply convoy was not intercepted and reached France unscathed.

Howe sent his flag captain ahead by fast frigate; he arrived in Plymouth

George III on Admiral Howe's flagship, the *Queen Charlotte*, by H P Briggs. Lord Howe is shown on the quarterdeck of his flagship, receiving the diamond sword from King George III. The King stands in the centre of the deck, with Queen Charlotte to the left, wearing a yellow silk dress with a red petticoat, together with other members of the Royal Family. *(© National Maritime Museum BHC0476)*

on 9 June and went straight to London with the news. Earl Chatham, First Lord of the Admiralty, took the news to King George who immediately wrote a letter of congratulations. And Chatham suggested to the monarch that he should visit Portsmouth to formally receive and review the victorious fleet.

The news was received rapturously in Britain and 'The Glorious First of June', as the battle came to be known, was perceived as having negated any threat of invasion from France and to have (re-)established Britain's superiority at sea. Firework displays took place all over London for several nights and the battle was celebrated in a number of plays, including one by Richard Sheridan,* weeks after news of the victory broke. And a gilded array of eminent artists, including Philippe de Loutherbourg, James Gillray, Mather Brown and Robert Cleveley rushed to Portsmouth to paint Howe and his ships from life.

Howe had arrived back at Portsmouth on 13 June. As the flagship anchored, a salute was fired from the town and another when he landed at the Sally Port. As he stepped onto dry land the band of the Gloucester Regiment played *See the Conquering Hero Comes* from Handel's *Judas Maccabaeus*. A Grand Ball was held on 16 June, at which Howe's daughter Maria had the honour of leading the dancers, and the House of Commons adjourned for 10 days from the 20th in order to accompany the King southwards.

King George and Queen Charlotte arrived on the 26th and the royal party, some of whose ladies wore small gold anchors on chains around their necks, was transported by barge to Spithead where they boarded the flagship, *Queen Charlotte*. George had specifically required that sailors from Howe's ship row him and his party out to the flagship, a signal honour to the crew. Once aboard, the King presented Howe with a sword liberally encrusted with jewels, valued at some 3,000 guineas;† Howe pointed at his men and stated that the credit really belonged to them. George inspected the ship after which he made a donation to the crew from his privy purse and all the men were invited to touch Admiral Howe's new sword. The six captured French vessels were proudly displayed to the King.

In the following days of celebration, the King attended the launch of the 98-gun HMS *Prince of Wales*, reviewed the Gloucester Regiment, made further gifts of money to Dockyard workers and finally embarked on the Fifth Rate frigate *Aquilon*‡ for a cruise on the Solent. Seven magnificent barges belonging to the King accompanied him and as they neared *Queen Charlotte*, Howe's flagship fired two guns to which the entire fleet responded with a simultaneous 21-gun salute. As the frigate took the royal party around the fleet, each ship' bands played martial airs. Even the *Aquilon* running aground on the Isle of Wight failed to dampen the fun. George feasted with the captains and royal family also dined privately with

* *The Glorious First of June*. It premiered on 2 July 1794 at the Drury Lane theatre and was based on newspaper accounts of the battle. The profits made from the play were donated to the families of those killed in the fighting.

† Howe also received, *inter alia*, the thanks of both Houses of Parliament and of the Common Council of London, the freedom of the Skinners' livery company (in two gold boxes valued at £100 each) and the freedom of the Goldsmiths' company.

‡ *Aquilon* had acted as a signal repeating vessel and fleet messenger during the battle. She also towed the 74-gun *Marlborough* to safety.

Howe and his immediate family. Finally, the King departed by road from Portsmouth to a cacophony of salutes and fireworks.

This is the only recorded example of a Royal Fleet Review immediately after a successful battle, and such was the appreciation of the victory that it became the first battle for which British naval officers were awarded a medal, the Naval Gold Medal. Flag officers each received a gold chain which suspended a gold medallion of neoclassical design showing Britannia on an ancient galley, crowned by winged victory. And captains who had shown particular valour or enterprise were awarded a similar device, to be worn from the button hole on a blue and white ribbon. To further commemorate the victory, the King decreed that admirals could wear gold lace rings of rank on their uniform cuffs. However, the conflict was far from over; indeed, Britain and France would be at war for the next 20 years.

1814 and Victory over Napoleon

By 1811, George III's descent into 'madness' and ill health had become so bad that his eldest son, also George, became Prince Regent and the King was confined to Windsor Castle, where he lived out the rest of his life. Napoleonic France was finally defeated and the emperor abdicated on 11 April 1814.* The Treaty of Paris, dated 30 May, ended the war between France and the Sixth Coalition. It seemed that Europe was finally at peace (although Britain was at war with America and the Royal Navy was blockading her coast). Nelson had become a national hero for his exploits at the Nile, Copenhagen and Trafalgar and the latter victory over the French and Spanish fleet in 1805 had ensured that 'the Royal Navy could roam the seas and oceans virtually unchallenged'.[12]

But Britain badly needed peace. The cost of 20 years of war coupled with the difficulties in trade due the Napoleon's 'Continental System' meant that Britain's economy was in tatters and the national debt had spiralled to unprecedented heights. A long period of peace was needed to recover.

To celebrate the signing of the peace treaty, a naval review was quickly arranged to take place in June at Portsmouth. The Prince Regent would preside and representatives of Britain's key allies in the war against France were invited. From Austria came foreign minister Prince von Metternich, from Russia, Tsar Alexander I, and from Prussia, King Frederick William III.† They were ferried from Europe to Dover by the royal yacht *Royal Sovereign*, together with other private vessels of the king, under the command of the Duke of Clarence, later King William the IV, the 'Sailor King', in his flagship HMS *Impregnable*, arriving on 7 June.

It transpired not to be an enjoyable occasion. The Tsar decided to stay with his sister at the Pulteney Hotel instead of in a royal residence. The Prince Regent and the Tsar soon found each other irritating and ended barely on speaking terms. The King of Prussia preferred to sleep on a

* Although Napoleon would return to France in March 1815 for the 'Hundred Days' until defeated at Waterloo on 18 June.

† The Prince Regent and all three potentates would also attend a military review in Hyde Park, London, on 20 June.

rough camp bed than in the state bed that had been prepared for him at the Regent's residence, Clarence House, and the king's victorious general, Blücher, got steaming drunk on brandy at the formal dinners. A banquet for them at the Guildhall cost £20,000.[13]* By the end of their stay, the honoured guests were becoming a burden. Prime Minister Lord Liverpool was moved to comment that 'when folks don't know how to behave, they would do better to stay at home'.[14]

The visit was intended to be a celebration of victory. But there was also a British sub-plot. The most powerful navy in the world would be on display; it was the same navy that had swept the French and Spanish fleets from the seas. And the unstated message was the power of Britain to close the seas to any other nation. Peace would be much better than war.

On 22 June, the royal guests were taken out to Spithead in a beautiful barge with sixteen rowers, all handsome men in white shirts, red breeches and stockings with blue velvet shoes and silver buckles. Once at sea, they observed at first hand four frigates, *Magicienne*, *Andromache*, *Amphion* and *Galetea*, conducting complex evolutions. The new 98-gun Second Rate HMS *Impregnable*[†] flew the prince's royal standard, no fewer than four 21-gun salutes were fired by all vessels present during the day and ships manned their yards. In total fifteen ships of the line and thirty-one frigates were in attendance, all veterans of the Napoleonic Wars. Six of the ships were captured prizes, *Ville de Paris*, *Andromache*, *Belle Poule*, *Cleopatre*, *Magicienne* and *Terpsichore*.

And it was not just the warships that were on parade. The guests were also shown the great armament and shipyard facilities that supported the fleet. They saw the huge mills where the blocks used in the rigging of warships were manufactured, the ordnance works and the tremendous array of naval armaments. At his request, Tsar Alexander visited the navy's Haslar Hospital to see for himself the treatments used there. Sir Richard Bickerton, now an admiral, was congratulated for his organisation of the events.

On the evening of the review the distinguished visitors assembled on the balcony of Government House and drank a toast to 'the British Nation'. And on departure the following day, the Regent knighted the mayor, Henry White, and left a sum of money for distribution to those in need.

But there had been no sign of any technological advance on previous Royal Reviews. The vessels which saluted the Prince Regent and his party were very little different from those that had assembled for George III in 1773. They were sailing ships every one.[‡] Nevertheless, the mighty naval power on display did usher in a period of relative peace. Indeed 'from around the time of the battle of Quiberon Bay in 1759 to the rise of German naval power in the late nineteenth and early twentieth centuries, Britain's navy unquestionably ruled the waves. The period 1815 [to the] 1890s is even known as the *Pax Britannica*.'[15] Furthermore, the historian

* About £1.5 million today, according to the Bank of England.

† This was the second ship of that name; the first, which had been present at the 1789 review, was wrecked in 1799.

‡ It is stated in many places that this was the last Royal Fleet Review which was comprised entirely of sailing ships, but this is not true.

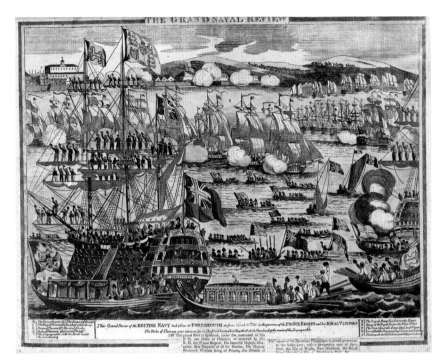

Etching of the June 1814 Grand Fleet Review, a premature celebration of victory over France and a demonstration of Britain's naval power. HMS *Impregnable* (launched 1810) is in the foreground. (© *National Maritime Museum PW4791*)

David Cannadine has averred that 'British ships were unchallenged by any western power. For the first time, that proudly boastful claim, made in 1745, that Britannia rules the waves, had serious and global substance to it.'[16]

1821 and the Coronation of George IV

The long reign of George III ended with his death on 29 January 1820. He had been king for 60 years; now the throne passed to the Prince Regent as George IV. He was largely unfit to govern and widely hated. In 1795 he had married Caroline of Brunswick; it proved a disastrous marriage and they separated in 1796 after the birth of their only child. Now aged 57, George IV was obese, addicted to laudanum, alcoholic and licentious. He thoroughly merited Shelley's line of description in his poem *England in 1819*; 'Princes, the dregs of their dull race.'[17]

George's coronation was delayed because he first tried to divorce his estranged wife (which he was talked out of because it would involve the revelation of his own multitudinous sordid affairs) and then requested and ensured the introduction of a Pains and Penalties Bill. The Bill would have annulled the marriage and stripped Caroline of the title of queen but it proved an extremely unpopular measure with the public and was withdrawn from Parliament.

The ceremony, which he had largely designed and planned himself, went ahead on 19 July 1821 at Westminster Abbey and Hall. But the King insisted on the exclusion of his wife. To ensure his veto, George hired prize-fighters, costumed as pages, to act as 'bouncers' to keep her out. The coronation was a fabulously expensive and ostentatious affair and, despite the monarch's unpopularity, it was marked throughout the realm, although often with riots in support of Queen Caroline as at, *inter alia*, Manchester and Lincoln.

There was no naval review to accompany the coronation, though some sources assert that there was a naval coronation review in 1820; moreover, these also claim that HMS *Beagle*, later to carry the naturalist Charles Darwin on his voyage of discovery, participated and led a fleet of ships up river and under the new London Bridge. Neither is likely. First, the coronation was in 1821 not 1820, and secondly, there is simply no evidence that such a commemoration took place. However, for the coronation 'the vicinity of the River Thames was enlivened by the constant discharge of royal salutes from a gun brig decorated with the colours of all nations moored between Blackfriars and Waterloo Bridges, which were [*sic*] continued firing every fifteen minutes from day break until after midnight'.[18] *Beagle* could be described as a brig and so the 'gun brig' could have been her. But there was no other Royal Navy warship involved, only 'rocket boats [which] were also rowed up and down the river all night discharging showers of fireworks'.[19]

And in Portsmouth, which the King had visited in September 1820 and where a local brewer George Garrett had been knighted for giving that day's royal welcome address, there was a full military celebration on coronation day. The fortress battery fired a fusillade of artillery volleys, whilst the navy ships in harbour fired 21-gun salutes, each vessel dressed with their colours.

Captains of the Royal Navy afloat or on half pay assembled to dine at the George Inn, with Commodore Sir Charles Paget in the chair;* and 500 attendees at the National Schools were treated to a dinner of roast beef and plum pudding after which the children sang 'God Save the King'. But there was no Royal Fleet Review.

George IV died on 26 June 1830. On his demise, *The Times* newspaper captured the majority opinion; 'there never was an individual less regretted by his fellow-creatures than this deceased king. What eye has wept for him? What heart has heaved one throb of unmercenary sorrow? ... If he ever had a friend – a devoted friend in any rank of life – we protest that the name of him or her never reached us.'[20]

His only legitimate child, Princess Charlotte of Wales, had died from post-partum complications in 1817, after delivering a stillborn son. His oldest brother, George III's second son Prince Frederick, Duke of York and Albany, had died childless in 1827. And so the succession passed to the third son of George III, Prince William, Duke of Clarence, who took the name William IV (and was popularly known as 'the sailor king'). When William died in June 1837 the reign of Shelly's 'Rulers who neither see nor feel nor know/ But leechlike to their fainting country cling'[21] came to an end.

* Paget, the son of Henry Bayly-Paget, 1st Earl of Uxbridge, had been appointed to the command of the royal yacht *Prince Regent* on 1 January 1819 and afterwards to the yacht *Royal George*.

Part Two:

VICTORIAN AND EDWARDIAN POMP

God of our fathers, known of old,
Lord of our far-flung battle-line,
Beneath whose awful Hand we hold
Dominion over palm and pine —
Lord God of Hosts, be with us yet,
Lest we forget — lest we forget!

Rudyard Kipling, *Recessional* (1897), on the occasion
of the Diamond Jubilee Royal Fleet Review.

Chapter 6

Emperors, Kings and Princes, 1842–1845

O N 20 JUNE 1837, Queen Victoria came to the throne, aged 18. She inherited a navy of some 292 ships (see Appendix 2), of which over half (157) were laid up 'in ordinary' (i.e. in reserve with no masts or rigging). A substantial number of these ships had been launched and placed straight into ordinary without ever being commissioned. The naval bases in the Medway, Portsmouth and Plymouth were full of such vessels.

Strikingly, twelve out of a total of eighteen First Rates – the largest line-of-battle ships – were laid up and those in commission were largely used for harbour service in naval ports, to provide appropriate flagships for the port admirals, or as depot ships. There was no battlefleet in home waters nor any grouping of partially-manned ships which could be quickly crewed up for action. There were twenty-four steam vessels but these were not warships but paddle ships, used as despatch vessels, tugs and the like. Ships that were in service were largely deployed abroad, principally in the Mediterranean at Malta. Others were involved in attempting to cut off the slave trade at source, around the coast of Africa.*

These naval dispositions reflected the government's priorities at the time. Europe was largely at peace and the principal foreign policy concerns were to protect the routes to, and borders of, India, the jewel in the crown of British possessions. Russia was considered the likely aggressor here, for the 'Great Game' of Russia's designs on India and its northern border was starting. And thanks to Peter the Great and his visit to England in 1698, Russia now had a navy of over seventy-two ships in the Black and Baltic Seas. Moreover, the routes to India were straddled by the lands of the Ottoman Empire and therefore Britain must protect Turkey, Russia's traditional enemy, even if this rambling and decrepit polity held little appeal to most Britons. The same thinking applied to Persia and Afghanistan, through which Russia could advance on India.

The French with eighty-two ships, although currently under a

* Britain had abol-
ished slavery in 1833
and all slaves were
freed from a manda-
tory 'apprenticeship'
in 1838.

monarchy, were always a potential issue. Thus, for all these reasons, the Mediterranean was considered the best strategic placement for the fleet. And the pressing need was still to rebuild Britain's economy from the depletions of 20 years of war with France.

Victoria was not crowned until the year after her accession (28 June 1838). There was no naval review to celebrate the coronation. Two years later she married Prince Albert of Saxe-Coburg and Gotha. But it was not until 1842 that she finally presided over the first Royal Fleet Review in her honour.

1842, The Grand Fleet Review

At the end of February, Queen, Prince and court were staying at the Royal Pavilion in Brighton. Victoria had with her as guests the Duke of Saxe-Coburg, her father-in-law, and her two cousins Prince Augustus and Prince Leopold; Prime Minister Sir Robert Peel was in attendance. At 0730 on Monday 28 February, the party boarded five carriages and set out for Portsmouth. Triumphal arches were erected in the approaches to Portsmouth and the streets were lined with troops. It was a miserable day, foggy and with heavy drizzle. Prince Albert, who became seasick the moment he stepped into a boat, must have been dreading it.★

Arriving at the port, they were greeted by First Lord of the Admiralty Thomas Hamilton, 9th Earl of Haddington, assorted other naval lords and the Duke of Wellington who had stayed overnight in Portsmouth at 'The George'.[1] The latter rode out to meet the carriages and led them into the town. It was windy and raining, conditions deemed too poor for them to

★ 'The Prince Consort hated the sight of the sea – where he was always deadly sick – and everything in connection with it' (Gambier, *Links in my life on land and sea*, p 281)

HMS *Queen* (1839) visited by Victoria, a brand new 110-gun three-decker in a painting by R S Thomas. Admiral Owen's red flag is shown flying from the main, together with the Red Ensign, Union Flag and the Royal Standard. As *Black Eagle* approached *Queen*, guns were fired in salute very close by and in the painting, both the ship on the right and the left are shown firing salutes. The ship on the far left flying the Blue Ensign and the flag of Admiral of the Blue is probably the *Formidable. Queen* is shown in the centre of the painting, broadside to port, with a carved figurehead showing the head of a queen wearing a crown. (© *National Maritime Museum BHC0629)*

proceed to Spithead and so, at 1500, Albert visited the gunnery training ship *Excellent*, after which the royal party boarded HMS *St Vincent*, the harbour guardship. As Victoria embarked, the Royal Standard was run up and all the ships in port manned their yards and fired a royal salute. The queen next visited the *Royal George*, a 120-gun First Rate launched in 1827, and again cannons were fired and masts and spars lined with sailors. As it then began to rain, the royal party moved indoors. Albert and his relatives went to see the block manufactory, the forge and the copper works and then joined the Queen at Admiralty House, where there was 'a select party'.[2] The royal visitors passed the night there and after darkness fell there was a *jeu de feu* as houses, the ships in port and the floating bridges of the dock were all illuminated. This seems to be the first time that a combined formal firework and light display was seen at a Royal Fleet Review.

The following day, 1 March, Prince Albert and his German kin rose early and visited Gosport to inspect the Victualling Department. They tasted ships' biscuit which, according to newspaper reports, they 'relished very much'.[3] Allegedly, Albert asked for some to be sent to the royal table. Then at 1000, they boarded the Admiralty steam paddle yacht, *Black Eagle*, for transfer to HMS *Queen*, flagship of Vice-Admiral Sir Edward William Campbell Rich Owen, who had a day earlier hauled down his flag as commander-in-chief of the Mediterranean Fleet. She was a 110-gun First Rate, originally ordered under the name *Royal Frederick* in 1827 and renamed while still on the stocks in honour of the new monarch.

Once more gunnery salutes were discharged and the royal party sat down on board to a '*dejeuner a la fourchette*'.* Afterwards, the Queen tasted the soup served to the tars on board and took a swig of rum ('three water grog') from a mess basin, stating that it was 'not strong enough',† which was apparently 'a remark which the sailors relished wonderfully, and will long be remembered in the navy'.[4] Throughout the review, a flotilla of small boats followed the royal party around, sightseers and local dignitaries on board. Victoria then returned to Admiralty House and received a loyal address from the mayor and corporation of Portsmouth.

The ships that Victoria reviewed were largely unchanged from those of her grandfather's time. They were all sailing vessels, although *Queen* was to be the last purely sailing battleship to be ordered.‡ The ceremonial was also much the same as that popularised by George III. But one highly visible thing had changed – the naval uniform. Instead of the random gaudy seen in previous reviews, there was now a standardised dress code for officers and men and it looked very different from those worn at the last review. The old officers' uniform had gone and they wore their cocked hats fore-and-aft instead of athwartships. Epaulettes had come in,§ and instead of breeches and buckled shoes they wore gold-laced trousers and black

* Fork buffet.

† This was not the first time Victoria had sampled sailors' fare. She visited HMS *Victory* in 1833 on board *Emerald* (tender to the royal yacht *Royal George*), aged 14, and tasted 'excellent beef, potatoes and grog as a sample of the sailors' rations' (Hibbert, *Queen Victoria*, p 37). Three water grog was a mixture of one part rum to three parts water.

‡ The all-sail HMS *Trafalgar* (120 guns) was launched after *Queen* in 1841 but had been ordered in 1825.

§ First officially introduced in 1795.

pumps. Sailors wore baggy trousers, short jackets, white-taped blue collars and black silk scarves, set off by a beribboned straw hat.

Administration of the navy had changed as well. The Navy and Victualling Boards, established by Pepys, had been abolished in 1832 and the whole of naval administration was now placed directly under the Admiralty. In the new system, each branch was headed by a senior official who reported to a member of the Admiralty Board (although the offices of the former naval boards continued to be housed in Somerset House until 1860).

1844, A Royal Progress

The year 1844 saw no less than four foreign sovereigns visit Britain. Not all were on formal state visits but all to a greater or lesser extent were exposed to the ships and facilities of the navy and saw the extent of British naval power.

The first to arrive, on 27 May, was the King of Saxony, the splendidly-named Frederick Augustus Albert Maria Clemens Joseph Vincenz Aloys Nepomuk Johann Baptista Nikolaus Raphael Peter Xavier Franz de Paula Venantius Felix of the House of Wettin, ruling as Frederick Augustus II. He alighted at Dover, having been conveyed across the channel by the Admiralty paddle steam packet *Princess Alice*. It was not an official state visit but the King was the guest of Queen Victoria and Prince Albert at Windsor Castle, explored many of the sights in London and in the university cities of Oxford and Cambridge, and toured widely in England, Wales and Scotland, including Lyme Regis in Dorset to purchase some of the fossils being unearthed there by Mary Anning, the famous self-taught palaeontologist.

From Dover, where he was given a tour of the castle and other fortifications, the King met with various of the nobility before arriving in Portsmouth on the 29th. Here, the port admiral, Sir Charles Rowley, played host at dinner and through the evening. On Friday 30th, Frederick Augustus was given a tour of the dockyard as well as inspecting some of the ships present. When he came to HMS *Victory*, the crew manned the yards and a royal salute of twenty-one guns was fired. The King then sailed to Ryde on the Isle of Wight on the admiral's 136-ton cutter yacht *Fanny* and dined and slept at the clubhouse of the Royal Yacht Squadron.

The next monarch to visit English shores was the Emperor of Russia, Nicholas I. He arrived at Woolwich on 1 June, from Rotterdam, on board the Dutch government steamer *Cyclops*, from which flew the imperial standard of a back double-headed eagle on a field of orange, the personal insignia of His Imperial Majesty Nicholas I, Tsar of All the Russias. His ship was accompanied by the King of the Netherlands' steamers *Merassie* and *Cerberus*. It was a formal visit but not necessarily a popular one.

British Russophobia grew throughout the nineteenth century, fuelled not just by rivalries over India and the Ottoman Empire but also because of the failure of the anti-Russian Polish Revolution of 1830–1. British public opinion was strongly pro-Polish throughout the whole struggle and continued to express its sympathy after the eventual defeat of the uprising. The Poles (many of whom sought refuge in France and Britain) stoked these feelings with regular leaks to the press of information about Russian atrocities in their country, and while this did not lead to any change in British foreign policy, it certainly made an impact on public perceptions of the Tsar and Russia.

A further issue was trade. Russia's rapid industrialisation meant that manufactured goods became available for export. 'Russia's developing commerce was already menacing; the day might come that the tsar's empire would prove itself an outright threat to Britain in India and the East.'[5]

When the Emperor's visit was first mooted, the satirical magazine *Punch* wrote that the Tsar 'should have guard of honour composed of Polish refugees'.[6] But Victoria was, in fact, quite taken with Nicholas – 'there is much about him which I cannot help liking',[7] she noted in a letter to her uncle – and overall, he impressed. The Tsar was entertained at Buckingham Palace* and Windsor Castle and accompanied the Queen, Prince Albert and the King of Saxony to the 'Italian Opera'. Their several suites required seven carriages for the journey. Nicholas was treated to a military review, went to Ascot races and then to Eton to see a pulling contest on the river. And a copper medal was struck to commemorate the Tsar's visit; in Latin it was engraved 'Nicholas I, Emperor of All Russia, friend and guest of Victoria, Queen of the Britons, 1844'.

Like Frederick Augustus before him, the Russian emperor was given a dockyard tour, this time at Woolwich before his departure back to Europe, arriving in company with six carriages and greeted by a royal salute. Nicholas was met by the Earl of Hardwick, Admiral Charles Philip Yorke, who conducted the emperor around his domain before the royal party boarded the Admiralty paddle yacht *Black Eagle*, whereupon Prince Albert said his farewells. The first lieutenant of the yacht was Prime Minister Sir Robert Peel's son, William, who was to win the Victoria Cross ten years later at the siege of Sevastopol. The Tsar gave him, and his captain and chief engineer, diamond rings for their trouble.

The Emperor's visit was not, however, an unqualified success 'for it was now that the tsar first openly raised the question of the eventual partition of the inheritance of the "Sick Man," as he called Turkey'.[8] Since the days of Catherine II 'Russians had dreamed of fulfilling their "historic mission" – to precipitate the dissolution of the Turkish Empire and gain control of Constantinople and the Straits, the "gates to our house"'.[9] The

* Where a room was named 'The 1844 Room', so called after the Russian Emperor Nicholas I had stayed (Rose, *King George V*, p 156). It was in this room that Asquith, Bonar Law, the Unionist leader Edward Carson and the Nationalist John Redmond met in July 1914 to try to resolve the Irish Home Rule question under the chairmanship of the Speaker of the House and at George V's invitation.

Tsar was determined that in the event of the collapse of the Ottoman Empire, Russia would see the fulfilment of her desires. Here were sown the first seeds of the Crimean War in which William Peel would so distinguish himself.

In August came the Crown Prince of Prussia, Prince Wilhelm (not the King of Prussia as stated in many sources).[10] On arrival, Wilhelm entered upon a whirlwind of visits and meetings, including attending the christening of Victoria's second son, Alfred (born 6 August), at Windsor Castle. He stayed at, *inter alia*, Buckingham Palace and Badminton, reviewed the Household troops in Hyde Park and went shooting with Prince Albert.

Finally came the day of his departure. He set out early, and went to see the National Gallery. The prince then called at Argyll House but found that Lord Aberdeen* was still at Windsor so went to Apsley House, and took leave of the Duke of Wellington. For some reason he next visited Barclay and Perkins's brewery† and then travelled to Greenwich where he was entertained to a whitebait dinner by Chevalier Hebeler, the Prussian Consul General, at the Crown and Sceptre Tavern. He drove over to Blackheath to take leave of the Princess Sophia,‡ returned to the Crown and Sceptre, and then embarked in the Queen's paddle steamer *Lightning* and set out for Ostend, amid the parting cheers of a crowd collected on the river bank. Wilhelm would come to the throne of Prussia in 1861 and, together with his chancellor, Bismarck, sow the seeds that led to the unification of Germany, the defeat of France in 1870 and, eventually, the First World War.

None of these three royal visits had involved a formal Royal Fleet Review, although two had included a demonstration of the Royal Navy's capabilities at Portsmouth and Woolwich. But now that would change; for the next and regal visitation of the year came from the traditional and hereditary enemy, France.

This hospitality was interestingly timed, for France was exciting British ire in several parts of the globe where British and French interests collided. In Tahiti the French Admiral Dupetit-Thouars had taken possession of the island, driving out the English missionary George Pritchard;§ conflict ensued and by May Britain and France were at odds. In North Africa, the French were fitting out an expedition against Morocco, which was perceived as a threat to British interests, especially as it would give them an Atlantic Ocean port. And the Prince de Joinville, son of Louis Philippe and a vice admiral in the French navy had recently published an article in the *Revue des deux Mondes* which outlined in detail how the British fleet could be defeated and an invasion force rushed across the Channel in the darkness of one night. There was a strong outcry against France in the press as a result.

On 6 October, King Louis Philippe of France arrived in England. He

* Secretary of State for Foreign Affairs.

† The Anchor brewery in Southwark which was acquired by Courage in 1955. Originally, it had been owned by Doctor Johnson's friend, Henry Thrale.

‡ A daughter of King George III and Queen Victoria's aunt.

§ In 1843, the French declared Tahiti a French protectorate and installed a governor at Papeete. Pritchard, who was advising the Tahitian queen, was driven out. The Tahitians fought fruitlessly against French intervention, writing to King Louis Philippe and Queen Victoria and asking in vain for British intervention. There followed the bloody French-Tahitian War which lasted from 1843 to 1847. Although the British did not militarily assist the Tahitians, they actively condemned France and war between the two powers in the Pacific briefly seemed likely.

had ascended to the throne in 1830 and, under the influence of his foreign minister François Pierre Guillaume Guizot, had sought to normalise relations with Britain. Guizot had built a good relationship with Lord Aberdeen, Peel's foreign secretary, and in 1843 had arranged a state visit to France by Queen Victoria and Prince Albert. They were accommodated at the Chateau d'Eu and Victoria had enjoyed her reception.

The British suite had crossed the Channel on board the Queen's newest royal yacht, *Victoria and Albert*. This was a paddle wheel yacht with sails, commissioned in July 1843, capable of 11.5kts and commanded by one of King William IV's bastards, Captain Lord Adolphus FitzClarence. As ever, Albert was seasick all voyage. The French king's visit was now the reciprocal of Victoria's.

Prior to his arrival, Louis Philippe sent a present to Victoria, an 'exceedingly handsome char-a-banc,* similar to those used by the royal family during the queen's visit last year to the Chateau d'Eu. It appears that, in the course of the numerous excursions made by King Louis Philippe and his royal guests in the neighbourhood of Eu,† the queen often expressed her admiration of those commodious and social vehicles'.[11] It reached England in mid-September at Portsmouth on a steam vessel, appropriately named *Monarch*.

The French king arrived at Portsmouth in his own royal yacht, the paddle frigate *Gomer*, built in 1841 and later converted for the King's use. Louis Philippe was seasick for most of the voyage. The King was accompanied by a squadron of the French fleet as escort and arrived at Gosport where the crew of the port flagship, *Victory*, manned the yards and he was greeted by Prince Albert.

The King was now given the signal honour of the royal salute. Cannons

* A char-a-banc was a long, four-wheeled carriage with several rows of forward-facing seats, originating in France in the early nineteenth century. It was pulled by up to six horses and was used by private owners to convey guests on excursions.

† Located in Normandy, close to the coast.

French royal yacht *Gomer*, a paddle frigate, used in the 1844 fleet review by King Louis Philippe from a painting by F Roux. *(Author's collection)*

fired in welcome and a large crowd gathered around, their cheers almost obliterating the sound of the gunfire. The *Spectator* magazine noted that 'the peaceful thunder of naval pomp harmlessly called to mind England's might, mingled with welcome in the praise of peace. Louis Philippe responded with a new emphatic declaration of his pacific faith, … which, he said, was only written in his heart'. It also commented that 'Louis Philippe is a man to remember that display of naval power and that universal echo of peace'.[12] This was, of course, the effect desired.

The royal party immediately travelled up to Windsor, where Louis was splendidly accommodated in quarters which included the queen's closet, the king's drawing-room, the king's closet, the council chamber and the ante throne room. As a further mark of honour, he slept in the state bed of George IV.

Meantime, the French officers of the squadron were feted. Amongst other treats, on the 9th they were entertained by Major-General the Hon Hercules Packenham, Lieutenant Governor of Portsmouth. The following day the port admiral, Sir Charles Rowley, threw a grand ball for them. And on the 11th Rear-Admiral Sir Hyde Parker gave another grand dance and celebration.

After his stay at Windsor, Louis Philippe, accompanied by the Queen and Prince Albert, returned by rail to Portsmouth where it was intended that Louis would entertain the Queen and Prince Consort aboard *Gomer*. But the weather at the coast was foul and the party could not transfer across in safety. Louis, prone to seasickness and anxious to return to France, decided to travel by train to Dover and leave from there by commercial packet. The French *L'Elan* would meanwhile be sent to Le Tréport to inform Queen Maria Amalia of the change of plan. At 1915 the King departed; his journey would not be smooth for New Cross station was ablaze and he had to proceed by carriage, eventually arriving in Dover at 0230 the next day where he lodged at the Ship Hotel. The weather was still bad and Louis had to suffer an impromptu address from the town council and mayor in his honour before taking the French *La Poste* steamer *Nord* back home, departing at 1100 and escorted by two British paddle steamers, *Ariel* and *Swallow*.

Meanwhile, back in Gosport the royal party were stranded in the docks and were unable to leave their fiercely-windswept position and so sheltered in the house of a Mr Grant, the Superintendent and Storekeeper, who had been hoping to entertain some friends while they observed the royal progress. Instead, he was prevailed upon to offer the hospitality of his house and victuals were hastily prepared and consumed. 'It was observed, that in spite of all these mischances and inconveniences the whole party were merry, and that every now and then a hearty laugh came from the room in which the principal persons were.'[13]

It was now Queen Victoria's turn to review the French squadron, which had remained behind after its king departed. Sailing to Cowes on the *Victoria and Albert* the next morning, Tuesday 15th, her yacht was preceded by the French *Caiman* and the brig *Favourite* and attended by several vessels from the Royal Yacht Squadron. As the party passed them, warships saluted with guns and flags and the French warships *Inflexible* (90 guns) and *Belle Poule*★ (60 guns) paid tribute in French fashion by firing off full broadsides. The latter ship had brought Napoleon's remains back from St Helena in 1840.

In the Spithead, the royal yacht closed the *Gomer* and the Queen and Prince Albert went on board, accompanied by three Lords of the Admiralty (Sir George Cockburn, Admiral Bowles, Third Naval Lord, and the Hon H T Lowry-Corry, Secretary to the Board), where they were received by Vice-Admiral Baron La Suisse with other French officers and given a tour of the ship. As they returned to their own vessel, the French squadron manned yards and again fired off full broadside salutes, a compliment which Victoria acknowledged by bowing and Albert by taking off his hat. They landed at Cowes not without incident, for a drunken spectating sailor ran his boat into their barge, and proceeded to Osborne House, whist the Lords of the Admiralty retuned to Portsmouth in the steamer *Comet*. The French ships departed the following day.

Neither of these reviews could be termed full-blown Royal Fleet Reviews; but the French visit had been a success, and the might of the Royal Navy had been seen and recognised. However, the benefit would be ephemeral. The fall of Peel's government in 1846 changed these intimate relations and the return of Palmerston to the Foreign Office led Guizot to believe that he was again exposed to the enmity in the British Cabinet.

Queen Victoria and Portsmouth were not yet finished for 1844. On 21 October she returned for the celebrations to mark Trafalgar Day and made a complete inspection of *Victory*. During its course, and whilst descending to the orlop deck, she was nearly knocked over by a powder monkey who was, as it turned out, running with a fresh supply of gunpowder for the royal salute.

1845, The Experimental Squadron and the Return of a Favour

When Victoria came to the throne massive wooden walls such as HMS *Queen* and *Trafalgar* were still being designed and laid down, and the navy was slow to embrace some of the advances of the Industrial Revolution. But large timbers, the result of centuries of careful planting and nurturing, had become scarce due the demands for shipbuilding during the Napoleonic war. And the limits of timber's ability to support sagging stresses was a constraint on ship length. Iron and steel came slowly into focus, as did coal.

Steam paddle ships had made an appearance in the commercial world but the Admiralty used them only as auxiliary vessels. The exposed paddle boxes meant they were vulnerable in battle; a screw ship had its vitals less exposed, and a paddle vessel could not mount a broadside. In 1842 the *Alecto*, a paddler, and the *Rattler*, screw propelled, were lashed stern to stern in a tug-of-war contest. *Rattler* won easily but this did not stop the Admiralty from continuing to develop paddle frigates, one of which was still with the fleet which fought in the Crimean conflict (HMS *Terrible*). The frigate *Penelope*, originally launched in 1829, was shortened by 65ft and fitted with paddles, barque-rigged with iron wire for standing rigging and given one funnel. But these experiments did not last long and *Penelope* was the only frigate so converted.

In 1845, HMS *Ajax* reached 7kts on trials. She had been built as a 74 in 1809 but was now fitted with an engine that turned a screw propeller. *Ajax* became the first screw-driven battleship. Steam screw warships began to be developed, still with full sailing rig, and the order 'up funnel down screw' became commonplace. *Emerald*, a frigate of 35 guns laid down in 1849 was ordered 'not to be advanced' in 1851 and finally built as a screw frigate in 1854; and HMS *Glasgow* was built as a 28-gun screw frigate in 1855. The penny had dropped and steam and screw were becoming the preferred method of propulsion.

Advancement in ship design proceeded by fits and starts and with not a little political interference. During the 1830s and 1840s, experimental squadrons (or evolutionary squadrons) were formed to test out various theses regarding novel techniques. In 1831 Admiral Edward Codrington formed such a grouping to evaluate new hull forms. There were others in 1832 and 1844. But now politics entered the ring. The Surveyor of the Navy was William Symonds, first appointed in 1832 by the Whig ministry. He was, at best, a gifted amateur, not a professional shipwright and his selection generated hostility, as did his arrogant mien. Nonetheless his improvements, such as watertight compartments, widening warships' beams and making their bottoms more wedge-shaped – to decrease the amount of ballast needed and to increase stability, speed, stowage and the weight of guns that could be carried – were welcomed in some quarters. When a new Board of Admiralty came to power with Peel's second Tory administration, they were determined to prove Symonds' designs a failure, as much for political reasons as for their known problems. Successive 'Experimental Squadrons' were sent out to support their case.*

Such a group was assembled at Spithead in the summer of 1845 under Vice-Admiral Edward Owen, last noted at the 1842 review, and Rear-Admiral Hyde Parker. The squadron comprised the pre-Symonds *Trafalgar*, *St Vincent*, *Rodney* and *Canopus*, along with Symonds' *Queen*, *Albion*, *Vanguard* and *Superb*. The objective of the squadron, as given out publicly, was 'to test the ships built by Sir William Symonds. The main improvement in them consists in a reduction of the midship section under water, and an increase in the plane of floatation, from which great stability is obtained, and additional accommodation for officers and men, with increased facility for the working and fighting of the guns.'[14] This squadron would now be the focus of not one but two Royal Reviews.

On 21 June 1845, First Naval Lord Thomas Hamilton, Earl of Haddington, accompanied by Vice-Admiral Sir William Hall Gage, another naval lord, and Haddington's private secretary, Captain the Hon Richard Saunders Dundas[†] arrived at Portsmouth at 2130, via the South Western Railway, and crossed the harbour to the port admiral's house where they were received by the C-in-C, Admiral Sir Charles Rowley, and stayed the night.

The following morning, with the Admiralty flag flying over the dock-yard gates, they boarded *Black Eagle* at 0800, to salutes from HMS *Victory* and *St Vincent*, and proceeded out of harbour to welcome Queen Victoria at Spithead.

The Queen was residing at Osborne House on the Isle of Wight, and from there boarded the royal yacht, *Victoria and Albert*, around 1120. With her were Prince Albert, her Equerry in Waiting Major General Wemyss, Colonel George Bowles, Master of the Household, and Lady Emma Portman, a Lady in Waiting. Under the command once more of Lord Adolphus Fitzclarence, the royal yacht steamed towards Spithead, pausing only to take on board the Lords of the Admiralty from their own vessel. At noon, the Queen and party arrived at Spithead to find the Experimental Squadron with manned yards and a 21-gun salute booming out precisely at twelve o'clock. As *The Times* of London put it 'Spithead at this time presented a most beautiful and animating appearance, the rigging of every ship being most gaily decorated, and with their crews stretched

* Symonds' designs depended on the art of their captains. They handled badly under less skilful ones, or those that disagreed with his philosophy, but well under skilled commanders, while his larger ships were fast but poor gun platforms due to rolling too rapidly.

† The son of the 2nd Viscount Melville, Dundas would later serve as First Naval Lord in the first Palmerston ministry, November 1857. After stepping down to be Second Naval Lord during the second Derby–Disraeli ministry, he became First Naval Lord in the second Palmerston ministry in June 1859 remaining in office until his death.

out upon the yards; while innumerable yachts of the Royal and other yacht squadrons, and swarms of crowded steamboats and shore boats, added increased liveliness to a scene already imposing'.[15]

On nearing the flagship, *St Vincent*, the royal party transferred by barge; as they set foot on board, the Royal Standard shot up to the mast head and a band played *God Save the Queen*, to cheers from the crew. 'The assembled fleet saluted', Victoria confided to her diary, 'which was a very fine sight and one could really be proud of having such splendid ships.'[16] Rear-Admiral Hyde Parker, second son of the admiral who had commanded Nelson, without distinction, at the battle of Copenhagen in 1801, conducted the queen around the flagship after which the royal suite transferred to *Trafalgar*, 120 guns, where Captain Martin had the honour of conducting his monarch on another ship's tour. The Queen remembered that she had seen the ship launched in 1841. On entering the bread room, Victoria asked to taste the chocolate, 'which she pronounced "very good".'[17] She then inspected the lieutenants' cabins where the Queen was particularly taken with that of the gunnery officer, Lieutenant Charles Joseph Frederick Ewart,* 'which is fitted up in particularly good taste'.[18] One wonders what that taste was, given that Queen Victoria's choice of dress and interior design was considered at the time to be very old fashioned, not to say dowdy.

Next, the royal party called upon 63-year-old Captain Nicholas Lockyer CB in *Albion* (90 guns). He had commanded *Albion* since November 1843 but now clearly had a bee in his bonnet. Victoria asked him, in the way of polite conversation one assumes, if he had a good ship's company. 'I had a good ship's company' he replied, laying strong emphasis on the word 'had'. The Queen was puzzled. 'Had' she queried, turning to the Earl of Haddington as if for an explanation. The First Naval Lord looked bewildered and Lockyer, undaunted, plunged on; 'yes, may it please your Majesty, I had a good ship's company, until it pleased their Lordships of the Admiralty to take away from me 100 of my best men'.[19]

Despite this *lèse-majesté*, Lockyer's ship was immaculate.

Every object on board the *Albion* was arranged in the most perfect order and good taste. The companion-ladder was lined with velvet, as were the various ladders on board, together with velvet side-lines. The decks were as white as it is possible for wood to appear, and every feature of the internal economy of the ship in that order and regularity which most palpably betokens smart officers and wholesome discipline.[20]

At 1300 the Queen disembarked from *Albion*, to raucous cheering, and all captains now repaired on board *St Vincent* for an 'extempore levee'[21] with the royal party. Finally, at 1410, the Lords of the Admiralty took leave of

* Ewart, who died in 1884 as an admiral, was a talented artist. This may explain the impact of his cabin! Several of his paintings are in major collections, including the Victoria and Albert Museum.

The Board of Admiralty yacht *Black Eagle*, a paddle steamer of 495 tons, depicted by TG Dutton. She was launched in 1831 as *Firebrand* and renamed in February 1842 in honour of the King of Prussia.
(© National Maritime Museum PY8662)

Her Majesty and embarked on board the *Black Eagle*. At the same time the royal yacht cast off, proceeding round the easternmost ship, and passed along the line to the westward, leaving Spithead to the roar of another 21-gun salute and the cheers of the thousands of crews of the warships.

The saluting was not yet over, for when the *Victoria and Albert* reached the Isle of Wight, there was further gunnery from West Cowes Castle, the Royal Yacht Squadron Battery and even from some yachts in harbour. The following day, Victoria would observe a mock battle, weather permitting. But for now, she had done her duty.

But then, on 15 July 1845, the Experimental Squadron was once more formally reviewed by Queen Victoria. All of the ships were sailing vessels; it would be the last time that a Royal Fleet Review comprised sailing ships only. And it was a doubly royal review, for Victoria and Albert were accompanied by the King and Queen of the Belgians, Leopold I and Louise-Marie. Leopold, of the Saxe-Coburg lineage, had initially married Princess Charlotte of Wales, the only legitimate child of George IV, and had settled in Britain where he had become (and still was) a trusted confidante of Victoria, before being offered the throne of Belgium in 1831.

It was a bright and sunny day; both Gosport and Portsmouth were crowded with visitors, 'train after train having for two days brought visitors, by hundreds at a time, from London, and more flocking in from the surrounding country'.[22] A special train also conveyed Major-General the

Prince George of Cambridge (Victoria's cousin) and another the Directors of the East India Company. Queen Victoria and Albert arrived by the royal train from London just before noon; the streets, quays and shores were all packed with onlookers and the naval and military authorities, including Prince George, were all drawn up in waiting to receive the Queen. But she ignored them and the royal suites embarked on *Victoria and Albert* without delay; the queen dowager, who had arrived the previous day, separately boarded *Princess Alice*. The two vessels immediately set out in company, followed by the Board of Admiralty in *Black Eagle* with *Fairy* (a small screw and iron royal yacht), and the East India Company in their yacht, *Tagus*. 'The shores were alive with people and the waters were covered with craft of all kinds – steamers, yachts, sailing vessels, and smaller boats.'[23]

At Spithead, the Experimental Squadron was drawn up in two lines, on short cables. Their yards were unmanned but HMS *Hibernia*, which was not of the squadron but lay to the west of all the warships present, manned hers. The royal yacht passed between the lines of warships and then rounded the bows of *Hibernia*. At that moment the signal was made to set sail and 'in a few minutes the anchors were all up, the canvass was flying and the vessels moved forward under studding-sails'.[24] First *Rodney* led the pack, then *Queen*. All the while, Victoria had been standing on a

Spithead, seen as Queen Victoria would have known it in a painting of 1855 by Edward Duncan. *(Courtesy of Birmingham Museums and Art Gallery)*

viewing platform between the paddles of her vessel, watching with 'evident interest'.[25]

Now the *Victoria and Albert* took the lead, and off Dunnose (a cape on the southeast coast of the Isle of Wight) the squadron reformed two lines with seamanlike ease and the royal yacht once more passed between them. This concluded the review; the Experimental Squadron continued on its way to its next destination, Ireland, whilst the royal party returned to port, preparatory to sailing over to Osborne, arriving at 1800. There they spent the following day at leisure and returned to London by train on Thursday morning.

The results of these experiments were, perhaps predictably, inconclusive and so in 1846 the Board instituted a 'Committee of Reference' to oversee Symonds and modify his designs according to the Board's wishes. In October 1847, Symonds resigned in pique.

Before leaving the year of 1845, it is worth asking the question as to why Victoria was asked, or saw fit, to review the same, politically charged, squadron twice within four weeks. Was it a move to support Sir Robert Peel in his attempts to reduce trade tariffs and relieve the discrimination suffered by Catholics; or in the machinations against Symonds? Victoria had not much cared for Peel at first* but had come to accept him. Albert liked Peel, and the older man had become something of a cross between tutor and friend. And Peel had set in motion the orders to provide her with a new yacht, urging Haddington to put matters in hand, as the queen much disliked the yacht *Royal George* that she had inherited from William IV. *Victoria and Albert* was laid down in 1842 as a result. Sir Robert had also suggested to Victoria that she purchase Osborne House (and, indeed, had found the property and brokered the transaction for her) to meet her need for an informal family home. She owed him a favour; was it as simple as that?

* And had caused Peel to decline the prime ministership in 1839 when she refused to change her ladies-in-waiting on the resignation of Melbourne's Whig government.

Chapter 7

Crimean Imbroglio, 1853–1856

DURING THE 1840s the British economy performed very well, driven by export trade and protected at sea by the Royal Navy. The number of jobs in the cotton industry, very export-oriented, increased from 260,000 in 1838 to 330,000 in 1850. During the same period, registered British merchant shipping rose from 2.8 million tons to 3.6 million. The railway mania of the time reached its zenith in the mid-1840s and between 1841 and 1851, annual gross domestic product grew from £452 million to £523 million. In 1830 the nominal value of British exports had been £38 million; by 1850 it had increased to £52 million. By the mid-nineteenth century, Britain manufactured half the pig iron in the world and mined half of the coal as well. It was clear that 'no other nation on the globe could compete or compare with such an extraordinarily vigorous and innovative economic performance'.[1]

But there were clouds on the horizon. In 1848, King Louis Philippe of France was forced to abdicate the throne. He tried to pass the crown to his nine-year-old grandson, also Philippe. The National Assembly of France initially planned to accept the youngster as king but strong public opposition made that impossible. The ex-king fled to England, disguised as 'Mr Smith', and on 26 February, the Second Republic was proclaimed. Louis Napoleon Bonaparte, nephew to the great emperor himself, was elected president on 10 December 1848. Three years later, on 2 December 1851, he declared himself president for life and subsequently Emperor Napoleon III in 1852.

Britain was worried about anyone named Napoleon; and the more so because 'the new Bonaparte had high ambition to remake Europe and extend French power around the world, to restore *La Glorie* of the first Napoleonic era. But before he did this, the French Navy had to neutralise Britain by exerting the maximum pressure on British home waters.'[2]

⋆ She had been first
named HMS
Windsor Castle; but
on the day of her
launch the duke
died and she was
renamed in his
honour.

HMS *Duke of
Wellington* (1852),
flagship of Admiral
Napier and the
Baltic Fleet.
Designed as a sailing
ship, she had a screw
and steam engine
fitted at the eleventh
hour. *(© National
Maritime Museum
PW8128)*

The French completed the defences at Cherbourg, making the port its
first battleship base on the Channel and an arsenal for a potential invasion
of Britain. It was a clear and present danger to British military planning and
an overt threat to her sovereignty of the seas. The Admiralty responded with
even bigger and better ships of the line. HMS *Agamemnon* was ordered in
1849 and completed three years later. Of 91 guns, she was the first British
battleship to be designed and built from the keel up with installed steam
engines as well as a full square rig on three masts. She was followed by HMS
Duke of Wellington,⋆ launched in 1853, which was twice the size of Nelson's
Victory and mounted 131 guns. It took 76 acres of trees to build her.[3] At the
time, she was the most powerful warship in the world, although the design
process which created her had started in 1841 under Symonds and was not
finished until she had been cut in half on the stocks in January 1852 to be
lengthened to receive steam engines and screw propulsion.

Not to be outdone, the French built ten new wooden steam battleships
and converted twenty-eight old ones. In turn, Britain built eighteen and
converted forty-one. It was a naval arms race which prefigured that
between Britain and Germany in the last years of the nineteenth and the
early twentieth centuries.

1853, The Queen's Ships and a Show of Arms

The government of Prime Minister George Hamilton-Gordon, 4th Earl of Aberdeen, was a coalition between the Whigs and Peelites (adherents to the policies of Sir Robert Peel, who had died in 1850). Aberdeen feared a resurgent France under a new Bonaparte and his potential foreign adventures. There were also growing concerns regarding the rising political dominance of the Russian Empire in eastern Europe and the corresponding decline of the Ottoman Empire.

Soon, these two fears ran together. Hoping to gain conservative Catholic support at home, in 1850 Napoleon III pressurised the Sublime Porte – the government of the Ottoman Empire – to increase the influence of the Roman Catholic Church in the management of the Christian holy places in Palestine. This was opposed by the Russian Tsar, Nicholas, who supported the Orthodox Christians there.

Riots in Bethlehem over whether French-backed Catholic monks or Russian-backed Orthodox ones should have custody over the Church of the Nativity led to deaths amongst the latter, which Tsar Nicholas portrayed as murder by the Turkish police. He demanded guarantees from Turkey that would effectively have meant an end to Ottoman independence of action and which were rejected. More importantly for Britain, it would have given Russia influence, maybe even a presence, across the trade routes to India.

In retaliation, diplomatic relations between the empire of the Sultan and that of the Tsar were broken off and at the end of July a Russian army was

Her Majesty's visit to the flagship of the Channel Fleet, 11 August 1853, showing *Duke of Wellington* flying the Royal Standard. Watercolour by W A Knell. *(© National Maritime Museum PW6120)*

despatched towards the Danube, on a crusade to protect the Holy Places from Islam, quickly occupying the Ottoman provinces of Moldavia and Wallachia (the so-called 'Danubian principalities'). It was a good time to send a message.

On Thursday 11 August 1853, the sun was shining and a zephyr breeze caressed a calm sea off Portsmouth. A huge fleet of warships was gathered offshore. 'The display of real force was greater than in any fleet we have ever mustered on the shores of England', thought the *Spectator* magazine.[4] There were ships present mounting a total of 1,076 guns, with engines having 'the power of 9,680 horses',[5] 40,207 tons of shipping and ships' companies numbering 10,423 hands altogether. On display were twenty-five ships of the line, thirteen of which were screw steamers, nine paddle wheel vessels and only three heavy sailing ships. 'The total steam-power employed' thought one correspondent, 'being stated at about half its actual value, probably represents a larger horse power than all the cavalry regiments in the service put together.'[6] They were gathered for a Royal Fleet Review.

For two or three days, Southampton and Portsmouth had been gradually filling up with intending spectators. Accommodation ran out; some visitors ended up sleeping on floors, some on chairs; and many did not sleep at all. Queen Victoria had come down from London and was staying at Osborne. Amongst her guests were, perversely or otherwise, two Russian princesses, the Tsar's eldest daughters Maria Nikolayevna and Olga Nikolayevna.

The arrangements for the day were coordinated by Rear-Admiral Maurice Frederick Fitzhardinghe Berkeley, the illegitimate second son of a liaison between the 5th Earl of Berkeley and a publican's daughter. Vice-Admiral Sir Thomas Cochrane flew his flag in the *Duke of Wellington*, Rear-Admiral A L Corry in *Agamemnon*. The previous day, the three sail-only battleships, *Queen*, *London* and *Prince Regent* had been towed out to the Nab to await their self-powered brethren. The naval forces rehearsed their manoeuvres. The Crown Prince of Prussia had arrived at 1600 on his own special train from London. He was greeted at Victoria Pier by Captain Crispin of the *Victoria and Albert* and a guard of honour. The prince entered a barge for embarkation in *Fairy* and was saluted by twenty-one guns from the platform battery as *Fairy* hoisted the Royal Prussian Standard before conveying the prince to Osborne.

On the big day, the South Western Railway Company began to run a steamboat service from Southampton carrying passengers hopeful of viewing events from the water. The Peninsular and Oriental Company was also afloat 'in one or more of their noble steamers, accompanied by a brilliant party'.[7] Military bands were in attendance.

About 0900, *Black Eagle* with Their Lordships on board, arrived; soon afterwards came two paddle sloops, *Stromboli* bearing the Peers of the

Realm and *Bulldog* bearing the House of Commons. This was the first time that the legislature had been a formal part of the procession, a role which now became a fixed part of Royal Fleet Reviews in the future. Next came *Fairy* with the Prince of Prussia and the Russian princesses on board and finally the paddle frigate *Gorgon*, set apart for the press together with other ships accommodating various naval and official personages.

Shortly after 1000, the *Victoria and Albert* hove into view, carrying the Queen and Prince Albert with their children; and in a line behind came the royal *Vivid*, *Elfin* (both steam paddle yachts) and finally *Fairy* (screw). The royal yacht bore straight down towards HMS *Duke of Wellington*. As she neared, the signal to fire the royal salute was hoisted on board the flagship 'and the effect of the combined roar of the great ships was overpowering to the senses'.[8] And as the Queen passed the Prussian warship *Gefion*, she too dressed yards and fired a salute.

Wilhelm of Prussia and the Russian suite now joined the *Victoria and Albert* preparatory to transfer by barge to Cochrane's flagship and they were soon visible to the crowds, gathered on the stern gallery. After an hour or so, the royal party returned to their yacht; and a public spectacle of manoeuvre and gunnery, a mock battle and the vanquishing of a simulated enemy took place, starting with Queen Victoria in *Victoria and Albert* leading her fleet out to sea.

The Times newspaper noted the spectacle:

the deep bass of the 68 and 84 pounders, chiming in at intervals with the sharper roar of the lighter guns, could be readily distinguished, and the observer could even note how these tremendous engines of destruction hurled forth a more projected and larger mass of flame and smoke into the wind's eye. Along the whole line of battle, nearly three miles long, the cannonading was kept up for many minutes with a fury which it is quite impossible to convey any idea of in words.[9]

Diplomats, Parliamentarians and royals all observed from their vessels at a safe distance and then retuned towards Portsmouth, where the *Victoria and Albert* was surrounded by gunboats to pay their own obeisances.

Then as a final act to the day, two second-class paddle frigates, *Magicienne* and *Vulture*, were attacked by the gunboats of the fleet off Southsea beach. The boats were manned and launched with astonishing rapidity. They bore down on the ships in two divisions, followed by the royal yacht and a crowd of boats of all kinds. One division attacked the stem, the other the stern, of the men of war. 'There was a great deal of firing on both sides and at length the victory of the boats was announced by a tremendous cheer.'[10] The day of spectacle was over. It was, thought one reporter, 'a great Peace Congress, headed by the queen'.[11]

Victoria invited Cochrane to dine with the royal party at Osborne the following day. On his return through Spithead on Saturday, in the royal steam tender *Sprightly*, he summoned by signal all the captains of the fleet engaged in the review and communicated to them personally that 'Her Majesty had been graciously pleased to express to him her most full and extreme satisfaction and gratification at all that had taken place during the review of Thursday'.[12] Victoria was amused.

As *The Times* observed, the import had surely got home:

> Is it imagined that the force of these squadrons has not been felt where it was most needed, in the Cabinet of St Petersburg and in the Conference of Vienna? The answer is obvious: these preparations for war, and the alacrity of the people of England to obey the old call of resistance to injustice and violence, have taken by surprise those foreign statesmen … and the maintenance of peace, to which we now look forward, is mainly due to the existence of a naval force, not used for any purpose of provocation, but ready and efficient for every necessary emergency.[13]

Except the message seemed not to have arrived.

1854, 'Black Charlie' and the Baltic

The dispute between Turkey and Russia rumbled on. Thanks to an arrangement brokered by the ambassadors of France and Britain, Russian access and privileges in the Holy Land were restored. But this did not deter the autocrats. Nicholas I wanted access to the Mediterranean from the Black Sea – and that could only be via Constantinople; religious difference was a useful excuse. Napoleon III wanted to make a reputation to rival his illustrious forebear and needed the support of the Catholic Church at home. Both refused to back down. Nicholas issued an ultimatum that the Orthodox subjects of the Empire be placed under his protection. Britain attempted to mediate and arranged a compromise that Nicholas agreed to. But then the Turks demanded changes; Nicholas refused and prepared for war. And having obtained promises of support from France and Britain, the Ottomans declared war on Russia in October 1853. It was not a wise decision.

On 30 November 1853, a Russian fleet under Admiral Pavel Nakhimov sailed out of Sebastopol, and found a Turkish flotilla off the south shore of the Black Sea at Sinope, where it was attempting to reinforce the garrison at Kars, under siege by Russian forces. Nakhimov sank the lot, killing 4,000 sailors; many of the dead, it was reported, were shot in the water.

There was outrage in Britain, coupled with a determination to keep Russia away from Britain's vital trade routes, and unwillingness to let

Russia gain territory at Ottoman expense. This was seen as a very real threat to Britain's interests. Indeed, according to historian David Cannadine 'the Crimean War came about because the British government had felt compelled to support the Ottoman Empire and take up arms against Russia, who seemed a constant threat to the British position in South Asia'.[14] At the time, the Lord Privy Seal, the Duke of Argyll, opined that if Russia were to gain the Straits 'the Black Sea would be a Russian lake, the Danube would be a Russian river and some of the richest provinces of Eastern Europe and of Western Asia would give Russia inexhaustible resources … she would possess inordinate power over the rest of Europe'.[15] For which read 'over Britain'. On 6 February 1854 Russia withdrew her ambassadors from Paris and London. The British government issued an ultimatum to Russia to withdraw from the occupied provinces on 27 February and on 27 March the French declared war on Russia. The following day, Britain did the same, with parliament informed that the country was 'to take up arms in conjunction with the Emperor of the French, for the defence of the sultan'.[16] The old enemy was now an ally.

Fearing an Ottoman collapse, France and Britain rushed forces to Gallipoli. They then moved north to Varna in June 1854, arriving just in time for the Russians to abandon Silistra. Aside from a minor skirmish at

Admiral Sir Charles Napier, painting by John Simpson. *(Author's collection)*

Review of the fleet at Spithead by Queen Victoria, 23 April 1856. Second attack of the gunboats on Southsea Castle. *(© National Maritime Museum PY8275)*

Köstence (today Constanta), there was little for the allies to do. Indeed, Karl Marx quipped, 'there they are, the French, doing nothing and the British helping them as fast as possible'.[17]

Meanwhile, a second expedition was planned, this time to the Baltic, in order to neutralise any threat from the powerful Russian Baltic Fleet, which had some twenty-eight ships of the line* at its disposal. Such a force might readily get out into the North Sea and threaten Britain's eastern coastline. And France was in no position to send ships to Britain's aid as all its available ships had already been despatched to the eastern Mediterranean. A fleet was thus assembled at Spithead, drawn mostly from the Lisbon station and augmented by token French support in the form of the 100-gun battleship *Austerlitz*, laid down in 1832 but not launched until 20 years later.

The Admiralty was desperately short of competent admirals to give the command to. In the end, and with much trepidation, they settled on 68-year-old Sir Charles Napier. According to an old *Encyclopaedia Britannica* entry, 'Sir Charles Napier was a man of undoubted energy and courage but of no less eccentricity and vanity. He caused great offence to many of his brother officers by his behaviour to his superior, Admiral Stopford, in the Syrian War, and was embroiled all his life in quarrels with the Admiralty.'[18]

An early enthusiast for steam power, a designer of his own ships and a fierce warrior, Napier was a large, untidy man of about 14 stone. He walked with a limp and a stoop due to leg and neck wounds and was known to the navy as 'Black Charlie' because of his swarthy appearance and dark side whiskers. His eccentric behaviour and enthusiasms, together with his lamentable personal hygiene and dress sense, also earned him the epithets 'Mad Charlie' and 'Dirty Charlie'. In February 1854, Napier hoisted his flag HMS *Duke of Wellington* and prepared for action.

Napier's send-off started with a banquet at the Reform Club in Pall Mall on 7 March. The First Lord of the Admiralty, Sir James Graham, was present, as were other government ministers and the French and British ensigns were both on display. Questions had been raised in Parliament as to the efficiency of the fleet and its manning levels, for impressment had now been abandoned for good. Both Prime Minister Lord Aberdeen and Black Charlie himself were at pains during the dinner to deprecate both claims.

———

It was the early morning of 11 March. Already, a large crowd had assembled at Portsmouth, 'crowding the shore, the pier, and every spot from which a peep could be obtained'.[19] Admiral Napier had first called at the Guildhall to receive an address from Portsmouth Corporation. Now he pressed with difficulty through the throng to gain the small steamer

* There were also eight frigates and ninety other vessels.

Sprightly, where his three married daughters awaited him, for conveyance to his flagship. Everywhere the roadstead was full of pleasure steamers, yachts and smaller craft, all waiting for a glimpse of the queen and her navy. Then, around 1300, the screw yacht *Fairy* burst onto the scene, carrying the Queen and the royal family from Osborne, followed by *Black Eagle*, another small royal yacht, *Elfin*, and *Fire Queen*, a paddle tender of the Commander-in-Chief Portsmouth, Admiral Sir Thomas Cochrane.

As the royal flotilla neared the fleet, the yards were manned and a gunnery salute fired, followed by cheers from the sailors themselves. *Fairy* hoisted the message that the Queen would receive the captains and admirals of the fleet on board and they took to their barges to execute the order. There 'the reception was brief, but cordial: the queen shook hands with each and spoke some parting words'.[20]

Victoria herself thought that

> at Spithead there was a good deal of smell. The scene was most animated and interesting; numberless boats in every direction, sailing and rowing, numbers of densely crowded steamers and the ships about to start like-wise surrounded by boats, bringing stores, ammunition, etc. We passed near the principal ships and then lay to, to receive all the officers; the admirals and captains, Sir J Graham presenting each as they came on board. It was an interesting moment, all seemed impressed with the solemnity of it. Leave was warmly taken on many sides.

However, Black Charlie lived up to his reputation; the Queen noted that 'Sir C Napier was in a great fuss and hurry, having hardly got any of his things. He told Captain Denman he had only got a fur cap and he actually got out of the train with a pair of worsted stockings dangling in his hand. He came on board without any epaulettes and his cocked hat worn the contrary way to what it is now.' But Napier was in fighting spirit nonetheless; on departing, the Queen 'observed that my good wishes would attend him; he said he hoped to bring back the Russian Fleet'.[21]

As soon as the officers regained their ships, the signal was raised to weigh anchor. Although most of the fleet had steam propulsion, they departed under sail 'with double-reefed topsails and courses, topgallant sails, jib, and driver'.[22] Victoria and her little group of vessels took position at the head of the squadron and led the fleet out as far as the Nab. There the leading ships shortened sail to let the second division come up, together with three paddle frigates, *Leopard* (18 guns), *Valorous* (16 guns) and *Dragon* (6 guns) which were to act as signal repeating ships. *Fairy* hove too, and as the battle fleet passed by the Queen's vessel each ship gave three cheers for her majesty; and sailed off towards the Kattegat.

Napier's command comprised sixteen warships. Eight were battleships, of sail and screw design, with four each of paddle and screw frigates. The *Duke of Wellington* and *Royal George* (built in 1827) were three-deckers of 131 and 121 guns respectively. The *Cressy* and *Euryalus* of 80 and 50 guns were also on passage to join the command; and on 16 March Admiral A L Corry sailed from Portsmouth with *Neptune* (120 guns). She had been built in 1832 and immediately put into ordinary. This was her first time at sea. Again, Queen Victoria, Prince Albert and the royal family came out in *Fairy* to see Corry off. Other planned sailings would bring Napier's command up to forty-four ships, 22,000 men and 2,200 guns; and of his battleships only *Neptune*, 120, *Royal George*, 120, *Prince Regent*, 90, *Boscawen*, 70, *Monarch*, 84, and *Cumberland*, 70 guns would be unaided by steam. As one reporter put it, they were 'noble vessels of the old school'.[23] It was a formidable fleet, once more sent to war by a Royal Fleet Review; and it was entirely unsuitable for the tasks set it by the Admiralty.

The one major success of Napier's campaign was the capture and destruction by French and British soldiers and sailors of the Russian fortress of Bomarsund on the Åland Islands, which were temporarily liberated from Russian rule and which Napier offered to Sweden.

But, despite his orders, Napier declined to attack the heavily fortified and defended naval bases at Sveaborg and Kronstadt, which his observations had established were probably impregnable without shallow-draught bomb vessels and monitors, which he did not have. Napier's fleet was one for a major ship-to-ship action; it was unsuited for bombardment of shore positions, as a later 1855 attempt on Sveaborg by an Anglo-French force would attest – an enormous expenditure of ammunition caused virtually no damage.

But at home in Britain, the press (and in particular *The Times*) led a hue and cry against the admiral, accusing him of inaction and lack of determination. And Napier felt that he was continually being second-guessed by the Admiralty, and especially by the First Lord of the Admiralty, Sir James Graham. Graham was in fact reacting to adverse press coverage. As the weather in the Baltic deteriorated and the wording of despatches between admiral and Admiralty became heated, Napier's disrespectful tone sealed his fate. He was ordered to haul down his flag in December 1854 and never served at sea again.

In fact, Napier had achieved much. He had successfully blockaded the Russian fleet, preventing them getting to sea. The 30,000 Russian troops in the area were unable to be transported to the Crimea. His training of the fleet had moulded the ships' personnel into a competent force for the following year's campaign; and not a single ship had been lost. One sees here glimpses of the fate of Admiral John Jellicoe in a later war. The Grand

Fleet at Scapa Flow throughout the 1914–18 conflict fought only one major battle, Jutland, with the German High Seas Fleet. But it kept them bottled up, and rendered them impotent. Jellicoe, both as C–in–C and as First Sea Lord, came to be vilified by the press for his inaction and like Napier was removed from power and denigrated. Napier died in 1860 and lies in the churchyard of All Saints' Church, Catherington, where there is a large tomb dedicated to the admiral and his wife Elizabeth.

1856, The Return from the Crimea

This is not the place to give a detailed analysis of the Crimean campaign, except to say that it highlighted desperate failings in the British army system of command, and in its commanders, and exposed the soldiers to terrible privations. Queen Victoria felt for them desperately. She herself and her household knitted socks, mittens and scarves by the hundred for the infantry and she offered *Victoria and Albert* as a troop transport, a proposal declined by the government.

The issue of transport was a vexed one for the Admiralty. When war against Russia was declared, the navy did not have sufficient capacity to transport the troops to the conflict zone. They had to hire in ships from commercial operators. One such ship was HMS *Himalaya*, which carried troops out in March 1854. She had been leased from Peninsular and Orient (P&O), her owners. They had originally intended her as an iron paddler but changed their minds at the last minute and instead decided on a single-screw iron ship. When launched in 1853 she was the largest passenger ship afloat, and one of the fastest, setting new time records for voyages to Malta and Alexandria. But *Himalaya* was also a guzzler of coal

HMS *Himalaya*, ex-P&O iron screw ship used as a trooper in the Crimean War. *(US Naval History and Heritage Command NH 71189)*

and had meagre freight capacity; and she had cost a great deal to build and fit out. P&O began to think that they would not get a return on the vessel and were happy to lease it to the government as a troop transport, first from Gibraltar to Constantinople and then from Queenstown to the Crimea. In 1855 the government bought the ship from P&O, stipulating that her engineers must stay with her for a year, and later she was taken over by the Royal Navy.

———•◦•———

Dissatisfaction with the conduct of the war and the casualties sustained grew in both Britain and France; indeed, in January 1855 there were riots in London. Lord Aberdeen's government fell on 30 January, when he perceived that he had lost a confidence vote, and the Crimean War finally ended with the Treaty of Paris, signed on 30 March 1856. The sailors and soldiers could come home and be recognised for their sacrifice and effort.

St George's Day 1856 was sunny, bright and clear. A large British fleet was assembled off Spithead. They included two ships of the navy's hydrographer's department. This may seem strange but in the absence of a naval intelligence staff, such pre-planning as existed was undertaken by the hydrographers. In 1853–4, the office had gathered and processed intelligence on the potential theatres of war and developed war plans, both strategic and operational. Officers from the hydrographer's staff were sent to both the Black Sea and Baltic war zones for surveying duties. The operational plans issued to Napier in 1854 had been written by the hydrographer's department.

The fleet anchored in two lines, occupying some six miles of water. At the southern end were two three-decker battleships, *Royal George* (120 guns) at the head of the starboard line, with the flag of Vice-Admiral Sir George Seymour, and the *Duke of Wellington* leading the port line. The vessels present encompassed twenty-six screw line-of-battle ships and nearly forty frigates, both paddle and screw. Two mortar frigates and four wrought-iron floating batteries with fifty 13in mortar vessels represented classes of ship which had been invented (or rediscovered) in the Black Sea to enable attacks on land positions from the fleet. It was the first time that such vessels had been seen at a royal review. *The Times* noted that the floating batteries were

> four low, flat, squat, black, unwieldy constructions, the *Trusty*, the *Glatton*, the *Thunder*, and the *Meteor*, remained motionless at anchor. Their appearance inspires a doubt whether they are capable of motion; they were, however, a feature of the scene, for to compensate for their shapelessness they had put on the gayest of toilettes; they were more brilliantly 'dressed' than any other vessels in the harbour. It was in vain;

beauty of form – the one thing needful for the eye of the amateur – was not there; their ugliness is irredeemable; garlands of roses would not give grace to these hippopotami.[24]

Additionally, there were twenty sloops, corvettes and brigs; and 164 screw gunboats. In total, 'upwards of 300 sail of men-of-war, having an aggregate tonnage of 150,000 tons, manned by 40,000 seamen, carrying 3,800 guns, and firing at one discharge a broadside of nearly 90 tons of solid iron' was present at Portsmouth.[25] And they were waiting to be welcomed by their Queen. The French were represented too, by the frigate *Du Chayla* under the flag of Rear-Admiral Edmond Jurien de la Gravière. He and his officers had already been entertained by the captains and admirals of the fleet at a banquet on shore.

Although it was a Wednesday, people had been pouring in to Portsmouth since Monday, by sea as well as by land. On the morning of the review, the South Western Railway started running from London to Portsmouth and Southampton at 0500 and Prince Albert and Queen Victoria had departed Vauxhall Station for Gosport at 0830. But to prove that nothing changes, the departure of the South Western Railway trains from London in the morning had been a disaster. An early train, with a huge line of third-class carriages in tow, broke down and had to be put into sidings at Andover. The following trains were all delayed, including those carrying the Queen. That caused the review to be late in starting.

Parliamentary business had been suspended for the day, in order that Peers and Commons could attend the review. However, by some mischance, members of the Houses of Parliament had been despatched by special train to Southampton, not Portsmouth. Worse, there was no tender there for them to take them to Spithead. Minsters and diplomats were not

Painting of HMS *Royal George* by Charles Cooper Penrose-Fitzgerald. She led the 1856 Review having been converted to steam in 1853. *(Author's collection)*

immune from the chaos either. The special cabs and omnibuses reserved to take them from the railway station to Southsea Common were hijacked by the crowds and they had to make their own way as best they could.

Prime Minster Lord Palmerston was not spared from transportation problems either. Arriving at Waterloo behind time, Palmerston found the train reserved for the Commons already in motion. 'A fellow member of the administration threw open a carriage door and Lord Palmerston had partly got in, when a policeman on duty rushed up to the carriage threw his arms round the noble lord, and without more ado, lifted him on to the platform, and the train proceeded without him.'[26] When the harassed premier finally reached Portsmouth and attempted to board the tender for his steamship, 'he was roughly accosted, and suspicions were expressed that he was trying it on to get on board without a ticket, but an, explanation taking place, his lordship proceeded without interruption'.[27]

The naval drama started early. At 0800 'the whole fleet, as if by magic, was dressed in flags and ensigns from their main-trucks to the water's surface and now the curtain seemed to have risen upon the glorious pageant of the day'.[28] Spectators poured onto the beaches and points of observation. Tents and brightly coloured pavilions sprang up on the water-side and wagons, barouches, phaetons and all manner of other things that run on wheels were drawn up at the littoral.

Only one thing was missing, the principal actor – Victoria herself; her train was an hour late and she arrived just before noon, to embark on the *Victoria and Albert*. De la Gravière had the honour of joining the Queen on board. This was the first Royal Review outing for a new *Victoria and*

HMY *Victoria and Albert* (II) of 1855 in a painting by WF Mitchell. *(Author's collection)*

Portsmouth Harbour in 1856, the year of the review of the returned Crimean Fleet, painting by JMW Turner, engraved by Thomas Lupton. *(Courtesy of Birmingham Museums and Art Gallery)*

Albert, still paddle-wheel driven and with three masts and two funnels, but more luxuriously fitted out. She had been laid down as *Windsor Castle* in 1854 and commissioned in March 1855. The original yacht was renamed *Osborne* and relegated to lesser duties.*

The royal yacht was accompanied by the Lords of the Admiralty in *Black Eagle*, black in name and deed for, although the Admiralty had issued an order to all the steamers present to use only anthracite coal (which produced 'cleaner' smoke), the instruction seemed to have passed their own vessel by. She arrived spouting 'a volume of black smoke that burst from her funnel as from a factory chimney'.[29]

As the Queen approached the serried ranks of ships, behind her followed the Commons in the troopship *Perseverance* and the Lords in another trooper, *Transit*, whist *Vivid* carried the foreign ambassadors. They were supposed to have been escorting the Queen's yacht but were late arriving in Portsmouth too. And with them, bearing many spectators and mixed all together, came a flock of steamers, including *Himalaya*.

The fleet was still drawn up in two lines as the Queen's yacht came out of the harbour. As the yacht neared, all the ships of the line manned their yards and as one unit fired a royal salute 'one of the finest effects produced during the day'.[30] Their hulls were completely shrouded in clouds of smoke and only the flash of the guns showed through as each vessel barked out its 21-gun salute. Before they had finished, *Victoria and Albert* had reached the south end of the line of ships and the men in the rigging broke out into cheering; the yacht then steamed back down the side of the port line and at the northern end took a course between the two ranks, followed by the gunboat flotillas.

* Lord Adolphus Fitzclarence retired too, after 25 years' service as captain of two royal yachts.

For some time, the royal yacht remained in a position near *Rodney* and *London*, which acted as pivot markers, about a mile from the Nab Light, as the screw battleships steamed up in regular order, turned on the pivot, each line following its leader, and returned into position. 'This was a pretty spectacle,' thought one observer, 'as some of the great ships were moving up to the queen's yacht while others were returning; and the whole swept along and turned short with astonishing ease and rapidity'.[31]

Next, Victoria was treated to the spectacle of a mock attack by the gunboats and the floating batteries on Southsea Castle. The gunboats had been specifically built for the Russian war, indeed the *Gleaner* class of 1854 were also known as 'Crimea Gun Boats'. They were wooden-hulled, with steam power and sails but shallow draught for coastal bombardment, and carried one 68pdr smoothbore muzzle-loader and one 32pdr of the same type, together with two 24pdr howitzers. The subsequent *Dapper* class and *Albacore* class were almost identical. The floating batteries were exactly that, powered by sail and steam but sometimes towed into position.

Smoke from forts and ships soon obliterated the view and, as the Queen had to return to London, the spectacle was abandoned, with a final cannonade of salute from the big ships as the royal yacht turned back to harbour. The review had lasted over five hours despite a late start and that evening the Commander-in-Chief, Sir George Seymour, entertained the admirals, captains, and other officers of the fleet at the Admiralty House with the French Admiral and his staff as the honoured guests.

So far, so traditional; the by-now commonplace elements of a Royal Fleet Review had all been played out. But the day closed with a splendid innovation. At 2100, on the signal of a single gunshot, 'the whole fleet at anchor burst into light as by magic, the jets one above another, main-topmast high aloft, and the ports of each opening at once, showed a vivid glare of blue lights between decks, and caused an unusual roar of cheering from the shore, which was echoed and given back with interest from the boats of the legion afloat'.[32] The very first full illumination of the fleet at a Royal Review had taken place – something which would now find its way into future celebrations.

Owing to the earlier chaos, the London-bound railway timetables were now thoroughly disrupted and the return trips were in turmoil. Members of Parliament again found their journey difficult and did not arrive back in London until the early hours of the following day. Other travellers reached London at three in the morning, some more at half-past six; the former had set out at nine o'clock and took six hours to cover 80 miles. The latter were detained standing outside the station until half-past midnight.

It had been a great display of British naval might and new types of ship. But there would not be another Royal Fleet Review for nearly ten years.

Chapter 8

France and Eastern Concerns, 1865–1878

PRINCE ALBERT DIED on 14 December 1861. The cause was diag-nosed at the time as typhoid, although he had been ill for the previous two years and it is likely that there were other contributing, or possibly primary, causes.* Victoria was distraught. Albert had taken much of the responsibility for the management of their affairs and had in many instances acted as the 'king'. The court was plunged into deep mourning and Victoria wore black for the rest of her life. She thought that she was unable to carry on without him and entered into a long period of almost hysterical grief, during which she refused to fulfil the duties of the monarch.

Her seclusion led to feelings running against the Queen during the 1860s. She was seen as selfish in her refusal to carry out her responsibili-ties, a view fanned by some newspapers and magazines. Comments were made such as 'what do we pay her for if she won't work' and 'she had better abdicate if she is incompetent to do her duty'.[1] It was a testing time for the institution of the British monarchy.

The 1860s were also a testing time for the Royal Navy. It had by now embraced steam engines as an auxiliary to sail. In June 1861 the Royal Navy had a strength of 398 ships, of which 49 were still on the stocks and 172 were laid up in ordinary. Of active ships, 144 had steam power in addi-tion to sail and just nineteen were sail only. Of the steam-powered vessels, twenty-eight were paddle driven and the remainder screw.[2] Steam-assisted sail and screw had become the navy's default propulsion method in the less than 30 years since Queen Victoria came to the throne.

But the ships produced still resembled in nearly all respects the wooden walls of Nelson or the navies of the Stuarts; while technological change also meant that guns became heavier and more powerful. Indeed, calibres were increasing by about an inch a year at the time. In response, defensive

* Modern opinion gives cancer or Crohn's disease as suspects.

armour plate came under consideration. Accordingly, in 1859 the French revolutionised the warship-building world by launching *La Glorie*, the first ocean-going ironclad. She had 4.7in armour plates, backed with 17in of timber, and in tests resisted hits from the most powerful guns of the time.

Britain immediately followed suit. The Admiralty selected seven wooden two-decked Second Rate vessels then under construction for conversion to armoured warships. One was HMS *Royal Alfred* (laid down 1852, launched 1864), a wooden-hulled vessel originally intended to be a 90-gun ship of the line. Instead she was equipped with iron plate backed by teak and fitted with a steam engine to complement her full rig of sails and triple masts. Her wooden sides were up to 29.5in thick and the plate was 4.5in at the front of her box battery and 6in protecting her broadside guns. But her armament still fired through gun ports in her sides just as at Trafalgar.

Nonetheless, her guns reflected a changing world, being comprised of ten 9in muzzle-loading rifles and eight 7in ones. At the end of the 1850s the Admiralty had been ambivalent about switching to breech-loading guns. Rifling, however, was accepted and many of the ships of this period were fitted with rifled muzzle-loading weapons, although Armstrong's had developed a rifled breech-loader by 1858. Hence *Royal Alfred* was fitted with muzzle-loaders.

With her reinforced hull and obsolescent guns, she was a sort of imperfect hybrid, but still technically an ironclad and, with her armament and protection, *Royal Alfred* was one of the most powerful of the wooden-hulled ironclads. She was not completed until 1867 and was scrapped 18 years later, having been laid up in 1875 due to the degradation of her machinery.

In any case, the Royal Navy had made both *La Glorie* and *Royal Alfred* immediately obsolete. HMS *Warrior*, launched in 1860, was the first armour-plated, iron-hulled warship. She was not intended to stand in the line of battle but was designed as a 40-gun armoured frigate, the precursor to the cruisers of later times. Conceptually, she was faster, better armoured and harder to hit than her rivals and superior to any then extant naval warship. With her launch, the Admiralty stopped the construction of all new wooden ships of the line, barring those already earmarked for conversion.

Warrior's gunnery lieutenant was John Arbuthnot 'Jackie' Fisher, who would later revolutionise battleship design with the launch of HMS *Dreadnought* in 1906. *Dreadnought* made a generation of warships immediately out-of-date, as did *Warrior* in her time. Indeed, Fisher wrote of her that 'it certainly was not then appreciated on board *Warrior* … . .that this, our first armour clad ship of war … would cause a fundamental change in what had been in vogue for something like a thousand years. For the navy that had been founded by Alfred the Great had lasted till then without any fundamental change till came this first ironclad battleship.'[3]

1865, a Show of Strength

Despite having been allied in their opposition to Russia ten years previously, the British remained suspicious of France and especially of Napoleon III. He increasingly advocated a bellicose position with regard to France's interests during the 1860s. The Emperor had built a powerful ironclad fleet with which he hoped to coerce British support for a wide-ranging reconstruction of the European state system, which Britain was anxious to avoid as being against her interests. Prime Minister Lord Palmerston had supported the idea of a Royal Navy visit to Cherbourg earlier in the summer, the intent being to demonstrate to Napoleon the power of the Royal Navy, implicit in its latest warship, *Royal Sovereign*, the first British turret-armed ship and the only one with a wooden hull. She had four gun turrets (one twin and two single mounting 10.5in smooth-bores), was based at Portsmouth for evaluation in 1865 and was a symbol of British offensive strategy; her protection and heavy guns made a profound impression on the French.

Now the French fleet were to make a reciprocal visit. There would be no 'royal' reception or review though. The Queen remained in purdah, refusing to involve herself in her ceremonial duties and bemoaning her burden with Albert gone.*

At 1000 on 28 August, the French fleet was observed off Spithead, led into the roadstead by the Imperial yacht, *Reine Hortense*, a steam corvette laid down as *Comte d'Eu* in 1844. She was built as a despatch boat and had been converted for her present duties in 1853. On board was Justin Napoleon Samuel Prosper de Chasseloup-Laubat, 4th Marquis of Chasseloup-Laubat, Minister of Marine and Colonies under Napoleon III, a keen imperialist who wished France to rival Britain's imperial reach. Next in line was the *Solferino*, named for the Crimean battle, a broadside ironclad warship, the second unit of the *Magenta* class. She was one of only two two-decked broadside ironclad battleships ever built and also the first ship in the world to be equipped with a spur ram. Her class was an enlarged version of the *Gloire* armoured frigate and intended to take a place in the line of battle. On board was the fleet commander, Admiral Count Bouet Villaumez.

The C-in-C Portsmouth, Admiral Sir Michael Seymour, in his paddle yacht *Fire Queen*, steamed out to greet them, his own fleet already at anchor. Steamers, yachts, yawls and cutters came out from the shore to mingle with the incoming ships as nine of the most powerful iron ships in the French navy, accompanied by four frigates, entered the Spithead and dropped anchor opposite the line 'in which the English ironclads lay … in as yet silent and grim array'.[4]

* In fact, the Queen was in Coburg at the time, in the seclusion of the royal shooting lodge at Rosenau.

As soon as the *Solferino* had anchored, the *Osborne* and the *Reine Hortense* headed towards each other and, midway between the fleets, dipped their ensigns in salutation. At this moment 'the English ships at Spithead were then, with almost magical rapidity, manned at every yard and a more stirring scene than that which greeted the spectator both on shore and afloat as they did so it is not easy to conceive'.[5]

The *Osborne* and *Reine Hortense* then headed for Portsmouth where the flag of the French Minister of Marine received a salute from *Victory* which was returned by *Solferino* 'with rigid punctuality belching forth flame in rapid flashes, and then the roar of the garrison artillery went booming across the water, dying away in reverberations which grew fainter and fainter until at last they totally ceased and the vexed air was quiet once more'.[6]

That evening, the capacious middle deck of HMS *Duke of Wellington* was cleared for a banquet hosted by Lord Edward Seymour, 12th Duke of Somerset, Lord Lieutenant of Devon and First Lord of the Admiralty in Prime Minister Palmerston's second administration. Seventy French and British naval officers dined together that night off a superb silver-gilt dinner service made by a Mr Hancock* of Bruton Street, London, at a cost of £24,000 and placed at the service of the Admiralty by him. The banquet ended at 2200 when the French minster departed for his ship, which was the signal for lighting up the *Duke of Wellington*, every one of whose portholes were immediately illuminated and blue lights exhibited at the same time all round her gunwale and at her yardarms.

There now followed a positive orgy of banquets. On the evening of the 30th, the Lords of the Admiralty gave a feast for all the officers of the French fleet in a marquee built in the courtyard of the Royal Naval College, Portsmouth. According to the *Spectator* magazine, 'healths were drunk and the speeches made. Nobody said anything remarkable but the Duke of Somerset and the French Minister of Marine, M de Chasseloup-Laubat, said pretty things of each other's sovereigns and navies, and the dinners on both occasions were said to have been remarkable, though the diners were not.'[7] When the French Minister proposed a toast to the queen, 'suddenly the fleet became a blaze of light, by means of red, white, and blue lights, placed in every port, rockets sent up in clusters, and so forth, for the space of twenty minutes … . after which the fleet suddenly faded away again'.[8]

Then, the following evening, a 'Grand Entertainment' was given by the mayor and corporation of Portsmouth. A ball was held in one of 'Edgington's tents', 138ft long and 36ft wide, floored over and lined with crimson and white cloth. It was decorated with flags and coloured lamps and at the upper end, behind the mayor's chair, was a bust of the Emperor Napoleon above a shield bearing the arms of the town of Portsmouth and with the mayor's chain and badge. On the mayor's right hand were the royal arms of Great Britain, supported by the standards of France, with the Imperial and British crowns. On his left hand were the arms of France, buttressed by the royal standards of England and of the Prince of Wales.

At the opposite end of the room were an exquisitely designed waterfall, fountain, and cascade, intermixed with ferns and evergreens. 'The company numbered about 2,000 ladies and gentlemen and the great majority of the latter wore naval or military uniforms, while the ladies, of course, were very richly and gaily dressed' reported the *Illustrated London News* and 'presented, while dancing, a splendid as well as a lively and animated sight'.[9]

Still the banqueting continued. On 1 September the troops of the garrison paraded in front of a French audience and a host of civilian spectators and a general salute was given to the French admiral and officers. And then in the evening, yet another banquet (at Admiralty House) and ball (at the Naval College) took place. This was apparently a more select affair, at least according to the *Illustrated London News*; 'this affair was more exclusive than Thursday's public ball' it reported. 'The 1,750 visitors included not only the rank, fashion and, let me add, beauty of the neighbourhood but was drawn from a very large area' and included 'a host of other distinguished persons connected with the aristocracy and the two services'.[10] The festivities did not finish until six in the morning; and the French fleet weighed at 1000. There must surely have been some *mal de mer* on that Channel crossing. Whatever was proven or not during this visit, the French would certainly have gone away impressed by the dura-bility of Royal Navy officer class in the field of feasting!

Not everybody was pleased, however. A dyspeptic press reporter thought that

> Portsmouth had done its best to look gay but the attempt was not very successful. At the best it is a town well described by the American epithet of 'one-horse' or 'tin-pot'. The place has a 'drunk-over-night' air about it, which even in its brightest and cleanest hours it never succeeds in shaking off entirely. Everybody appears to be more or less closely connected with the sale of intoxicating liquors and to be in the habit of promoting consumption by his own example.

The writer also noted that 'there were very few sailors about Portsmouth. In fact, the authorities know that if the French and English tars got drinking together there would be quarrels and blows. So leave to go on shore was granted sparingly and I doubt whether one in twenty of the French fleet saw much more of England than they could catch sight of from the deck.'[11]

An ordinary 'John Bull' of a boatman perhaps reflected the view of the populace at large. He did not care much for the Anglo-French alliance, and 'unconsciously followed the maxim of Talleyrand and held to the view that the guests of today will be the enemies of tomorrow'. He also expressed his opinion that the Frenchmen 'weren't no good; that their iron plates were put one over another like tiles on a roof, and that the *Royal Sovereign* could sink the whole lot of them in a day'.[12]

Was this a Royal Fleet Review? Certainly not, in the absence of the physical form of the monarch. But in the feasting, the lavish decoration and illumination and in the determination to put on a 'good show' it must surely rank as having the same import and function, with the Queen present in spirit and, given the toasts, in spirits too.

1867, the Sultan of Turkey gets Seasick

In July 1867 the Sultan of Turkey, Abdülaziz, made a visit to Britain. He had ascended to his somewhat precarious throne in 1861 and was a great admirer of Western culture. He was also an ardent navalist and by 1875 had made the Ottoman navy the third largest fleet in the world.* Abdülaziz aimed to cultivate good relations with the Second French Empire and the British Empire and in 1867 went on a European tour, the first sultan to do so, visiting Paris (where he took in the *Exposition Universelle*) and then on to Britain.[†]

The visit was very much in line with British foreign policy, for the

* Twenty-one battleships and 173 warships of other types.

† He also visited Berlin, Brussels and Vienna on his way home.

desire to keep the Ottoman Empire intact to prevent Russian aggrandise-
ment and access to the Mediterranean was still uppermost in the government's mind, especially now that the Suez Canal was soon to open to
commercial traffic. This would significantly reduce the time taken to reach
Asia and India in particular and the preservation of some sort of British
influence over it was seen as crucial. The visit was thus doubly important
as the Sultan was accompanied by the Khedive (Viceroy) of the
autonomous Ottoman Khedivate of Egypt and Sudan, Ismail Pasha,
through whose lands the Suez Canal ran.

The problem was that Victoria continued to refuse to undertake public
duties. She was in retreat at Balmoral for the summer and that was where
she intended to stay. However, Prime Minister Edward George Geoffrey
Smith-Stanley, 14th Earl of Derby, was able to persuade her that 'English
influence which was then paramount at Constantinople, might well be
damaged if the Sultan was shown less respect than he had been in Berlin
or Paris'.[13] Victoria agreed to come down to Osborne and a great Royal
Naval Review was planned for the Turks' delight.

The Sultan arrived at Dover on board Napoleon III's royal yacht, *Reine
Hortense*, on 12 July, to be met by the Prince of Wales and the Duke of
Cambridge who accompanied him on the train to Charing Cross station.
During his ten days in Britain, the sultan was accommodated at
Buckingham Palace, where a number of staterooms had been specially
redecorated in honour of his visit.

The problem was the weather. It had been steadily becoming worse for
two days, with little chance of its moderating; in-shore boats could not
communicate with the fleet and a postponement was only prevented by
the announcement that Wednesday 17 July was absolutely the only time at
the Sultan's disposal. A review would go ahead on that day come hell or
high water.

The Sultan and the Khedive travelled separately to Portsmouth. But
once again, railway problems interfered. Although he had left much earlier,
the Khedive arrived at the same time as the Sultan and the separate reception planned for each, by first the Admiralty and then the mayor and
corporation of the town, became an unseemly melee.

In the meantime, the weather worsened and a wind got up with 'a
violence that soon cleared the water of all sailing craft except a very few
of the most adventurous yachts and rose into perfect fury as each one of
the dull grey masses of rain cloud that kept gathering to windward broke
over or near the scene'.[14] It was decided that the original plans could not
be adhered to and there would instead be the briefest inspection of the
fleet at anchor.

There was a further complication, as the Sultan had been promised that
he would be made a member of the Order of the Garter* as a mark of

* Founded by Edward III, this was and is an honour entirely in the sovereign's gift and regarded as the most prestigious British order of chivalry.

respect. Victoria had cavilled, suggesting the Star of India; but the government prevailed and the presentation was to take place on *Victoria and Albert* during the review.*

At midday *Osborne*, carrying the Sultan, followed by another yacht with the Khedive, and three P&O steamers, *Tanjore*, *Ripon* and *Syria*, bearing the foreign ministers and diplomats, the House of Commons and the House of Lords respectively, followed in their wake. As they cleared the harbour mouth on one side were the old wooden walls of *Victory*, *St Vincent* and *Duke of Wellington*; on the other a long line of spectators crowding the seashore. And stretching away in the foreground was 'a monster avenue of vessels'.[15] On the Isle of Wight shore was the long line of fifteen ironclads, and in an exact parallel on the Hampshire side were a corresponding number of 'the finest screw liners afloat',[16] while the same number of gunboats extended the columns still further. All the warships were flying the White Ensign instead of the previously-used red, white and blue squadron flags.

At the head of the line of ironclads was the flagship of the Channel Squadron, the huge five-masted HMS *Minotaur*. Originally ordered in September 1861 as HMS *Elephant*, in honour of the ship once commanded by Nelson 70 years before, her name was changed to *Minotaur* during construction. Launched two years' later she was an armoured frigate, iron-hulled with five masts, a single screw, two telescopic funnels and a rounded ram. *Minotaur* was armed with a mix of 7in and 9in rifled muzzle-loading guns. All four 9in and twenty 7in guns were mounted on the main deck while four 7in guns were fitted on the upper deck as chase guns. The ship also carried eight brass howitzers for use in saluting. She was never to be tried in battle, however, which was possibly just as well. She had a small radius of action, as her Penn trunk engine was prodigious user of coal (although could it drive her at up to 14kts in short bursts) and

* Possibly because, as the Sultan was the Caliph of the Muslim world, the more usual venue of the Chapel of the Knights of the Garter at Windsor Castle was deemed inappropriate.

HMS *Minotaur*, flagship of the Channel Fleet in 1867. *(US Naval History and Heritage Command NH 59979)*

she could not manage more than 9.5kts under canvas. Furthermore, *Minotaur* was reputed to be 'almost unmanageable under sail'.[17]

The flagship was the first vessel to commence firing the royal salute, which then rolled up the line of warships. *Achilles* (sister to *Minotaur*), *Warrior* and her sister-ship *Black Prince* 'the latter of which combines the long low black hull, and the grim and frowning battery, with graceful curves, comparatively light spars, and bows that sit on the water with real beauty of outline'.[18] The experimental turret ship *Royal Sovereign*, under the command of Captain Cowper Coles, 'excited great interest' waxed one reporter. 'In appearance, it must be said, she looks the image of a butter boat with three pats of butter, but the simile is strangely in contrast with the fact that the heaviest artillery in the fleet, then present, could have barely made a dent even on the small target exposed to them'.[19]

While all this was happening, the Sultan himself, the intended beneficiary of the display, was generally down below deck in his vessel being violently seasick. Nonetheless, when the line of yachts and steamers came to the shore off Osborne, where the Queen had allowed a band to play for the first time in nearly six years, the Sultan was able to board *Victoria and Albert*, narrowly missing a further downpour in which 'another furious squall of whistling wind and stinging rain seemed to beat straight down on the sea'.[20] The flag of the Ottoman ruler ran up alongside that of Queen Victoria, and the Queen, accompanied by the Prince of Wales, the Duke of Cambridge, Prince Arthur (Victoria's seventh child), Prince Leopold (eighth child), Prince Louis of Hesse (married to Victoria's third child, Alice), Princess Beatrice (Victoria's youngest offspring) and three Ladies in Waiting, invested the Sultan with the Order of the Garter.

Despite the weather, and the annulment of an order for the fleet to weigh anchor, a display of British might was still possible. Headed now by the royal yacht, the procession reformed and steamed down through the path marked out by the fleet. Manning the yards was impossible, given the weather, as was any display of bunting in face of the gale; although a Danish frigate, in the lee of the Isle of Wight, actually did manage to accomplish both tributes.

Once again, the cannons roared out with royal salutes. Then, after passing through the fleet, the royal yacht came to anchor and a spectacular display of a mock attack by gunboats against the shore forts took place. 'In a moment the roar began, from one end to the other, and the smoke came rolling down, ship by ship fading spectrally away in the gloom. From the far end came a mingled mass of sound, from the nearer ships came incessant but distinguishable peals.'[21] Victoria wrote that 'they all saluted so violently that I thought the windows would break. The sultan remained below, not feeling very comfortable.'[22]

Queen Victoria
investing the Sultan
of Turkey with the
insignia of the
Order of the Garter
in 1867. Behind her
on the left stand the
Prince of Wales, the
Duke of Cambridge,
Prince Arthur,
Prince Leopold,
Prince Louis of
Hesse and Princess
Beatrice with three
Ladies in Waiting.
The Sultan's son
stands near him.
From a painting by
G H Thomas.
(Author's collection)

The attack over, the royal yacht returned to Osborne and Victoria took her leave of the Sultan who, after a further salute from the fleet, arrived at Portsmouth Harbour, passing as he entered just under the *Syria* and *Ripon* and where he was roundly cheered as he proudly sported the broad blue ribbon of the Garter on his chest.

So ended the 1867 Royal Fleet Review; however, it was not the end of the festivities for the Sultan. That evening he travelled up to London, where he was entertained the following day by Lord Mayor Thomas Gabriel (a timber merchant) in a dinner at the Guildhall. Perhaps appropriately, one of the guests was the chairman of the P&O Navigation Company, Arthur Anderson, whose steamers had done such good service the day before.

A bronze medal was designed for the Corporation of London by J S and A B Wyon to celebrate the visit of the Sultan, depicting Londinia greeting Turkey with St Paul's Cathedral and the Hagia Sophia mosque in the background. And the central-battery ironclad HMS *Sultan*, laid down just after the Turkish European tour, was named in his honour.

Victoria returned to her funereal seclusion. In 1869, Prime Minister Gladstone made a determined effort to persuade her to perform her duties, which she ignored, possibly because she disliked both the man and his politics. In 1870, Victoria flatly refused to attend the State Opening of Parliament. The royal reputation was now at a low, not assisted by the louche lifestyle of the Prince of Wales which excited much unfavourable comment.

Perhaps as a result, Victoria did consent to open Parliament in 1871, and in 1872, a public ceremony of thanksgiving for the recovery of her eldest son, Edward Prince of Wales, from typhoid, which she attended, did much to restore her reputation. Suddenly, she was visible again as queen and the populace once more took her to their hearts.

1873, the Shah of Persia receives the Garter

Persia, lying as it did on the borders of both Russia and India, was a country in which both British and Russian imperial power vied for influence. The Persians themselves were worried about the potential intervention of the great powers, especially Russia, with which they had agreed a fragile peace after two Russo-Persian wars. Persia had lost its Caucasian provinces to Russia and the Persian regime was still concerned by Russian intentions towards it.

For Britain, keeping that part of western Persia which bordered the Persian Gulf free from Russian control or incursion and ensuring that a power more hostile to Britain than Turkey did not gain influence in the Middle East, and thus sit astride the route to India, were the main foreign policy goals regarding the country. As late as 1903, Henry Petty-Fitzmaurice, 5th Marquess of Lansdowne, the Secretary of State for Foreign Affairs, stated that Britain operated 'a sort of "Munroe doctrine"' regarding the Persian Gulf, declaring that an encroachment by any other power 'would be regarded as a great menace'.[23] Thus, the visit to Europe by the Shah of Persia, Naser al-Din Shah Qajar, which began in Austria in May 1873, was a significant political event.

The Shah of Persia, Naser al-Din Shah Qajar. *(Author's collection)*

However, despite her recent public appearances, Queen Victoria was not inclined to receive the visitor from the East. Eventually she was 'with great difficulty persuaded to welcome Shah of Persia for reasons which [Prime Minister] Gladstone assured her were of the upmost political importance'.[24] She was also less than pleased about the cost of entertaining the Shah and his entourage; and not all that happy that the Prince of Wales advised her to invest him with the Order of the Garter – of which there were only ever supposed to be twenty-four living members. Victoria had also been warned that he was rude to women, had bad manners, ate with his fingers and cooked over open fires in his rooms. None of this proved to be the case, although when Baroness Burdett-Coutts was presented to him he looked closely in her face and then, summoning up the only two words of French he knew, exclaimed '*quelle horreur*'.[25]

But the visit gained even greater consequence just before the arrival of the Persian ruler, for the shah announced the signing of the Reuter Concession. The ever improvident and perpetually short of money ruler had agreed with a British entrepreneur, Baron Paul Julius de Reuter (born Israel Beer Josaphat), a concession whereby the baron would have control over Persian roads, telegraphs, mills, factories, extraction of resources and other public works for five years in exchange for an up-front payment and 60 per cent of all the net revenue for the next 20 years. The concession was so immense that even imperialists like Lord Curzon characterised it as the most complete grant ever made of control of resources by any country to a foreigner; as one newspaper declared 'never was there such a bargain or such a monopoly'.[26]*

The Shah and his entourage sailed from Ostend to Dover on Wednesday 18 June in the paddle steamer *Vigilant*, accompanied by Admiral Leopold McClintock (Admiral Superintendent of Portsmouth Dockyard and known for his discoveries in the Canadian Arctic Archipelago) and, as translator, Sir Henry Creswicke Rawlinson (a former officer in the East India Company's army and a noted orientalist who deciphered the Old Persian portion of the trilingual cuneiform inscription of Darius I the Great at Bīsitūn). Two further vessels carried the remainder of the Shah's suite.

As they approached England the *Vigilant* was met by three ironclads, 'chief among them the huge, unsightly hull of the *Devastation*, the last born of these grim monsters of the deep'.[27] *Devastation* was a turret ship, one of a type which included her close sister HMS *Thunderer* and her slightly larger sister HMS *Dreadnought*, and can be fairly regarded as the models for subsequent mainstream battleship layout and development

Turrets were considered revolutionary (pun intended) and Captain Cowper Coles (who had commanded *Royal Sovereign* at the 1867 Royal Review) had pushed the concept with zeal. In 1865 a committee had recommended that some aspects of his suggestions be pursued. *Monarch* (launched 1868) and *Captain* (1869) were the result, with tragic consequences for the latter. She was a masted turret ship, designed and built to Coles's designs and against the wishes of the Admiralty Controller's and Chief Constructor's departments. HMS *Captain* was completed in April 1870 and capsized in September the same year, because of design and construction errors that led to inadequate stability. Nearly 500 lives were lost and Coles himself was amongst the dead. This tragedy could have put back the cause of turret ships by some distance. Fortunately, the Admiralty persisted and HMS *Devastation* was the first turret ship constructed to an Admiralty design. Launched in 1871, she and *Thunderer*, were also the first mastless† turret ships built for the Royal Navy.

Devastation was armed with four 'Woolwich Infants' mounted in two turrets. Weighing 30 tons each, these massive muzzle-loading rifled guns, nicknamed with typically British litotes for their size, took a cartridge 2ft 6in long, with 130lb of powder, to throw a 700lb shot from a barrel 12in in diameter. Admiral Phipps Hornby had taken her on a round-Britain cruise which generated much favourable publicity (an Aberdeen dancing master composed the *Devastation Galop* in honour of her visit) and 'her uncompromising appearance was such that it was popularly believed that she was the model for the warship appearing on boxes of [Bryant & May's] *England's Glory* matches'.[28] The Shah was fascinated by her at first sight and expressed the desire to examine *Devastation* more closely. Signals were sent

* The Shah was forced to revoke the agreement after a year following a public outcry.

† In the sense that they had no sailing rig, but did have a mast for boat handling and signalling.

and *Vigilant* closed on the warship, over which the paddle steamer could look down on the 'iron raft'.[29]

Then, as the Shah observed her through opera glasses, *Devastation* manned as if for action. The iron bulwarks on the lower deck were cleared away, so as to leave free play for the guns and a boarding party was drawn up on the upper deck, with cutlasses and hatchets drawn. *Vigilant* dropped astern and as she did the turrets moved slowly around and 'there echoes out a bang loud enough to wake all the Rip Van Winkles in the world, as the great gun of the fore turret is fired on the port side'.[30] As the smoke cleared another salvo was fired, this time to starboard, and 'the shock must have been greatly felt on board the *Vigilant*, for ... one of the doors in her bulwarks, which ... had been carelessly fastened, [was] shaken into the water by the concussion'.[31] The 'Woolwich Infants' had spoken.

As the flotilla approached Dover around 1320 'a fleet of mighty ironclads was seen guarding the approaches. The sea was swarming with smaller steamers and vessels, come out to take part in the welcome.' *Vigilant* passed between the two magnificent lines in which the squadron was drawn out, including some of the largest and most remarkable ships in the navy';[32] these lines included the battleships *Agincourt*, *Northumberland*, *Sultan*, *Hector* and *Hercules* with the turret ship *Monarch* and *Black Prince*. Twenty-one-gun salutes crashed out from the fleet, echoed by the shore batteries at Dover.

There was a high-powered welcoming party which included the Prince of Wales, the Duke of Edinburgh and the Foreign Secretary, Granville George Leveson-Gower, 2nd Earl Granville. But all were kept waiting as the Shah personally oversaw the unloading, and re-loading onto a train, of his personal treasures which he had brought with him from Tehran.

The inspection of the fleet at Spithead by the Shah of Persia in *Victoria and Albert*, 23 June 1873. Etching from the *Illustrated London News. (Alamy DDRH85)*

HM Turret Ship *Devastation* at Spithead on the occasion of the naval review in honour of the Shah of Persia, 23 June 1873. She was the first ship to be built for the navy without sails. The royal yacht *Victoria and Albert* is shown on the extreme left. Painting by EW Cooke. *(© National Maritime Museum BHC3287)*

From here he was transported to Buckingham Palace. The Shah was particularly taken by the lawn mower, an 'agricultural machine, like a cart, drawn by a horse, that cuts down the grass in strips a yard broad, which falls into the cart'.[33] From the palace, Naser al-Din Shah Qajar embarked on a series of meetings and other engagements. He was entertained to a banquet at the Guildhall; at Windsor, Queen Victoria invested him with the Order of the Garter; and he was taken to Woolwich to see where the 'Infants' were manufactured. Here the Shah was asked by the Duke of Cambridge to select an artillery piece to keep and take home. He chose 'a nine pounder of the newest pattern'.[34]

On Monday 23 June, the Shah rose early and with royal accompaniment made the three-hour carriage journey to Portsmouth, where he was greeted by an address from the mayor and corporation and more artillery salutes. Boarding *Victoria and Albert*, he was able to view three long lines of ironclads, forty-four ships in total including twenty-one gunboats, all under the command of Admiral Geoffrey Thomas Phipps Hornby with his flag in *Agincourt*, identical sister to *Minotaur*.

Phipps Hornby was considered to be one of the best handlers of a fleet ever. Fisher, who served under him, certainly thought so. 'That great man was the finest admiral afloat since Nelson,' Fisher later wrote, adding 'he was astounding. He would tell you what you were going to do wrong before you did it; and you couldn't say you weren't going to do it because you had put your helm over and the ship had begun to move the wrong way.'[35]

Victoria and Albert sailed up the lines of ships, eleven ironclads of the First Division and twelve of the Second. Their guns boomed out in tribute: 'the thunder of their guns was heard far inland and strangely echoed among the Welsh hills [*sic*]. In the towns along the coast the windows of the houses shook as if from an earthquake.'[36]

The Shah went on board the flagship and afterwards *Sultan*; on *Agincourt* he was most impressed with the display of 'action stations'. 'They blew a fife to make ready for battle. In an instant all the sailors came from above on to the lower deck, and with the greatest speed went through the gun exercise. They turned those enormous guns about with the implements of which they made use, so as to astonish us.'[37]

At the conclusion of the ship tours, the Shah was conveyed by barge back to the royal yacht; he thought himself lucky to survive the trip.

> A small steamer towed us. On reaching our ship it passed the ladder and went on under the very paddle wheel, which was in motion. We had a narrow escape of being struck by one of the paddles; had this happened we must all have been drowned. Thank God, however, the wheel was stopped; we escaped the danger, got on deck, and returned to Portsmouth where, in a room, another breakfast was laid out, of which we partook.[38]

But his tour of inspection was not yet finished. Next the Shah was taken to the dockyard where 'they were constructing a very large ship of war, into which we went'.[39] This was HMS *Blonde*, which in honour of the

HMS *Shah*, originally HMS *Blonde*, renamed in honour of the Shah of Persia's visit in 1873. *(US Naval History and Heritage Command NH 71214)*

Shah's visit was renamed *Shah*.* Launched the previous September, she was
an unarmoured, iron-hulled, wooden-sheathed frigate, the largest square-
rigged, unarmoured iron vessel ever built for the Royal Navy. From there,
the Shah returned to London, a concert at the Albert Hall and yet more
receptions and meetings. And after a stay in Britain of 18 days, he left via
Portsmouth on the French vessel *Rapide* escorted by a Royal Navy
squadron until met by the fleet of the Third Republic.

Thus ended three weeks of pageantry, designed to impress a ruler whose
country was important in the 'Great Game' with Russia. The Queen had
not attended the review in person but there had been a full house of royal
princes and dukes present. The fleet that they and the Shah observed was
much changed from the last Royal Review. As one newspaper noted
'when the sultan and the khedive, in 1867, saw our Channel Fleet, there
was still one line of wooden men-o'-war and frigates but not a single spec-
imen of this class was now brought out. Yet the fleet which the shah beheld
that Monday was stronger than the combined fleets of Europe.'[40]

1878, Turkey and Russia, again

Russia continued to cast envious eyes towards the Ottoman Empire, especially the Balkans and as a means of access to the Mediterranean. By mid-
October 1876, Russia's intentions to wage war sooner rather than later
against the Turks – with all that this implied for the defence of India and
the Mediterranean Sea communications – were sufficiently clear for Prime
Minister Benjamin Disraeli to take steps towards implementing a defensive
military policy. His Cabinet was not unanimous on the issue but nonetheless a military mission was secretly despatched to design and possibly
prepare fortifications at Gallipoli and Bujuk-Checkmedji for the defence
of Constantinople. The Inspector-General of Fortifications, Sir Lintorn
Simmons, was appointed commander-in-chief designate of any expeditionary force that might subsequently be sent to occupy those positions.
Major-General Sir Garnet Wolseley was seconded to the India Office as
Military Member of the Home Council to advise on Indian military
policy and strategy, and the Viceroy of India, Lord Lytton, was warned that
since war might be declared within three weeks he should be prepared to
strike at Russian interests in Central Asia.

A last-minute conference of European powers failed to halt the journey
to conflict and in April 1877 Russia and Turkey were once more at war.
Before long, Russian troops took control in Bulgaria and were soon at
Constantinople's gates. Disraeli sent Admiral Phipps Hornby and the
Mediterranean Fleet to assist the Turks, with orders to guard the
Dardanelles, basing himself at Besika Bay and then Vourla. Here he suffered
from the uncertainty of the British government which sent him puzzling
and contradictory orders reflecting the difference of opinion between

* *Shah* would fight a
single-ship action
with the Peruvian
ironclad *Huascar* in
1876; and tradition
has it that her masts
became *Victory's*
lower masts during
an early twentieth-
century restoration.

Disraeli and his Foreign Secretary, Lord Derby (incidentally Hornby's cousin). This saw the fleet ordered both in and out of the Dardanelles and the Sea of Marmara before eventually anchoring (in part) off Constantinople.

Turkey sued for peace and the resultant Treaty of San Stefano of 3 March 1878 created the independent Principality of Bulgaria (in reality a Russian client state) and gave Russia much influence in the Balkans and the Black Sea. The agreement was also believed to compel Turkey to pay a massive indemnity and hand over to Russia several Aegean ports, thus providing the Russians with bases in the eastern Mediterranean, anathema to Britain. Perhaps unsurprisingly, it was around this time that the term 'Jingo' came into usage, an epithet directed at those who supported inter-vention against the Russians, expressed in the music-hall song by McDermott and Hunt, whose chorus was:

> We don't want to fight but by Jingo if we do
> We've got the ships, we've got the men, we've got the money too
> We've fought the Bear before, and while we're Britons true
> The Russians shall not have Constantinople.

Throughout the Russo-Turkish War, Disraeli and Queen Victoria had favoured the Turks. She encouraged and supported the hawks in her government and urged them to hold a 'bold and united front to the enemy'.[41] Disraeli called up the reserves on 27 March and Victoria came out of seclusion to preside over reviews of troops. The prime minister also sent ground forces to Malta and in June entered into a secret undertaking with Turkey to defend her against any further Russian aggression; in return Britain gained Cyprus, which Disraeli called 'a *place d'armes* from which Russia's designs on a disintegrating Turkish empire could be resisted'.[42] He also successfully had the San Stefano treaty referred to a European congress (the Congress of Berlin, at which a much watered-down peace treaty was signed on 13 July). It was in the wake of these febrile times that Victoria committed to a Royal Fleet Review, the first that she would personally attend since 1867.

At 1400 on 13 August, the Queen, with Princess Beatrice and a lady in waiting, boarded her barge at Osborne for transfer to *Victoria and Albert*. There she was joined by the Prince and Princess of Wales with their chil-dren and Prince Arthur, together with her naval ADC Sir Harry Keppel. The ships that she was to inspect belonged to the Reserve Squadron, commanded by Admiral Sir Astley Cooper Key, who had completed his term as C-in-C of the North American Station in March and was placed in charge of Reserve Squadron, which might be needed to intervene in matters Turkish and Russian.

Key had his flag in HMS *Hercules*, one of ten central-battery ironclads in the squadron which included *Warrior*. His flag captain was the future iconoclastic First Sea Lord, Captain John Arbuthnot Fisher. There were also eight turret ships, six sloops and gunboats and two novelties, the torpedo boats *Vesuvius* and *Lightning*, the former under the command of a future Admiral of the Fleet, Lieutenant William Henry May.

It was a wretched afternoon with constant showers and quite windy. But the Queen enjoyed herself. 'It was a beautiful sight, as we passed up the line at Spithead, the men all cheering. The ironclads looked splendid and the turret ships and gun boats, very extraordinary,'[43] she confided to her journal.

There were many pleasure boats out to see the spectacle, despite the weather, and as had become normal on these occasions the House of Lords and House of Commons were present in ships reserved for them. But the conditions were considered too poor to allow the fleet to engage in any manoeuvres and so the Queen contented herself with sailing through the two lines of the squadron and on reaching the Nab, turning around to sail through them again.

Off Osborne, the Prince and Princess of Wales took their leave but the *Victoria and Albert* sailed on and went as far as Yarmouth. Victoria thought it a 'very pleasant evening'.[44] The Queen had enjoyed the new torpedo boats; 'I must not forget to mention the two torpedo boats, *Vesuvius* and *Lightning*, which rushed about at the rate of 21kts an hour! They are painted grey and are very low in the water.'[45] The speed she claimed for them is unlikely. *Vesuvius*'s compound steam engines drove two propeller shafts but she could only manage a shade under 10kts at best. Launched in 1874, she was intended for night attacks against enemy harbours, most likely French, and was armed with a single tube for Whitehead torpedoes in her bow. The Admiralty had purchased a licence to build Whitehead's torpedo, with production beginning at the Royal Arsenal at Woolwich in 1872. *Vesuvius* was the first ship designed for torpedo attack but her slow speed rendered her useless for the role envisaged and she was used as a test bed for torpedo trials, attached to HMS *Vernon*.*

Lightning had a claimed top speed of 18.5kts, so it may have been her which caught the Queen's eye. She had been designed and built by a

---

* *Vernon* was established on 26 April 1876 as the Royal Navy's Torpedo Branch, also known as the Torpedo School, named after HMS *Vernon* which originally served as part of its floating base.

Torpedo boat HMS *Lightning* (1876) in an illustration from *Scientific American*, 7 July 1877. Queen Victoria admired her performance at the 1878 Royal Review. *(Author's collection)*

company that would become famous for its small naval craft, John Thornycroft, and entered service in 1876. As Victoria saw her, she had two drop collars to launch torpedoes. These were replaced in 1879 by a single torpedo tube in the bow. Soon all navies were acquiring these small, lethal, craft, particularly from Thornycroft's. 'No high-pressure salesmanship was needed to sell torpedo boats in the nineteenth century; on the contrary, the customers queued up.'[46]

HMY *Osborne II* (launched 1870 and the last royal paddle steamer ever built) and the Thornycroft torpedo boat # 3, launched in 1878. A single torpedo tube was mounted forward. *(US Naval History and Heritage Command NH 76925)*

At the start of this chapter, the Royal Navy was in the process of moving to steam power as an assist to sail. By the end of it, there were ironclads without sails, ships with only turrets and no sail-only powered ships in active service. Torpedoes were being slowly adopted by the navy, although no one yet understood the revolution in warfare at sea that they would cause.

Queen Victoria had seen all of this, willingly or otherwise. And all the while, the Russian threat had been ever-present and the French continued to trouble. But even that small part of the fleet present at the 1878 Review, was still 'a force almost equal to the entire maritime resources of any one continental power, not alone numerically, but also as to fighting capacity'.[47]

Chapter 9

Golden Years, 1887–1896

The Training
Squadron at the
Golden Jubilee
Review. HMS
Martin (1850–1907),
renamed *Kingfisher*
(1890, possibly the
left-most ship); *Sea-
flower* (1873–1908);
Liberty (1850–1905);
Pilot (1879–1907);
Sealark (1875–98).
*(US Naval History
and Heritage
Command
NH 88849)*

THE QUEEN'S CONTINUED SECLUSION had led to a resur-
gence of criticism in the press of her avoidance of public appearances,
from which she still shrank. Indeed 'at a Liberal parliamentary dinner a
large number of guests remained in their seats when the loyal toast was
proposed and several of them … hissed'.[1]

She had at first refused to consider celebrating the fiftieth anniversary of
her coming to the throne, complaining of backache, rheumatism and
tiredness. But the Prince of Wales encouraged her to embrace the occasion
and in the end Victoria agreed, excepting that she would not perform any
ceremony on the actual day itself because that was the day William IV had
died and as a personal rule she avoided such anniversaries.

By March 1887, planning was well in hand and Victoria was persuaded to undertake some public duties. She laid the foundation stone of Aston Webb and Ingress Bell's magnificent law courts in Birmingham on 23 March. She performed a similar service for T E Collcutt's Imperial Institute in London two weeks after the Jubilee. Special medals were stuck. Convicts were set free in her honour. But in May, when she travelled through the East End to open the Hall of the People's Palace on the Mile End Road she was booed by the crowd.*

On 21 June, the Golden Jubilee was celebrated at Westminster Abbey with due pomp and ceremony. Victoria had declined to wear a crown but Prince Alfred, now Commander-in-Chief, Mediterranean Fleet, convinced her to dress up and she eventually wore a bonnet set off with white lace and diamonds. On her return to the palace, there was a late luncheon and a naval parade. And a month later, on 23 July, the Jubilee was to be celebrated with a Royal Naval Review.

But behind the scenes there were naval issues. The Royal Navy had not fought a major sea action since Trafalgar. Naval thinking was stale and the fleet not in the best of maintenance. Some design blind alleys and strategic misconceptions had led to ship types which were less than optimal. Indeed, former Chief Constructor of the Navy Edward James Reed, now an MP and perhaps not without an axe to grind, observed that only six or seven of the ships present at the review were 'fit to go to war'.[2] Successive governments stood accused of failing to sufficiently fund the navy. Particular issues were outdated and poorly designed ships and weapons, insufficient numbers of trained officers and ratings to man all of the ships involved and the related inability of the fleet to carry out coordinated exercises.

This latter point was brought home in the preparations for the review. On 20 July, HMS *Black Prince* collided with *Agincourt*; no serious damage resulted. But then HMS *Ajax* struck the turret ship HMS *Devastation*. It occurred when *Devastation* fouled *Ajax* when taking up her position at the head of the line and some considerable harm was done. Then, during the review, the royal yacht itself smashed into the troopship *Orontes* with the Crown Prince of Germany, the future Kaiser Wilhelm II, on board. The *Daily News* was moved to comment that 'foreign visitors should be kept out of the way until our bumping races of ironclads have come to an end'.[3]

The Queen was oblivious to these problems. At Osborne, in the afternoon of 22 July, Victoria received a deputation from the navy, who brought an Address and 'an album containing the drawings of the present they are going to give me, viz, two models of ships in silver. Old Sir Alexander Milne,† who was very nervous, read the Address in a strong, Scotch voice.'[4]

The following day, Victoria and her party, which included the German crown prince, had an early lunch and then embarked in *Alberta* for transfer

* The People's Palace was a concert room, library and singing gallery all in one. Prime Minister Salisbury apologised to the Queen, saying that 'London contains a much larger number of the worst kind of rough … probably socialists and the worst Irish' (quoted in Ackroyd, *Dominion*, p 326).

† Admiral of the Fleet Sir Alexander Milne. He served as First Naval Lord in the first Gladstone ministry of November 1872, remaining in office under the second Disraeli ministry and identifying the critical need for trade protection at times of war, demanding new cruisers to protect British merchant shipping. His son Archibald Berkley-Milne also became an admiral (*vide infra*).

to *Victoria and Albert*, meeting there the Empress Eugenie* who was so
keen to see the review that she had slept on board. The Prince and
Princess of Wales travelled separately in *Osborne* with their suite. The royal
yacht led *Osborne*, followed by *Alberta* and *Elfin* carrying other royal guests,
towards the fleet.

The ships spread out before them made a magnificent spectacle. There
were 134 vessels in all, which included twenty-six armoured ships, nine
unarmoured, three 'torpedo cruisers',† thirty-eight first class torpedo
boats, thirty-eight gunboats, one torpedo gunboat, twelve troopships, one
paddle frigate and six ships of the Training Squadron. Royal Naval
personnel involved totalled approximately 13,938, together with 2,263
Royal Marine Artillery and Infantry, and a further 2,342 non-combatants.

The Houses of Lords and Commons were present, as was by now traditional, and P&O provided their latest steamer, SS *Victoria*, a *Jubilee*-class
liner, the largest ship the company had ever built, together with other
passenger vessels. P&O themselves hosted 120 distinguished guests on
board including several eminent MPs, two would-be prime ministers and
the Governor of the Bank of England, Sir Mark Wilks Collet.

Amongst other passenger ships, the Indian troopship *Malabar* carried
serving officers in the army and their families. The ship was one of five
purpose-built iron-hulled troopships paid for by the Indian Government
and launched in 1866 as a response to the need to move soldiers quickly
to and from India, as demonstrated in the Indian Mutiny of 1857. *Malabar*
and her sister-ships, *Crocodile*, *Euphrates*, *Jumna* and *Serapis*, were all of the
same design and tonnage and were distinguished by different coloured
ribands around the hull, which in the case of *Malabar* was black; all also

carried the 'Star of India' on their bows. Each ship could transport a full battalion of infantry with its married families, or about 1,200 people.

Victoria thought the fleet 'an enormous force and certainly a truly magnificent sight. Each large ship manned yards, as we passed. There were thousands of spectators in steamers chartered for the occasion.'[5] Standing near to the Queen was Admiral Phipps Hornby with First Lord of the Admiralty Lord George Hamilton; Hornby provided a running commentary to his monarch as they passed through the lines of warships. The Board of Admiralty was also present on the Admiralty paddle yacht *Enchantress*, but had transferred to *Victoria and Albert* at the commencement of the review.

The ships that formed the lanes through which Victoria passed were swung round by the tide broadside to the lines they had formed. 'A vista of four miles of ironclads, decorated with thousands of flags, was thus produced, in which each ship stood out clearly defined in all her majesty of form and gaiety of colour.'[6]

Rather prosaically, the Queen commented that 'when we reached the end of the line, which extended beyond Ryde, we steamed back slowly and had tea. We then anchored.'[7] Next, the royal yacht flew the signal, 'Captains repair on board'; ships' barges conveyed their commanders to *Victoria and Albert* to be received by the Queen and the Prince and Princess of Wales, who had now joined her, and 'which took a long time' according to Victoria. 'We only got home at nine. I was very tired.'[8]

Fourth (junior) Sea Lord Captain Lord Charles Beresford managed to give the press a good story around this time. Anxious to tell his wife that

'Captains repair on board' by R T Pritchett. A captain's barge can be seen heading for HMY *Victoria and Albert* with HMS *Hero* to the left of the image. *(Author's collection)*

The Indian
troopship HMS
Malabar of 1866,
which carried
spectators at the
Golden Jubilee
Review. *(Author's
collection)*

★ Remarkably, some
of this class survived
to take part in the
First World War.
HMS *Bustard*, for
example, refitted
with a 6in and a
4.7in gun, served
with the Dover
Patrol.

he had been delayed on board the royal yacht and that she should transfer
from *Enchantress* to *Lancashire Witch* and await him, he had a signal, a long
and complex hoist, sent to that effect and which was read by all the fleet,
wary of some new instruction from on high. One newspaper commented
that 'in spite of these instructions having been signalled in all pomp from
the vessel flying the flag of the sovereign and Lord High Admiral of the
Fleet … surrounded by the naval strength of England in review assembled,
there is reason to believe they were not obeyed, for Lady Charles
Beresford was observed to be on board *Enchantress* as she steamed into
Portsmouth'.[9]

But along with the pomp and the unintentional comedy, there was
tragedy. The blasting off of 21-gun salutes was a commonplace occurrence
in Royal Reviews. HMS *Kite* was an *Ant*-class 'flat-iron' gunboat,★
launched in 1871 and designed for harbour defence or coastal bombardment. She mounted a single 10in 18-ton muzzle-loader, fitted forward on
a hydraulic mount that allowed it to be lowered for a sea passage to
improve the vessel's seaworthiness. As she fired off her tribute to the

Queen, a saluting charge exploded prematurely and four men were badly
injured, one of whom later died in hospital.

Amongst the lines of warships the Queen had seen that day lurked a
new, strange and different vessel. This was *Nautilus*, a Nordenfelt experimental steam-driven submarine, built by the Naval Construction
Company at Barrow. She was the third Nordenfelt to be built in British
yards, the first two having been purchased by the Turkish navy. The British
naval attaché noted that the Ottomans had little faith in the boats and that
'the general opinion of naval officers is much opposed to them'.[10] Captain
Lord Beresford had gone aboard her at Tilbury Docks in January; she had
submerged as planned but then refused to rise to the surface. 'The Thames
mud held us fast. In this emergency I suggested rolling her by moving the
people quickly from side to side.' This expedient eventually succeeded but
'by the time she came to the surface the air was very foul'.[11] In reality, the
Nordenfelts were not particularly successful. When operating near the
surface they were fast and manageable, but when completely submerged
they lacked longitudinal stability. At Victoria's previous review, she had
marvelled at the new-fangled torpedo boats, based around the new
Whitehead torpedo. Now she could see the embryo of the weapon which
would make the torpedo such a killer in two world wars. *Nautilus*'s career
was not long. After the review she sailed for Russia, becoming a total loss
on the coast of Jutland during the passage. The Tsar's government refused
Nordenfelt's claims for compensation and denied that it had ever intended
to purchase the vessel.

Another interesting ship was HMS *Inflexible*, commissioned in 1881 and
flagship for the day. She was fitted with engines of 8,000 horsepower,
armed with four 16in 80-ton muzzle-loading guns in two turrets,
protected with armour plates nearly 2ft thick and able to steam at up to
15kts. She was the first Royal Navy ship to be completely lit by electricity
but also came equipped with a pair of masts and yards, so that 18,500ft^2 of
sail could be deployed. She also had a ram.

HMS *Minotaur* was again present, this time as the flagship of Vice-
Admiral Sir William Nathan Wrighte Hewett, who had earned the Victoria
Cross at the siege of Sevastopol in 1854.* It was to be her last review duty
for *Minotaur* was paid off at the end of 1887 in Portsmouth and assigned
to the Reserve until 1893, when she became a training ship at Portland.

Near to *Inflexible* in the line of ships was HMS *Collingwood* of the new
'Admiral' class fitted with four 12in breech-loading guns in two twin open
barbettes together with three 6in guns on each of her broadsides and
capable of 16.8kts. All the 'Admiral'-class battleships had breech-loading
guns. They were not the first RN battleships to carry them; that honour
belonged to the two *Colossus*-class ships which came into service in 1882.
They had twin turrets with 12in guns; the larger six-ship 'Admiral' class

* Gazetted 1857.
Hewett was in
command of the
Channel Fleet from
1886 until his death
in May 1888.

followed them into service in the late 1880s with *Collingwood* only commissioned just before the Golden Jubilee Review.

The Royal Navy had in fact briefly adopted breech-loaders in the 1850s but they failed repeatedly and the switch back to muzzle-loaders was made in response. For much of the nineteenth century, the race between armour and artillery dictated gun design. Muzzle-loading guns using black powder produced a relatively low muzzle velocity; this meant that the gun had to fire a very heavy projectile to punch through the increasing levels of armour being fitted to warships. Hence the Victorian obsession with relating the weight of the guns (see *Inflexible* or the 'Woolwich Infants', *vide supra*), for a heavier gun was necessary to withstand the blast of firing a more massive projectile.

The development of a slower-burning powder at the beginning of the 1880s meant that longer, lighter guns firing less massive projectiles could be constructed. The high muzzle velocity resultant made up for the lower weight of the shell. Only breech loading was practical for this type of gun and the Royal Navy moved from massive muzzle loaders of 16- to 18-calibre to a new generation of 30-calibre guns, with the further benefit of an increase in the rate of fire possible. The momentum to change to breech-loading was accelerated by an accident which occurred on board HMS *Thunderer* on 2 January 1879. She was exercising with the Mediterranean Fleet in the Sea of Marmara when one of her 12in 38-ton guns mounted in the forward turret burst, killing two officers and eight men and wounding several others.

The implications of the accident – the possibility that a class of weapon that armed the navy's most powerful ships was fatally defective – caused the Admiralty to appoint a commission of officers and scientific experts to investigate the cause. This body decided that the accident had been the result of an error in loading discipline which had caused the gun to be fired when loaded with two complete rounds of powder and projectile.

It had been intended, on the fateful day in January, that the two guns would be fired simultaneously, both being loaded with a charge of 110lbs of powder and an 800lb Palliser projectile. One gun, however, missed fire; but nobody noticed. The noise and the smoke made by the discharge of one gun was so great that it was difficult for anyone to know that both guns had not been fired. The gun crews, drilled to run their guns in directly they were fired, had not observed that one of the guns had not gone off. Both guns were reloaded through the muzzle, by a hydraulic system, and the weapon with the double charge burst when the next round was fired.

The surviving gun was brought back to Britain and subjected to trials, with a view of ascertaining under what other conditions it would burst. These tests were conducted at Woolwich Arsenal. When double loaded, it

burst as had its sister. These accidents strengthened the feeling in favour of a return to breech-loaders for it was certain that no such mistake as double-loading could be made with a breech-loading gun. This report added weight to the drive for breech loading; the change was made and even *Thunderer* and her sisters were upgraded, receiving new 10in weapons. A technology which had served the navy for some 500 years, the armament of Drake and Nelson, was finally replaced, a casualty of the escalating war between guns and armour.

Partial view of the fleet at the Golden Jubilee Review, probably HMS *Hercules* in the foreground. *(National Museum of the Royal Navy)*

For a dramatic conclusion to the review's show of strength there was an illumination of the fleet. At a signal rocket being sent up from the flagship, 'a ribbon of fire was drawn around the vessels of every sort that formed the fleet'. At another signal from the *Inflexible*, 'thousands of rockets, sent up from every quarter, filled the air, while ship after ship shone forth outlined in red and blue fires'. And as a finale, 'the great ironclads turned their electric lights [to] fall upon the shore and showed how that keen and searching glare could make all that came within its scope as visible as if it were daylight'.[12] Such a display was rather wasted on the Queen, however; 'there were illuminations, but we could not see much of them, though they were said to be very fine' she noted in her journal.[13]

The display of naval strength seemed to please the press, despite the reservations expressed by Edward Reed and others. According to the *Spectator*, 'even if compared with the fleets that any one of the other nations of Europe could today put afloat, the ships gathered at Spithead must be admitted to surpass them greatly in strength, and this though our squadrons in the Mediterranean, in the Pacific, on the American, African, and China stations remain unimpaired in strength and numbers'.[14] And as a piece of public relations for the navy, the occasion was a success. 'On the whole, the review was one of which Englishmen have every right to be proud. It proved beyond a doubt that England possesses a fleet which, in time of danger, could afford the fullest protection to her coasts', noted one observer.[15]

An estimated 50,000 onlookers enjoyed the spectacle from sea or shore. Or at least, all except one did. Despite his viewing point on the royal yacht, Prince Wilhelm of Germany was most put out that he wasn't accorded the precedence he thought he deserved. Peevishly, he said of Queen Victoria (his maternal grandmother) that it was 'high time the old woman died ... . She causes trouble more than one would think. Well, England should look out when I have a say about things ... One cannot have enough hatred for England.'[16]

SMS *Charlotte*, the first German blue-water cruiser. *(US Naval History and Heritage Command NH 64260)*

The presence of the man who would become ruler of Germany less than a year later was prophetic, for Germany was taking its first faltering steps towards a blue-water navy. It was only in 1887 that command of the Imperial German Navy was entrusted to specialist naval, rather than army, officers. Initially the ships and tactics of the force were based around coastal defence. But as Germany joined the race for colonies abroad, so it needed blue water ships to seize and defend them. Typical of this new breed of ship was SMS *Charlotte*, commissioned in 1886. Of 3,700 tons and 275ft length, she carried eighteen 5.9in guns and had accommodation for a crew in excess of 500. Germany was set on a road that would lead to the naval race of the early 1900s and, eventually, be a cause of the First World War.

1889, the Seeds of War

Two years later Wilhelm was back in Britain, this time as His Imperial and Royal Majesty The German Emperor, King of Prussia. Following her humiliating defeat in the Franco-Prussian war of 1870–1, the France of the Third Republic endeavoured to make colonial gains as part of rebuilding her self-confidence and world status. But relations with a unified Germany were such that in 1887 France looked to Russia for support. In concluding the so-called Reinsurance Treaty with Germany in 1887, Russia insisted on maintaining for France the same conditions that Germany had stipulated for its ally, Austria. France and Russia were now bound together by mutual agreement, and they possessed the second and third largest naval fleets on the planet.

Perhaps unsurprisingly, this led to considerable agitation for increased naval expenditure as well a sustained political campaign aimed at both raising awareness of the Royal Navy and reforming its perceived weaknesses. For example, on 10 May 1888 a notice headed 'strictly non-political – great Britain's danger' appeared in *The Times*. Placed there by a group of naval officers and city businessmen led by Captain Lord Charles Beresford and Admiral Sir Geoffrey Phipps Hornby, it asked 'Englishmen of all classes and politics' to consider whether or not the Royal Navy was adequately equipped and funded to protect Britain and its trade in time of war.

This question was followed with a dire warning: 'a great war may at any moment burst upon us, in which we may have to fight for our very existence.' The two basic assumptions underlying the notice – that war was imminent and the country unprepared – formed the underlying theme of discussions relating to national defence of the British Empire.

A major meeting to discuss such issues was advertised and many serving officers choose to speak, attacking the system of 'government by party' which, they claimed, had left the navy in such a poor condition. Public agitation grew and Queen Victoria added her voice, berating Prime

Minster Robert Arthur Talbot Gascoyne-Cecil, 3rd Marquess of Salisbury, about the concerns raised. Salisbury promised to act.

In early 1889, Salisbury was able to redeem the pledge he had made to the Queen in December the previous year. Money was going to be spent on improving the navy and a new huge building programme under the Naval Defence Act would be set in train. It would 'put your majesty's fleet in a completely commanding position'.[17] In a speech at the Guildhall he stated that 'in a sensitive commercial community like ours, alarm is almost as destructive as danger and what we have to provide is not only safety for our citizens but a sense that safety exists'.[18] In other words, it was necessary to ensure that Britain retained sovereignty of the seas to protect her trade position.

He persuaded the Cabinet to support a new Naval Defence Act* which would spend an extra £20 million† on the Royal Navy over the following four years. Since the battle of Trafalgar, Britain had been content with having a fleet which gave a one-third advantage over the world's next largest (usually France). Henceforth, the yardstick would be the 'Two Power Standard' by which the Royal Navy was always to be kept 'to a standard of strength equivalent to the next two biggest navies in the world'.[19] As First Lord of the Admiralty Lord George Hamilton later recalled 'it was deemed impolite to mention either France or Russia by name'.[20]

The Act called for ten battleships, thirty-eight cruisers, eighteen torpedo gunboats and four fast gunboats; it represented the greatest ever peacetime expansion of Britain as a naval power. The new *Royal Sovereign* class battleships provided for by the bill would be the most powerful ever constructed. 'With a navy thus augmented, it was hoped that the Franco-Russian combination could be faced down, the empire's communications protected, the Mediterranean fleet made a match for the Toulon fleet, French invasion fears dispelled and the Jingoes silenced.'[21]

There was then the issue of Germany. Kaiser Wilhelm had badly slighted Edward Prince of Wales in Vienna in 1888 and Victoria was furious with him. Moreover, Wilhelm was rattling Germany's sabre, seeking colonial expansion and was soon to drop Otto von Bismarck, the navigator of German policy for many years. He was, in all meanings of the term, a loose cannon. But the Kaiser made it known that he wanted to visit Britain. Victoria, smouldering from the insult to her eldest son, was adamant that he should not come. But Salisbury insisted that he must be invited as he believed that Britain needed good relations with German as a counterweight to the Franco-Russian axis. 'It is in your majesty's interests', he told the Queen, 'to make his penitential return as easy to him as possible.'[22]

Eventually Victoria issued an invitation but only to Cowes, not Windsor. Meanwhile, Salisbury learned that Wilhelm cared deeply about uniforms; he persuaded Victoria to appoint the Kaiser to the rank of admiral in the

* Which received the Royal Assent on 31 May 1889.

† About £2.5 billion at today's prices, according to the Bank of England.

Royal Navy. Wilhelm was ecstatic, 'fancy wearing the same uniform as Nelson and St Vincent,' he gushed.[23] And in honour of the visit of this new admiral, a Royal Fleet Review would be staged on 5 August 1889.

Wilhelm arrived at Cowes on 2 August in his royal yacht *Hohenzollern*, commanded by his younger brother Prince Henry, where he was greeted by the Prince of Wales in *Osborne*. With the Kaiser came a German naval squadron whose flagship was SMS *Baden*. She was one of four *Sachsen-*class armoured frigates of the German navy, commissioned in September 1883. The class were armed with a main battery of six 10in guns in two open barbettes.

Come the appointed day, the British fleet was assembled at Spithead. Victoria had chosen not to attend the review personally, although in the end she in fact relented and 'decided to go out in the *Alberta* and see the German ships, which were all anchored close to Osborne Bay, so at five embarked … Went round and through the German ships, who all played *God save the Queen* in turn as we passed them. Home at seven, heard all had gone off well.'[24]

But the review was really about Wilhelm. 'The Emperor of Germany, just gazetted an Admiral of the English Fleet, and the Prince of Wales steaming down the gaily decked avenue of ironclads, and holding a reception of all the captains of the fleet on board the *Howe*, the principal flagship.'[25] Wilhelm also held a *soirée* for commanders of all ships on board his yacht. One captain who was granted that distinction, C C Penrose-

SMS *Baden* (1880), one of four *Sachsen-*class armoured frigates. She was the flagship of the German Squadron at the 1889 review of the British fleet by Wilhelm II. From a lithograph by Hugo Graf. (*Author's collection*)

The White Star liner
RMS *Teutonic*,
which as an AMC
was present at the
Kaiser's review. The
German emperor
was given a guided
tour of her by the
Prince of Wales.
(Author's collection)

Fitzgerald of HMS *Inflexible*, later recalled that 'they had the honour of receiving a hearty shake from the unmailed fist, before it had become stained with innocent blood, and before the blasphemous hypocrite – prince of spies and father of lies – had been found out, and his villainous character exposed.'[26]

The Kaiser showed intense interest and curiosity in all he saw. When looking at a new quick-firing gun on board the *Teutonic*, he turned around to his brother and exclaimed 'we must have one like that, and quick, too'.[27]* RMS *Teutonic* was a White Star liner built by Harland and Wolff for the Atlantic crossing trade. When she was launched on 19 January 1889, she became the first White Star ship without square-rigged sails. The ship was completed on 25 July 1889, just in time for the Spithead review. The Kaiser was given a two-hour tour of the new ship hosted by Edward, Prince of Wales. *Teutonic* had been built with government help under the Auxiliary Armed Cruiser Agreement and was Britain's first armed merchant cruiser (AMC), armed with eight 4.7in quick-firing guns. These were removed after the review and on 7 August she set sail on her maiden voyage to New York City.

Next, the royal yacht took up a position in Sandown Bay, with Wilhelm standing on her paddle box resplendent in his new admiral's uniform; there the Kaiser saw a line of ships 10 miles long file by him, the vessels keeping an exact distance between them 'as if they were regiments swinging past a saluting post'.[28]

The British flagship was the 'Admiral'-class battleship HMS *Howe*. This was effectively her shakedown cruise for she had only been commissioned the previous month. Admiral Sir John Edmund Commerell VC flew his

* Some sources
suggest he was
referring to the ship
itself.

flag in her; he had earned his Victoria Cross in the Crimean conflict and 'famously disregarded dress regulations and saluting formalities and made no secret of his antipathy to long range gunnery'.[29] This antipathy was shared by many senior officers; they still believed in the Nelsonian tradition of close engagement, despite the fact the *Howe*'s main guns had an effective range of some 12,000 yards. *Howe*'s officers were an interesting group. Her captain was Compton Domvile, who would become C-in-C of the Mediterranean Fleet. The ship's commander was Francis Bridgeman, who became First Sea Lord in 1911. The future King George V, then Prince George, was an honorary member of the ship's wardroom. C-in-C Grand Fleet during the First World War and later First Sea Lord, John Rushworth Jellicoe, was a lieutenant commander aboard. And Christopher 'Kit' Cradock who was to be the first Royal Navy admiral to die in battle in the Great War, at this point in his career a lieutenant on half pay, made a 'pier-head jump'* to join *Howe* for the review.

But despite this high-powered wardroom, the ship, and her class, were a disappointment. The big guns were prone to exploding when fired (in the proofing stage) and the bows were cut so low that in only moderate seas, the waves broke heavily over the decks. These and other defects, Admiral Reginald Bacon concluded, made the 'Admiral' class 'really useless as seagoing fighting ships'.[30] *Howe* became known to the navy as 'No-how'. Some other ships were not all they seemed to be either. Five cruisers of

* A 'pier-head jump' is when a crew member is posted to join the ship's company at the very last moment, almost literally as she is leaving the quayside.

The 1885 battleship HMS *Howe*, flagship for the review by Kaiser Wilhelm II on 3 August 1889, depicted here at Queenstown, Ireland, as guardship. Notice the huge, open barbette-mounted 13.5in guns. *(Author's collection)*

the *Orlando* class, ordered under the 1885 programme, paraded with no main guns and were forced to use wooden replicas instead.

The fleet now departed for manoeuvres off the coast of Ireland where they practised fighting off an attempt to capture Dublin, Waterford and Belfast. The Kaiser tarried long enough to attend the Cowes Regatta, make Queen Victoria an honorary colonel of the *Garde Dragoner** and have *Baden's* band play for the Queen's entertainment. Then he departed back to Germany; but surely this display of naval magnificence, even if the show was better than the reality, must have caused the realisation in the Kaiser's febrile mind that he too must have such sea-going might to enhance his and his realm's global heft.

1891, the French Fleet at Spithead

By 1891, Russia and France were moving politically and militarily closer to each other, the strange bedfellows of an autocratic dictatorship and an anti-monarchist state. The Kaiser had forced Bismarck's resignation in March 1890 and Germany, assuming that ideological differences and a lack of common interest would keep Republican France and Tsarist Russia apart, allowed its Reinsurance Treaty with Russia to lapse that same year.

But France, frightened of another German attack such as had defeated her in 1870–1, wanted support against Germany. Russia was worried about aggression, especially in the Balkans, by Austria-Hungary. The two powers slowly came closer together, upsetting the system of alliances that had been established by Otto von Bismarck to protect Germany against potential threats on two fronts. By August 1891, both states had made a preliminary agreement to consult in case of aggression against either of them (this was followed by a formal treaty in 1894).

Britain sat outside these alliances; as quondam prime minister Palmerston noted in 1848, 'we have no eternal allies, and we have no perpetual enemies. Our interests are eternal and perpetual, and those inter-ests it is our duty to follow.'[31] But she was increasingly nervous regarding Germany's long-term intentions. And both Russia and France acknowl-edged that Britain's powerful fleet could be decisive in any conflict between them and Germany/Austria-Hungary.

It was against this background that the French fleet made a goodwill visit to Britain in 1891, having previously visited St Petersburg at the end of July. Queen Victoria had delayed her planned departure to Balmoral in order to undertake an inspection of the combined fleets and the Admiralty had ordered the Channel Squadron to assemble at Spithead to greet their French equivalents from the Northern Fleet.

The French arrived on 19 August, led by the old battleship *Marengo*, flying the flag of Admiral Alfred Albert Gervais. It was a peculiar choice of flagship for she was an aging wooden-hulled, armoured frigate of the

* The Queen presented Prince Henry with the Order of the Garter and Wilhelm gave Prince George the Black Eagle in this cosy exchange of honours.

Océan class, built for the French Navy in the mid to late 1860s. She carried
her main armament in four barbettes on the upper deck, one gun at each
corner of the battery, with the remaining guns on the battery deck below
the barbettes. The six larger guns were 10.8in, the smaller four 9.4in and
four 4.7in.

The most recent ship in the French fleet was the *Marceau*, an ironclad
turret ship launched in 1890, but laid down eight years previously. The ship
was armed with a main battery of four 13.4in guns. These weapons were
mounted in individual barbettes in a lozenge arrangement, with one gun
forward, one aft, and two amidships. The secondary battery consisted of
sixteen 5.46in quick-firing guns, shooting through unarmoured embra-
sures in the hull.

The French visit evoked massive interest, although it was perhaps ironic
that the review would take place under the guns of the Royal Navy's
Portsmouth base. Here, in response to heightened Anglo-French tensions
in the 1860s, Britain had invested enormous sums to protect the base with
massive fortifications on both the land side and on artificial islands
constructed in the sea approaches.

Huge crowds attended to watch although the weather was appalling and
newspapers noted the qualitative and quantitative differences between the
two fleets. The different colour schemes elicited the comment that the
grey of the French hulls, though easier to see at night than the English
black, was less easy to see by day, and that the French ships were far less
visible even when near at hand. And 'some of the great French ships are
said to be even uglier than our own monsters, and that is saying a great
deal'.[32] The *Spectator* commented on the relative merits of mounting heavy
armament in turrets (as with the latest French ships) or in barbettes, noting
that the heavier weight of turrets meant they had to be mounted lower
down[33] and that the French seamen, mainly Breton, were 'physically, …
fine fellows enough, painstaking and docile, but with little of the gaiety
and exuberance of British seamen'.[34] It also noted 'French engine-room
complements are said to show a marked superiority in education and
intelligence over the average class of hand shipped for duty as stokers and
assistants in our vessels' and that 'the officers are educated gentlemen,
brim-full of the latest theories of naval war and practice and, as the recent
French naval manoeuvres showed, exceedingly competent in the practical
management of their ships'.[35]

Certainly, Queen Victoria found the French pleasant enough. 'Admiral
Gervais is a tall good-looking man of about forty-five, thin, *distingué*', she
noted in her journal.[36] On the evening of the 20th, she entertained the
French suite to dinner at Osborne and 'after dinner I spoke first to the
admiral, who is very pleasing and full of conversation, and then Mr
Waddington called up the principal captains who were all very civil and

The very model of a Victorian admiral. Admiral Sir Michael Culme-Seymour, 3rd Baronet. He was the flag officer at the 1891 review and commanded the Channel Fleet between between 1890 and 1892 and the Mediterranean Fleet from 1896. *(Author's collection)*

some particularly so. The one who commands the Training Ship seemed a particularly nice man, and had seen me at Cherbourg in '56!'[37]

On 21 August, the morning of the review dawned with rain and developed into a dull, cheerless day. The French fleet had been anchored in Osborne Bay but now moved to Spithead and joined with their Royal Navy hosts, where the combined fleets anchored in three lines, the southern most of which consisted of the brand-new British *Trafalgar*-class ironclad battleship HMS *Nile*, the 'Admiral'-class ships *Anson, Rodney, Howe* and *Camperdown*, the *Orlando*-class armoured cruisers *Immortalité* and *Aurora*, the third class cruiser *Pallas* and the torpedo depot ship *Hecla*. Admiral Sir Michael Culme-Seymour, commanding the Channel Fleet, flew his flag in *Camperdown*.

Victoria was meant to review the fleets at 1500 but this was delayed due to rain until 1600 when 'at length the rain ceased and the sun made a brave but ineffectual struggle to emerge from the dense clouds in which he was enveloped'.[38] The royal party embarked aboard *Alberta* at Trinity Pier, East Cowes, for transfer to *Victoria and Albert*. Soon the royal paddle yacht, led by a Trinity House vessel and followed by *Alberta, Elfin* and *Enchantress*, was amongst the massed fleets, which were 'dressed from stem to stern rainbow fashion and the many coloured flags contributed a pretty and effective picture';[39] and the royal salute roared out from British and French ships alike.

Victoria, however, was less impressed; she had done this many a time. To her 'it was not interesting passing up between the two lines of ships, English and French'. And the French particularly 'are certainly not smart looking'.[40] Moreover, she thought that

the peculiar shape of the French ships and the dull grey colour of the paint, makes them look more like powerful forts than floating batteries. The *Marceaux* is the largest and the one of which they are the most proud. We had our tea in the deck cabin … It came on to rain a little … The yacht stopped, to enable the various admirals and captains to come on board, make their bow, and take leave. I received them on deck, and expressed to the French Admiral, Gervais, my gratification at what I had seen.[41]

In dealing with the French, the Royal Navy seemed to believe that feasting them was a *sine qua non*. As in previous French visits, there was a formal dinner on board the flagship and the town and corporation of Portsmouth gave a dinner for 700, where a choir sang the *Marseillaise* and two Royal Marine bands provided music for dancing.

The Mayor of Portsmouth also laid on a repast for the matelots of the fleets. 'This entertainment must, indeed, have proved especially gratifying to the tars of both nations, for it confirmed two well-worn beliefs. The menu demonstrated that Englishmen do actually live on nothing but *rosbif* and plum pudding'; while the fact that the French sailors insisted on kissing as many of the townsmen of Portsmouth as they could get at during the triumphal procession back to their ships, 'confirmed the stories of Gallic embracement between man and man which are current in England'.[42] No national stereotyping in this reporter's thinking. But the Royal Navy did win some bragging rights. The French cruiser *Surcouf* ran aground and British seamen and marines were sent on board to assist in freeing her.

The review was deemed a success. But 'as a political event it has no significance', thought one observer, 'unless to show that our sole desire is to see peace maintained'.

The prominence of the navy was furthered during 1891 by a Great Royal Naval Exhibition, held between May and October. This extravaganza was fathered by the Naval Defence Act of 1889. Various strands of navalist propaganda and promotion had followed the success in securing additional funds for naval expansion and this was one of the most significant. In order to maintain the momentum behind the strengthening of naval prowess, it was decided that a spectacular naval show would be held in Chelsea, in the grounds of the Royal Hospital. This five-month event tapped into domestic pride in the navy, which crossed class boundaries, as well as fears of invasion from the Continent and a loss of prestige in international relations.

Advertised widely, it attracted over two million visitors; 70,000 catalogues, 305,000 official programmes and over 6,000 souvenir medals were

HMS *Nile*, head of the southern line at August 1891 review. She had only just been commissioned (in the June) and carried four 13.5in breech-loading guns in two turrets, whose muzzles were only 3ft 6in above the deck and were very hard to fight in a seaway owing to the spray breaking over the forward turret. (*Author's collection*)

purchased by the public. After costs were covered, the Exhibition raised some £50,000 for naval charities and boosted awareness of matters naval to the highest degree. The exhibition displayed paintings, models and memorabilia lent by private owners, as well as stands at which many of the main armament suppliers and shipbuilders displayed their wares. A large lake was constructed on which scale models of the battleships HMS *Edinburgh* and *Majestic* staged mock battles while smaller vessels ran the gauntlet between two sea-forts. These displays were extremely popular for their noisy spectacle. Landings by naval brigades were enacted, sailors and marines coming ashore. Here were born the field gun drills, breaking down and reassembling their components for use when necessary, activities which formed the basis of naval tattoos until 1999, when the last Royal Navy Command Field Gun competition took place during the final Royal Tournament at Earls Court.*

The exhibition was strongly supported by Queen Victoria and was opened by Edward, Prince of Wales, and his wife – who did so by pressing a switch to light up a model of the Eddystone Lighthouse. The exhibition was subsequently visited by the Queen herself.

The considerable propaganda and status acquired by the Royal Navy impacted on fashion, design and social behaviour and standing, positioning the navy as very much the 'senior service' and leading directly to the formation of the Navy League and a 'cult of personality' among admirals, which would reach its apogee at the end of the century.

1896, a Chinese Visitor

China was an important trading partner for India; but not in a good way. India exported opium to China and in return received Chinese silver bullion.† This enervated the Chinese population and undermined the country's currency. In attempting to stop this trade, the Chinese found themselves on the losing side in the two 'Opium Wars' against Britain of 1839–42 and 1856–60. In the latter, Britain was joined by an opportunistic France and the results included the establishment of more than eighty 'Treaty Ports'. All foreign traders gained rights to travel within China and China was opened to free European trade.

China slowly began to industrialise. She badly needed railways and other infrastructure, but also warships and arms for self-defence, particularly against ever-increasing Japanese greed. Thus, when an important member of the Chinese court came to Europe, it was appropriate that Britain gave him a warm welcome; and an invitation to see the Royal Navy on manoeuvres.

The visitor in question was Li Hung Chang (also known as Li Hongzhang) a Chinese general who ended several major rebellions and was a leading statesman of the late Qing Empire.‡ He served in important

* A reduced version of the sport is still run at HMS *Collingwood* as the annual Royal Navy and Royal Marines Charity Trophy.

† By 1856 this trade accounted for 22 per cent of all British India's revenues.

‡ Unusually for a Chinese he stood over 6ft tall.

positions of the Imperial Court, once holding the office of the Viceroy of Zhili, and known in the west for his diplomatic negotiation skills. In 1896, Li attended the coronation of Nicholas II of Russia on behalf of the Qing Empire and then toured Europe, Canada and the United States.

In Britain, he was received by Prime Minister Lord Salisbury, met ex-PM Gladstone at the latter's country seat, attended a banquet in London given by China merchants and toured the country by train. He visited the shipbuilding yards at Barrow-in-Furness and Newcastle and even sailed on Lake Windermere in a day steamer.

It had been planned to hold the annual naval fleet manoeuvres between 8 July and 25 August. They were now partially reconfigured as a Royal Fleet Review, in order that Li could be given the honour of attendance at such a prestigious event. Others were less impressed. In the House of Commons, the MP for Paddington North, John Aird, demanded of George Goschen, First Lord of the Admiralty, 'whether it is contemplated making such arrangements in connection with the forthcoming naval manoeuvres as will afford the representatives of the people an opportunity of forming a judgment on the efficiency of the navy'. Perhaps not wishing to have to stump up for the entertainment costs, Goschen answered that

> I do not know whether my hon Friend has more in his mind than a sight of the ships at anchor. If so, I may say that it is not contemplated to have a pageant or review, but the ships … will, on the completion of the manoeuvres, be at Spithead for a few days, about the 4th, 5th, and 6th of August, previous to their dispersion, and facilities could be given to hon Members to see them there if they wished it, but without a ceremonial.[43]

No free tea and buns for Members of Parliament.

On 4 August Admiral Lord Walter Talbot Kerr, Commander-in-Chief of the Channel Squadron and flying his flag in HMS *Majestic*, had assembled fifty ships of all types and sizes at Spithead. *Majestic*, sent down the slipway in 1895 and laid down as a result of the continuation of the Naval Defence Act funding, was the largest battleship launched at the time. She mounted four 12in in two turrets placed on pear-shaped barbettes and twelve 6in guns. The name ship of a highly successful class of nine, she was capable of 16kts and, like her sisters, the first British ships to incorporate Harvey armour, which allowed them to carry a much more comprehensive level of protection.

It was a fine, bright day. After luncheon, Queen Victoria and her party had boarded *Alberta* at Trinity Pier and steamed to Spithead and 'through the really splendid fleet'.[44] They went very close to some of the larger ships including the new cruiser *Blenheim*. She had a particular resonance for the

HMS *Blenheim*, a
Blake-class protected
cruiser comm-
issioned in 1891.
She was capable of
22kts and carried
two 9.2in guns
together with ten
6in quick-firers.
(Author's collection)

queen because Prince Henry of Battenberg, her son-in-law by marriage
to Princess Beatrice, died from malaria in January 1896 while on active
duty on board HMS *Blonde* off Sierra Leone. *Blenheim* repatriated his body
from the Canary Islands and Victoria appointed the commanding officer,
Captain Edmund S Poe, to the fourth class of the Royal Victorian Order
as a mark of appreciation for this service. The royal party then turned to
pass through the torpedo boats, a type which always seemed to exert a
peculiar fascination for the Queen. In the evening, Victoria hosted a dinner
at Osborne which Lord Walter Kerr attended, the first time he had been
to the house since he served on *Victoria and Albert* as a lieutenant, in 1859.

The following day, the Queen received Li Hung Chang for lunch in the
Durbar Room. Afterwards, Li was made a member of the Royal Victorian
Order, speeches were exchanged and, sticking strictly to the script, Victoria
emphasised that 'it will always be my earnest desire to maintain the most
friendly relations with China and to promote commercial interests
between our two countries'.[45]

Four years later, Britain and China were at war.

Chapter 10

Diamond Jubilee
1897–1901

A T 1115 ON 22 JUNE 1897 a cannon boomed out in Hyde Park. It signalled the departure from Buckingham Palace of Queen Victoria for St Paul's Cathedral and a service to celebrate her 60 years on the throne. The streets and houses on the route were thronged with spectators, cheering or applauding as she passed and the Queen, 78 years old, small, plump and as always dressed in black, lightened for this day with grey panels, was moved to tears by her reception. The cannon shot also indicated the start of a week of festivities in honour of the Queen which would include a fleet review at Spithead.

Victoria had initially been lukewarm to the idea of a celebration of her Diamond Jubilee; and there had been some tough negotiations between the officials of the Royal Household and the government, with the former anxious to avoid the expenses incurred to the Privy Purse of the Golden Jubilee. In the end, the costs were split and Colonial Secretary Joseph Chamberlain proposed that the event double as a 'Festival of the British Empire' to celebrate Britain's colonies. When Chamberlain suggested restricting the Jubilee's foreign guest list to the heads and representatives of the countries in the British Empire, the Queen – eager to avoid the problems of taking in unwelcome royal relations at Buckingham Palace and Windsor Castle – came around to the idea.*

Despite her initial reluctance, Victoria enjoyed herself, as did the public. Newspapers waxed lyrical over the Diamond Jubilee celebrations. 'Wherever the English language is spoken, wherever the British Flag flies' ran a typical example, 'representatives were present to do honour and homage to the sovereign who had done so much to shed lustre on England's history.'[1] The Queen, who spent much of the day in tears of emotion replied, 'From my heart I thank my beloved people. May God bless them. Victoria R and I.'

* Inevitably, the guest list expanded to include foreign royalty after all.

The previous evening, Victoria had entertained a glittering array of guests at the palace.

> Dressed for dinner. I wore a dress of which the whole front was embroidered in gold, which had been specially worked in India, diamonds in my cap, and a diamond necklace, etc. The dinner was in the supper room at little tables of twelve each. All the family, foreign royalties, special ambassadors and envoys were invited. I sat between the Archduke Franz Ferdinand and the Prince of Naples. After dinner went into the Ball Room.[2]

There she met the colonial prime ministers, invited at Chamberlain's suggestion. Telegrams of congratulation kept pouring in; she is said to have received some 1,300.

Four days later, on 26 June, Admiral Sir Nowell Salmon VC, Commander-in-Chief Portsmouth, had the Diamond Jubilee fleet drawn up in six lines A–G (with letter E somehow excluded), four of them some five miles long. Column A was exclusively comprised of visiting foreign warships, fourteen in total, including ships from the USA, Germany, France and even Siam (see Appendix 3 for details). The latter country was represented by the *Maha Chakrkri*, which was not only a 2,500-ton cruiser, built by Ramage and Ferguson at Leith in 1892, carrying six 4.7in guns and about a dozen other small quick-firing weapons, together with a ram, but also the royal yacht of Siam's ruler King Somdetch Phra Paramindr Maha Chulalongkorn.* Whilst he was visiting European capitals as part of a grand tour (which would bring him to England on 30 July) his yacht attended the review. Her commander was a Royal Navy officer, Captain Cumming, assisted by Lieutenants (RN) Walsh and Saunders and around 200 Siamese crew. Cumming had sailed her to Europe from Bangkok.

Five rows of Royal Navy ships completed the scene, stretching from Portsmouth to Ryde on the Isle of Wight. Two lines comprised fifty-nine battleships and cruisers. There were thirty-eight third class cruisers and gunboats in column D, forty-eight destroyers and gunboats in column F and twenty torpedo boats in column G. One hundred and sixty-five British warships (according to the official programme)[†] filled the sea as far as the eye could see, dressed overall; and all this done without taking ships from foreign stations, for the Royal Navy boasted 451 ships in total (not counting torpedo boats) of which 212 were in active commission (see Appendix 4). The power and the glory of the Royal Navy was on magnificent display on a dull and misty morning; for spectators, the ends of the lines could not be seen, just lines of dark hulls, white upper works and yellow funnels melting away into the distant haze.

There were also auxiliaries, passenger liners and day boats galore.

* The king had been tutored in his youth by Anna Leonowens. Her memoirs became the basis for the novel *Anna and the King of Siam* and later the musical *The King and I*.

† Some sources state 173.

Amongst the ships crammed with spectators was the General Steam Navigation Company's paddle steamer SS *Philomel*. She had been hired for the day by the Civil Service Cooperative Society. The package included first-class rail travel on the 0850 from Waterloo to Southampton (returning after the illuminations) and breakfast, lunch and dinner on board.

The civil servants of those days clearly didn't stint themselves. Dinner (served at 1800) included mock turtle soup, salmon, cucumber and tomato salad, rib of beef, lamb and mint sauce, braised beef with jelly, chicken salad, steak and pigeon and veal and ham pies, galantine of fowl, salad, cheese, jellies and cream, pastry, dessert, coffee. To wash this down there were no less than four champagnes offered; vintage F Epervier 1894 and 1889, Perrier Jouet and Moët & Chandon.[3]

RMS *Campania*,* launched in 1892 and the pride of the Cunard Fleet, was also present as were a mass of small craft jammed with day-trippers, milling around the black hulls of battleships riding at anchor. There was even a boat arranged by the Admiralty especially for the press. As one observer had it, 'looking down these spacious water avenues, the spectators saw an endless succession of battleships, cruisers, destroyers, gunboats, and torpedo boats, all ranged with the precision of a military camp. Practically the historical anchorage of Spithead was filled to the point of safety with our armed ships.'[4]

There were soldiers afloat too. Troops came from every corner of the empire for the celebration and detrained in Portsmouth. Behind the band of the Shropshire Light Infantry playing *The Soldiers of the Queen* they marched to Clarence Pier to board the paddle steamer *Koh-i-Noor* for the review, watched by packed pavements of spectators.

Admiral Salmon had his flag in HMS *Renown*, a second class battleship; small and with a main armament of four 10in weapons, she had been completed in the January of the Jubilee year and was intended to command cruiser squadrons operating on foreign stations. Salmon himself was a veteran of the defence of the British Residency in the siege of Lucknow during the Indian Mutiny, where he had won his Victoria Cross. He shared with Admiral Lord Walter Kerr (*vide supra*) the distinction of being one of three officers later to achieve high rank in the navy to be awarded the India 1857–1858 campaign medal with the 'Relief of Lucknow' clasp.

His fleet was different in composition from that of the Golden Jubilee Review. There were battleships for sure but also a predominance of cruisers, armoured, first, second and third class. Victoria's navy had seventy-five such vessels in commission, another sixty-six in reserve and seven more under construction. And of the foreign vessels present, the Americans had sent their armoured cruiser USS *Brooklyn* (1895), 'the new American cruiser, whose four very long, thin funnels and curious build greatly inter-

* During the First World War she would serve with the Grand Fleet as a proto-aircraft carrier.

ested the sightseers';[5] the French despatched the cruiser *Pothuau* and the Russians, *Rossiya*. And from Germany came the armoured frigate *König Wilhelm* (1868) under the command of Rear-Admiral Prince Albert William Henry of Prussia, the Kaiser's brother.

The composition of the fleet was now mainly decided by the needs of empire. First, cruisers of medium size and exceptional endurance to patrol the colonial outposts of Britain's territories and keep the sea lanes free for trade. The Victorians divided these vessels into three classes, plus armoured cruisers – in reality small battleships – which could be used as an admiral's flagship and fight anything that they could not outrun. Secondly, gun vessels, heavy guns on shallow keels for coastal bombardment or defence and policing the imperial waterways. And thirdly, the battle fleet to fight the foreign foe, the chief candidate for which was still at this time France.

Cruisers were not meant to be used in the line of battle. They were

intended to impose control and sovereignty of the sea, rather than the gaining of it. In peacetime they signified presence, a visible symbol of the fleet and by extension the power of the British nation. In war time cruisers were to be used to prosecute economic warfare, both defensive and offensive, and in being the eyes of the fleet, finding the enemy, assessing its composition and passing that intelligence to the fleet commander who would then engage the enemy with his heavy ships.

Britain's very latest protected cruiser was present at the review, HMS *Powerful,* commissioned the previous month. She sported two 9.2in guns and twelve 6in; plated with Harvey armour, she had a range of 7,000 nautical miles at 14kts. Two years later, with her sister *Terrible*, both ships would become public favourites for the part their crews played in the relief of Ladysmith during the Boer War, an incident which made *Powerful's* captain, the Hon Hedworth Lambton, a national figure and also a rich man. Lambton, son of the second Earl of Durham, attracted the attention of the beautiful socialite Valerie, Lady Meux, who had ordered six 12pdr guns to be sent to South Africa for him at her own expense. When

Brand new at the Diamond Jubilee Review, the first of the two *Powerful*-class protected cruisers, HMS *Powerful*, designed to counter Russian commerce raiders. *(US Naval History and Heritage Command NH 57872)*

Lambton, back in England, had called upon her to give his thanks, an association was established between the 44-year-old naval captain and a widow nine years his senior.

In 1900, Lady Meux had inherited significant wealth on the death of her husband, Sir Henry Bruce Meux Bt. Valerie had married Henry in secret. She was an actress – a word synonymous with mistress, even prostitute, in those times – and from a poor background. Polite society never accepted her and she took to playing the socialite, spending huge sums of money on entertainments and driving herself round London in a carriage pulled by two zebras. Known as a beauty, she was painted no less than three times by James McNeil Whistler. After meeting Lambton, she left her entire estate to him in her will on condition that he change his name to Meux.

The battlefleet lined up at Queen Victoria's Diamond Jubilee Review at Spithead, 26 June 1897. On the left of the royal yacht HMS *Renown* heads the line of *Majestic*-class battleships. Captains' barges can be seen heading to the reception on *Victoria and Albert*. Painting by Charles Dixon. (© *National Maritime Museum BHC0645*)

On her death in 1910, Lambton/Meux became an extremely wealthy man.

The ships present at the review were a significant advance on those at the Golden Jubilee. Captain Lord Beresford, who had been one of the agitators for the increased naval funding of the 1889 Naval Defence Act, wrote that 'the fleet of 1887 was in no way adequate to our needs at that time and many of the ships assembled for review could not have taken their places in the fighting line'.[6] But even now, the glittering array of ships hid some problems. Beresford noted that

of the older ships that figure in the 1897 review, the *Inflexible* and the *Alexandra*, armed with muzzle loading guns … and the armoured

cruisers *Black Prince*, *Agincourt*, *Minotaur* and *Northampton* also armed with muzzle loaders, … are quite useless and all seven of the muzzle loading ships in this review are of no value as fighting ships while so armed.[7]

These ships had all been ground-breaking in their time but were now practically obsolete. *Alexandra*, of 1875, a central-battery battleship was the second most massively protected ship at the review, with 12in of armour amidships,* and the flagship of the First Reserve Fleet until 1899; she was broken up as late as 1908. *Inflexible* had 24in of iron at its thickest point.

So, all was assembled for the Royal Review. With one exception: the Queen. Victoria was not present, feeling tired from the Jubilee celebrations.† Some modern accounts suggest that she watched the spectacle from Osborne with a telescope but in fact on the day of the Royal Diamond Jubilee Fleet Review the Queen was at Windsor Castle. Many of her relations and family went but she stayed away, noting in her journal only that 'all those who went to the Naval Review only got back at nine, having had a very unpleasant time owing to a terrific thunderstorm'.[8] She did however find the time to present her son and admiral Alfred, Duke of Edinburgh, with a field marshal's baton, in the teeth of opposition from the Admiralty which disapproved of such military gewgaws.

* Although this was iron armour, weaker than the compound or steel armour of later vessels.

† Her journal is ambiguous about this point; the author suspects that she had never intended to attend.

HMS *Terrible* was the second of the *Powerful*-class cruisers, seen here from the stern bedecked with flags for the 1897 review. *(Picture courtesy of Julian Mannering)*

The *Majestic*-class
battleship HMS
Mars, commissioned
in the same month
as the Diamond
Jubilee Review.
(Author's collection)

Instead the salute of the fleet was taken by Edward, Prince of Wales. Two special trains brought the prince, representatives of the colonies and other notables to the Dockyard Station where they were welcomed by no less than six Admirals of the Fleet. Edward was accompanied by his sister, Empress Friedrich of Prussia, mother of Wilhelm II. As they boarded the royal yacht the British and German royal standards were hoisted.

At 1400 the old paddle yacht *Victoria and Albert** left Portsmouth harbour and proceeded to pass through lines A and B, and thence B and C, and on to the western end of the column. Next the yacht passed through lines C and D to the eastern end of the line and returned to B to anchor next to the flagship, HMS *Renown*. As the royal yacht first entered the lines, all ships present began firing a 21-gun salute. The noise must have been immense. Edward's vessel was led by the Trinity House yacht *Irene* and followed by *Alberta*, *Osborne* and *Elfin*, all with royal family members and their guests aboard. Next came *Enchantress* with the Board of Admiralty embarked, *Fire Queen* (C-in-C Portsmouth guests), *Eldorado* (carrying the foreign ambassadors), *Danube* (with the House of Lords on board) and Cunard's *Campania* (with the House of Commons). The P&O iron-built liner *Carthage* (1881) was also of the party and carried Indian princes and yet more royal guests.

Finally, *Victoria and Albert* anchored abreast of the flagship, and the royal yacht signalled for all commanders to repair on board; there followed the traditional reception aboard *Victoria and Albert* for captains and admirals.

In amongst the daytime pageantry, the engineer and designer the Honourable Charles Algernon Parsons[†] staged an adventuresome publicity stunt by sailing his steam turbine-driven vessel *Turbinia*, whose revolutionary engines gave her speeds much faster than any ship of the

* A new royal yacht, at long last screw driven, *Victoria and Albert III*, was laid down in December of the Diamond Jubilee year. Queen Victoria had resisted changing vessels as *Victoria and Albert II* reminded her of happy times with Albert and their life together. For that reason, some of the ornamentation and fittings of the old vessel were transferred to the new.

† He was the youngest son of the 3rd Earl of Rosse, the astronomer William Parsons.

time, between the lines of navy ships and up and down in front of the crowd. Admiralty and royalty alike saw his escapade and his little craft easily evaded a navy picket boat which tried to pursue her, almost swamping it in its wake. The picket boat was commanded by Sub Lieutenant Humphrey Hugh Smith of HMS *Majestic*. He noted that *Turbinia* was 'out to do all she could to advertise the advantage of the turbine … in point of speed and I gave her every opportunity of satisfying her desires at my expense'.[9]

Parsons' élan paid off for, after further high-speed trials attended by the Admiralty, Parsons set up the Turbinia Works at Wallsend, and built turbine engines for two steam-turbine powered destroyers *Viper* and *Cobra*, both launched in 1899.* The first turbine-powered merchant vessel, the Clyde steamer TS *King Edward*, followed in 1901 and in 1905 the Admiralty confirmed that all future Royal Navy vessels would utilise steam turbines.

Whilst the review progressed, a programme of music was given by the Band of the Royal Artillery at Fort Gilkicker. Two pieces had been composed especially for the occasion. Joseph Philip Paul Zavertal Ladislao, Master of the Royal Artillery Band since 1881, presented *March Queen Victoria*; and the great Edward Elgar was commissioned by Novello's to write his *Imperial March* Opus 32 for the jubilee. He appropriately marked the score *Pomposo*. Rather less pompously, the band also gave its listeners H Trotère's[†] *Rum Tum Tum* polka, perhaps a shade insensitively as 'Tum-Tum' was a common nickname for the corpulent Prince of Wales.

At the end of the review at sea, the Prince made the general signal

* Both were wrecked in 1901 within months of each other, *Cobra* being lost with all hands.

† Rather more prosaically, he had been born as Henry Trotter.

The old battleship HMS *Alexandra* (1875), the most massively armoured ship at the review. (© *National Maritime Museum BHC3184)*

'Splice the Mainbrace'.* 'This signal had not been made previously within the memory of any officer or man serving in the fleet'[10] and was received with much enthusiasm.

The conclusion of the review was not the end of the merriment at Portsmouth, however. As darkness fell, there was the now habitual illumination of the fleet. This was considered the best attempted yet. Electric light picked out the hulls, fighting tops, masts and spars, and funnels of the vessels. For some twenty miles the water bore rows of ships, seemingly outlined in fire, and the USS *Brooklyn* flew from her two masts two large flags, the English and the American. On these she turned her powerful searchlights and the illuminated Union Jack and Stars and Stripes were visible in amity to the whole fleet.

Turbinia in a painting by Eduardo de Martino. This painting was first hung at Osborne House and is now in the Royal Collection. *(Author's collection)*

* The main brace on a sailing ship handled the main yard carrying the primary sail. If it gave out during a storm, a splice was the fastest way to repair it. The best sailors on board were used for this difficult task and were then rewarded with an extra ration of rum. In navalese, the term came to mean any special issue of spirits to the crew.

The gate-crasher at 34kts. *Turbinia*, the interloper which proved a point. *(Author's collection)*

It had all been a great festival of pomp and splendour. *The Times* correspondent wrote that 'weary but glad at heart at the brilliant success which
from first to last had crowned the proceedings, the few spectators who
remained to witness their solemn and impressive closing retired at last to
rest, full of inspiring thoughts about the empire and the bond of sea power,
and of loyal respect and sympathy for the beloved sovereign, in whose
person, even more than in her office, its unity is so nobly embodied'.[11]

The revels continued on 30 June. There was an athletics programme for
naval ratings and soldiers which included various foot races, a tug of war
and 'musical dumb-bells by the boys of *St Vincent*',* all accompanied by the
band of the King's Shropshire Light Infantry. That evening, the festivities
ended with an Admiralty Ball comprising twenty dances which included
ten waltzes, a barn dance *The Darkies' Holiday*, and concluded with the
galop *John Peel*.

Despite all this jollity, not everyone was happy. Sailors generally disliked
naval reviews. 'It is a well-known fact that a naval review at Spithead always
produces the most damnable weather,' wrote Humphrey Smith, adding
'then a ship is always moored miles from anywhere and when that
anywhere is reached there is a huge congested mass of boasts and human
beings all struggling together to render the confusion even more
confounded … and nothing to do on board except spitting and polishing
ad infinitum'.[12]

Cost was also an issue. The Admiralty spent £23,324 10s 3d on accommodation and entertainment for their guests, together with the illuminations and fireworks,[13] which was six and a half times the cost of the
Golden Jubilee celebrations. But for their Lordships, the review was more
than just a celebration of the Queen's reign, it was a public relations
activity too, a reminder to the British public of why they should support
expenditure on their splendid navy.

Even given these costs, the House of Commons felt that the arrangements for their spectating were *infra dignitatem*, despite the fact that they
were accommodated aboard *Campania*. Rather than the luxury they
expected, 'instead they were tumbled into a steamer already half full of
ordinary sightseers, run through the fleet, and then bundled out of their
boat in the rain, in order that the more privileged occupants of the steamer
might be able to get back in good time to see the illuminations'.[14] MPs
were also upset that their gustatory needs were not catered for satisfacto-
rily. The Treasury had allowed one shilling and fourpence per head for
food and drink which would apparently '[provide] luncheons on the tariff
of a beef and ham shop'.[15] Fortunately, Cunard stepped in; they 'treated the
Commons to a decent lunch and saved the Treasury the expense of the
frugal fare they had provided [for]'.[16]

Nonetheless, all estates joined in their admiration for the naval might on

* A 120-gun First
Rate ship of the line
launched on
11 March 1815 and
used as a training
ship since 1862.

display. 'The review was probably the most magnificent naval spectacle ever beheld', thought the anonymous journalists of the *Spectator* magazine, 'and the country, though not boastful or aggressive, has experienced a thrill of intense pride. Here was a fleet ready and able to face any naval force in the world and yet all our distant foreign squadrons are in full strength, and we have in the Mediterranean an unusually powerful fleet.'[17]

Si vis pacem, para bellum.

1899, the Kaiser Comes to Call

The year 1899 was not without its challenges for Britain. From 12 October, the country was at war in South Africa in a conflict which would demonstrate to the world that the army had not progressed much since its struggles in the Crimea. The Royal Navy blockade, and the stopping of a German mail ship off the African coast for inspection, fired public indignation in the Kaiser's realm. In Samoa, Germany, Britain and the United States were locked in a dispute over who should control the Samoa Islands. Germany had passed the first of what would be five Naval Laws in 1898, which allowed funding for a navy which by 1903 was meant to comprise nineteen battleships, of which seven were new builds, two additional large cruisers and seven more light cruisers for a fleet of sixty-nine warships; many saw this as a threat to Britain's dominance of the northern seas. Germany's economic transformation and rapid industrial growth was also seen as a risk – to British trade. Not everyone felt antagonistic to German ambition, however. 'He [the Kaiser] has a right to a big navy, even if we have to go to the expense of additional squadrons, just as his people have a right to undersell us throughout the world if they can,' was one view.[18]

However, France and Russia were still seen as threatening British interests and Germany as a potential counterweight to them. An editorial in November summed up that view:

> The Emperor for diplomatic purposes is Central Europe, and neither France nor Russia, nor both combined, will challenge the greatest of maritime powers with Central Europe looking on. The risk would be too great, the probable ultimate gain too small. If their two fleets were destroyed, Germany could attack France or Russia at points which neither could defend … [and] Russia would be cut off from her possessions in the Far East, and France would lose not only all hold, but all possibility of future hold upon her vast North African dominion.[19]

Furthermore, Wilhelm himself still professed his love for England.

It was against this background that the German ruler visited Britain in November, by invitation. An agreement on Samoa was to be reached

The Kaiser's royal
yacht SMY
Hohenzollern (II) in
use from 1893.
(Author's collection)

before his departure for Britain and a settlement was finalised in London
by 9 November and signed on the 14th.

On 19 November 1899, the Kaiser's yacht SMY *Hohenzollern* steamed
into Portsmouth Harbour, accompanied by a squadron of German
warships. To greet him was a double line of Royal Navy vessels; the battleships *Howe, Trafalgar, Collingwood,* and *Sans Pareil,* and the Particular
Service Squadron cruisers *Australia, Juno, St George, Cambrian,* and *Minerva,*
awaiting their voyage to South Africa and the maintenance of the
blockade. As the *Daily Mail* put it 'not many of them, and not the most
expensive things in this class of goods. But they look pretty good samples
for shop-window purposes.'[20]

To justify those comments, note might be taken of HMS *Sans Pareil.* She
was a *Victoria*-class battleship launched in 1887, sister to the ill-fated name
ship of the class which was sunk in a ramming accident in 1893. In the
design of these ships, several retrograde steps were taken. Her main armament of two 16.25in guns was mounted in a single turret, the great weight
of which meant that it had to be positioned low down so as not to detract
from the ship's stability, and that a similar large gun and turret could not
be carried aft. Instead, the after gun was a 10in gun protected by a gun
shield. Her low foredeck disappeared from view in even slight seas as a
result of having to mount the turret so low. And although the largest guns
afloat at the time, *Sans Pareil's* gun barrels were found to be so heavy that
they drooped when installed on their mountings and could fire only
seventy-five rounds before barrel wear became excessive. Unsurprisingly,
Sans Pareil was the last British battleship ever to be equipped with her
main armament in a single turret. Her active life was short. By April 1895

she had been paid off and named as port guardship at Sheerness. She was scrapped in 1907.

Wilhelm disembarked at the South Railway Jetty, where 3,000 soldiers, sailors and marines formed a guard of honour to welcome him. The Kaiser was met by Prince Arthur, Duke of Connaught, Queen Victoria's seventh child. 'The scene on the jetty and in the harbour was a particularly striking one. Extra rigging had been put up on the *Victory*'s masts so that Nelson's old ship had somewhat the appearance she must have presented in her fighting days', effused the *Daily Mail*.[21]

The following day, Wilhelm, his wife and two children, and Secretary of State for Foreign Affairs Bernhard von Bülow, departed by train for a five-day stay at Windsor Castle, where a banquet for 144 persons was held in his honour on the 21st. The Kaiser held talks with acting Foreign Secretary A J Balfour and the Queen and went shooting. The royal party then spent three days at Sandringham (more shooting) before departing for Germany via Holland on *Hohenzollern*, now moored in the Medway at Queenborough. The Kaiser had 'gone away delighted both with his social and political reception'.[22] So, there was a royal visit; but no royal review.

⸻

Queen Victoria died at half past six in the evening of 22 January 1901, at her beloved Osborne House. She had ruled Britain for nigh on 64 years. Loved and unloved by the country, an empress and a queen, a grieving

Osborne House, designed by Prince Albert and Thomas Cubitt and Queen Victoria's preferred residence for her fleet reviews. Edward VII hated the house and presented it to the nation in 1902. In 1903 it became Royal Naval College, Osborne. *(Library of Congress LC-DIG-ppmsc-08987)*

widow for over 38 long years, she was an icon by the time of her death, familiar yet so distant to many countries and races across the globe. Nearly all her active naval officers and men had served no other monarch. And over her reign, Queen Victoria had seen, or been a factor in, sixteen Royal Fleet Reviews. No British sovereign would ever achieve that distinction again.

On the 24th, all the fleet at Spithead and in Portsmouth Harbour was dressed overall to honour their new king. Guards and bands were paraded, ships' companies manned ship and salutes of twenty-one guns were fired in honour of King Edward VII's accession.

The old Queen's body lay in state in the dining room at Osborne, hastily converted to a mortuary chapel, and guarded by four soldiers of the Queen's Company, Grenadier Guards. On 1 February it was carried to Trinity Pier and placed on board *Alberta*. As she sailed across the Solent, the minute guns of the anchored warships each boomed in single melancholy tribute. Sailors manned ship in silence and bands paraded on the quarterdecks. Behind *Alberta* came *Victoria and Albert* bearing the new king. *Alberta*'s captain flew the Royal Standard at half-mast; Edward challenged him why. 'Sir, the queen is dead', he answered. Edward replied 'but the king lives'.[23]

Chapter 11

———◆◇◆———

Edwardian Splendour, 1902–1909

A S THE NINETEENTH CENTURY turned into the twentieth, the
Royal Navy was at the peak of its power and glory. The considerable
propaganda and status obtained for the navy from events such as the Great
Naval Exhibition and the Golden and Diamond Jubilee Reviews had
established the service in the public eye as both senior to, and more high
profile than, the army, and given sailors a social position and standing that
they had previously only aspired to.

The Navy League, founded in 1893 to aid recruitment and act as a pro-
naval pressure group, had steadily expanded its membership. Its self-
appointed mission was to keep a 'watchful eye on the nation's greatest asset
and prod politicians to keep ahead of rival powers',[1] or, as the League itself
defined it, 'to bring home to every man, woman and child in the United
Kingdom that the bulk of the raw material used in our manufacturing and
two thirds of the food we eat is transported across the sea'. For many, 'if
Britain did not keep to the two-power standard it was believed that she
would face disaster; the empire would collapse and the survival of the
country would be jeopardised because food imports would be at the
mercy of others'.[2]

Naval commanders' exploits were front-page news. The navy was sexy
and its characters famous. For senior officers, on or before retirement,
knighthoods, company directorships and wealth were virtually assured. To
the public it became <u>their</u> navy, and admirals became stars as sportsmen are
today. The entertainment industry took up the strain and songs and verse
praised the Royal Navy and its ships with lyrics such as *Stand by to reckon
up your battleships, ten, twenty, thirty there they go …* , words to a popular song
of the time by Henry Newbolt and Charles Villiers Stanford.* People
responded to and copied the navy's tropes, *inter alia* beards and, perhaps the
most toe-curling, the sailor suits which little boys and girls were forced
into. Cigarette packets and matchboxes† carried images of ships and sailors.

* Sir Charles Villiers
Stanford, *Songs of the
Fleet*, opus 117, iv
The Little Admiral.

† Such as Player's
Navy Cut cigarettes
and tobacco, intro-
duced in 1883 and
which bore an
increasingly debased
likeness of Able
Seaman Thomas
Huntley Wood from
the 1882 battleship
HMS *Edinburgh*.

Cigarette cards featured admirals and ships. Jolly tars danced across biscuit tins and advertising posters.

To be an admiral was a wonderful thing. A flag officer could have authority over thousands of men, many thousands of pounds of weaponry, and the life and death of both friend and enemy lay in his hands. He made and unmade careers from the lowest sailor to the highest-ranking subordinate. He was possessed of plenipotentiary powers and when abroad on service represented the monarch and government. In the far-flung corners of the world, away from communication with London, flag officers made and unmade foreign policy. He was the Supreme Being wherever he went, so much so that Admiral Algernon Charles Fieschi 'Pompo' Heneage* refused to kneel for divine service in his naval uniform, as a British admiral did not recognise a superior. 'Pompo' always changed into civvies for such events. Flag officers had personal servants, their own barges and crews, a suite of officers to fulfil their every desire or order and untrammelled authority over their ships and captains. Their orders were unquestionable, divine writ, omniscient and omnipotent, and if no admiral was present then this mantle of greatness fell to a commodore or the senior captain afloat.

The British flag flew over 20 per cent of the earth's surface and 25 per cent of its people, and the size of the Royal Navy meant that Britain could project its power wherever it chose to. But all this pomp masked a sad truth. The navy had become a hidebound organisation, fossilised in the past, rigidly hierarchical and obsessed by petty rules.

Ships were not assessed on their ability to fight but more on how spick and span they were. They had to positively gleam and sparkle. As Admiral Percy Scott related,

> it was customary for a commander to spend half his pay, or more, in buying paint to adorn HM ships, and it was the only road to promotion. A ship had to look pretty; prettiness was necessary to promotion, and as the Admiralty did not supply sufficient paint or cleaning material for keeping the ship up to the required standard, the officers had to find the money for buying the necessary housemaiding material.[3]

*Commander-in-Chief, Pacific Station, in 1887 and Commander-in-Chief, The Nore, in 1892.

† £255,000 in today's money, according to the Bank of England.

Scott added that 'the prettiest ship I have ever seen was the [Duke of Edinburgh's flagship] HMS *Alexandra*. I was informed that £2,000† had been spent by the officers on her decoration.'[4]

Gunnery practice was abhorred (and often ignored) as it made the ship dirty. Many captains, sent to fire off practice ammunition at sea, simply threw it overboard. When at sea, manoeuvres were balletic and formal, unreflective of the sort of fighting that modern warfare would call for and devised top down by the admiral in charge. Absolute adherence to the admiral's plans was required and formation sailing was the rule. Orders were gospel and not to be questioned. The admiral knew best and initiative was completely discouraged. Captains followed orders religiously and likewise ships' officers followed their commanders' orders without question. Percy Scott noted that

> the rule was that the senior officer made out a fixed routine which all ships had to follow, irrespective of the time they had been in commission. What exercises the ships are to perform; what clothes the officers and men are to wear; what boats the ships are to use; what awnings the ships are to spread; when the men are to wash their clothes; when and how the washed clothes are to be hung up, and when they are to be taken down. All these are matters over which captains of ships have no jurisdiction; they are settled by the senior admiral present.[5]

The correct form of dress was a problem. Following the introduction of Ball, Mess dress and Mess undress in 1891, officers in the Royal Navy of the 1890s had no fewer than seven different dress codes to follow depending on the occasion. The garments and their usages were all listed in Admiralty regulations. Just buying the clothing necessary would put a strain on many bank balances and to be inappropriately dressed would lead to a reprimand at best and punishment or restriction of privileges at worst.

This obsession with dress extended to the ratings too. Men traditionally made their own working garments but as the nineteenth century progressed the number of outfits grew with it and the Admiralty saw fit to regulate the exact size allowed for a trouser leg or a collar. By 1891 an officer inspecting his division often carried a ruler with him marked with the various regulation uniform measurements.

All of this obsessive behaviour would have appealed to the new king, for Edward loved dressing up, uniforms and regalia, and had a comprehensive knowledge of the correct form. In 1906, when Edward was visiting the King of Greece in Corfu, Lord Charles Beresford, by then commander of the Mediterranean Fleet, arrived to escort the royal yacht. Beresford welcomed the King of Greece onto his flagship without changing into his full-dress uniform. Edward was furious at this act of discourtesy to a fellow monarch and made a formal complaint to the Admiralty.

1902, the Coronation Review of Edward VII

In 1902, Britain was the greatest power on earth with the largest navy. Her age-old enemy remained France. In 1898 there was a war scare over the so-called 'Fashoda Incident' when British and French forces on the White Nile nearly came to blows over the occupation of a small colonial outpost. Both empires stood on the verge of war with choleric bellicosity on both sides. Under heavy pressure the French withdrew, accepting Anglo-

Egyptian control over the area. Amongst those involved on the British side were Herbert Kitchener, later Secretary of State for War, 1914–16, and Lieutenant Walter Cowan RN, who won a DSO for his command of the British naval forces at Fashoda, later an admiral in the Baltic campaign of 1919.* Russia remained an enigma and a threat, but would soon be humiliated in a war with Japan.

Meanwhile, Germany had passed another Naval Law in 1900 which further added to its fleet. The plan was now to have thirty-eight battleships (eleven new to be built), fourteen large cruisers (two additional), thirty-eight small cruisers (eight extra) and a new ninety-six torpedo boats, all by 1920.

Threatened by the German expansion and that of France and Russia too, Britain signed a naval treaty with Japan on 31 January 1902;† both parties had a common interest in defence against Russian aggression. 'The agreement ensured joint Anglo-Japanese naval superiority in the Far East over France and Russia'[6] and saved Britain the cost of a dedicated Pacific Squadron.‡ But it also marked the end of her Palmerstonian 'splendid isolation'.

* See S R Dunn, *Battle in the Baltic* (Barnsley: Seaforth Publishing, 2020).

† It was renewed in 1905 and 1911.

‡ The Pacific Station was abolished in October 1903.

§ Not appendicitis as is sometimes stated.

The coronation of Edward VII was arranged for 26 June 1902. The programmes were printed, souvenirs manufactured and commemorative medals cast. A fleet review was planned and ships and men were organised; the brand-new (commissioned 7 June) 12in-gunned battleship HMS *London* was designated to be flagship. But on 23 June, Edward was taken ill with high fever and excruciating stomach pain. It turned out to be an abscess;§ when operated on, over a pint of pus was released. The corona-

The Japanese cruiser *Takasago* at Portsmouth. Laid down in 1896 by Armstrong Whitworth in the UK, she mounted two 20.3cm (8in) guns together with ten 12cm (4.7in) and twelve QF Hotchkiss guns at a maximum speed of just over 23kts. *(Author's collection)*

tion was postponed and the King went to recuperate on board *Victoria and Albert* (the third).

Plans for a celebratory Royal Fleet Review were also thrown into confusion. Special trains had to be hastily cancelled, printed orders rescinded, fetes and events scratched. Fortunately for the matelots, the Admiralty decreed that 'the original instructions as to observing 26 and 27 June as holidays, issuing of extra grog and remission of punishments are to hold good'.[7]

The notice of the deferment did not reach some of the colonies in time. Captain Percy Scott of HMS *Terrible* wrote; 'on the 26th June, 1902, we were at Hong Kong, and everyone was anxious to do something to commemorate the coronation of King Edward VII. I remembered having written "*Scylla*" in human letters on the rocks at Candia, and decided to write "God save the King" on the *Terrible*'s side in the same way. The four-teen letters took about two hundred and fifty men'.[8]

Some six weeks later, at 1100 on 9 August, the Gold State Coach was pulled by eight horses from Buckingham Palace to Westminster Abbey. As Edward VII and his wife Alexandra entered that sacred place, the boys of Westminster School shouted out '*Vivat Regina Alexandra*' and '*Vivat Rex Edwardus*', as was traditional. A congregation of 8,000, which had been seated in place for three hours, witnessed Edward formally invested with the throne. They heard the first performance of Sir Hubert Parry's anthem, *I Was Glad*, especially written for the event. The director of music, Sir Frederick Bridge, misjudged the timing and had finished the anthem before the King had arrived; he had to repeat it when the right moment came. His organist saved the day by improvising in the interim.

Edward Elgar and Arthur Christopher Benson, a housemaster at Eton, had written (at the King's request) a *Coronation Ode* (Opus 44) for the June coronation, which included the now famous *Land of Hope and Glory*. Owing to the delay, the full score did not receive its first performance until October. Part three, *Britain Ask of Thyself*, contained the lines;

See that thy navies speed, to the sound of the battle-song;
Then, when the winds are up, and the shuddering bulwarks reel,
Smite the mountainous wave, and scatter the flying foam,
Big with the battle-thunder that echoeth loud, loud and long.

A Royal Fleet Review was held two weeks after the coronation.

At 1400 on Saturday 16 August, King Edward VII, wearing the uniform of an admiral of the fleet, accompanied by the Prince of Wales in a

rear-admiral's uniform and Queen Alexandra, boarded the royal yacht
Victoria and Albert.

The King had already had a busy 24 hours. The previous evening, he had
received Admiral Lord Walter Kerr* on board to present him with the
insignia of the Knight Grand Cross of the Order of the Bath (GCB),
awarded in the Coronation Honours List. And on the morning of the fleet
review, Edward had received three Boer commanders, Louis Botha,
Christiaan de Wet and Koos de la Rey. This was a remarkable gesture of
reconciliation, for the Treaty of Vereeniging which ended the Second Boer
War had only been concluded on 31 May. Together with their nemesis,
Lord Kitchener, the three Boer generals were then taken on board HMS
Wildfire (a screw yacht tender) for transfer to the Admiralty yacht
Enchantress to observe the review and the might that had been ranged
against them.

Awaiting the King in the Solent were six lines of ships, each three and
a half miles long, all under the command of Admiral Sir Charles Frederick
Hotham, C-in-C Portsmouth and with his flag in the battleship *Royal
Sovereign*.† Hotham had directed the naval ceremonial events at the funeral
of Queen Victoria, for which he was made a Knight Grand Cross of the
Royal Victorian Order. *Royal Sovereign*, name ship of a class of seven, was

* So also *vide supra*;
Kerr had served as
Second Naval Lord
in May 1899 and
First Naval Lord
from August 1899.

† HMS *London*
having sailed for the
Mediterranean.

another ship which owned its genesis to the 1889 Naval Defence Act. Launched in 1891, her main armament of four 13.5in guns was housed in two barbettes, rather than turrets, at either end of the ship, which allowed a higher freeboard, greatly increasing her capacity for fighting in rough weather. However, the class rolled like pigs in anything but a calm sea and *Royal Sovereign* was fitted with bilge keels in 1894–5 in an attempt to obviate this problem. The secondary armament was ten 6in quick firers. Despite a main armour belt which ran for two-thirds of their length, they were the fastest capital ships in the world in their time.

Under Hotham's orders were twenty battleships, twenty-four cruisers, fifteen gunboats, ten training ships, seven torpedo boats and thirty-two torpedo boat destroyers, the latter a new innovation and appearing in number at a fleet review for the first time. The Royal Navy had built its first destroyers in 1893, two ships each of three types, *Daring*, *Havock* and *Ferret*, known as '26-knotters'. These, and all succeeding classes up to 1903, were of 'turtleback' design, making them very wet ships. They were powered by steam driven reciprocal engines, coal fired. The *Viper* class of two in 1899 were the first destroyers to be fitted with turbine power.

They were called into existence to combat the growing threat posed by small, fast, cheap torpedo-carrying craft, known as torpedo boats. Large numbers of these might, it was thought, overwhelm a battleship's defences and sink it, or distract the battleship and make it vulnerable to the

The first destroyers; HMS *Ferret* of 1893, with her forward mounted 12pdr gun prominent. She took part in the Coronation Review with New Zealand-born Lieutenant Arthur William Tomlinson in temporary command. (© *Imperial War Museum Q 21251*)

The *Eclipse*-class
protected cruiser
HMS *Juno*, which
took part in the
Coronation Review
of 1902 under the
command of
Captain David
Beatty. She still has
small-calibre
weapons in her
fighting tops. *(US
Naval History and
Heritage Command
NH 60133)*

opposing fleet. The role of the torpedo boat destroyers, soon abbreviated
to just 'destroyers', was to sally ahead of the battlefleet and deal with the
torpedo boat threat before they could attack the large big-gun ships. They
sprang from the ever-fertile brain of then Third Sea Lord 'Jackie' Fisher,
who in 1892 ordered the development of a new type of ship equipped
with novel water-tube boilers and small-calibre quick-firing guns. Fifty-
two were under construction at the time of the Diamond Jubilee Review.
Now they had their own prominent place at the coronation celebrations.

Amongst the cruisers was HMS *Juno* (launched 1895, eleven 6in guns)
under the command of Captain David Beatty,* a dashing young officer of
whom much would soon be heard. HMS *Calliope* (1884) was with the
fleet; under the heroic Captain Henry Kane she was the only vessel to
avoid being sunk or stranded in the tropical cyclone that struck Apia,
Samoa, in 1889. The ram-equipped battleship *Camperdown* (1885) was on
display, which had used its underwater weapon to disastrous effect when it
accidentally rammed and sank HMS *Victoria*, killing Admiral Tryon and
357 others, on 22 June 1893 off the Lebanon.

Line D included the turret battleship *Devastation* (1871), 'that dangerous
looking death trap, which it is to be hoped will reach the scrapyard before
the next great naval war'.[9] She was in fact not to be stricken for another
five years.

Line 'F' of the assembly comprised a number of foreign warships,
including two vessels of Britain's new ally, Japan, the French-built
armoured cruiser *Azuma* and the British-built protected cruiser *Takasago*.
And a sixth column of vessels awaiting the King was comprised of
merchant ships, including RMS *Ophir*, a twin-screw ocean liner of the

* Beatty had been
wounded in the
Boxer Rebellion of
1900 and required
surgery to his arm.
He was advanced to
the rank of captain
for his actions at
Tientsin; *Juno* was
his first appointment
in that rank.

Orient Steam Navigation Company. The previous year she had taken the Duke and Duchess of Cornwall and York (the future King George V and Queen Mary) on their tour of the British Empire; one of the two escorting warships had been HMS *Juno*. Now she was crammed with spectators who had each paid 15 guineas* for the privilege of a place on board. Members of both Houses of Parliament viewed the spectacle from the P&O steamship *India*, chartered for that purpose by the Admiralty. In rather less luxury were the mayor and corporation of Portsmouth, accommodated in the Naval Ordnance Store Vessel *Buffalo*. The Admiralty had even chartered a ship, SS *Nubia*, for the benefit of 206 carefully-selected dockyard workers; the democratic intent of this gesture was somewhat compromised as it was arranged that they should be strictly segregated on the vessel by class. P&O's ageing *Carthage* was again at a royal review, fresh from service as a transport and hospital ship during the Boxer Rebellion in China. She was employed in carrying minor guests but rather disgraced herself by hitting the quay at Southampton when landing them.†

There were also spectators from overseas, especially Germany. The HAPAG (Hamburg-Amerikanische Packetfahrt-Actien-Gesellschaft) company had first started excursions to British reviews in 1897. Now they were there in force including the SS *Auguste Victoria*, four decks, a promenade deck and 180 cabins; HAPAG had even manged to secure special berths close to the lines of warships.

All together the ships present for the review covered some 20 square miles, excluding the 100 passenger ships which were scheduled to depart from Southampton to Spithead packed with spectators. Indeed,

* Just under £2,000 in today's money.

† A year later she was sold for scrap.

RMS *Ophir*, in her guise as a royal yacht for the Duke and Duchess of Cornwall and York (inset) on their tour of the British Empire. At the 1902 Coronation Review she carried spectators at 15 guineas a head. *(Author's collection)*

Portsmouth was awash with visitors. The London and South West Railway ran sixty-seven special trains from Waterloo; as the *Daily Express* commented 'on Saturday all regular railway traffic will be suspended and from an early hour of the day an immense procession of excursion trains will put such a concourse of spectators into the old town as it has probably never witnessed'.[10]

Tour operators such as Thomas Cook and Henry Lunn organised 'package deals' and hired vessels from which their customers could observe the review. Many of these proved to be a problem, sailing amongst the fleet and getting in the way. Admiral Hotham was moved to complain to the Admiralty that 'I personally have observed this lack of consideration, having to suddenly change course to avoid being run down by the SS *Duchess of Fife*'.[11]

At 1430, the royal yacht joined the fleet, followed by *Alberta* and *Osborne* and with the Board of Admiralty in *Enchantress* in the rear. The King was greeted by sailors manning their ships, which were decorated from end to end with flags, and a 21-gun salute from all the assembled vessels. The manning of the ships had been the subject of detailed orders from the Admiralty, which had specified that initially 'the rail should be manned from fore to aft' together with the bridge and the tops. 'On the first dip of the signal, men to go aloft' and when 'the signal being hauled down, men to lie out'.[12]

Victoria and Albert steamed east between a line of gunboats and cruisers on the one side and a line of battleships and cruisers on the other. Reaching the end of the lines, the royal yachts and the accompanying vessels returned past the line of foreign representatives, then east, and once more back again. On this occasion the King sailed past the merchant vessels, from whose decks many people witnessed the spectacle, as did an estimated crowd of 100,000 on the shore or in pleasure steamers and small boats at sea.

The royal progress lasted for two hours and the 61-year-old Edward, despite his recent illness, remained standing on the upper deck for the greater part of it, taking the salute. As the *Walsall Advertiser* put it, 'the king standing erect on the upper bridge of *Victoria and Albert* and punctiliously saluting each ship as he passes in response to the ringing cheers that greet him'.[13] Each ship's company cheered the King individually, and then the men of the entire fleet, by signal from the flagship, cheered together, 'producing an effect not readily to be forgotten'.[14]

At the close of the review the admirals and captains present, including those of foreign navies, were received on *Victoria and Albert* by the King and a message was signalled to the fleet 'expressing [Edward's] "extreme satisfaction" at the appearance of the ships and the ships' companies'.[15]

The traditional light show finale included a display by searchlights. The

Admiralty had experimented with alternative makes of paint beforehand and ships were instructed to paint the lights' protective glass in five different colours. But the effect was marred by the weather; 'the illuminations of the fleet in the evening were completely spoiled by a thunderstorm, followed by torrents of rain'.[16] One Lilian Brandon was a spectator at the review. On 18 August she wrote 'what a fiasco the illuminations were … the elements certainly do not seem to be favourably inclined towards the king'.[17] But the weather did have a side benefit in that it 'enhanced their beauty by the strange atmospheric effects produced. A truly magnificent climax was reached by the elevation of the rainbow-hued beams of the searchlights so as to form a colossal gothic arch over the royal yacht.'[18]

The Monday was to have seen the exhibition of a complex series of manoeuvres called the 'Gridiron' – very clever and pretty but of limited use in battle. In any event, it was scratched, owing to the misty and squally weather. Nonetheless, the King again inspected the squadrons under way and signalled his farewell to the departing foreign warships.

Thus ended the first-ever Coronation Review. Once again, Britain's naval might had been on display without the need to recall ships from home or out of reserve. King Edward VII and Queen Alexandra departed in the royal yacht for a cruise to Scotland, calling at Portland, Milford Haven, the Isle of Man and various ports on the west coast of Scotland. They disembarked at Invergordon for Balmoral, and *Victoria and Albert* sailed to Queensferry to await the Queen and her autumn cruise.

It had been a remarkable spectacle; as a post-event report noted 'nothing on a similar scale has ever previously been attempted by the Admiralty'.[19] And the cost, at £28,701-9s.-6d plus another £6,200 on illuminations of fleet,[20] was considerable. But it was also splendid publicity for the navy in its campaign to increase expenditure on new ships and weaponry, a battle that would soon grow in intensity.

1905, Entente Cordiale

Edward VII loved France and was fluent in its language. He enjoyed the people, the food and the freedom he had found there as a younger man. When he became king, he took it as a personal mission to rebuild British relations with France. As his biographer Jane Ridley has written, 'he was … responsible for making possible the *Entente Cordiale* with France'.[21]

In May 1903, Edward personally arranged to visit Paris in what was possibly the most important political intervention that he made during his reign. When he arrived, he was booed and the crowd shouted '*Vivent les Boers*'. On his departure, after a round of dinners, opera, horse racing and bonhomie, they shouted '*Vive le Roi*'. 'In a little over twenty-four hours, the English milord had conquered Paris,' noted Ridley.[22]

Edward's intervention paved the way to a formal compact, generally known as the *Entente Cordiale*, a series of agreements signed on 8 April 1904 between Britain and the French Republic which saw a significant improvement in Anglo-French relations. In particular, the concordats granted freedom of action to the UK in Egypt and to France in Morocco. This pleased the French who had imperial ambitions in North Africa. For the British it eased France out of Egypt where the Suez Canal,* and the route to India that it provided, which remained a paramount foreign policy concern.

However, the ceding of influence in Morocco to France nettled Germany for she believed that the Anglo-French *Entente* went a long way towards the creation of a new diplomatic balance for Europe. An international convention had guaranteed the independence of Morocco in 1880; Germany saw that the friendship between two of Europe's most powerful nations threatened to override this. And more, it posed a challenge to Germany's own influence in Europe and the world.

On 31 March 1905, Kaiser Wilhelm II disembarked into an open boat from the steamer *Hamburg* and was taken through the breakers to the shores of Tangier. Here he mounted a white horse (which nearly threw him) and headed for the sultan's palace, where he declared that he had come to recognise Morocco's independence. That done, he promptly left. His landing, which sparked an international crisis, had been intended to set Britain and France at odds. In fact, it had the opposite effect, strengthening the bond between the two countries due to their mutual suspicion of Germany. One way of displaying this alliance and its power to Germany and the rest of the world was naval cooperation.

In July 1905 the British Channel Fleet visited Brest; the visit was well received at home and in France. 'Considering the history of the two nations, there is also something which appeals strongly to those who believe that international hatred need not be eternal', noted the *Spectator*. 'We English bated the French and the Scotch about equally, and now, while we cannot distinguish between the Scotch and the English, we are feeling, sincerely feeling, that circumstances are driving Englishmen and Frenchmen to become fast friends.'[23]

In the spirit of reciprocity, in August a French fleet came to Britain. To greet them, the Channel Fleet of twelve battleships and eight cruisers under Vice-Admiral Sir Arthur Wilson VC in the *Duncan*-class battleship HMS *Exmouth*, armed with four 12in and sixteen 6in guns (and at the time one of the fastest battleships in the world), together with HMS *Sapphire* (a new *Topaze*-class protected cruiser) and twenty-four destroyers, were ordered to assemble at Spithead by 3 August.

The French Northern Squadron of eighteen vessels arrived at Portsmouth on 7 August. It was led by Admiral Leonce Albert Caillard who had been commander of the French navy in Algeria during the

* The Suez Canal had opened in 1869 but an inability to pay his bank debts led Egyptian ruler Isma'il Pasha to sell his 44 per cent share in the Canal for £4,000,000 (about £91.3 million in 2018) to the government of Britain in 1875, although French shareholders still held the majority. Local unrest caused the British to invade in 1882 and take full control, although nominally Egypt remained part of the Ottoman Empire.

Front cover of the souvenir programme for the visit of the French fleet and review of 1905. *(Author's collection)*

Morocco crisis. He flew his flag in the battleship *Masséna*, launched in 1895, one of five vessels ordered in response to the British *Royal Sovereign* class. They fell sadly short of their target, however. The ships suffered from a lack of uniformity of equipment, which made them hard to maintain in service, and their mixed gun batteries comprising several calibres (two 12in, two 10.8in, eight 5.5in and eight 3.9in) made gunnery in war conditions difficult, since the shell splashes were hard to differentiate and thus accuracy problematic to discern. They were in any case poor gun platforms as they rolled excessively and were plagued by difficulties in seakeeping and mechanical issues. And the French arrival was not trouble free; the two 12in, two 10.8in-gunned battleship *Jauréguiberry* grounded.

Cover page of *The Graphic* magazine of 19 August 1905 with a depiction of the arrival of the French fleet. Original artwork by W L Wylie. *(Author's collection)*

The French battleship *Masséna*, commissioned in 1898 and the flagship of Admiral Caillard at the 1905 joint fleet review. Her class were ordered in response to the British *Royal Sovereign*s. *Masséna* significantly exceeded her design weight and suffered from serious stability problems which prevented accurate firing of her guns. Unsurprisingly, she was considered to be an unsuccessful design and was scuttled as a breakwater in 1915. *(US Naval History and Heritage Command NH 74863)*

Edward had always disliked Osborne House and as soon as he could he gave it to the nation; he much preferred to travel to Portsmouth or Southampton by royal train and stay on board *Victoria and Albert*. For this purpose, new carriages were built in 1902 to replace those of 1869. At the

King's instruction, they were designed internally to resemble the royal yacht, with white enamel paint and polished brass. Externally, the carriages were painted carmine-lake and cream in colour with double-door entrances and a vestibule. The headstocks behind the buffers were in the shape of lions' heads, covered in gold leaf. In this luxury did the King now travel to his duties.

Thus it was on *Victoria and Albert* that Edward personally received the French admiral, who was conveyed there in the new Admiralty yacht *Enchantress** as soon as his squadron had anchored. And that evening, he and his officers were entertained on the royal yacht. In his honour, the Channel Fleet was illuminated from the time that Caillard left his flagship until the point of his return. The following day, the French admiral and his captains feasted with the Board of Admiralty on board their yacht *Enchantress*. The remaining French senior officers dined 'as convenient' with the Channel Fleet. Some had previously been given luncheon at the Royal Yacht Squadron.

To formally commemorate the French visit, a Royal Review of the combined French and British Squadrons was arranged for Wednesday 9th. Portsmouth had been 'lavishly decorated, and many festivities have been arranged'[24] in readiness for the event and 'great preparations have been made for giving the officers and crews an enthusiastic welcome to England'.[25] Much of the entertainment seemed, as usual for a French visit, to involve eating.

At 1030, the royal yacht, preceded as was traditional by the Trinity House yacht and followed by that of the Admiralty together with *Osborne* and *Alberta*, passed down between the two flagships and returned on the Isle of Wight side of the French ships to its buoy. As the yacht approached the warships, all present thundered out a 21-gun salute. The procession was

* The Belfast-built *Enchantress* had been launched in 1903. She could manage 18kts, had slim and elegantly raked funnels, a bowsprit, sumptuous polished wood and brass, and carried three 3pdr signalling guns.

The *Duncan*-class battleship HMS *Albemarle*, sister-ship to *Exmouth* which served as flagship to of the Channel Fleet during its visit in 1905. Note the four 12in guns in two turrets and sixteen 6in guns in casemates. *(Author's collection)*

watched by a large crowd on land and at sea. One of the largest passenger vessels present, with the most important guests, was the Union Castle Line *Armadale Castle*, 12,973grt and newly built. At the other end of the spectrum, the local Church Lads Brigade commander had begged that his boys be allowed to view the fleets at anchor. The gunboats *Ant* (of 1873 vintage) and *Insolent* (1881) were detailed for that purpose.

In Portsmouth, after the King's inspection of the combined fleets, the sailors were entertained at a fete at North End Recreation Ground and in the evening the officers went to a banquet at the Town Hall, attended by the Prince of Wales. The band of HMS *Excellent* and the bugles of the Royal Marine Light Infantry and the Royal Marine Artillery sounded the dinner call and the meal was followed at 2130 by a ball.

On 10 August, the Lord Mayor of London had entertained the French officers at the Guildhall; and a day later, Admiral Caillard and 120 French officers, with thirty from the Royal Navy accompanying them, were feasted at Windsor Castle as guests of the King himself. A special train was laid on to take them to Windsor, departing at 0900 and returning at 1455. Meanwhile, 120 French and 80 British matelots, together with ten officers from each nation, had their turn with lunch at the Guildhall that same Friday. Again, a special train was provided.

And on the 12th, a garden party was held in Victoria Park for the visiting officers and men which included a performance by the Portsmouth Theatre Company. At the same time, Admiral Caillard and his officers were hosted at the Houses of Parliament by 200 MPs, led by the Lord Chancellor (Hardinge Giffard, 1st Earl of Halsbury) and the Speaker of the House of Commons (the Rt Hon James William Lowther).

Perhaps with an eye to France's public image in Britain, Caillard and some of his suite paid homage to the memory of Nelson as they passed through Trafalgar Square. At Westminster, they dined in Westminster Hall; this had a special status, for 'the Hall of Rufus is not lightly used, and the fact that it has been given over to the entertainment of the officers of the French Fleet, with the heartiest approval of the whole nation, is not without its significance'.[26]

The French departed Portsmouth on 14 August. It had been a successful visit on both sides; '[a] note of provocation or defiance has been entirely absent, and on all sides the Agreement between the two nations has been fully recognised as a league of peace, a mutual insurance against the calamities of war'.[27]

However, there was some concern expressed regarding the cost. The total bill to the Treasury for the entertainments provided was £6,271-18s-7d,* against an estimate of £4,011. The cost overrun was ascribed to 'additional trains', the press (who totalled sixty-two persons), the Lord Mayor's party (154) and 'French Ladies' (eleven in number).[28] And the expense

* Perhaps £750,000 in today's money.

would have been further increased had it not been for the public-spirited hospitality offered to the French by the Duke of Norfolk at Arundel Castle, Arthur Lee MP* at his house 'Rookesby' and Sir Arthur Conan Doyle at his house 'Undershaw' in Hindhead.

Trafalgar 100

The year 1905, marking the 100th anniversary of the battle of Trafalgar and the immortalisation of Lord Nelson, saw commemorations across the country but, significantly, with the *Entente Cordiale* just entered into, no member of the royal family took part. On 21 October, the Trafalgar Dinner held at the Royal Naval College was the greatest ever. In London, Nelson's column was adorned with flags and streamers like some giant stone maypole. The Navy League was at its peak of membership and its most assertive political tone. For the centenary, Henry Wood wrote his *Fantasia on British Sea Songs* for the Promenade Concerts. And there were local celebrations up and down the land.

Nor were the celebrations confined to Britain. In Brisbane in Australia, for example, one Lieutenant Pascoe, grandson of Nelson's flag lieutenant at Trafalgar, hoisted the flags of Nelson's last signal; and the YMCA 'had made elaborate preparations to celebrate the day, and held two functions in His Majesty's Theatre, where crowded audiences gathered in the afternoon and evening for a concert and a display of pictures connected with the life of Nelson and the British navy. A dinner for members of the Naval Brigade formed part of the day's proceeding.'[29]

At London's Earl's Court, a 'Naval, Shipping and Fisheries Exhibition' was held, intended to mark the anniversary and promote interest in all things maritime. The president of the exhibition was the Lord Mayor of London, Charles Johnston, and the vice president Admiral Sir Edmund Fremantle, Commander-in-Chief Plymouth in 1896 and honorary Rear-Admiral of the United Kingdom. In an 'historic and loan relic section' were featured an item billed as the quilt from Nelson's bed on board *Victory* and a 'scenic interpretation' of the battle and the admiral's death, as well as Captain Cook's chart rule and plane table. There were fishery displays, and an 8ft-long model of the *Empress Queen*, the largest and fastest paddle-driven cross-Channel steamer ever built, part of the Isle of Man Steam Packet Company fleet. There was also an Amerind village with canoes and a selection of amusement rides.

The nation was proud; and so were its seamen. But the Royal Navy was about to experience a revolution.

1907, Winds of Change

The revolution was called Admiral Sir John Fisher, popularly known as 'Jackie'. Fisher (eventually Admiral of the Fleet Sir John Arbuthnot Fisher,

* Who in 1917 gave his house 'Chequers' to the nation for use by the sitting prime minister.

First Baron Fisher of Kilverston) was the man who created the modern navy. The fleet which served throughout the First Word War was his creation. Appointed First Sea Lord (and thus executive head of the navy) in 1904, he set about reshaping the service.

Fisher was the son of a Ceylonese tea planter, from a poor background, a man who rose to high rank through ability not connections or his position in society. He was volcanic in temperament, Old Testament in expression, intolerant of fools or anyone who disagreed with him and a compulsive and skilful dancer. He was a loyal friend to those who agreed with him; and an implacable enemy to those who didn't, and one man detested him with a passion – Admiral Lord Charles Beresford.

Fisher's rift with Beresford probably had its genesis in an incident when Fisher commanded the Mediterranean Fleet with Beresford as his number two. Beresford's flagship made a hash of anchoring on coming into port. Fisher signalled in public and *en clair* 'Your flagship is to proceed to sea and come in again in a seamanlike manner'. The pompous and self-important Beresford never forgave this public humiliation and the two men became sworn enemies. When Fisher was allowed to serve a second term as First Sea Lord, ensuring that Beresford would never hold that position, the dislike clotted into vitriolic hatred.

Left: Admiral Sir John Fisher. *(Library of Congress LC-B2-3330-5).*
Right: Fisher's arch enemy, Admiral Lord Beresford. *(Author's collection)*

Charles William de la Poer Beresford, 'Charlie B' to his admirers, was a man of limited intellect, great snobbery, a family pedigree going back to the Norman Conquest, a large estate in Ireland and an MP to boot. He saw Fisher as an inferior and an *arriviste*, whilst Fisher was jealous of Beresford's inherited wealth. Beresford did everything he could to destroy Fisher and his reforms, was a frequent 'leaker' to the press and used his position in Parliament to undermine his enemy. The war between these two outsized characters split the service and officers had to take sides. Fisher's chosen few, called 'the Fishpond', were attacked by Beresfordites and vice versa. Fisher called Beresford's supporters 'the Syndicate of Discontent'. The schism caused fault lines through the Navy. A Fisherite serving under a Beresfordite would have limited chance of successful advancement and the reverse was also true.

The feud was pursued with malevolent determination and it caused the ruin of more than a few careers and reputations. Beresford eventually was able to force a Committee for Imperial Defence (CID) subcommittee review chaired by Prime Minister Asquith and its half-hearted endorsement of Fisher caused him to step down in early 1910. But in the meantime, Fisher had turned the Royal Navy on its head and created a modern

HMS Dreadnought, the ship that changed the naval world. With ten 12in guns in five turrets and turbine engines, she made all other battleships obsolete overnight.
(US Naval History and Heritage Command NH 61017)

fighting force beyond the dreams of the Navy League at the end of the previous century.

With the launch of HMS *Dreadnought* in 1906, the first all-big-gun battleship in the world, he produced the definitive capital ship rendering obsolete all others – including the ones in Britain's own navy. His modernising enthusiasm changed training programmes for officers and men (the Fisher-Selborne scheme), introduced oil-fired engines and turbines, made engineer officer a respectable position and reconfigured the navy's forces.

Fisher recognised that the most likely enemy that Britain would have to face was not France, now an ally thanks in part to Edward VII, but Germany. Admiral Tirpitz, with the enthusiastic backing of Wilhelm II, was creating an Imperial German Navy designed to raise his country to first-class naval status. With other factors, including violent anti-British feeling during the Boer War and the German government's refusal to consider an alliance except on terms that guaranteed Germany a free hand and hegemony in Europe, Fisher was convinced that Germany was now the most probable foe. His political master, Lord Selborne, certainly agreed with him. In a memo to the Cabinet, Selborne noted that 'the great new German navy is being built up from the point of view of war with us'.[30]

To ensure that Britain had the necessary concentration of forces, Fisher instigated a reorganisation of the fleets. He recalled ships from far-flung postings, concentrated the navy where he expected it to have to fight (the Channel and the North Sea) and scrapped 150 ships (and, of course, the positions of commanding them) deeming them 'too weak to fight and too slow to run away'. Five battleships were withdrawn from the China Station in 1904. The standing South American, North American and Pacific squadrons were abolished. As Andrew Lambert has written, 'by early 1906 the centre of naval effort was shifting from the Mediterranean to the North Sea; Germany was not only the most likely but also the only realistic enemy. Russia was no longer a naval power and the French navy had collapsed.'[31]

Fisher created a new entity – the Home Fleet – to be based at Sheerness, where easy access to the North Sea and the German coastline could be obtained and which was announced by the Admiralty on 24 October 1906. He stripped the Mediterranean, Atlantic and Channel Fleets of battleships and cruisers to make up this new force and backed it up with ships from the reserve. The commander of the Atlantic Fleet at the time was Beresford, who was less than pleased to lose his ships and status and returned to Parliament as an MP. Brought back to office to keep him from doing mischief there, he went to the Mediterranean and spent his time inveigling against Fisher. From there he took command of the much-

* The Channel Fleet was eventually merged into the Home Fleet in 1909 and Beresford was ordered to haul down his flag.

reduced Channel Fleet where Beresford waged an increasingly acrimo-
nious and public campaign against 'Jackie' and all his works.*

As Percy Scott put it:

> Lord Charles Beresford's grievance against the Admiralty was that they
> were forming another fleet in home waters under the name of the
> Home Fleet, and that it was not to be under his command. He explained
> to me that this Home Fleet was a fraud on the public and a danger to
> the State; that so grave was the disorganisation and confusion, that, if the
> country had been suddenly attacked, the navy, in his opinion, would
> have suffered a reverse, if not a severe defeat. Lord Charles appeared to
> be of opinion that he could either enforce his views on the Admiralty,
> or procure the retirement of the Sea Lords; that the Admiralty were not
> to remain in control of the navy unless they accepted him as a dictator
> of what they should do. He was, in fact, to be an admiralissimo.[32]

The flagship of the Home Fleet was HMS *Dreadnought*, the ship that revolutionised the naval world. King Edward himself had launched her just
eighteen months earlier. Wearing a bicorne hat and the full-dress uniform
of an admiral of the fleet, Edward had to twice swing a bottle of Australian
wine against the ship before it would shatter and christen the latest battleship for the navy. He then took up a hammer and chisel made from the
timbers of HMS *Victory* and severed the last cord holding her in place; and
touched off a revolution. *Dreadnought* had been laid down on 2 October
1905, just under a year after Fisher had taken office, and was ready for
launching four months later. She sported, for the first time on any battleship, an all-big-gun armament of ten 12in guns in five turrets, virtually no
secondary armament, turbine engines and even moved the officers'
accommodation forward, breaking a long naval tradition.

At a stroke, her armament destroyed several naval shibboleths.
Throughout the late nineteenth century British gunnery prize shooting had
been at 2,000 yards and battle practice was only 3,000 yards in 1904, the
year that the Japanese fleet opened an accurate fire at 18,000 yards during
the Russo-Japanese War. British admirals still expected to close the enemy
and pepper them with quick-firing weapons, in the Nelsonian tradition.

It was for this reason that all RN battleships carried a limited number
of heavy guns and a preponderance of quick-firing weapons, usually 6in.
So did the latest cruisers, such as the *Drake* class of 1900 which carried
two 9.2in guns and sixteen 6in. The larger weapons were intended to
serve as 'hull-crackers'. The idea was that they would 'crack' the enemy's
armour plate in order that the smaller side-mounted guns could pour in
a broadside.

Worse, ships carried mixed armaments, such as the 12in and 10.8in combination seen on the French battleships in 1905 (*vide supra*). This made rangefinding impossible as no-one could tell the splashes apart at distance. Gun smoke made it worse. Individual gun captains were expected to sight and fire their own guns and each gun fired when ready, exacerbating the aiming and ranging problems. *Dreadnought* solved this problem, having no smaller-calibre weapons apart from light anti-torpedo boat guns. Fisher actively promoted improvements in gunnery, including centralisation of gunnery control in director towers, high above the ship (and giving British warships a distinctive profile with their tripod masts).

Overnight, *Dreadnought* made all other battleships obsolete and sparked a rush to build *Dreadnought*-type vessels which spread across the globe; and from April 1907 to May 1912 she was the flagship of the Home Fleet.

On 3 May 1907, a fleet review was held at Spithead which, although containing over sixty ships, was not royal. It was occasioned by the Imperial Conference in London in which King Edward VII and Prime Minister Henry Campbell-Bannerman hosted the premiers from Britain's major imperial colonies around the world between 15 April and 14 May.

Edward did not attend the naval excursion, but all the premiers were entertained aboard HMS *Dreadnought* and an imposing spectacle was provided by the Home Fleet, despite constant rain. The politicians observed a mock attack on the flagship by torpedo boats and submarines. They also saw the destroyer *Coquette*, 335 tons, destabilised by a heavy wash of sea and crash into a coal hulk which was crowded with spectators. She was damaged but fortunately no one was hurt.

But the King was present on 3 August 1907 when *Dreadnought*, flying the flag of the Home Fleet C-in-C, the quietly intelligent Yorkshireman Admiral Sir Francis Bridgeman (last noted as a commander on HMS *Howe*, *vide supra*), headed an assembly of 188 vessels in the Solent (which included a Swedish squadron) the lines of which 'covered twenty-four miles and constituted a sight of the most impressive character'.[33]

As ever, Edward sailed between the lines of warships in *Victoria and Albert*, receiving the royal salute and cheers of the men as he passed by. Additionally, during the review, King Edward, Queen Alexandra and the Prince of Wales all boarded *Dreadnought* to both 'experience the smooth speed generated by the turbines and to marvel at the quality of the gunnery which the stability made possible'.[34] Apparently, the Queen was so impressed by the ship's marksmanship that she ordered the targets towed in and hung from the fantail, a gesture which a rival battleship's captain described as 'cheap swagger'.[35] But the boasting was justified; *Dreadnought*, British-built and designed, was the best battleship in the world.

Fisher's protégé, Rear-Admiral John Jellicoe, just appointed to be second-in-command of the Atlantic Fleet, was received by the King on board *Victoria and Albert* and appointed a Knight Commander of the Royal Victorian Order (a distinction within the sole gift of the monarch) no doubt to his patron's pleasure.

Finally, Edward expressed 'his satisfaction at the efficient condition of the fleet'.[36] And *The Times* mused that 'although not a perfect model of fighting efficiency … the fleet exhibited abundant promise and a very large measure of achievement'.[37]

But why was there a review in 1907? There was no great anniversary to celebrate, no coronation, no major visiting royalty; yes, Edward was there anyway as he always visited in Cowes Week. But what was the review for? The answer can be found in a question asked in Parliament by Sir Berkeley Sheffield; replying for the government, Edmund Robertson, Parliamentary and Financial Secretary to the Admiralty, noted that 'His Majesty the King having intimated his gracious intention to inspect the Home Fleet, orders were given as soon as His Majesty's commands were received'.[38] The King wanted a Royal Fleet Review.

Fisher had been under sustained attack by Beresford, his parliamentary friends and some quarters of the press, who accused him of hazarding the security of the nation by the changes he was making to *materiel* and dispositions. Edward VII liked Fisher; they corresponded, they talked. And Fisher revered the old king. 'King Edward had faith in me and supported me,' wrote Fisher, adding 'he gave me his unfaltering support right through unswervingly'.[39] Moreover, Edward disliked Beresford. They had unintentionally shared a mistress, Daisy Greville, Countess of Warwick; this led to a dispute which ended with Edward excluding Beresford from his royal circles and Edward never forgave the matter. King Edward VII, in the author's view, conducted a fleet review to give support and royal imprimatur to Fisher's new creation.

1909, Contention – A Navy or a Pension?

Herbert Henry Asquith had become Prime Minister of Britain in April 1908. He and his Chancellor of the Exchequer, David Lloyd George, were set on a redistributive policy which would allow for the introduction of old age pensions and a number of other socially reforming policies.

In a major speech in December 1908, Asquith announced that the upcoming budget would reflect this agenda, and a so-called 'People's Budget' was submitted to Parliament by Lloyd George the following year. This greatly expanded social welfare programmes. To pay for them, the budget significantly increased both direct and indirect taxes. These included a 20 per cent tax on the unearned increase in value in land, payable at death of the owner or sale of the land. There would also be a tax of a halfpenny in the pound on undeveloped land. A graduated income tax was to be imposed, and there were increases in imposts on tobacco, beer and spirits. The proposed budget divided the country and provoked bitter debate through the summer of 1909.

The focus on social spending ran counter to a widespread belief that more money was needed for the navy to fund spending on *Dreadnought*-type warships, in competition with a significant German building programme which now included such vessels. On 8 December 1908, First Lord of the Admiralty Reginald McKenna had recommended to the Cabinet a new shipbuilding programme of six dreadnoughts for 1909–10. This would have brought the navy's strength of such ships to eighteen in 1912; but Germany was thought to have plans to build seventeen (possibly twenty-one) by then – the two-power standard would not apply, and indeed Britain may be outnumbered!

Winston Churchill (President of the Board of Trade) and Lloyd George opposed increased spending, proposing only four such ships, and a public battle broke out with navy-supporting sources calling for at least eight ships to be laid down – the 'We want eight and we won't wait'* campaign, led by the Navy League. Space does not allow the recounting of the full tale; it became a bitter argument, with proponents of increased social spending set against those who argued that old age pensions were less important than a strong navy. Sufficient to say that eventually eight were agreed upon, across two years; but the two-power standard was quietly consigned to the history books.

Showcasing the navy to cultivate public opinion during this period of debate was important public relations and no less than four naval reviews were held during the year; but only two may be called Royal. Both of these occurred at Spithead during the summer.

First, the Admiralty staged a special event at Spithead to display the fleet to the attendees at the Imperial Press Conference of 5 June. This event was intended to encourage closer relations between newspapermen in Britain and the Dominions but the Admiralty clearly saw it as a good way to promote the navy and its associated need for funding at the height of the Anglo-German naval race. The Admiralty laid on 144 warships in seven lines, over 18 miles of ships; there were sham fights and mock torpedo attacks. Via the instrument of the press, the might of the king's navy was demonstrated to the Imperial family.

Next, there was a Grand Naval Pageant on the Thames between 17 and 24 July; the fleet was officially invited to London by the Lord Mayor, but this was perhaps a pretext for a display which was part advertisement, part exhibition. There was no royal and naval precedent for the event, it was pure public relations by the navy.

On Saturday 17 July, Tower Bridge was opened at 1300 to let the

* A phrase coined by the Conservative MP George Wyndham.

warships through. There were small cruisers and destroyers moored at Woolwich and Greenwich, more destroyers opposite Tower of London, a line of torpedo boats stretching up river to Somerset House and Westminster Bridge. Two submarines were positioned at Temple Pier and four at Westminster while the great battleships were anchored in lines at Southend. By 1500, 150 boats had assembled in the Thames. It was designed as mass entertainment, on a Saturday, and remained there for a week, staging mocks fights and illuminations while naval parades marched through London. An estimated four million spectators viewed the naval extravaganza, many from pleasure steamers which charged a guinea per head for a trip around the fleet.

Meanwhile, the royals gathered at Cowes for the regatta as normal. On 28 July, HMY *Alberta* transported the Princess of Wales from Portsmouth. On the 30th, Edward arrived at Portsmouth from Goodwood, where he had been taking in the racing, travelling as usual in his royal train. All ships in harbour were dressed for review and as the King boarded *Victoria and Albert* the fleet fired off a royal salute. The same day, the Duke and Duchess of Connaught and his children Prince Arthur with Princess Patricia embarked on the new royal yacht *Alexandra*, twin screw and launched in 1907. On Saturday 31st, *Alberta* returned to Portsmouth carrying the Princess of Wales and the King and Queen of Spain, Alfonso XIII and Victoria Eugenie of Battenberg. From there, they and the rest of the royal party, together with the Board of Admiralty, joined *Victoria and Albert* and the Spanish Royal Standard was worn and saluted as a mark of respect.

A line of battleships
at the 1909 review.
(Author's collection)

The *Invincible*-class
battlecruiser HMS
Indomitable, one of
Fisher's greyhounds.
*(US Naval History
and Heritage
Command
NH 60003)*

King Edward's
review of the fleet at
Spithead, 1909. A
general view of the
lines, showing the
Indomitable in the
centre with the
armoured cruisers
Drake astern and
Shannon on the right
of the picture.
*(© National Maritime
Museum P00022)*

Waiting for them in the Solent were 153 warships from the Home and Atlantic fleets under the command of Commander-in-Chief Portsmouth, Admiral Sir Arthur Fanshawe KCB. There were twenty-four battleships, of which four were Dreadnoughts, sixteen armoured cruisers, eight protected cruisers, four scouts, forty-eight destroyers, eight auxiliaries and forty-two submarines; these latter had been much pushed for by Fisher. But the centrepiece of the fleet was Fisher's three new 'Dreadnought Cruisers', *Indomitable*, *Invincible* and *Inflexible*, all laid down in 1906. They were the logical next extension of Fisher's battleship ideas, ships that could catch anything that they could fight, and quickly withdraw from any ship too well armed to engage. Fisher called them his 'new testament' ships, 'greyhounds to catch hares'. Each carried eight 12in guns and sacrificed armour protection for speed ('speed *is* armour', claimed Fisher). Four screws and steam turbines drove them at around 25kts.

The first of the breed, *Indomitable*, crossed the Atlantic in 1908 with the Prince of Wales (the future George V) on board. For reason best known to themselves, both he and his private secretary worked a shift in the stoke-hold. On the return journey she averaged a fraction below 25kts, almost equalling the record for the voyage of 25.08kts set by RMS *Lusitania*. George told Fisher (whom he actually disliked) 'she is indeed a grand ship and the finest steamer I have ever seen'.[40]

In the light of the criticism heaped upon the lightly-armoured battle-cruisers after the loss of three of their type at Jutland, it should be recalled that Fisher had not intended them as 'line-of-battle' ships. They were orig-inally to lead a cluster of light cruisers, which would act as their 'eyes', sweeping the seas for enemy commerce raiders and sinking them. Thus their initial appellation was 'Dreadnought Cruisers'; they were only chris-tened 'Battlecruisers' by Admiralty order on 25 November 1911, not least so that the fleet of capital ships would seem, for public consumption, to be larger than it was.

The ships laid out in six lines before Edward looked different in many respects to those which had greeted his mother in her later years, not least in their paintwork. In Nelson's time, captains had wide discretion as to how they painted and decorated their ships. By late in Victoria's reign, a standardised pattern of black hulls (with white upper works and buff-yellow funnels in the Mediterranean) was adopted. But in 1903 most British warships turned grey. In home waters, ships were painted a dark shade generally called 'battleship grey'. On some hotter stations, lighter shades were permitted as being cooler.* A grey fleet now lay awaiting on the dull green waters of the Solent.

At 1130, the royal yacht departed Portsmouth harbour, preceded as always by the Trinity House vessel *Irene* and followed by *Alexandra*, *Alberta*, *Enchantress* and *Firequeen*.

* Torpedo boats and torpedo boat destroyers remained black until after the battle of Jutland in 1916.

There was a large crowd ashore and afloat. Special trains had been laid on from the newly-constructed 'South Station' at Waterloo with four platforms in constant use.

Members of Parliament and the Lords too had their own special arrangements; they were taken aboard the White Star Line passenger liner *Adriatic*, which had been chartered especially for them at a cost of £800. Lunch was served to them in harbour in Southampton at 1300, after which the ship sailed to tag onto the end of the line of royal yachts. The Admiralty was determined to ensure that MPs and peers received a good view, and a favourable impression, of the fleet they were being asked to pay for. The Upper Promenade Deck had been placed out of bounds, however, for use as a 'Ladies' Cloak Room'.

These arrangements did not find favour with some who opposed the increased annual naval expenditure Estimates. Questions regarding the costs were asked in the House of Commons. Opposition MP Stanley Wilson pointedly inquired 'under which Admiralty vote, and which sub-head, will be included the expenditure necessary for the provision of free railway tickets and for other entertainment for members of parliament and their families on the occasion of the naval review'; to which First Lord Reginald McKenna dead-batted the reply 'the expenditure will be borne under sub-head Z of Vote 11, "Miscellaneous Payments and Allowances"'. Arnold Herbert, MP for Wycombe, wanted to know 'are we to understand that, in future, when we ask for money for the navy, we are really voting money which can be used for our own entertainment'?[41] These cavils aside, the *Adriatic* was full!

Some deserving Royal Navy and Royal Marine officers were allowed to view the fleet from RFA (Royal Fleet Auxiliary) *Harlequin*, and the press was accommodated in HMS *Seahorse*, a fleet tug tender. This led to an embarrassment; the earthly needs of the Fourth Estate had been overlooked and some of the ship's messes sold their provisions to the ravenous press at a good profit.*

At 1425, *Victoria and Albert* entered the lines of waiting ships, all with flags out, bands mounted and sides manned. She sailed east to west along line B, back along row A and then west again to pick up the royal yacht buoys off the coast of the Isle of Wight. Here she was close to HMS *Dreadnought*, flying the flag of Home Fleet C-in-C Admiral Sir William Henry May, and at the head of the lines of submarines and destroyers moored in the Fairway. Immediately the royal vessel dropped anchor, a 21-gun salute roared out from the whole fleet. The review concluded, there only remained the traditional illumination of the fleet and all was over for the day.

But there was to be a second review almost immediately afterwards. The Tsar of Russia was in France, visiting his ally and its president. At Edward's

* This was an embarrassment to the Admiralty who were endeavouring to keep the press 'onside'. The extent of their regret can be seen in the fact that First Lord of the Admiralty McKenna apologised to the press in Parliament.

invitation he then sailed in the Russian royal yacht *Standart* to Cowes, accompanied by two armoured cruisers, the British-built *Rurik* (four 10in, eight 8in guns) and the French-built *Admiral Makarov* (two 8in, eight 6in), and another yacht, the secondary royal vessel *Polar Star*, all arriving on 2 August. That evening the tsar dined with Edward on *Victoria and Albert*, accompanied by First Lord of the Admiralty McKenna and Prime Minister Asquith, who received a wigging from the King over Lloyd George's recent speech in Limehouse where he had berated the House of Lords for objecting to his budget proposals.

The Tsar's visit was contentious. Radicals attacked the King for entertaining a reactionary autocrat. But Foreign Secretary Sir Edward Grey put it differently; 'the king's influence with the tsar and the friendship of the British government are really a support to [prime minister] Stolypin … and to the Duma and all friends of constitutional progress in Russia'.[42]

On 3 August the two monarchs jointly reviewed the British fleet, sailing through three lines of warships as before in *Victoria and Albert*. Pennants dipped, saluting cannons boomed and bands played 'God Save the King' and 'God Save the Tsar', sailors cheered and waved their caps while the whiplash-slim Tsar, wearing a white British admiral's uniform, stood next to the portly King.

Cowes Week immediately followed the review. Ashore and afloat there were dinner parties and balls. Steam launches with gleaming brass funnels and slender cutters and gigs, pulled by crews at long white oars, ran between the yachts and the Royal Yacht Squadron steps. The area was

At the 1909 Royal Fleet Review, the last pre-dreadnought battleships built for the Royal Navy. HMS *Agamemnon* (front) with *Lord Nelson* were commissioned in 1908, two years after *Dreadnought* had made them obsolete. To their rear is the *Bellerophon*-class dreadnought HMS *Temeraire*, commissioned in 1909. *(Author's collection)*

awash with boats of all kinds. To enhance security, the three Dreadnought cruisers had been ordered to remain at Spithead after the departure of the fleet on 3 August 'at His Majesty's pleasure'.[43] Together with the battleship *Bellerophon*, and all under the command of Rear-Admiral the Hon Stanley Colville, they were to provide a private honour guard for the Tsar and King. One Inspector Quinn had been directed by the Chief Commissioner of Police to wait on Admiral Colville 'to concert the necessary arrangements for preventing unauthorised persons from approaching the yachts'.[44] Picket boats and whalers circled the two royal yachts to mount a permanent water-borne guard.

The security extended to all aspects of the Tsar's visit. The King's grandsons, Prince Edward and Prince Albert, were attending the Royal Naval College Osborne at this time and were scheduled to show the Russian party around the facilities. At the last moment, Albert was found to be suffering from a cold which turned into whooping cough. It was feared he could infect the Tsar's haemophiliac son Alexis, so only Edward was allowed into the Russian party's presence. According to Edward's later account 'because of assassination plots … the Imperial government would not risk the Little Father's life in the great metropolis. Therefore, the meeting was set for Cowes … which could be sealed off completely … I do remember being astonished at the elaborate police guard thrown around his every movement when I showed him around Osborne College.'[45]

Eventually, the Tsar departed on the 5th, with 'much saluting and band playing',[46] reported the King's naval equerry, Captain Godfrey-Faussett; and finally, on the 9th the royal yacht took Edward to the railway station and his luxurious train. He departed to yet more gunfire from *Victory* and ships in harbour. Edward would never preside over a Royal Fleet Review again.

Edward VII died on 6 May 1910. 'Jackie' Fisher, by now in retirement, missed him deeply; 'He was a noble man and every inch a king', he wrote afterwards.[47] As Lord Redesdale told the admiral, 'He was the best friend you ever had'.[48] The King's influence and support helped create a new, modernised Royal Navy.

Part Three:

GEORGIAN APOTHEOSIS AND DECLINE

After His Lieges, in all His Lands,
Had laid their hands between His hands,
And His ships thundered service and devotion,
The Tide Wave, ranging the Planet, spoke
On all Our foreshores as it broke: –
'Know now what Man I gave you – I, the Ocean!'

Rudyard Kipling, *The King and the Sea*, July 1935,
on the occasion of the Silver Jubilee Fleet
Review of George V.

Chapter 12

Countdown to War, 1911–1914

GEORGE V had not been intended for the throne; he was Edward and Alexandra's second son, the 'back-up' to the heir. His elder brother, Albert Victor, called Eddy by the family, was considered backward, lazy and obtuse. As second son, George was expected to follow a career in the navy but, because of concern regarding Eddy, it was deemed unwise to separate him from his brother as George was considered a good influence upon him.

Both brothers were therefore sent to join the cadet training ship HMS *Britannia* in 1877, where Eddy was nicknamed 'Herring' and George 'Sprat'. George was small, knock-kneed and shy, Eddy considered stupid; both were bullied by other cadets who resented their exalted status and privileged position within the strict regime on the ship. They were forced to fag for senior boys, and George later said that 'other boys made a point of taking it out on us in the grounds that they'd never be able to do it again'.[1]

On passing out they went on a round-the-world cruise and on their return Eddy was sent to Cambridge and George began a naval career. He served on the royal yacht *Osborne*, sat his gunnery exams at HMS *Excellent* and in 1890 was posted to the North American Station as officer in charge of HMS *Thrush*, a composite gunboat of sail and screw propulsion. In 1891 George was advanced to the rank of commander and in 1892, he took command of the *Apollo*-class protected cruiser *Melampus* (two 6in, six 4.7in guns), acting as coastguard ship off Kingston, Jamaica. He was happy in his life. He had a career, position and was far away from the court and its stultifying routine. But then his brother died of pneumonia.

George was now second in line to the throne. His naval career was over (apart from a brief flourish as captain commanding the *Edgar*-class cruiser HMS *Crescent* for a few weeks in 1898); his rank would now be ceremonial only. Like it or not, he returned to court. But he never lost his joy in things naval and in the old traditions of the service. He disliked Fisher for his reforming zeal and was greatly pleased that 'Jackie' was out of office when he ascended to the throne. Fisher reciprocated the feeling, calling George V and Queen Mary 'futile and fertile'.[2]

On becoming king, George soon showed where his heart lay by visiting the annual manoeuvres of the combined Home, Mediterranean and Atlantic Fleets at Torbay in July 1910. This was not a formal Royal Fleet Review but nonetheless, on 26 July the King was treated to a 21-gun salute from the assembled ships and spent the 27th and 28th on board the flagship HMS *Dreadnought*, Captain Herbert Richmond, in company with Admiral William Henry May, C-in-C Home Fleet. From her, he observed the sea exercises which included, amongst other notable warships, the 1st Cruiser Squadron, comprising *Indomitable* (flag), *Inflexible* and *Invincible*.

This might well have been instructive for the former naval commander and now king, as May was an innovative tactician and had initiated an extensive series of exercises of considerable scale and comprehensiveness. These encompassed examination of the cruising formations from which deployment into battle formation could most rapidly be made, the use of flotillas in a tactical offensive, the employment of fast squadrons in action and the alternative of divisional or squadron-based command in place of the single line under one commander.

The King's visit was also made instructive certainly, worrying possibly, by the activities of the British aviator Claude Grahame-White, who flew his airplane over the assembled fleet at Mount's Bay, buzzing *Dreadnought* as he passed by. Grahame-White, a pioneer of aviation and the first man to make a night flight (during the *Daily Mail*-sponsored 1910 London to Manchester air race) was trying to make a point regarding the lack of defence that ships would have against an aerial attack. As will be seen, it was noted.

As king, George was soon confronted by two difficult problems. First, the conflict between Lords and Commons over the passage of Lloyd George's redistributive budget; here Asquith bullied the King into agreeing to create hundreds of new peers to ensure its passage unless the House of Lords backed down. And secondly, German aggression over Morocco – the 'Agadir incident', which might have led to war.

This was a crisis triggered by the deployment of a large force of French troops to the interior of Morocco in April 1911. Germany did not necessarily object to France's expansion but wanted territorial compensation for herself. Berlin threatened war, sent the gunboat *Panther* to Agadir followed by the cruiser *Berlin*, and roused German nationalists to bellicosity. Negotiations between Germany and France resolved the issue: but the British government, in the person of Lloyd George, made it clear that Britain would not stand idly by if Germany threatened French or British interests. 'If Britain is treated badly … as if she is of no account in the cabinet of nations, then I say emphatically that peace at that price would

Arrival of the fleet for the 1911 Coronation Review by A C Burlton Cull. It depicts the fleet drawn up in parallel lines for the King and Queen to sail past in the *Victoria and Albert II.* *(Author's collection)*

be a humiliation intolerable for a great country like ours to endure,' Lloyd George thundered in a speech at the Mansion House in London. The speech was interpreted by Germany as a warning that she could not impose an unreasonable settlement on France.

The British Cabinet, however, was alarmed at Germany's aggressiveness toward their French ally. Relations between Berlin and London were strained and Prime Minister Asquith called for a presentation of war plans by the army and navy to the Committee of Imperial Defence. Here the navy, represented by Admiral Sir Arthur Knyvet Wilson VC, First Sea Lord, performed badly and the blame was placed by Asquith and others on the lack of a naval staff, a function which had been resisted by Fisher and his hand-picked successor Wilson. The navy's political master, McKenna, supported his admiral and by October both had been fired as a result, McKenna being replaced by Winston Churchill who, incidentally, George V liked even less than Fisher. Edward VII had said of Churchill that he was 'almost more of a cad in office than he was in opposition' and George V agreed.[3] Eventually, the King came to regard Churchill as 'an able but awkward minister'.[4]

But Churchill lay in the future. On 22 June 1911, George Frederick Ernest Albert was crowned king. And as with his father, a Royal Naval Coronation Review was arranged, to take place two days later.

The foreign representation at this assembly had mostly arrived at least a couple of days beforehand. Seventeen warships from countries including, *inter alia*, Denmark, France, Germany, Greece, Japan, Russia and the USA, were anchored in the Solent (see also Appendix 5).

The Americans sent USS *Delaware*,* a dreadnought battleship with ten 12in guns, commissioned a year earlier. The French despatched the pre-dreadnought *Danton*, commissioned that month but already obsolescent, while the Greek cruiser *Georgios Averof* arrived without any ammunition for her 9.2in and 7.5in British-made guns; she was to collect it while there. Shortly after the review she grounded in Plymouth Sound and suffered a near-mutiny while docked for repair.

On the 20th the Admiralty arranged a welcoming garden party at Admiralty House, Portsmouth, for the foreign officers present and many of the British ones. These overseas emissaries and their vessels joined with thirty-two Royal Navy battleships, twenty-four armoured cruisers, eight protected cruisers and four unarmoured cruisers, together with sixty-seven destroyers, twelve torpedo boats and eight submarines from the Home and Atlantic Fleets, all under the command of Admiral Arthur William Moore, C-in-C Portsmouth, the Home Fleet contingent sailing under Admiral Sir Francis Bridgeman and the Atlantic under Vice-Admiral John Jellicoe. The lines of British warships alone stretched for 26 miles.

On 21 June, many foreign and RN officers travelled to London to view the Coronation itself and the following day, Coronation Day, was decreed a Sunday (it was actually a Thursday) with extra grog served to the sailors.

* She would serve with the Grand Fleet during the First World War.

The American representative at the Coronation Review, USS *Delaware*. *(Library of Congress LOT 10775)*

A royal salute was fired at 1200 and the fleet was illuminated that evening
between 2130 and 2300. An athletics event was held that same day.

The 24th dawned a grey, cool morning which threatened rain. The
King and Queen arrived at the great naval dockyard of Portsmouth
during the morning of Saturday 24 June and, with their household in
attendance, embarked in *Victoria and Albert*. As the Royal Standard was
broken on the yacht, HMS *Victory* alone fired a royal salute. Admirals
Moore and Bridgeman were then received on board the royal vessel by
George and were no doubt gratified to be advanced within the Royal
Victorian Order to GCVO;* and another fourteen flag officers afloat in
the review lines were presented to the King. As with Queen Victoria's
Golden Jubilee review of 1887, participating ships had been cautioned to
burn Welsh coal only, to reduce smoke and thus the collisions which
marred that event.

At 1400 *Victoria and Albert* left the harbour and half-an-hour later
entered the lines of the fleet, led by the Trinity House *Irene* and followed
by *Alexandra*, *Enchantress* and *Firequeen*. There were 165 vessels at Spithead
to greet them, anchored in seven columns each nearly five miles long. The
procession around the fleet took some two hours. Ships were dressed
overall and upper decks manned and from each vessel in succession the
new king was greeted by three rousing cheers. A new king, but a continuing navy tradition now stretching back centuries.

Not all went as it should. A 21-gun salute was to commence as the royal
yacht entered the lines; but the cruiser *Euryalus* fired prematurely due to
an error by her Gunner, Mr Thomas Sandover; he was immediately placed
under arrest and a court of enquiry called for. But generally, 'the imposing
appearance of the new battleships justifies one in saying that a more
impressive-looking fleet was never seen'.[5] Of new ships on show, the
destroyer *Swift*** had a remarkable top speed of 35kts under light condi-

tions. 'D'-class submarines were much admired, not least for the fact that they were fitted with wireless telegraphy and 'it is said that the E-class, which are now building, will carry quick-firing guns, a development undreamed of when submarines were invented'.[6]

Anchoring near to *Dreadnought*, whose captain Sydney Fremantle was the son of the admiral who had been part of the board of the Diamond Jubilee Earl's Court extravaganza, *Victoria and Albert* now received on board all flag officers, and the captains of the foreign ships to a reception with the King. George later issued a congratulatory message which emphasised 'the marked precision of the lines'.[7]

As always, there were crowds of spectators ashore and afloat. For those on land, 150 members of St John's Ambulance Brigade were mobilised to ensure the wellbeing of spectators, and afloat, for the first time many of the hired pleasure vessels were actually given berths for anchorage within the review field, to prevent them interfering with the lines. The Admiralty itself hired two steamers for its guests, the British-India Steam Navigation Company SS *Rewa** and the P&O SS *Dongola* with Rear-Admirals Cradock and Tupper respectively on board to provide expert commentary for Their Lordships' guests.

Thomas Cook offered a package deal which encompassed the coronation processions in London as well as the Spithead review. Guests travelled by special train from Waterloo to Southampton Docks and boarded RMS *Armadale Castle* which put to sea, anchored and served dinner on board

* She became a hospital ship during the First World War. On 4 January 1918, she was hit and sunk by a torpedo from the German U-boat *U-55*.

HMY *Victoria and Albert* passing through the lines of the fleet at the Coronation Review 1911. *(National Museum of the Royal Navy)*

(accompanied by an orchestra). On the day of the review she cruised between the lines of warships except when required to moor up in her allocated position to allow unimpeded passage for the King.

There were privileged spectators on board His Majesty's ships too. As but one example, the light cruiser HMS *Gloucester* was a *Bristol*-class vessel launched in 1909. The class were originally intended to have a uniform 4in gun armament but two 6in guns were added to give them an advantage over German light cruisers. This was not a success. The ships were cramped, were 'lively' gun platforms and the mixed-calibre armament caused problems with fire control. Additionally, the 4in guns were mounted too near the waterline to be usefully worked in heavy seas. Her captain, Walter Cowan, had invited an eclectic collection of personal guests on board. These included four officers of the Gloucestershire Regiment (sartorially distinguished for their uniform caps which had the badge front and back), Sir Reginald Wingate (quondam Governor-General of the Sudan and Sirdar of the Egyptian Army), Slatin Pasha (the Austrian-born Major-General Rudolf Anton Carl Freiherr von Slatin, held captive by the Mahdi and his successors for 11 years and freed with Wingate's help), and Sir Henry Rawlinson and his wife. 'Rawly' was General Officer Commanding the 3rd Division of the British Army (and the future commander of the Fourth Army at the battles of the Somme and Amiens). At 1800 the King and Queen departed Portsmouth by rail and, once more, the fleet was lit up from night fall until 2300. But this was not the end to the festivities; the Lord Mayor of Portsmouth gave a banquet at the Town Hall on the 27th to round off the celebrations.

Once again, the navy had put on a fine show. But the costs reflected it. At an additional £31,800 for accommodation, entertainment and extra policemen, they were the highest yet. Indeed, from the 1912 Naval Estimates onwards, 'ceremonies and visits' became a separate budget item. But the publicity for the naval cause, fanned across Britain from 267 accredited press reporters,[8] also the highest yet, was superb at a time when the government of the day was intent on increasing social spending.

And so a second Coronation Royal Fleet Review passed into history; another tradition had been established, to sit alongside illuminations, dressing and manning ship, and royal salutes aplenty. Kaiser Wilhelm II of Germany had been an invited guest; but his attitude to Britain had hardened. As he left Portsmouth he uttered 'threats and curses against England'[9] to Vice-Admiral Prince Louis of Battenberg. Ominous clouds were gathering.

1912, Another Revolution

George V was present at another two Royal Fleet Reviews less than a year later and there he witnessed, probably unwittingly, another revolution, one on a par with that viewed by his father in 1907 when Fisher proudly displayed his *Dreadnought* to an astounded world.

The first was a review with a difference in several ways, setting aside a latent revolution. It was set off Torbay; the second was staged for a specific audience – Members of Parliament. In October 1911, Reginald McKenna, urbane and polished, a financial man who left operational matters to the sailors, was replaced as First Lord by Winston Spencer Churchill, a 37-year-old rising minister. Churchill's appointment did not find widespread approval. He was regarded by many as a self-advertiser, a politician on the make. Churchill brought energy and enthusiasm and had Fisher whispering in his ear as an *eminence gris*. But he also took day-to-day control of matters traditionally left to the professional officers of the Admiralty Board which created unnecessary tensions.

The world was a fragile place in 1912. The Balkans would soon erupt into the First Balkan War. And Britain and Germany were now locked in a naval arms race, laying down new large ships at an ever-increasing rate. The Naval Estimates for 1911 had totalled £13.2 million; Churchill presented 1912's Estimates in March at £12.5 million and claimed a decrease. This was possible only due to some financial *legerdemain* and the First Lord noted that if 'other powers' (by which he meant Germany) increased their own building programmes he would have to return to the House with supplementary monetary requests.

On 1 April 1912, Britain was building ten battleships, six battlecruisers, eight protected cruisers, two unarmoured cruisers, thirty-one destroyers and fifteen submarines. To these, the new expenditures would add four large armoured ships, eight light armoured cruisers, twenty destroyers and 'a number of submarines', together with 2,000 additional men.[10]

The Liberal Party had, of course, come to power promising reduced armament expenditure and increased money for social programmes. The Liberal-leaning newspaper *Daily News* noted the Estimates as 'a financial disaster' and the *Morning Leader* as 'a grave disappointment'. But *The Times* thought that 'it was impossible to make the reductions which the [Liberal Party] desired'.[11]

The Admiralty needed to get MPs on-side with this impressive and expensive programme; they wanted to showcase the fleet that the money voted was bringing, so no less than two Royal Fleet Reviews were arranged for 1912. Nonetheless, the Treasury fought a rearguard action to prevent expenditure on what it saw as an unnecessary function. There had, in fact, been continuous warfare between Treasury and Admiralty since 1911 over the question. This newly-proposed Parliamentary inspection seemed particularly wasteful to the mandarins. 'I can conceive of no reason at all why it should take place this year' wrote the Secretary of the Treasury to the Admiralty.[12] He was ignored.

The first review took place in Torbay over 7–11 May and contained several innovations. On Friday 10 May, the King dived in a submarine. No monarch had ever (at least voluntarily) gone underwater before. He boarded HMS *D-4* and submerged. For ten minutes the King and his naval cadet second son, Prince Albert, 'enjoyed the sensation of a voyage beneath the waves, travelling a distance of two miles'.[13] To show that some politicians had mettle too, Churchill and A J Balfour (quondam prime minister and leader of the opposition) had dived in another 'D'-class sub a day earlier. 'Probably no two statesmen have ever found themselves companions in similar circumstances,' observed the *Morning Post*.[14] It was a recognition of the submarine as more than one of 'Fisher's toys' (to use Beresford's insult); and a prefiguring of the damage to Britain's trade and food supply that U-boats would cause in two World Wars.

The second 'first' presented for parliamentarians and the King's delectation was even more far-reaching, for it would render obsolete these massive financial investments in capital ships within the following 30 years. On 9 May, Commander Charles Rumney Samson of the naval wing of the Royal Flying Corps took off from HMS *Hibernia*[*] in his modified Short Brothers S38 'hydro-aeroplane' to become the first pilot to take off from a ship underway at sea. The S38 T2 aircraft had air-bag floats to enable landing on water and was launched via a trolley-shuttle system off a ramp which stretched from *Hibernia*'s bridge to bow, over her forward 12in guns.[†] Samson already held the honour of being the first British pilot to take off from a ship, flying a Short Improved S27 from a ramp mounted on the foredeck of the battleship *Africa*, which was at anchor in the River Medway, on 10 January 1912. Now he was the first man to achieve the feat from a moving ship.

But his demonstration did not end there. Five aircraft, including Samson's floatplane, braved intermittent fog and flew over the royal yacht

[*] She was a *King Edward VII*-class pre-dreadnought, one of the 'Wobbly Eight'. 'These ships were quite useless owing to their roll and the proximity of their guns to the waterline. They were useful only in reasonably calm weather or against shore targets' (Agar, *Footprints in the Sea*, p 46).

[†] The aircraft had been towed out to the battleship sitting on her launching platform and was then hoisted aboard.

HMS *Hibernia* with Commander Samson's Short S38 plane, the occasion of the first flight from a moving ship. *(Author's collection)*

where Lieutenant Gregory in a Short biplane released a '300lb packet labelled "dynamite"'[15] next to *Victoria and Albert*.* Air-to-ship bombing had just been invented. Samson then landed his craft next to the royal yacht. It was the nascent dawn of airpower. A stunned Prime Minister Herbert Asquith told reporters, with a certain amount of hyperbole, 'I have just come from witnessing a spectacle to which I suppose there has never been a parallel in the history of the world'.[16]

The following month two naval seaplanes flew from Sheerness to Portsmouth; one accomplished the journey without stopping and at an average speed of 62mph. And in September, four naval seaplanes took part in the annual army manoeuvres. Air power had arrived.

Then in July, a second fleet review was organised at Spithead. This was specifically arranged for members of both Houses of Parliament and they were given a special invitation and ringside seats. As this was regarded as a private visit, no press facilities were provided. Four battle squadrons, four cruiser squadrons, and two flotillas of destroyers were present but fog prevented the fleet from putting to sea for gunnery practice. Some 3,075 reservists were called up for the event. The politicians attending were taken around the fleet in RMS *Armadale Castle* or RFA *Harlequin* and visited a battleship. There was even another flying demonstration, floatplanes passing over the fleet. Readers will by now understand the general format.

A view from the shore of the 1912 fleet review in Torbay *(Press Association 1376973)*

* The other aircraft included a Deperdussin monoplane, a Short monoplane and a Short biplane.

The cover of a
commemorative
brochure for the
1912 'Parliament-
arians' review',
published by Gale &
Polden Limited.
(Author's collection)

The requisite impression was made and considerable publicity obtained as postcards and memorabilia programmes proliferated. It all went to reassure that the money spent on the navy was well spent.

There was a further, non-royal, review in 1912. In August the Admiralty sent eleven warships (including the 2nd Battle Squadron) under Vice-Admiral John Jellicoe to Glasgow, to participate in the celebrations on the occasion of the 100th anniversary of the launch of Henry Bell's paddle steamer *Comet*, deemed the first commercial steam ship. Jellicoe flew his flag in HMS *Hercules* (1910), a *Colossus*-class dreadnought battleship mounting ten 12in guns in five turrets. On 31 August the Lord Provost of Glasgow formally inspected the squadron. The Admiralty had clearly noted the likelihood of favourable associated publicity.

In 1913, there was even a 'Mercantile Review' on the occasion of George V and Queen Mary visiting Liverpool on 11 July to open the newly-built Gladstone Graving Dock. Over 100 ships were assembled in the River Mersey, including Cunard's RMS *Mauretania* and *Lusitania* and the White Star Line's *Ceramic*. Cunard masters who were not members of the Royal Naval Reserve were given naval uniforms for the day and the ships were drawn up in lines, just like a naval review. The King inspected them and boarded *Mauretania* for a full tour of the ship.

1914, War

Europe had just about survived two Balkan Wars in 1912 and 1913 without coming to blows. But Austro-Hungary feared Serbian irredentism as a threat to its integrity; Germany was afraid of a rapidly industrialising Russia on its eastern flank and a revanchist France to its west, the latter two bound together by alliance and linked to Britain via the *Entente Cordiale*. Britain was apprehensive of Germany gaining possession of Channel and/or Atlantic ports. Tensions simmered.

It was summer. From 24 June 1914, a British naval squadron was visiting Kiel. Then on 28 June, when Gavrilo Princip, a Bosnian Serb, assassinated Archduke Franz Ferdinand, heir presumptive to the Austro-Hungarian throne, an unstoppable stone began to roll downhill.

In Britain, a Royal Fleet Review had been organised to take place on 20 July as part of a trial mobilisation of the fleet. Partly for reasons of cost saving the ships of the Royal Navy were now divided into three fleets – First, Second and Third – and three 'unified home commands' had been instituted on 31 July 1912. The Commander-in-Chiefs of these organisa-tions (Home, Channel, Atlantic) reported to the Commander-in-Chief, Home Fleets, Admiral Sir George Callaghan. The First Fleet was effectively the ships comprising the main battlefleet, soon to be known as the Grand Fleet, the modern battle line and its consorts. The Second Fleet was ships manned by nucleus crews whose complements could be rapidly brought up to strength by drafts from naval barracks and reservists, while the Third Fleet comprised ships laid up under Care and Maintenance Parties, older vessels considered of limited worth but necessary to 'keep up the numbers' for public consumption and as a reserve.

With the world situation as it was, the timing of the review was fortuitous, and directly as a result of the need for economy. It had been arranged in October the previous year as a substitute for the usual summer manoeuvres, a more expensive exercise.* Thus from 15 July, as well as calling up the reserves for the usual two weeks of training, the Admiralty conducted a full trial mobilisation of all three fleets and combined this with a Royal Review, another advertisement for the navy and its power. It would have the added effect, perhaps, of demonstrating Britain's strength to Germany and others in such trying times.

As in 1912, the Admiralty wished to show Members of Parliament what their money had paid for but on this occasion the Treasury won out and denied them the extra funding of £2,500 that this would require. 'My Lords see no sufficient justification for the expenditure this year'[17] the Secretary to the Treasury wrote to his opposite number at the Admiralty. The press did get to attend this time though. They were to be accommodated on RFA *Harlequin*, once more pressed into service, but were sternly enjoined that no food would be provided and they had to bring their own provisions.

Once more, the US Navy was invited and initially Captain William Freeland Fullam with the battleships *Missouri* and *Illinois* was tasked with this mission, as they were on a training voyage in European waters. But as the world slipped towards war the Americans decided that it would be injudicious to be present; the 'Great Neutral' did not wish to be seen to take sides, and on 16 July American Ambassador to London Walter Page wrote that Fullam was anchored at Gravesend and had 'disabled his engines and can't get them fixed in time'.[18]

The navy's ships had largely gathered by 17 July. The First Fleet was led by HMS *Iron Duke*, flying Callaghan's flag, the Second and Third Fleets by the pre-dreadnought *Lord Nelson*. *Iron Duke* (1912) carried ten 13.5in as main armament, supported by twelve 6in, and her Parsons turbines drove her at a top speed of 21.25kts; she was the very latest thing in battleship design afloat at the time.

Reservists had been called up for their training from far and wide. They expected to spend a busy fortnight training and on manoeuvres before going home. Their presence allowed the navy to turn out the largest number of ships ever brought together in one place for review. Over 200 vessels participated, including twenty-four dreadnoughts and battle-

* In order to obtain Cabinet approval for the 1914–15 Naval Estimates, First Lord Winston Churchill had agreed to a reduction of £1 million, which meant omitting three light cruisers and twelve torpedo boats and cutting out the summer manoeuvres in favour of a test mobilisation of the reserves.

cruisers, twenty-five pre-dreadnoughts and eighteen large cruisers. They
formed twelve lines stretching from the Isle of Wight to Portsmouth.
Between 70,000 and 80,000 Royal Navy personnel were present at
various times in the largest fleet ever assembled in British waters.
Midshipman V J Robinson of the cruiser HMS *Cumberland* thought 'I bet
they would make a foreigner think twice about attacking us'.[19]

But many of the ships were perhaps less than fit for fighting purposes.
HMS *Canopus* (1897) of the Third Fleet had been reactivated out of
reserve for the trial mobilisation. Her newly-arrived captain noted that

> from the point of view of fighting efficiency, the armament of the
> *Canopus* consisted of four 12in and ten 6in. Her speed obtained at full
> speed trial … was approximately 15 knots, but owing to age and wear
> 12 knots was found her best for any consecutive steaming. The crew
> were composed of some active service petty officers and ratings but
> mostly of Royal Naval Reserve, Fleet Reserve and pensioners. The offi-
> cers were principally of the Royal Navy, as heads of departments, and of
> the Royal Naval Reserve, as junior lieutenants, with a small number of
> Royal Naval Mids[hipmen].[20]

First Lord Winston Churchill was present in *Enchantress*, bibulously entertaining senior officers at lunch and dinner. And on the evening of 18 July
seventeen admirals dined with the King on board the royal yacht. After
dinner, Admiral Callaghan took the King around the fleet in his barge,
while Vice-Admiral Lewis Bayly performed a similar service for Prime
Minister Asquith.

Then at 2100 all ships exercised searchlight drill, the beams forming
arches and waving in unison, for the entertainment of the huge throngs of
spectators ashore. The King enjoyed it so much, he asked for the display to
be repeated as he wanted to see the lights from ashore and at sea.

On the 20th, George V sailed from harbour on board *Victoria and Albert*. As usual, royal salutes boomed out and once again he steamed down the long lines of ships as they lay at anchor, to receive the cheers of the sailors and gun salutes from the ships. Behind came *Alexandra* and *Enchantress*, the latter with Churchill aboard. There followed the second royal fly-past in history as Commander Samson, now Officer Commanding the Eastchurch (Mobile) Squadron of the Royal Naval Air Service (formed on the first of the month), led a flight of four planes from Calshot. In an effort to increase the popularity of flying in the navy, Samson and his pilots offered rides to any spectator who was interested. There were also airships overhead from Farnborough and Kingsnorth.

The royal yacht then steamed to the Nab Lightship and dropped anchor 'while squadron after squadron passed by and faded out to sea to their … areas for exercises and manoeuvres'.[21] Led by HMS *Lion* and three other battlecruisers, it took six hours for the fleet to pass the King's vessel. One of those saluting the King was the pre-dreadnought battleship HMS *Exmouth* (1901), which carried the poet and writer Rudyard Kipling as an invited guest.

There were many foreign dignities present. These included Prince Henry, brother of the Kaiser, who had called on his cousin at Buckingham

HMS *Lord Nelson*, flagship of the Second and Third Fleets at the 1914 Spithead Review. She carried a mixed armament of four 12in and ten 9.2in guns. *Lord Nelson* is shown here from the port side showing her 12in main and 9.2in secondary battery. *(US Naval History and Heritage Command NH 59907)*

Palace and been assured by King George that Britain would remain neutral in the event of a European conflict. Many saw such a conflict as inconceivable. 'With no other country in the world do we maintain such active and important commercial relations as with the British Empire' commented Arthur von Gwinner, a director of Deutsche Bank, just two years earlier.[22] Lieutenant Augustus Agar on HMS *Hibernia* later wrote 'I remember passing the Needles and catching sight of the kaiser's racing yacht *Meteor* which had just arrived to take part in the sailing races at Cowes … Little did we realise that within a few days the British navy would be at war on a global scale for the first time for over a hundred years.'[23]

The Austro-Hungarian ultimatum and mobilisation to humiliate and destroy Serbia, and the 'blank cheque' given to her by Germany, saw war clouds close over Europe. In Britain, it had been planned that the navy should return to peacetime status after the review and trials; on the weekend of 25–27 July the fleet was meant to disperse following the completion of the manoeuvres and reservists return to their homes and families. The First and Second Fleets were to assemble at Portland for a flag officers' conference and the Third Fleet to sail to their home ports to pay off their crews. But as the global situation worsened, and with Churchill away from his office and at the seaside building sandcastles with his wife and children, Admiral Prince Louis of Battenberg, now First Sea Lord, issued the instruction that 'no ship to leave harbour until further orders' to the C-in-C Home Fleets (the famous signal, 'Stand the fleet fast', for which Churchill later tried to take credit, despite having been out of communication at the time of its issue).

The Grand Fleet sped to the north to take station at Scapa Flow in the Orkneys. The 10th Cruiser Squadron took its patrol position at the top of the North Sea. The 6th Destroyer Flotilla blocked the English Channel; old battleships and cruisers guarded the Kent and Channel coasts from invasion and prepared to escort the BEF* to France. On 29 July the Admiralty issued the 'preparatory to war' signal. And on 4 August, Britain declared war on Germany, its quondam friend with whom it shared ties of royal kinship, whilst fighting alongside her traditional enemies, Russia and France.

In his diary for that fateful day, King George showed concern for his second son, Bertie, serving as a midshipman in HMS *Collingwood*; 'Please God that it may soon be over and that He will protect dear Bertie's life,'[24]† and to Admiral Jellicoe, now appointed C-in-C Grand Fleet, he signalled:

At this grave moment in our national history, I send to you and through you to the officers and men of the fleets of which you have assumed command, the assurance of my confidence that under your direction they will revive the old glories of the Royal Navy and prove once again the sure shield of Britain and her Empire in the hour of trial. George RI.[25]

* British Expeditionary Force, the first six infantry divisions and five cavalry brigades to be sent to France at the outbreak of war.

† Bertie was at Jutland on 31 May 1916. He rose from his sick bed to attend to his duties in a gun turret and was Mentioned in Despatches.

Chapter 13

Finance and Silver Jubilee, 1919–1935

B RITAIN WAS WRECKED by the 1914–18 conflict; she won the war but lost the peace. There was only one winner: the United States of America. For much of the war she had managed to sell to both sides, at great profit, and loaned substantial amounts in return for depleting her customers' gold reserves, especially Britain's.

The United States had long been a debtor country but emerged from the war as a net creditor to the tune of $6.4 billion. Before the war the centre of the world capital market was London and the Bank of England was the world's most important financial institution; after the conflict leadership shifted to New York, and the role of the Federal Reserve was enhanced.

At the end of the war, France owed America £550 million and Italy owed £300 million. As for Britain, she was indebted to the USA by £842 million. The war had bankrupted her, not least because she gave so much of her precious treasure to her allies to keep them in the conflict. There was no chance of getting back the £568 million which was owed by now communist Russia. France was indebted to Britain by £508 million which she was in no position to pay; Italy was also indebted to Britain by £467 million and Belgium £98 million. Some £20 million was due from Serbia and the countries that would become Yugoslavia and £79 million elsewhere. In total, Britain was owed £1,740 million, possibly £10 billion at today's values. As Winston Churchill put it, victory 'proved only less ruinous to the victor than to the vanquished'.[1] Moreover, the National Debt, which in 1914 had stood at £650 million, had swollen to £7,435 million by 1919.

This change in the international order of things, with America emerging as top dog, had cost the USA only 53,400 men killed in combat. But the war had cost Britain 723,000 men (921,000 including Empire dead) with another 1,662,625 wounded (2,090,212 including the

191

Empire).* The flower of her manhood had been destroyed on the Western Front and elsewhere.

The navy had not fought the second Trafalgar that the public (and many in the Royal Navy) expected of it; indeed, the big ships had spent much of their time lying to their anchors in Scapa Flow. But the Royal Navy had (at times only just) maintained command of the sea – Edward III's 'sovereignty of the seas' – and through this had enforced a strict blockade of war *materiel* and food on Germany and her associates. By the 'turnip winter' of 1916, this had reduced German households to starvation levels. When the German army's morale finally cracked on the Western Front in 1918 it was a direct corollary of the collapse of morale they saw in their families and friends at home through the navy's blockade as much as through anything else.†

To mark the end of the war, a committee chaired by Lord Curzon, acting Foreign Secretary, decided that 'with a view to the more wide-spread and general celebration of the Conclusion of Peace, it is desirable that Saturday, the Nineteenth day of July instant, should be observed as a Bank Holiday and as a Public Holiday throughout the United Kingdom'. It became known as 'Peace Day'. The army took the prime spot. On the morning of the 19th, thousands of spectators gathered in London, many having arrived overnight. They witnessed a spectacle never seen before, with nearly 15,000 troops taking part in a victory parade, led by Allied commanders Pershing (Head of the US Expeditionary Force), Foch (Allied Supreme Commander) and Haig (British Commander-in-Chief). Admiral Beatty and his bulldog led the naval contingent and the WRNS mascot was a little girl in uniform with medals. Bands played, and the central parks of London hosted performances and entertained the crowds. That morning the King issued his own personal message 'To these, the sick and wounded who cannot take part in the festival of victory, I send out greetings and bid them good cheer, assuring them that the wounds and scars so honourable in themselves, inspire in the hearts of their fellow countrymen the warmest feelings of gratitude and respect'. The end of the victory parade saw the unveiling of Sir Edwin Lutyens' wood and plaster Cenotaph in Whitehall.‡ All around the country there were other commemorations, street parties, festive sports and general exultation.§

The navy was determined not to be left out and a fleet review was organised at short notice for 17–21 July, not at Spithead but off the town of Southend and in the mouth of the Thames Estuary. Around fifty ships participated, representative of those which had battled for command of the seas for over four years. Some vessels were opened to the public, who were ferried across from Southend Pier.

There was a wide cross section of the Royal Navy present, from the repair ship HMS *Assistance* to the latest submarines and battleships. Moored immediately next to *Assistance* and just off Southend Pier, was a

* Figures taken from Ferguson, *The Pity of War*, table 32.

† See S R Dunn, *Blockade* (Barnsley: Seaforth Publishing, 2016); S R Dunn, *Southern Thunder* (Barnsley: Seaforth Publishing, 2019) for further detail.

‡ To be replaced by one of Portland Stone in 1920.

§ Not all thought this appropriate. Upon release from the military, soldiers found mass unemployment at home and little appreciation for their sacrifice. Luton Town Hall was burnt down on Peace Day by some veterans who shared those views.

ship type that had not existed before the war, the aircraft carrier HMS *Furious*. From 1912, and Lieutenant Gregory's bombing of the royal yacht, aircraft now played an important role in the fleet and had their own specialist ships to fly from. *Furious* had started life as one of 'Jackie' Fisher's more madcap ideas, the 'large light cruiser', fast, lightly armoured and armed with two massive 18in guns. She was modified and became an aircraft carrier while under construction. Her forward turret was removed and a flight deck was added in its place; aircraft had to manoeuvre around the superstructure to land. It was on *Furious* that Squadron Commander Edwin Dunning landed a Sopwith Pup on 2 August 1917, becoming the first person to land an aircraft on a moving ship. Later in the war, the rear turret was also removed and a second flight deck installed aft of the superstructure, although this proved unsatisfactory due to air turbulence.

Next to *Furious* was another ship which had been revolutionary at launch, the battleship and class name ship *Queen Elizabeth*; four of the class were present, the others being *Barham*, *Malaya* and *Valiant*. Armed with eight 15in guns and commissioned in 1915–16 they were well armed, well armoured, fast, and were described in the 1919 edition of *Jane's Fighting Ships* as the 'most successful type of capital ship yet designed',[2] and they were the first Royal Navy battleships to be planned as solely fuelled by oil. Previous classes had used fuel oil, which was still relatively scarce, as a supplement to coal. But Fisher had long been convinced that oil was the future, despite the fact the Britain had none. Oil was cleaner, needed fewer

Charles Dixon's painting shows the assembly of a fleet off Southend in July 1919 to celebrate the Armistice as they shape a south-westerly course, standing in from the sea to take up their berths. Towards the right of the picture is Admiral Madden's flagship *Queen Elizabeth*. In the foreground are three 'K'-class submarines, *K-2*, *K-5* and *K-6*. Astern of the flagship are ships of the 2nd Battle Squadron: *Erin*, *King George V*, *Conqueror*, *Orion*, *Thunderer* and *Monarch*. (© *Maritime Originals, www. maritimeoriginals.com & www.maritime prints.com*)

HMS *Furious*, 'large light cruiser' turned aircraft carrier. *(Library of Congress LC-B2- 4991-8)*

men to manage it and a ton of oil had 1.4 times the thermal value of a ton of coal. As the navy sought to adopt oil power, the search for sources of it became crucial to Fisher.

Fisher had retired in 1910 but had continued to press Churchill with his views on the benefits of oil and the need to secure its supply. Churchill was not slow to respond. On 17 June 1914 he introduced a bill into the House of Commons which allowed for the partial nationalisation of the Anglo-Persian oil company. The government would invest £2.2 million into the company in exchange for 51 per cent of its shares. After considerable debate, the bill passed by 254 votes to 18. Britain was in the oil business.

Next in line, lying off Shoeburyness, were three *Royal Sovereign*-class battleships *Revenge*, *Royal Oak* and *Royal Sovereign* herself, laid down under the 1914–15 Naval Estimates. Again, wholly oil fired and carrying eight 15in guns they were the latest battleships in the British fleet. The battle-cruisers *Lion* (Beatty's flagship at Jutland) and *Tiger* were in attendance, as was the 2nd Battle Squadron comprising the older battleships *Erin*, *King George V*, *Orion*, *Thunderer* and *Monarch*. *Erin*, with her ten 13.5in guns, had originally been ordered by the Ottoman navy as *Resadiye* but was seized in the dockyard at Churchill?s orders and taken up for the Royal Navy. This was one of the proximate causes of Turkey eventually joining the war on the German side.

At the other end of the scale there were five destroyer flotillas present, DFs 1–5. Such ships had been the workhorses of the fleet, in short supply and overworked throughout the war. Some of them were still <u>at</u> war, for throughout 1919, a total of eighty-five destroyers, from a variety of flotillas, were deployed fighting communist Russia in the Baltic Sea.*

There were four submarine flotillas on show, numbers 1–4. These included the disastrous 'K'-class (known to the tars as 'Kalamity-class'), oil fired, steam powered, with two funnels and with an 'as designed' armament of two 4in guns as well as eight torpedo tubes. *K-12* was there; she had survived the disastrous 'Battle of May Island' on the night of 31 January 1918 when two 'K'-class boats were sunk, and four others and a scout cruiser damaged. But overall, Royal Navy submarines, so neglected and ill-considered before the war, had sunk 54 enemy warships and 274 other vessels in all theatres of war. Finally, over the anchorage flew airships, hovering menacingly above the fleet.

The assembled ships were under the command of Admiral Sir Charles Madden, C-in-C Atlantic Fleet and a future First Sea Lord, with his flag in *Queen Elizabeth*. On Peace Day itself a 21-gun salute was fired by the fleet, which was illuminated at night, together with a firework display put on for the viewers from the shore. There were yacht races, pageants and even swimming competitions. But there was no king. George did not visit Southend or inspect the assembled ships, a slight which is difficult to understand at this distance. So this was not a Royal Fleet Review and technically does not belong in this book. But an event so important as the ending of the Great War cannot be overlooked and the navy's celebration of it deserves to be recorded and understood. As Corelli Barnett has written, 'the year 1919 appeared to witness the apogee of English supremacy at sea. Sixty-one battleships flew the white ensign, more that the French and United States fleets put together. There were 120 cruisers and light cruisers and 466 destroyers to escort the fleet and protect the tens of thousands of miles of sea routes that converged on Britain … England

* See Dunn S R, *Battle in the Baltic* (Barnsley: Seaforth Publishing, 2020).

The oil-fuelled *Queen Elizabeth*-class battleship HMS *Barham* (1915) at Scapa Flow in 1917, with other battleships and cruisers of the Grand Fleet. The triangular fabric pieces fitted to her masts and funnels were intended to hinder the obtaining of a clean 'cut' by coincidence-type rangefinders, by obscuring clear vertical lines. However, the Germans did not use coincidence but stereoscopic rangefinders, which would not find this problematic at all. *(U.S. Naval History and Heritage Command NH 50155)*

and the empire rested secure behind the overwhelming power of the Royal Navy.'[3] All this was about to be thrown away.

1922 to 1924, Austerity and Cuts

There were two Royal Fleet Reviews in the 1920s, in 1922 and 1924, with another for the Dominion premiers in 1923. All were held under the cloud of economic depression, unemployment and significant cuts to naval operating budgets.

Cost reductions had begun as soon as the war ended. Chancellor of the Exchequer Andrew Bonar Law wrote to First Lord of the Admiralty Eric Geddes on 23 November 1918 that he was 'most anxious that the cutting down of unnecessary war expenditure should take place at once'.[4] And the day before, Geddes himself had recommended to the Admiralty Board that 'as a purely temporary measure … a twenty per cent cut in manpower on the pre-war numbers'[5] should be adopted as a goal.

Naval expenditure fell from £344 million in 1918–19 to £154 million in 1919–20. By March 1922, following what became known as the 'Geddes Axe' of the year before (which had reduced the 1920–1 Naval Estimates to £76 million), First Lord of the Admiralty Leo Amery was able to report to the House of Commons that 'the policy of this country ever since the war has been one of drastic reduction in naval armaments. We had relegated to scrap or otherwise disposed of nearly two and a half million tons of warships. We had broken off all new construction of capital ships with the Armistice.'[6]

But he went on to express concern that other countries had not followed Britain's lead:

> Two other great Powers, rich in every resource, human and material, for the building up of sea power, had not only initiated but had carried far towards completion great programmes of new construction. On the slipways of America and Japan whole battle fleets were being hurried forward, incorporating in their armament and design the complete revolution wrought in naval construction by the lessons of the war, and calculated from the hour of their completion to reduce to obsolescence, if not, indeed, to utter powerlessness, the splendid navy which for four long years had maintained inviolate our mastery of the seas.[7]

Britain could not afford, it was said, to keep up with such building programmes.

Such apprehensions led to the Washington Naval Treaty of 1922, signed the month before Amery's speech by the governments of the United Kingdom, the United States, France, Italy, and Japan. It limited the construction of battleships, battlecruisers and aircraft carriers.

The key clauses of the treaty were that of a ten-year pause or 'holiday' in the construction of capital ships (battleships and battlecruisers), including the immediate suspension of all building of capital ships; the scrapping of existing or planned capital ships to give a 5 to 5 to 3 to 1.75 to 0.75 ratio of tonnage with respect to Britain, the United States, Japan, France and Italy respectively.

There were also limitations placed on size and armament of ships. Capital ships were to be no more than 35,000 tons standard displacement and guns of larger than 16in calibre were not permitted. Aircraft carriers were restricted to 27,000 tons and could carry no more than ten heavy guns, of a maximum calibre of 8in. All other warships were limited to a maximum displacement of 10,000 tons and a gun calibre of no bigger than 8in.

There was collateral damage too. Giving way to American pressure, Britain did not renew her naval treaty with Japan which was to expire in 1922. Prime Minister Lloyd George and his government felt that renewing the agreement carried the certainty of American ill will. Not renewing it would make Japan a potential enemy and meant the Royal Navy had to protect the Pacific once more. Furthermore, the acceptance of the ratios for fleet size placed future British freedom of action in a straitjacket by making it impossible to build against future naval threats which had nothing to do with the size of the American fleet.

Thus did Britain give away her birthright for a mess of pottage; the politicians wanted cost savings and as a result the country was denuded of her 'strong and sure shield'. It would no longer be possible for Britain to have adequate fleets in the North Sea, the Mediterranean and the Far East simultaneously.

It was against this background that, on 4 July 1922, King George boarded the royal train for Portsmouth and then sailed in *Victoria and Albert* to rendezvous with the fleet assembled off Portland. No longer was the elegant royal yacht *Alexandra* of the company; she too had fallen victim to austerity, being paid off at Portsmouth a month earlier for reasons of economy.[*]

Once again under the command of Admiral Madden, there were eight battleships, two battlecruisers and ten light cruisers of the Atlantic Fleet gathered for review and exercises. On the 5th, the King sailed around his ships, receiving the usual gunnery salutes and cheers from his ships, manned and decorated as they had been for centuries past. He then made visits to the flagship HMS *Queen Elizabeth* and Admiral Madden, *Barham* and finally the battlecruiser HMS *Hood* (Rear-Admiral Sir Walter Cowan), the 'Mighty Hood'. On each ship the King briefly met and chatted to a representative sample of officers and men. On *Hood*, he announced that the ship and *Repulse*, another battlecruiser, were to repre-

[*] She was sold to become the Norwegian luxury cruising yacht *Prins Olav*.

The 'Mighty Hood',
HMS *Hood*, the
navy's cock-of-the-
walk in the inter-
war years, depicted
in a painting by
Commander Eric
Erskine Campbell
Tufnell RN. *(U.S.
Naval History and
Heritage Command
NH 86392)*

sent the Royal Navy at Rio de Janeiro in September for the centennial
celebrations of Brazilian independence and International Exhibition,
which was to include an Olympic-style sports competition between the
attending navies. 'National prestige was at stake', wrote her biographer
'and neither expense nor effort was spared to equip the Battlecruiser
Squadron for the voyage or strip the fleet of her finest sportsmen.'[8]
Honour was satisfied when the British ships' contingent won the tournament, the result decided on the final day when Royal Navy boxers beat
their American opponents.

The *Hood* was an inter-war icon for the Royal Navy. Commissioned in
1920, over 46,000 tons* with eight 15in guns, launched by the widow of
Rear-Admiral Horace Hood[†] and named for one of his forebears, Samuel
Hood, she was the *non plus ultra* of Fisher's dreams, the ultimate 'greyhound
of the sea'. She became the face of the navy all over the world, following
several showing-the-flag exercises between the 1920s and 1930s, including
training exercises in the Mediterranean Sea and a circumnavigation of the
world with the Special Service Squadron in 1923 and 1924. But although
impressive, she also carried the fatal flaws built into the whole battlecruiser
concept. She was now intended to be a 'ship-of-the-line'; but she had the
limited armour of her predecessors. It would prove fatal when *Hood* met
the *Bismarck* in 1941.

But that lay in the future. On Thursday 6th, George boarded the flagship and the fleet put to sea for exercises, watched by the King from the
bridge of the battleship. As an ex-sailor he must have enjoyed it immensely.

* By way of
comparison, the
battleship *Barham*
was a little over
33,000 tons.

† Who died when
his battlecruiser
Invincible blew up at
Jutland.

HMS *Argus*, seen here in dazzle paint, the world's first through deck aircraft carrier. *(Library of Congress LC-B2-4991-9)*

There was a non-royal fleet review in 1923, staged for the Premiers of the eight Dominions (now including the Republic of Ireland) attending the Imperial Conference held between 1 October and 8 November.

This was a somewhat fractious affair in which the Dominions seized much more independence from Britain than they had previously enjoyed. In naval terms it is of interest only for the attempt by Britain to persuade India, New Zealand and Australia to fund the development of a major naval base at Singapore. The conference 'took note of the deep interest' shown by Australia in the project and more so in New Zealand Prime Minister William Massey's announcement of a contribution of £100,000 to its construction.[9]* The Dominions also wanted to have their cake and eat it to. They reaffirmed the need to provide 'adequate protection of their territories and trade of the counties comprising the British Empire' but expressed 'earnest desire for further limitation of armaments'.[10]

The premiers were taken to a fleet review in their honour on board HMS *Princess Margaret*, an ex-passenger liner, used as a minelayer during the war and again in 1919 during the Baltic campaign. First Lord of the Admiralty Leo Amery accompanied them and the ministers would have observed one novelty, HMS *Argus*, the world's first through-deck aircraft carrier. Commissioned in September 1918, she would serve until 1944. *Argus* was converted from an ocean liner, under construction when the war began, and was the first example of what became the standard arrangement for aircraft carriers, to wit, a full-length flight deck that allowed wheeled aircraft to take off and land.

1924, The Reserve Fleet

The Treaty of Versailles imposed draconian terms on Germany, largely at the insistence of France. She had no wish for a third German invasion and Premier Clemenceau's treaty aim was simple; reduce and maintain Germany in a state from which she could not be a further threat to France. This meant the levy of enormous reparations on Germany, payments which many believed were unsustainable. One of those who thought so was the economist John Maynard Keynes. In his seminal book *The*

* The base was never completed, for reasons of cost.

Economic Consequences of the Peace, published in December 1919, Keynes predicted that the stiff war reparations and harsh terms imposed on Germany by the treaty would lead to the financial collapse of the country, which in turn would have serious economic and political impact on Europe and the world.

Keynes was largely correct. In 1923 French and Belgian troops occupied the Ruhr, ostensibly as a result of Germany falling behind schedule in the reparation deliveries of timber and telegraph poles, but really because they wanted the coal mined there. Britain, always sceptical about the treaty's onerous terms, did not participate in the occupation, in the belief that an economic restoration of Germany was important to the revival of the European and world economies – a recovery which was very necessary for Britain's own economic fortunes. France, however, persisted in implementing the Treaty of Versailles by securing the Ruhr as a hedge against further German default.

The American Charles G Dawes, a banker and politician, was asked to head a committee to propose the actions that should be taken to resolve the impasse and its recommendations involved American banks injecting significant capital into German industry, which was then able to rebuild and expand. (It is worth noting that the capital inflow to German industry effectively transferred the burdens of Germany's war reparations from German government and industry to American bond investors. It also ensured that the future augmentation of German national power was paid for by the United States.) In July 1924, an Inter-Allied conference (aka the Inter-Allied Commission) was held in London to consider and ratify the Dawes Plan, chaired by British Prime Minister Ramsay MacDonald.*

MacDonald, leader of the Labour Party and the party's first prime minister, had come to power in the January at the head of a minority government. During the late war, he had opposed the voting of war credits and became unpopular, being accused of treason and cowardice. Even his golf club barred him from membership. He had also opposed the Treaty of Versailles, stating that 'we are beholding an act of madness unparalleled in history'.[11]

With British unemployment high and industry stagnating, the country was racked by a series of strikes, especially in the coal industry, which would culminate in the General Strike of 1926. In these circumstances, there was unlikely to be anything but further cost-cutting for a steadily shrinking navy.

July and August were also the months chosen by the Admiralty for a mobilisation of the Reserve Fleet and combined fleet exercises, the first since the end of the war. And such a gathering of ships and men would be an ideal time for a formal review, in front of the King and the Inter-Allied

* The Dawes Plan and the subsequent Young Plan re-adjusted and reduced German reparations until they were effectively abolished by the Lausanne conference of 1932.

Commission, a demonstration to the potentates from abroad, perhaps, that Britain still had teeth.

Ships began to gather; on 23 July Admiral Sir John de Robeck with his flag in *Queen Elizabeth* arrived with the Atlantic Fleet. The following day came the Reserve Fleet under Vice-Admiral the Honourable Victor Albert Stanley,* with his flag in the 13.5in-gunned battleship HMS *Centurion*. The Commander-in-Chief Portsmouth, Admiral Sir Sydney Fremantle, flew his flag ashore in *Victory* and exercised overall control of the review. King George V and his suite travelled to Portsmouth by royal train on the 25th.

The King arrived at 1930 to board *Victoria and Albert*; as the Royal Standard was raised, all ships in harbour fired a 21-gun salute, as did the garrison ashore. All vessels were dressed with masthead flags and that evening the fleet was illuminated at 2200, giving a 'searchlight display' for the benefit of the watchers on land and in the royal yacht.

The following day, the royal yacht sailed at 1400, preceded by the Trinity House vessel *Patricia* and followed by *Enchantress*. Accompanying George were the Prince of Wales and the Duke of Connaught. As the *Victoria and Albert* left harbour, she was escorted by three aircraft of the Fleet Air Arm[†] overhead. The ex-liner, ex-minelayer *Princess Margaret* had once again been pressed into service to convey the Admiralty's guests and she also carried the members of the Allied Commission. Other important visitors were embarked on *Harlequin* and the paddle steamer RFA *Nimble* (1906), built as SS *Roslin Castle* for her owner's Firth of Forth ferry service. On 25 March 1908 she had been purchased by the Admiralty for £15,500 for service as a tender based at Sheerness and was renamed.

The *New York Times* reported that 'the 194 warships … .were arrayed in ten four-mile lines which the royal yacht *Victoria and Albert*, … steamed by'.[12] whilst the *Argus* in far-distant Melbourne noted that 'the procession steamed for five miles among the warships which were gaily dressed. The crews cheered and the guns fired their salutes. Thousands of people lined the shores.'[13]

---

* Stanley was the second son of the fourteenth Earl of Derby, three times Prime Minister. Queen Victoria had been his godmother.

† The Royal Naval Air Service and the Royal Flying Corps had merged on 1 April 1918 to form the Royal Air Force, an organisation which proved antithetical to the navy. In April 1924 the Fleet Air Arm was formed, comprising those RAF units that normally embarked on aircraft carriers and other fighting ships.

Two aircraft carriers, *Hermes* (1919) and *Eagle** were present, the former the first ever aircraft carrier to be laid down as such from inception. One journalist described her as a 'craft strange to eyes inexpert … which seemed all deck and mighty little superstructure'.[14] Their aircraft performed manoeuvres over the fleet as the review progressed which was a 'picturesque feature' according to one newspaper.[15] All five *Queen Elizabeth*-class battleships were there, although about to transfer to the Mediterranean Fleet. But overall it was a sadly depleted fleet compared to its pre-war glory. There had been forty-nine battleships at the July 1914 review; now there were ten; 1924 offered one battlecruiser (*Tiger*, with her battle scrolls of Dogger Bank and Jutland adorning a turret) instead of four; nine cruisers instead of thirty-five. But war had changed the composition of the fleet. There were thirty-seven minesweepers present (a class which barely existed before the war), two aircraft carriers and numerous submarines. Amongst the latter was HMS *M-1*, the bastard offspring of the 'K'-class submarines (of which four were in attendance). She mounted a huge 12in gun in a turret; she sank a year later when this was ripped off in a collision with a merchant ship, with the loss of her entire crew.

It took the King 75 minutes to traverse the lineaments of his fleet. As the royal yacht first approached *Queen Elizabeth*, at the head of the columns, all ships fired a royal salute. There followed the usual reception on board the royal yacht and then the King's party returned to port, leaving by train at 1700. The following day the fleet dispersed for exercises.

* She had been ordered by Chile as the *Almirante Latorre*-class battle-ship *Almirante Cochrane* in 1912 and was laid down before the war. In early 1918 she was purchased by Britain for conversion to an aircraft carrier, which was only completed in 1924.

HMS *Hermes*, the world's first purpose-deigned aircraft carrier, pictured in 1931. *(US Naval History and Heritage Command NH 60474)*

But to some, the occasion had looked a little threadbare; 'the naval treaties had deprived Britannia of her trident and here was a gathering comprised for the most part of lines of small craft, destroyers, submarines and minesweepers', thought the naval author Eric Talbot-Booth.[16]

There would be no more reviews that decade, although in 1926 King George did present the Royal Navy with new Colours, and the country continued to drag itself through an economic mire.

1935, The Silver Jubilee of George V

A concatenation of circumstances reduced Britain to near catastrophic economic performance in the late 1920s and early 1930. The return to the Gold Standard in 1925, driven by Chancellor of the Exchequer Churchill, was a move of stupidity and national vanity. The General Strike of 1926 was an act of self-harm. Britain's finances were desperate; in 1928, 40 per cent of public expenditure was used to pay interest or repay capital on wartime debts.

The Wall Street Crash of 1929 and the US erection of tariff barriers led to industrial stagnation around the world. In an attempt to save money, Royal Navy wages were cut for many categories of sailors, leading to the Invergordon Mutiny of 1931.

Britain was forced off the Gold Standard that same year and by 1932 unemployment reached 3.4 million men, roughly one worker in six. By 1934 it was nearly 26 per cent. Prime ministers and governments came and went. There were four ministries between 1924 and 1935, the latter two being National Governments under MacDonald.

Expenditure on the British armed forces had been severely limited, not least by the 'Ten Year Rule', established in August 1919, which directed military and naval heads to plan on the basis that there would be peace for the next decade. Every year, the ten years were rolled forward and in 1928 Winston Churchill, as Chancellor of the Exchequer, successfully urged the Cabinet to make the rule self-perpetuating. This provided a fig leaf for politicians to ignore the pressing demands of aging equipment and declining military strength.

The Royal Navy had survived Churchill's five years at the Treasury (1924–9) shrunken in numbers, even in categories of vessels not limited by the Washington Treaty, and obsolescent in much of its *materiel*, especially in cruisers. The Geneva Naval Conference of 1927 failed to reach agreement on total tonnage of cruisers, destroyers and submarines; but the Royal Navy was soon threatened by further cutbacks. Indeed, Ramsay MacDonald's Labour government, which had come to power with the 1929 General Election, seemed actually eager to give away British power.

Britain's cruiser strength, so vital for the protection of empire and trade routes, had been capped at fifty ships by the Washington Treaty. This was a huge concern to the Naval Staff and in late 1929 First Sea Lord Sir Charles Madden was moved to ask the First Lord to inform the Prime Minister that 'our cruiser requirements are seventy … based on war experience and security. In view, however, of the apparently quiet conditions, we have agreed to limit the number of cruisers to fifty for the period of this agreement, viz, seven years.'[17] Privately Madden said that he had conceded because he only had forty-eight cruisers anyway.

Nevertheless, a second naval treaty was signed in 1930, the London Treaty for the Limitation and Reduction of Naval Armament. This restricted submarines to 2,000 tons displacement,* limited the number of permissible 'heavy cruisers' (defined as guns of 8in, Britain being permitted eighteen) and capped destroyer tonnage and gun size. It further stipulated that no new capital ships were to be laid down until 1937. And in 1932 this was followed by the Second Geneva Naval Conference which targeted further reductions but broke down, not least because Japan announced its intention to withdraw from the 1922 and 1930 Naval Treaties when they expired in 1936; indeed, planning started on the giant battleships of the *Yamato* class. Thus, 'the maiming of British seapower, begun by the Conservatives in Washington in 1922, continued by Churchill between 1924 and 1929, was completed by the Labour Government in [the Treaty of] London in 1930'.[18]

But serving officers were seriously concerned at the continued cuts. In a speech at the Lord Mayor of Bristol's Banquet in the summer of 1930, Captain Henry Harwood RN commented that 'should war unfortunately occur, it must be remembered that the food supply of these islands will not last three weeks unless the fighting services … are able to secure its safe passage. The cost of these services is the insurance premium which the three fighting services ask from the Empire.'[19] In April 1931 the First Sea Lord, Admiral Sir Frederick Field, averred in a report to the Committee of Imperial Defence that the Royal Navy had declined not only in relative strength compared to other Great Powers but 'owing to the operation of the ten-year-decision and the clamant need for economy, our absolute strength also has … been so diminished as to render the fleet incapable, in the event of war, of efficiently affording protection to our trade'.[20] Under this pressure, in 1932 the Cabinet abandoned the rule but instead issued a stricture that defence expenditure would not be increased owing to the economic impact of the Great Depression.

Meanwhile, in Germany Adolf Hitler became Chancellor in 1933 (*Führer* from 2 August 1934), the Weimar Republic having proved unequal to the task of meeting Germany's Versailles war debts and a worldwide economic depression. One of his first acts was to withdraw Germany from the League of Nations and from arms reduction conversations. The European political landscape became preoccupied with thoughts of German *revanche* and

* The British government had proposed the abolition of submarines, as they had in 1921, a move supported by the unlikely alliance of Ramsay MacDonald and King George V. The proposal floundered on the opposition of the French who regarded the submarine as their principal weapon at the time.

Britain signed a further naval treaty with Hitler's Germany in June 1935. The Anglo-German Naval Agreement regulated the size of the *Kriegsmarine* in relation to the Royal Navy by fixing a ratio whereby the total tonnage of the Kriegsmarine was to be 35 per cent of the total tonnage of the Royal Navy, and 45 per cent of submarines, on an ongoing basis.

By May 1935, George V had been on the throne of Britain for 25 years. Given the economic circumstances, and his own preference for a quiet life with his stamp collections and his shooting, the King did not favour a large celebration of the event. But the National Government of Ramsay MacDonald, although in its dying days,* urged a Silver Jubilee together with a naval review. If inspired by respect, their position also owed something to political opportunism; a display of patriotic enthusiasm would play well ahead of the forthcoming general election and may serve to warn the bellicose dictators, Hitler and Mussolini, that they should beware of provoking Britain and her navy.

Thus it was that on 6 May there was a Silver Jubilee thanksgiving service at St Paul's Cathedral. Amongst the attendees was Neville Chamberlain, Chancellor of the Exchequer, one of 4,406 invited worshippers. He looked across at the foreign ambassadors and thought to himself 'this'll show 'em'.[21] On the 8th there was a further ceremony at St James Palace, devoted to the Empire overseas, and the following day both Houses of Parliament assembled in Westminster Hall where the Speaker of the House of Commons Edward Algernon Fitzroy addressed the King.

The Royal Fleet Review was planned for 16 and 17 July, and was to be associated with a call up of the reserves and combined manoeuvres. Cost issues immediately arose. The Admiralty wished to retain the reserves for twelve days' service on the Reserve Fleet ships at standard notice. The extra cost of so-doing would be £17,000 but it was suggested that 'the calling up … should be on a voluntary basis'. The economic situation was such that 'in the present state of the labour market it is not anticipated that there will be any difficulty in obtaining the 5,575 reservists required and it is proposed that the financial estimates should be based on this number called up'.[22] The cost of fuel was another issue for debate. Nonetheless, on 8 July, reservists joined their ships and two days later went to sea for exercises. On the 11th they began to congregate at Spithead, joined on the 13th by elements of the Home and Mediterranean Fleet.

From the Mediterranean came the battleships *Queen Elizabeth* (flagship of Admiral Sir William Fisher), *Royal Sovereign*, *Resolution*, *Revenge* and *Ramillies*, and from the Home Fleet came the battlecruisers *Hood* and *Renown*, with the battleships *Barham*, *Valiant* and the unusual *Nelson* and *Rodney* (with the flag of Admiral the Earl of Cork and Orrery).

* MacDonald would resign owing to ill-health in June and Stanley Baldwin took up the premiership.

These latter two ships were the progeny of the 1922 Washington Naval Treaty. They had been designed to fit within the 35,000-ton limit and were unique in British battleship construction, being the only ships to carry a main armament of 16in guns, and the only ones to have all the main armament forward of the superstructure, in three triple turrets. Immediately after the war, the Admiralty drew up plans for massive, heavily armoured battlecruisers and battleships, far larger and more powerful than all previous vessels. The 'G3'-class battlecruisers would carry 16in guns, and the proposed 'N3'-class battleships would carry nine 18in guns, making them the most powerful vessels afloat. These ambitions were abruptly terminated by the Washington Treaty and the battlecruisers were cancelled, while the battleships became the *Nelson* class, whose sharply cut-off shape, harking back to the old *Victoria*-class such as *Sans Pareil* (1887, *vide supra*), led to them being known as 'Cherry Trees' because they had been cut down by Washington.

By 16 July, 157 warships were assembled, joined by 60 merchant vessels and hundreds of smaller craft. No foreign ships had been invited. On the surface it was an impressive show of strength. The *Daily Telegraph* called it 'a royal pageant of surpassing grandeur',[23] whilst the *Times* waxed lyrical about a navy which had 'charted the seas of the world, rid them of pirates, established trade routes and preserved Britain from invasion for 800 years'.[24] But more perceptive viewers expressed the real truth. The quondam spy and now journalist Hector C Bywater noted that the fleet was 'sadly deficient in the heavier elements of fighting power typified by big guns and armour and … contains an unduly large proportion of antique material which is no longer really effective'.[25] As the historian Stephen Roskill wrote, 'the assemblage of 160 warships looked impressive and included two aircraft carriers but to the knowledgeable it was painfully obvious that the proportion of new ships present was small and that few of

The 6in cruiser HMS *Leander*, lead ship of a class of four, the most modern ships at the 1935 review and dressed overall.
(© National Maritime Museum N31788)

the older ones (many of which were of First World War vintage) had been
fully modernised. In truth the shop window was mainly filled with obsolescent goods.'[26] Navalist Eric Talbot-Booth observed that although there
were 'close to 150 ships certainly [present] but the Reserve Fleet had to be
brought out and, more serious still, the Mediterranean had to be denuded
of its ships in order to provide anything to review'.[27] In truth, thanks to the
Washington Naval Treaty, the RN now possessed only fifteen capital ships,
of which almost all were in need of serious modernisation.

Additionally, decades of lack of investment had taken their toll and
among the few recent ships on show were four *Leander*-class light cruisers,
6in guns, 7,000 tons and completed the previous year. Even the old and
iconic HMS *Iron Duke* was called up, Jellicoe's flagship at Jutland. She had
been recommissioned as a gunnery training ship in 1929 and in November
1931, under the terms of the London Naval Treaty, had been disarmed and
continued in her role unarmed. Vessels of the Merchant Navy and the
fishing fleet, formally invited for the first time at the specific request of the
king, filled out the ranks and were assigned a more active role.

The review followed the traditional pattern. The King arrived by train,
alighting at Cosham and continuing his journey by motor car; with him
were three of his sons, the Prince of Wales, the Duke of York and the Duke
of Kent. On the 15th he received all flag officers, some merchant masters
and a selection of fishing skippers who had served in the 1914–18 war. The
following day, with a vast crowd in attendance, the review commenced
with a reception on board the royal yacht for the Board of Admiralty and
flag officers. At 1600 *Victoria and Albert* entered the lines; all ships were
dressed overall with their companies manning ship and each gave three
cheers as the royal yacht passed. At 1800, the review area was reopened for
the public in their pleasure boats and at 2200 the fleet was illuminated.

The light display reached new levels of sophistication; 'from 2200 until
midnight the whole fleet was illuminated and such a sight has never been
witnessed before, not even in the days of the Crystal Palace fireworks. Ship
after ship broke out into a glory of coloured lights and decorative
schemes.'[28] There were imperial crowns with the colours of the jewels
correctly formed, crests of ships, and sudden blackouts followed by thousands of rockets. Bluejackets manned ship and held aloft red flares and at
the conclusions of the show, a single searchlight on *Victoria and Albert* lit
up the Royal Standard.

Cadet Dudley Davenport was serving on *Iron Duke* and recalled the
scenes in his diary.

Turned out at 0545 and scrubbed focsle … after breakfast we gave all
the brightwork a final polish and generally cleaned up … after lunch we
fell in on deck … All the ships with saluting guns fired a royal salute

The Cunard ship RMS *Berengaria* represented the line at the 1935 review. Built as *Imperator* for the Hamburg-Amerika Line, she made her maiden voyage from Cuxhaven to New York on 20 June 1913. From August 1914, she was in Hamburg harbour for the duration of the war. In May 1919 she was seized by US Navy as a troop transport and in February 1920 handed over to the Shipping Controller in London, as reparation for the sinking of the *Lusitania*, and sold to the Cunard Line where she became the company's flagship. *(Author's collection)*

of twenty-one guns [but] the noise was not as bad as we were led to expect … we had to fall in for manning ship, my position on Y-turret grid on the quarter deck was an excellent one as we could see the yacht approaching … as the V&A approached the band played *God Save the King* and the guard presented arms in the royal salute. When the king was halfway past, we gave three cheers. You could just see the king on the bridge, saluting. After supper we watched the illuminations … after half hour all the lights were turned off and red flares were lit on deck, each held by a sailor at the guardrail. These did not look very good except for the first few seconds … the ships remained illuminated for the rest of the time until midnight.[29]

Rear-Admiral Andrew Browne Cunningham was at the review in the cruiser *Coventry*. He recalled that 'the concentration, which was eleven heavy ships and eighteen cruisers, was imposing enough, but nothing to compare with the review in 1914'. But he was impressed by a fly-past of the Fleet Air Arm as *Victoria and Albert* moored to her buoy; 'a hundred aircraft … roared overhead in formation and came dipping down in salute in a long glide'.[30]

Official guests were accommodated on a variety of vessels, including the fifteen passenger liners which were present; Rudyard Kipling and his wife watched the review from the Cunarder RMS *Berengaria** with Sir Percy Bates, the Chairman of Cunard, an old friend. Amongst Kipling's fellow passengers were scions of the Wills tobacco empire, Doxford marine engines, Lady Brocklebank (shipping), five members of Canada's Eaton family (owners of the country's largest department store chain), Mrs

* Previously the German liner *Imperator* (1912), she had been handed over to Cunard as part of the war reparations.

Oswald Mosely and three teenage daughters of John Brooke Molesworth Parnell, 6th Baron Congleton – the Hon Mary, aged 16, the Hon Jean, 13 and the Hon Shelia, just 11. Cunard also offered a three-day cruise to enjoy the festive experience in RMS *Lancastria*. Lord Jellicoe was on board a Mediterranean Fleet ship to observe in order to see both review and exercises. And Sir Maurice Hankey, Cabinet Secretary, was in the new *Leander*-class cruiser HMS *Neptune*.

Other important Admiralty guests were accommodated aboard the hospital ship RFA *Maine*;[*] but their experience was marred by a complete breakdown in the catering arrangements which produced outraged protests in Parliament and an apology from the First Lord of the Admiralty Bolton Eyres-Monsell.

No foreign warships had been invited but the German Norddeutscher Lloyd liner SS *Columbus* was present, crowded with sightseers who included, no doubt, a sprinkling of members of the German and Italian intelligence services.

For the first time the wider world was able to share in the festivities too, for the national broadcasting service, the BBC, recorded eyewitness accounts of the scene in real time. A series of broadcasts were given by two naval officers located in the foretop of HMS *Royal Sovereign*. From this lofty perch, a short-wave portable radiotelephony transmitter, installed in the battleship for the purpose, was used to relay the commentary to a receiver at Southsea Castle. The signals were then transmitted by land-line to Broadcasting House, and subsequently distributed in the ordinary manner via the normal extant radio stations. In this way, the scene as the King took the royal salute, steaming up and down the lines of warships, and enhanced by four microphones used to pick up the gun salutes and cheers, were described to home and empire, as were the illuminations at night.

In the evening, all flag officers dined with the King. And the following day, at 0800, the royal yacht led the fleet out of harbour for exercises. It was the last time the he would be at sea with his beloved navy. In his final message to his sailors, George V stated that 'I shall not easily forget the impressive spectacle of the review in which I am pleased to think the Merchant Navy have, for the first time, taken part, while the success with which the fleet exercises have been carried out today bears witness to the traditional efficiency of the Royal Navy.'[31]

George V died less than a year later, on 20 January 1936.[†] A dull, decent man, although a domestic tyrant, who would have been happy as a career sailor, he had presided over seven Royal Fleet Reviews and seen the navy change from the largest and best in the world to something rather less.

[*] Formerly the SS *Panama* (1902), purchased by the navy in 1920.

[†] Two days after the death of the great voice of his empire, Rudyard Kipling.

Chapter 14

German *Revanche,*
1936–1944

O N THE DEATH OF GEORGE V, the throne passed to his eldest son, Edward Albert Christian George Andrew Patrick David, who took the title King Edward VIII. Edward was already known for a series of public affairs with unsuitable or married women through the 1920s. At the time of his accession, he was having an affair with a twice-married and once-divorced American woman, Wallis Simpson. By October 1936, it became clear to the Establishment (although not to the public owing to voluntary press silence) that Edward wanted to marry Mrs Simpson. This would cause a constitutional crisis, as remarriage after divorce was opposed by the Church of England of which the King was the titular head.

Nonetheless, Edward's coronation had been set for 12 May 1937 and the usual commemorative paraphernalia had been produced or was in production. No fleet review date had yet been set to celebrate the event and it is thought that the new king was not very keen on one anyway. But between 11 and 13 November 1936, Edward visited the fleet off Portland and it would appear that the occasion was intended to be a full formal fleet review with the usual traditions.

Edward arrived at Weymouth by train. The country had suffered several days of heavy rain and many streets around the station and in the town were flooded. He was greeted by Sir Samuel Hoare, First Lord of the Admiralty, and Admiral Sir Ernle Chatfield,* First Sea Lord, and forty warships of the Home Fleet were arrayed in the bay to greet the monarch.

Wind and rain continued to sweep the area and a howling gale was blowing; as a result, it was decided not to dress the ships all over but that they should wear masthead flags only. Similarly, it was deemed too boisterous for sailors to man ship. The planned sailing down the line of ships in the C-in-C's barge was also scratched owing to the conditions. Instead, Edward visited a number of ships, starting with the flagship *Nelson*, where he was piped aboard in the manner of an admiral by bosuns and quarter-

* Beatty's flag captain at Jutland.

masters. Apart from *Nelson*, in the morning the King reviewed the battle-ship *Royal Oak*, the cruisers *Orion* and *Cairo* and the carrier *Courageous*, where 1,000 men were paraded on deck for inspection in a very heavy rain squall. After lunch aboard the flagship, he continued with the battle-ship *Royal Sovereign*, new cruisers *Leander* and *Neptune*, the net laying vessel *Guardian* and the new minelaying submarine *Narwhal* as well as the shore base, HMS *Osprey*. Here Edward 'inspected the anti-submarine school and the latest secret weapons for locating underwater craft'.[1]

Edward hosted a dinner on board *Victoria and Albert* for flag officers and captains in the early evening before going to an all-ranks ship's smoking concert on board *Courageous*. Here he decided to break from the programme and pushed his way through the throng of sailors and 'started community singing to the accompaniment of a seaman's mouth organ'. Returning to the platform Edward 'made an impromptu speech which brought the house down'.[2] Next, and showing commendable energy, the King attended an 'at home' for officers of the fleet on board *Nelson* before returning to the royal yacht to sleep, the only time he did so as king.

Three days later, Edward invited Prime Minister Stanley Baldwin to Buckingham Palace and expressed his desire to marry Mrs Simpson when she obtained a divorce. Baldwin informed him that his subjects would deem the marriage morally unacceptable and that he could not support it; and on 10 December, Edward VIII signed the instruments of abdication from the throne. He had been king for just 326 days – and seen one fleet review.

He left England for exile two days later; *Victoria and Albert* was laid up for the winter so the Royal Navy provided one last service; Edward travelled to the Continent on the destroyer HMS *Fury* from the Home Fleet. Her captain, Cecil Howe, had to hurriedly borrow linen, crockery and glasses from the royal yacht and smuggled on board a surgeon commander in case the ex-king should need medical attention while afloat.

As Edward departed, his brother was proclaimed king. All Royal Navy ships were ordered to fire a royal salute at 1500* and ships were to be dressed with masthead flags

1937, The Coronation of an Unexpected King

Like his father, Albert Frederick Arthur George had not been intended for kingship as he was the second son. He was reluctantly thrust into the lime-light by his brother's abdication. Taking the regnal name George VI, his formal coronation was held on the day originally intended for his brother's enthronement, 12 May 1937. It was followed eight days later by a Royal Fleet Review at Spithead.

The political situation in Europe cast a cloud over both proceedings. In 1933, Germany had withdrawn from the League of Nations and the World Disarmament Conference. Two years later Hitler announced that, ignoring

* Excepting those vessels in Spanish waters, where gunfire might have been taken amiss, as Spain was ravaged by civil war.

the Treaty of Versailles, the German army would expand to 600,000 men, six times the permitted number. This would be accompanied by the development of an air force and an increase in size of the navy; such increases were also against the terms of the treaty.

Britain, France, Italy, and the League of Nations condemned these violations of Versailles, but did nothing to prevent them. Then followed the Anglo-German Naval Agreement of 18 June (*vide supra* Chapter 13). The League of Nations was not consulted by either country over this treaty, giving further emphasis to its impotence. Meanwhile, also in June 1935, Italy invaded Abyssinia and became another violator of the post-war peace agreements.

In March 1936, Germany had reoccupied the demilitarised zone in the Rhineland, again in spite of Versailles. Hitler also gave support to General Franco's Nationalists during the Spanish Civil War. And in August 1936, in response to a growing economic crisis caused by his rearmament efforts, Hitler privately ordered Göring to prepare and implement a Four-Year Plan to equip Germany for war by 1940. It was clear to all that a German revanche was fast approaching.

The royal yacht photographed from HMS *London* as she passed down the lines, 20 May 1937. *London*'s original 4in QF gun single mounts can be seen in the foreground as can sailors manning ship; they are holding the hand of the man next to them, as was traditional. *(Alamy EW5NDF)*

The 1916 battlecruiser HMS *Repulse*, dressed overall for the 1937 Coronation Review. She had just returned from a refit. (© *National Maritime Museum N31984)*

In December 1936, the 1922 and 1930 Naval Treaties were allowed to lapse and the major powers moved towards rearmament. In Britain this effectively started with the 1936/37 Naval Estimates as the government turned to a policy of deterrent rearmament in parallel with, from 1937, appeasement to try to delay the evil day.

Thus on 20 May 1937, the might of the Royal Navy was turned out to greet its new monarch. The Reserve Fleet had been activated for exercises between 15 and 18 May and elements of the Home* and Mediterranean Fleets joined them in the Solent. It was a patent signal to potential aggressors. There were 145 British and Empire ships assembled that day; eighty-six of them had been present at the Silver Jubilee two years earlier. But there were new ships too. The 'Town'-class cruisers *Southampton* and *Newcastle*, commissioned that year, were on display. With their twelve 6in guns in four triple turrets and eight 4in quickfirers, they were London Treaty light cruisers with a standard displacement just under 10,000 tons. Lightly armoured, they were a new class of 'eggshells armed with hammers'.[†] There were some new submarines too and representatives of the latest 'G', 'H' and 'I'-class destroyers. The battlecruiser HMS *Repulse* (1916) was also present, just out of an extensive three-year refit.

The 'County'-class heavy cruiser *London* (1927), eight 8in guns and again just under 10,000 tons displacement, a Washington Treaty cruiser, was on show, flying the flag of Vice-Admiral Charles Kennedy-Purvis, commanding the 1st Cruiser Squadron in the Mediterranean and a future Deputy First Sea Lord. The difficulty of packing her armament into such a displacement resulted in the class being poorly protected with the additional burden of a high silhouette. Admiral Roger Roland Charles Backhouse, commanding the Home Fleet and to be appointed First Sea Lord the following year, flew his flag in the Treaty battleship HMS *Nelson*, sister-ship to *Rodney*. On the day of the review, the King appointed him a Knight Grand Cross of the Royal Victorian Order. Another future First

* The Home Fleet paid a brief visit to the Thames on passage for a public display.

† As battlecruisers had once been dubbed.

Overleaf: HMS *Nelson*, flagship at the 1937 review. Anchored in the background are two *Queen Elizabeth*-class battleships and two cruisers of the *London* class. (*Author's collection*)

The treaty-busting German 'pocket battleship' *Admiral Graf Spee. (US Naval History and Heritage Command NH 81110)*

* Under the Treaty of Versailles, Germany was to retain six battleships of the *Deutschland* or *Lothringen* type, six light cruisers, twelve destroyers and twelve torpedo boats. No submarines were to be included. She was not to build ships beyond the following displacements; armoured ships, 10,000 tons; light cruisers, 6,000 tons; destroyers, 800 tons; and torpedo boats, 200 tons.

Sea Lord, Admiral Sir Dudley Pound, in charge of the Mediterranean Fleet, wore his flag in *Queen Elizabeth*. Yet again, the old HMS *Iron Duke*, battleship turned training ship, was in the lines, immediately in front of the 'Mighty *Hood*'.

Unlike the Silver Jubilee of 1935, foreign warships had been invited and eighteen attended. Argentina, Cuba, Denmark, Estonia, Finland, France, Germany, Greece, Japan, Netherlands, Portugal, Poland, Romania, Spain, Sweden, Turkey, the USA and the USSR were all represented. Germany sent the heavy cruiser *Admiral Graf Spee* (1934), a *Deutschland*-class *Panzerschiff* (armoured ship), nicknamed a 'pocket battleship' and launched in 1934. Her construction showed how Germany had ignored the confines of the Versailles Treaty* (she was not a signatory to the Washington and London treaties), in contrast to the latest British cruisers which kept to the 1922 and 1930 agreed limitations. With a design displacement of just under 15,000 tons (against a Treaty limit of 10,000 tons) she mounted six 11in guns in two triple turrets. Unusually, she had eight diesel engines which drove her at 28.5kts. She could outshoot any cruiser in the Royal Navy's inventory.

France despatched *Dunkerque*, commissioned only at the beginning of the month. She carried eight 13in guns, in two quadruple turrets mounted, like HMS *Nelson* and *Rodney*'s three, forward of the superstructure. Her design, as with theirs, was constrained by Washington Treaty limits. Argentina was represented by *Moreno*, launched in 1911 and completed four years later. She was American-built with the typical

The 1911 Argentinian 12in battleship *Moreno*, one of the foreign visitors paying tribute to the new king, a 'strange vestigial sea monster'.
(© National Maritime Museum N32221)

American lattice foremast and mounted twelve 12in guns with a 6in secondary battery. *Moreno*'s presence at the review moved the *New York Times'* reporter Hanson Baldwin to describe her as a 'a strange vestigial sea monster in this company of more modern fighting ships'.[3]

The Americans also sent an older ship, albeit modernised, the USS *New York* (1912) which had served with the Grand Fleet during the latter part of the last war as part of Battleship Division Nine, commanded by Rear-Admiral Hugh Rodman. Now retired, Rodman came too as the senior USN representative. He and his vessel were given pride of place at the head of the line of foreign warships and parallel to the flagships of the Home and Mediterranean fleets.

Each of the three Royal Navy Fleets assembled incorporated aircraft

The French battle-ship *Dunkerque* represented her country at the 1937 Coronation Review. *(Author's collection)*

carriers. *Courageous* and *Furious*, both once Fisher's 'large light cruisers', were with the Home Fleet; Another such, *Glorious*,* came from the Mediterranean; and the Reserve Fleet sported the outdated *Pegasus*, a seaplane carrier of 1913 vintage originally named *Ark Royal*, and *Hermes*.

Watching the spectacle from the head of the eight columns of warships were six charted vessels carrying government guests and members of the Imperial Conference then sitting in London. *SS Strathmore*, *Vandyck*, *Laurentic*, *Cameronia*, *Portsdown* and *Whippingham*. SS *Vandyck* carried MPs and about twenty admirals, including Sir Walter Cowan of Baltic fame and Andrew Browne Cunningham, another future First Sea Lord. Ex-Prime Minister Ramsay MacDonald and W L Mackenzie King, Prime Minister of Canada, were accommodated on *Enchantress*. All these ships were to follow the royal yacht through the lines of ships.

A total of twenty-four liners, floating grandstands to all intents, were on hand together with dozens of private yachts and other vessels, moored down the Isle of Wight side of the assembled company. These included the Duke of Westminster's *Flying Cloud* which was one of the largest private yachts in the world; but as befitted one of the richest men in the country, she obtained a prime position at the very end of column D, exactly where the royal yacht would turn at the western extremity of its voyage.

HMS *Rodney* at the 1937 fleet review. The ships in the background are from the Mediterranean Fleet. She was sister-ship to the Home Fleet flagship *Nelson* and the location of Commander Woodrooffe's famous broadcast.
(© *Imperial War Museum* MH5)

HMS *Barham*, *Ramillies* and the French *Dunkerque* at the 1937 review. (*Author's collection*)

The actual formality of the review took the traditional course. In the morning, George received the two admirals commanding the fleets, together with the C-in-C Portsmouth, Admiral William Wordsworth Fisher,* on board *Victoria and Albert*. After lunch, the King, accompanied by his wife and his two daughters and with the Duke and Duchess of Kent in company, entered the lines of the fleet at 1530. As the royal yacht approached, and at a signal from her, the royal salute was fired. Every ship was manned and 'three cheers' rang out in succession as *Victoria and Albert* passed through the lines. At 1710 she moored at the eastern head of the columns and there was a fly-past by the Fleet Air Arm. Dinner on board the royal yacht followed and at 2200 the fleet was illuminated.

This act provoked great hilarity from those fortunate enough to be following the review on BBC radio. The commentator was retired Lieutenant-Commander Tommy Woodrooffe. He had been granted the privilege of broadcasting the event from his old ship, HMS *Rodney*. The emotion of reunion had clearly proved too stimulating for him and he had imbibed freely in the wardroom. As the fleet was illuminated, he incoherently and repeatedly shouted 'the fleet's lit up'; as was he! Slurring deeply, he continued 'We've forgotten the whole Royal Review … we've forgotten the Royal Review … the whole thing is lit up by fairy lamps. It's fantastic, it isn't the fleet at all. It's just … it's fairyland, the whole fleet is in fairyland.' At this point he is heard telling someone to shut up. He then rambled on until the lights were switched off for a moment, at which

* Known as 'the Great Agrippa' on account of his height, Fisher died in office a month later.

he ejaculated 'It's gone! It's gone! There's no fleet! It's, eh, it's disappeared! No magician who ever could have waved his wand could have waved it with more acumen than he has now at the present moment. The fleet's gone. It's disappeared.' Finally, he breathlessly intoned 'There's nothing between us and heaven. There's nothing at all.' After four minutes of this, a BBC minion managed to reach the transmitting equipment and the broadcast abruptly ended.

Next day the King visited four of the capital ships present and at 1400 the royal yacht returned to harbour and the fleet dispersed. The third Coronation Review in British history had concluded.

1938 and 1939, The Road to War

The period immediately preceding the Second World War included two

HMS *Courageous* at the 1937 fleet review. She was originally a 'large light cruiser' mounting four 15in guns. The Washington naval treaty allowed for the conversion of battleships to carriers, which was actioned in 1924. *(© Imperial War Museum MH3)*

Royal Fleet Reviews, both of which in retrospect seem rather hurried affairs, without the usual pomp and ceremony.

In March 1938, Germany annexed Austria. Many people believed that Czechoslovakia would be next. And on 2 May 1938, Hitler embarked on a six-day Italian state visit to Rome, Naples, and Florence in a display of Axis solidarity. The carefully staged visit featured a parade by the Italian armed forces, a review of the Italian navy (the world's fifth largest) and a horse-drawn carriage ride into the centre of Rome. Bonds of common interest between Mussolini and Hitler were cemented and Germany drew up a major naval rearmament programme, the 'Z Plan', to bring the navy closer to equality with Britain by the mid-1940s.

Against this background of simmering trouble and gathering menace in Europe, King George VI and Queen Elizabeth made their first official visit

abroad, to France. It was explicitly designed to rekindle the relationship between France and Britain. Playing on the theme of the Great War, and the threats now once again gathering around France, the visit started with the unveiling of the Britannia monument at Boulogne on 19 July and ended with the inauguration of the Australian War Memorial at Villers-Bretonneux on the Somme on 22 July. There were also receptions and galas, a garden party, a visit to the Louvre and a huge military review at Versailles. The not-so-hidden messages of this royal progress were that Britain and France were again united and still had military capability (although Prime Minister Chamberlain had already made it clear in the House of Commons that he was not prepared to risk an unwinnable war to preserve France's ally, Czechoslovakia).

Before George had departed for France, he helped showcase Britain's naval capabilities to the world in a Royal Naval Review off Weymouth and Portland. During 20 and 22 June, King George and the Duke of Kent (George's younger brother) stayed aboard *Victoria and Albert* and George reviewed the fleet and accompanied it for some of the planned fleet exercises. There was another Grand Concert on board *Courageous* and the King boarded *Nelson* to view the manoeuvres from the bridge of the battleship.

The Admiralty issued a press release on the 21st which advanced the likely fiction that 'the king took command of eighty ships of the Home Fleet today, and out in the English Channel from the bridge of the 33,500 ton flagship *Nelson*, saw the latest fighting and manoeuvring principles put into practise'. They added a picture of HMS *Sheffield* of the 2nd Cruiser Squadron firing her anti-aircraft guns against a DH-82 'Queen Bee' (a radio-controlled Tiger Moth variant) target.[4]

After the King had departed, the fleet embarked on a series of exercises in the Channel which, between 5 and 10 July, replicated a surprise attack and attempted landing in 'hostile territory'. Units of the Home Fleet played the attacker and the defenders were drawn from the commands at Portsmouth and Plymouth. Troops from the Southern Command also participated. Invasion was on some naval minds.

Against this background, the Cabinet met in July and discussed the replacement of the 40-year-old *Victoria and Albert*. With over three million men unemployed, and growing threat of war on the continent, the timing seems strange; but the royal yacht, after much loyal service, was in poor shape. Her eighteen Belleville boilers were obsolescent and could no longer hold much pressure, which had of necessity been reduced with a concomitant impact on speed. The decision was taken to spend £900,000 on a replacement vessel. The King had made it clear that whilst he approved of the decision, he did not want to press it if there was a risk of it interfering with rearmament.

Tension in Europe continued to rise. Hitler massed German troops on the Czechoslovak border. On 27 September, First Sea Lord Admiral Sir Roger Backhouse received Chamberlain's assent to mobilise the fleet (both forgot to inform First Lord Duff Cooper). Chamberlain and French Premier Daladier met the German chancellor the following day. And on 29 September, Germany, Great Britain, France and Italy signed the so-called 'Munich Agreement'. It allowed the cession to Germany of the 'Sudeten German territory' of Czechoslovakia.* Hitler had announced that the Sudetenland was his last territorial claim in Europe and the choice to Britain and France had seemed to be between war and appeasement. In March 1939, Hitler took the rest of the country anyway.

In March 1939, Britain and France gave guarantees of support to Poland if and when her independence was threatened. Britain doubled the size of the Territorial Army and created a Ministry of Supply to expedite the provision of equipment to the armed forces. The Italian invasion of Albania on 7 April 1939 led to British and French guarantees being extended to Greece and Romania too. On 28 April, Hitler renounced the Polish non-aggression treaty and Anglo-German naval agreement and the following month Italy and Germany signed a treaty of alliance, 'The Pact of Steel'. War no longer seemed a distant prospect and in May Britain reintroduced limited military conscription under the Military Training Act. Some hoped that any outbreak of hostilities might be delayed. Demonstrating appropriate sangfroid, Peter Malden Studd,† captain of Cambridge University cricket first XI, commented that he 'hoped to God that Hitler wouldn't declare war before the cricket season was over'.[5]

On 9 August 1939, over 130 Royal Navy ships assembled off Portland. The vast majority were from the Reserve Fleet, mobilised for fleet manoeuvres. Some 12,000 reservists had been called out in a few days and the government was in the processes of requisitioning eighty merchant ships and fishing vessels for war work. 'With other British fleets scattered in home and foreign waters in a full state of preparedness and going about their normal occupations' noted the *Sydney Morning Herald*, 'the fact that the king … was able to review 133 ships – a complete navy in itself – served to emphasise the extent of the nation's seapower'.[6] No doubt many hoped that Hitler would take notice.

The 15in-gunned battleships *Ramillies* and *Revenge* had been 'loaned' from the Home Fleet and the whole Reserve Fleet turned out under Vice-Admiral Max Horton, three years later to command in the Western Approaches. Amazingly, the old *Iron Duke* was once again present. Other famous vessels on display included the veteran 'C'-class cruiser *Cardiff*, which had led the German fleet into Scapa Flow and the destroyer *Warwick*, in which Admiral Roger Keyes had worn his flag at Zeebrugge. Once again

* Hitler claimed it was to unite the German-speaking peoples; the coal and iron ore of the region was possibly a more attractive boon to an energy-poor Germany.

† Later Lord Mayor of London 1970–1.

together, standing in fourteen lines in the sunlight which followed a dismal bout of rain and mist, the aging ships awaited their monarch.

The King had travelled overnight from Scotland, where he had been holidaying at Balmoral, by train. On arrival at Portland, he was greeted by First Lord of the Admiralty, Lord Stanhope, and First Sea Lord Admiral Sir Dudley Pound and at 1045 boarded his barge to join *Victoria and Albert*. As the Royal Standard broke from the royal yacht's masthead, a 21-gun salute thundered out from the assembled host and echoed across the bay.

At 1430 the King rejoined his barge and, escorted by the motor torpedo boats (MTBs) numbers 22 (ahead) and 102 (astern), and for the next two hours passed along the lines of warships. Each ship gave out three cheers as the monarch sailed by, watched by an assembly of private yachts and pleasure steamers off to the northeast.

One declared purpose of the review was so that the King could meet some sixty commanding officers, who were gathered on the recently refitted light cruiser *Effingham* (1921) for that purpose, and to inspect the reserve warships prior to re-commissioning. There was a political purpose too. The Chief of the French Naval Staff, Admiral Jean Louis Xavier François Darlan, was warmly greeted as an ally, having arrived in the destroyer *Volta*, and participated in the ceremony.* He was seated in the stern sheets of the royal barge in a place of honour. Once again, the King boarded *Courageous* where he inspected 1,500 reservists chosen by ballot to represent each ship or flotilla of the Reserve Fleet. King George also inspected the submarine HMS *Otway*, went aboard the destroyer *Exmouth* and finally the trawler *Myrtle*.

At 1645, the fleet fired off a final salute and the King departed for Weymouth. Duty done, George VI returned to Scotland by train, eight hours after he had arrived. When he reached his destination, Ballater Station, the following morning, his train had travelled nearly 1,500 miles. The King was impressed by what he had seen. 'It is wonderful the way in which the men have come for duty at this time' he wrote to his mother, 'and I feel sure it will be a deterrent factor in Hitler's mind to start a war.'[7]

Meanwhile, dressing lines came down and cables were shortened. At 1900, led by *Revenge*, *Ramillies* and *Iron Duke*, the reserve ships departed for combined exercises with the Home Fleet in the North Sea and thereafter dispersed to their war stations. For many of the reservists (and indeed the regulars too) it would be a long time before they saw their homes again.

On 1 September, Germany invaded Poland, the first shots fired by the old pre-dreadnought battleship SMS *Schleswig-Holstein*, launched in 1906 and immediately obsolescent. Britain issued an ultimatum to Germany that evening. And on 3 September 1939, Britain and France went to war with Germany.

* Much good this did, for Darlan went on to be the commander of Vichy forces in North Africa. King George VI disliked him, stating that 'nobody trusted him and he had shifty eyes' (quoted in Bradford, *King George VI*, p 350).

1944, Operation Overlord and D-Day

Many of the lessons learned in the 1914–18 war had been either forgotten or rendered impossible to execute by the naval reduction treaties. The Royal Naval entered the war deficient in cruisers and especially in the small ships – convoy escorts, destroyers, anti-submarine vessels and minesweepers – that the Great War had shown to be so desperately required. As a result, the navy, starved of resources between the wars, was ill-equipped to fight the all-important Battle of the Atlantic against the Nazi U-boat fleet. But huge building programmes, and fifty old destroyers sent from the USA in exchange for 99-year leases for American bases in British possessions,* together with Lend-Lease, helped plug the gap until America joined the war. The navy made huge sacrifices, lost many ships, but acquitted itself well. And by 1944, the Allies were ready to carry the fight into the heart of Europe.

On 6 June 1944 the Allied invasion force set out for France from many locations on the southern English coastline, stretching from Falmouth to the Thames Estuary and including the Solent. There were twenty-three cruisers covering the landing, seventeen of them RN. Seven battleships provided fire support (four of them British, *Nelson, Rodney, Ramillies* and *Warspite*). Within the fleet were 139 destroyers and escorts (eighty-five of them British and Dominion). There was even a Great War-style monitor *Roberts* (1941) with her 15in guns. There were Free French, Norwegian, Polish and Dutch naval forces in company. In all, 4,000 landing craft had been prepared.

There are a number of on-line sources which aver that George VI inspected the D-Day invasion fleet, in great secrecy, before it departed for Normandy. This is untrue. These was no Royal Review of the invasion fleet. What did happen was as follows. On 15 May, the King attended a high-level invasion presentation and planning meeting at St Paul's School, joining over 150 high-ranking officers. The commanders sat on wooden benches, with chairs placed at the front for King George, Churchill, Field Marshal Smuts and General Brooke (Chief of the Imperial General Staff). Closing the meeting, George made a speech, which was well received, and ended by asking for God's blessing on the venture. Before he departed, the King had a private conversation with supreme commander Eisenhower.

Next, on 24 May and under the code name 'Operation Aerolite', George VI motored to the 'stone frigate' HMS *Mastodon*, which was used to train landing craft crews. He met with the overall naval commander, Admiral Bertram Ramsey, and some of the officers and men. Taking to a barge, the King travelled down the Beaulieu River into the Solent passing many moored landing craft. He visited two command ships, observed the landing craft gathered in Portsmouth Harbour and lunched with Rear-Admiral Philip Vian on board the cruiser *Scylla*. George now boarded a

* Newfoundland, Bermuda, the Bahamas, Jamaica, Antigua, St Lucia, Trinidad and British Guiana. King George VI was 'much disturbed over it as the USA is asking for more facilities than were originally agreed to and wishes to fortify and have garrisons in Bermuda and Trinidad'(quoted in Bradford, *King George VI*, p 332).

naval rescue launch and from a distance viewed landing craft in Southampton Water and the Hamble. It was extremely informal and few people knew of the tour; and it was not a Royal Fleet Review.

Prime Minister Winston Churchill was determined to sail with the invasion fleet which Eisenhower forbade; to get around this, Churchill decided to appoint himself to the cruiser HMS *Belfast*. George seized on that idea and wanted to join his prime minister; but then realised that this was impractical and set himself to persuade Churchill out of the idea too. Admiral Ramsey was also determined that neither man should go.

On 2 June, George wrote to Churchill as his monarch; the letter shows how much he himself had wanted to support his forces.

> My Dear Winston,
>
> I want to make one more appeal to you not to go to sea on D-Day. Please consider my own position. I am a younger man than you, I am a sailor, and as king I am the head of all three services. There is nothing I would like better than to go to sea but I have agreed to stay at home; is it fair that you should then do exactly what I should have liked to do myself?
>
> You said yesterday afternoon that it would be a fine thing for the king to lead his troops into battle, as in old days; if the king cannot do this, it does not seem to me right that his prime minister should take his place.
>
> Then there is your own position. You will see very little, you will seem a considerable risk, you will be inaccessible at a critical time when vital decisions might have to be taken, and however unobtrusive you may be, your very presence on board is bound to be a very heavy additional responsibility to the admiral and captain.
>
> As I said in my previous letter, your being there would add immeasurably to my anxieties, and your going without consulting your colleagues in the Cabinet would put them in a very difficult position which they would justifiably resent.
>
> I ask you most earnestly to consider the whole question again, and not let your personal wishes, which I very well understand, lead you to depart from your own high standard of duty to the state.[8]

Grumpily, Churchill complied.*

* The prime minister finally visited Normandy on 12 June, taken across the Channel in the 'K'-class destroyer HMS *Kelvin*.

Eventually, King George VI did publicly visit the D-Day forces; on 16 June, the King embarked on the cruiser *Arethusa* at Portsmouth and sailed for France, accompanied by First Sea Lord Admiral Andrew Browne Cunningham. The monarch was driven ashore in a DUKW amphibious truck to be greeted by General Montgomery and lunched with him in his caravan at his tactical headquarters.

But there was no Royal Fleet Review.

Part Four:

———◦❖◦———

THE EBB TIDE

Kingdoms which long have stood,
And slow to strength and power attain'd at last,
Thus from the summit of high fortune's flood
They ebb to ruin fast.

Robert Southey, *The Ebb Tide* (1799)

Chapter 15

Decline ... , 1945–1977

IN 1945 Britain was in a parlous economic condition, her resources spent. The war was over, but the conflict had stripped her of virtually all her foreign financial resources; moreover, the country had built up 'sterling credits' – debts owed to other countries that were to be repaid in foreign currencies – amounting to several billion pounds. Industry too was in disarray. Railways and coal mines were short of new equipment and in bad repair and the manufacturing base was on its knees.

With nothing to export, Britain had no way to pay for imports of any sort, even food, and within weeks of the Japanese surrender the Americans ended Lend-Lease, which Britain had depended upon for its necessities as well as its armaments. John Maynard Keynes was sent to negotiate a $3.75 billion loan from the United States* and a smaller one from Canada. Britain was effectively bankrupt.

By 1947 the situation was worse. Dreadful weather led to a fuel crisis with electricity cuts of five hours a day imposed. Unemployment rose to 2.5 million and production fell. The loan from the USA, meant to last for four years, was almost exhausted. Chancellor Hugh Dalton told the Cabinet that it would run out before the end of the year and in August announced a suspension of the convertibility of the pound. Imports were severely restricted by government fiat. Bread, unrationed during the war, was now controlled. Britain was forced to withdraw its long-term financial and military support of Greece in its civil war against communism.

Unintentionally or otherwise, this move by Britain's Labour government precipitated the Truman Doctrine, whereby President Harry S Truman established that the United States would provide political, military and economic assistance to all democratic nations under threat from external or internal authoritarian forces. This *volte-face* in American's traditional policy was due to Truman's desire to counter Soviet geopolitical expansion. On its heels came the Marshall Plan, whereby the United States would undertake a massive programme of financial aid to the European

* The loan was at 2 per cent interest, repayable in fifty annual instalments from 1951. In return, Britain had to end imperial preference and make sterling convertible for current transactions from July 1947, a condition which was likely to place a huge strain on the country's reserves.

continent and Britain.* Europe and Britain were saved; this was not altruistic, America wanted allies and bulwarks, Britain especially, in its Cold War struggle with Russia.

It was against this background that Britain's military planners and their political chiefs had to decide strategy. In 1948 they articulated what was named the 'Three Pillars Strategy'. This was based on the premise that the security of the British Commonwealth depended upon three key points; defence of the UK, maintaining vital sea communications and securing the Middle East as a defensive and striking base against the Soviet Union.

An embryonic NATO had been founded in March 1947 when the Treaty of Dunkirk was signed by France and Britain; it was a Treaty of Alliance and Mutual Assistance in the event of a possible attack by Germany or the Soviet Union. In 1948, this pact was expanded to include the Benelux countries and the USA and formally agreed the following year. Strategy now emphasised the deterrent value of US atomic supremacy over the Soviet Union and the growth of NATO forces to a level capable of overcoming a Soviet invasion of Western Europe.

In 1952, the Korean War led to a British rearmament programme and defence spending was planned to rise rapidly from 1951, to approximately 10 per cent of gross national product. But the cost implications of such an effort were untenable for Britain; following the end of the war in 1953 it was obvious that military expenditure on this level was beyond the country's capacity.

George VI died on 6 February 1952, to be succeeded by his 25-year-old daughter, Elizabeth, who became Queen Elizabeth II. Her coronation took place the following year on 2 June. And as 'invented tradition' dictated, it was followed by a Royal Fleet Review on Monday 15 June 1953, at Spithead.

The fleet which would greet the new monarch was radically different from the one which her father had reviewed in 1938 and 1939. The fleet flagship, wearing the flag of Admiral Sir George E Creasy (Commander-in-Chief, Home Fleet and NATO Commander-in-Chief Eastern Atlantic), was – as traditional – a battleship, HMS *Vanguard* (1944). But she was the only battleship present. All the others, familiar from pre-war reviews, *Nelson*, *Rodney*, *Revenge*, *Ramillies* and their kin, even the old *Iron Duke*, had been stricken in the late 1940s. The C-in-C Mediterranean Fleet, Admiral Earl Mountbatten of Burma, flew his flag in a light cruiser, HMS *Glasgow*, of 1936 vintage.

Instead the new capital ships were aircraft carriers and eight were represented at Spithead, HMCS *Magnificent*, HMS *Perseus*, *Eagle*, *Theseus*, *Implacable*, *Illustrious*, *Indomitable* and *Indefatigable*. The latter two took

* Britain received $2.7bn under the Marshall Plan. This was 'estimated to have saved 1.2m jobs and raised national income by ten per cent' (*Olympic Britain, Social and economic change since the 1908 and 1948 London Games*, House of Commons Library, 2012).

The front page of the Coronation Review souvenir programme with HMS *Vanguard* in the background. *(Author's collection)*

Ships assemble for the Coronation Review, 9 June 1953. (© Imperial War Museum A 32574)

names previously given to Fisher's 'greyhounds of the sea', his battle-cruisers, and now fulfilled something of a similar function. Experience in the Pacific and at home had shown that huge expensive battlewagons could not survive without extensive air cover. This had been noted as early as 1942, when Assistant Chief of the Naval Staff Rear-Admiral Henry Harwood wrote that 'every battleship or pair of battleships must have an attendant carrier to provide fighter protection'.[1] Aircraft carriers also gave the fleet the opportunity to strike where, when and how they liked.★

★ To update 'Jackie' Fisher's dictum regarding speed.

But not all of the carriers were what they seemed. The light aircraft carrier HMS *Perseus* (1944) had been completed in 1945 and thus 'missed'

The last battleship. HMS *Vanguard*, completed in 1946. Note her beautiful hull lines. She was placed in reserve three years after the 1953 review and broken up in 1960. (Collection R A Burt)

the war. Instead she was used for aircraft ferry duties and catapult testing. Having returned from America with a cargo of Grumman TBF Avengers, part of the Mutual Defence Assistance Act* of 1949 and 1950, she was fitted with temporary grandstand seating specially for the use of VIPs at the review. Sea cadets were drafted on board to sell programmes to the guests.

The flagship, HMS *Vanguard*, was a beautiful ship, completed in 1946; she had an elegant sheer and with a slight flare to her bow, eight 15in guns (of First World War vintage however, taken from the Admiralty Armament Reserve and some once fitted to the 'large light cruisers' *Glorious* and *Courageous* before their conversion to carriers) and sixteen 5.25in. Her design had evolved from the earlier *King George V* class and incorporated much of the fully-developed design for two planned battleships, *Lion* and *Temeraire*, laid down in 1939 but never completed. At 813ft length and over 51,000 long tons (deep load), she was the last battleship to be built in the world and the biggest and fastest British battleship yet commissioned; but *Vanguard* saw no action in war. Her career highlight was to take King George VI and the royal family to South Africa in 1947. Three years after the Coronation Review, she too would be laid up and she was scrapped in 1960.

Only one battleship greeted the Queen; but there was no royal yacht at all. Despite Chamberlain's decision in 1938 to build a new one, the war supervened. *Victoria and Albert III* spent the war moored at Portsmouth, mainly as an accommodation ship for the gunnery school at Whale Island, and in October 1945 was declared unseaworthy. No decision was taken on a replacement until June 1951 when it was decided, for reasons of economy, to build a new vessel based on the existing designs of two North

* Which followed on from the Marshall Plan and the formation of NATO.

HMS *Surprise* was converted into a royal yacht for the occasion of the 1953 Coronation Review. (© *Imperial War Museum FL019520*)

Sea ferries and a start was made in 1952 at John Brown's shipyard. She would not be commissioned as HMY *Britannia* until January 1954.

Instead, the Queen was to inspect the fleet from HMS *Surprise*, originally a 'Loch'-class frigate, completed as a despatch boat or 'C-in-C's yacht'. She was repainted light blue, the two 4in guns in her 'B' turret were removed and a glass-enclosed platform built there for the monarch, from which to observe the festivities. The Board of Admiralty too had to rough it; *Enchantress* was gone and they were instead confined to HMS *Redpole* (1943), a *Black Swan*-class sloop performing the duty of Admiralty yacht.

There were other changes obvious to the naked eye. There was a significant increase in Commonwealth representation, a reflection of the rapid development of the Dominion navies during the war. The personnel strength of the Royal Canadian Navy was now more than three times what it was in 1939 and Canada sent six ships. Australia and New Zealand sent a warship each, India three and Pakistan two. The profusion of radio and radar aerials in all classes of ship demonstrated the importance of electronic equipment in modern sea warfare and ships now boasted a considerable increase of anti-aircraft armament, born of war experience.

Observation also gave another cause for reflection; of the vessels present, not all of them were warships or in current commission. The impact of defence cuts could be seen. Half the fleet was now held in reserve, from which some had been reactivated for the review, appearing with guns and other equipment still protectively wrapped in vacuum-shrunk plastic. To make up the numbers, ocean liners, merchant vessels (twenty-nine in number), fishing craft (nine) and lifeboats (four) were included in the lines, which even incorporated the Isle of Wight car ferry *Farringford*.

The Admiralty was clearly aware of the need to make the number of ships present seem impressive and were at pains to have as many of the Mediterranean Fleet attend as was expedient; but there was a problem. In the summer of 1952, an army coup had taken control of Egypt and deposed the king in favour of his son with the Revolutionary Command Council as a ruling junta. All political parties were banned, a new constitution was proclaimed in February 1953 and some British property was seized. The Suez Canal and influence in the Mediterranean were key British interests and these now appeared threatened.

As a consequence, the Admiralty was forced to leave sufficient forces in the Mediterranean to lift 3 Commando Brigade to Port Said, provide Task Force 52 to protect the Suez Canal and form Task Force 56 as a mobile reserve. The remaining vessels would depart from Gibraltar on 18 May for their Home Ports (for leave) and then Spithead; it was noted that they could not reach Egypt in under nine days, or seven days if they sailed from Portsmouth. As a result, the light aircraft carrier *Theseus* of the Home Fleet and a destroyer were instructed to be at 48 hours' notice from 1 May, and Mediterranean Fleet units would sail for Malta immediately after the review.

Despite the strained economic circumstances surrounding the review, there were new ships on show. The latest aircraft carrier, HMS *Eagle*, had only been accepted into service the previous year (although first laid down in 1942). There were four *Daring*-class destroyers, newly commissioned that year, armed with six 4.5in guns, capable of 34.5kts and the largest destroyers the navy had ever built. They were the 'equivalent to the light cruisers of former days, with a complement of 300 and a mass of complex equipment, dedicated to the location and destruction of an underwater enemy, which supplements their powerful surface armament'.[2] The 'Weapon'-class destroyers *Battleaxe*, *Scorpion* and *Crossbow* were also there, completed at the end of the 1940s and armed with two Squid anti-submarine mortars. 'The appearance of these ships is almost as revolutionary as was that of the *Nelson*-class battleships of twenty-five years ago,' noted one commentator. 'Their somewhat insect-like appearance is the logical outcome of a technique evolved in the hard school of the Western Approaches, whereby submarines are killed by ahead-throwing weapons which have superseded the depth charge throwers and traps of the past.'[3]

The fleet had begun to assemble on Monday 8 June. The 10th was the Duke of Edinburgh's birthday and all ships dressed overall and fired a royal salute at noon. That same day the representatives of foreign navies began to arrive, sixteen ships in total from all over the world (see Appendix 6). Despite the Cold War, the USSR sent the cruiser *Sverdlov*, armed with twelve 6in guns in four triple turrets. She fired a 21-gun salute as she

HMS *Broadsword*, a 'Weapon'-class destroyer, was built by Yarrow at Scotstoun and completed in 1948. She served in home waters until 1953 when she entered reserve. The picture shows her after her conversion to a radar picket in 1957–8. *(Author's collection)*

steamed up the Solent and on landing her captain, Olimpey Rudakov, paid his respects to the port admiral and drove through the streets to Portsmouth Guildhall to visit the Lord Mayor.

The following day was the Queen's official birthday, another excuse to dress ship and fire another royal salute. Some vessels were opened to visitors. And on Saturday 13th there was a display of naval aircraft at Lee-on-Solent air station. That same day, at the Lord Mayor's invitation, '300 officers and men from the *Sverdlov* yesterday drove in coaches to a Portsmouth cinema to see a Coronation colour film'.[4] Captain Rudakov would not allow visitors on his ship, however.

On Sunday evening the Queen arrived by car; she was received by Admiral Sir John Hereward Edelstan, C-in-C Portsmouth, together with the Lord Mayor of Portsmouth. Ships were again dressed overall and a royal salute was fired as the Royal Standard broke above HMS *Surprise*. Interestingly, the Duke of Edinburgh journeyed separately and in a different car.

On the 15th, the review adhered to time-worn custom. The Queen received the Board of Admiralty in *Surprise*. At 1300 there was a luncheon party aboard (for the first time at a Royal Review, a small party of WRNS acted as stewardesses). At 1430, the Queen Mother, Princess Margaret and others members of the royal suite came by train and boarded the *ersatz* royal yacht. And at 1500, preceded by the Trinity House vessel *Patricia* (with Sir Winston Churchill on board in his capacity as an Elder Brother of that august body) and followed by *Redpole*, the little convoy left harbour. As they approached the lines of the fleet, 156 ships in nine lines,

Commissioned in the coronation year, the *Daring*-class destroyer HMS *Dainty*. (*Author's collection*)

SS *St Patrick*, celebratory bunting flying, carried passengers around the Coronation Review. *(© National Maritime Museum N37183)*

a 21-gun salute rang out across the waters, as it had many times before. Following on behind were the sloop HMS *Starling* (1942) with Admiralty invitees, another sloop HMS *Fleetwood* (1936) with the C–in–C Portsmouth's guests, the frigate HMS *Helmsdale* (1943) with the Mayor and corporation of Portsmouth and associates, and five chartered vessels carrying government guests and Admiralty staff.

After *Surprise* had anchored at around 1710, there was a fly-past of naval aircraft, thirty-eight squadrons comprising 300 aircraft which passed over *Surprise* at 45-second intervals, and not just fixed-wing; a swarm of Westland WS-51 Dragonfly* air-sea rescue helicopters flew low over the monarch, sounding like angry insects. There was a sherry party on board the royal yacht and at 2030 the Queen dined on board *Vanguard* (where again WRNS waited at table). Finally, at 2230 the fleet was illuminated and a firework display followed.

As in days past there were many, many spectators ashore and afloat. For the latter paddle steamer ferries were pressed into service and, for those prepared to pay a little more, vessels such as SS *St Patrick* (1948) took passengers around the review and then anchored up as floating grandstand. And 163 private yachts were allocated specific anchorages on the Isle of Wight side of the assembled fleet.

Many commercial organisations took advantage of the event to entertain their customers and contacts. Once such was the Pirelli-General Cable Works Company from nearby Southampton. They had first opened there in 1914 and were soon at work supplying cables for thousands of field telephones used in the trenches of the First World War. And during the Second World War the firm supplied 3.5 million miles of wire to the Royal Corps of Signals, provided special wiring rigs for Avro Lancaster bombers and designed and installed a submarine fuel pipeline to deliver fuel for the vehicles involved in the D-Day landings (code named 'Pluto'). Now they hosted nearly 500 guests including Sir Harry and Lady Railing, chairman of GEC, and Ross McWhirter, later to found the *Guinness Book of Records* with his twin.†

* A licence-built version of the American Sikorsky S-51.

† Who was murdered by the IRA in 1975.

The review was generally well received. One naval correspondent enthused:

> There are few spectacles more satisfying to the great majority of Englishmen than a Review of Her Majesty's Fleet in the historic anchorage at Spithead. Apart from pride in what many of us consider to be the finest service in the world, it is reassuring to be able actually to look at a major part of the weapon which has served the nation well for many centuries in the exercise of British sea-power.[5]

But there were also some clouds in the sky. Britain's navy had now sunk to being ranked only third in the world. The *Spectator* magazine thought that 'the responsibility for an important part of the immemorial task of the fleet has been entrusted to an international organisation [i.e. NATO] in which Great Britain is a senior, but by no means the controlling, partner. This is a sobering thought.'[6] For the first time the Royal Navy was sharing sovereignty of the seas with other powers.

During the period 1887–1914 and in the inter-war years, Royal Fleet Reviews had been used as much as anything as advertising for the navy, a

A swarm of dragons; Westland WS-51 Dragonfly helicopters fly over HMS *Manxman* at the 1953 Coronation Naval Review. *(Press Association 6397534)*

constant reminder to legislators and public that protection needed money put behind it and to show the nation what their cash had purchased. Cavils aside, the 1953 event certainly put on a show, although without the confected manoeuvres that often accompanied pre-war demonstrations. But did it secure the navy's place at the table of the Treasury? Time would soon tell.

1957 and 1965, Regression

Although not a Royal Fleet Review, the Queen met her new royal yacht *Britannia* for the second time (she had launched her in 1953) on 2 May 1954. With Prince Charles and Princess Anne embarked, *Britannia* had slipped from Portsmouth and headed for the Mediterranean where she met with, and took on board, the Queen, who was returning from a Commonwealth tour on the Shaw Savill liner SS *Gothic*.

Her uncle, Admiral Lord Louis Mountbatten, Commander-in-Chief Mediterranean Fleet, was in charge of the arrangements for the Queen's subsequent escort into Malta and was determined that the event should show some of the navy's old dash and spirit. He personally involved himself in the planning of what he called 'The Precise Manoeuvre' and the fleet was drilled to within an inch of its life in rehearsals. Ships' captains were encouraged to incline to showmanship and to operate within (rather than outside) the prescribed distances of separation and above the designated stationing speeds. They practised at 25kts and with cruisers positioned at only two cables (400 yards) apart, with smaller ships even closer at 300 yards. There was simply no room for error; perfect timing, from the firing of gun salutes to executing wheel overs and speed changes, was critical for the required panache of the occasion (and personal safety).

The fleet escort, led by the C-in-C in the 6in cruiser *Glasgow*, approached *Britannia* and her close escort in two columns at high speed from ahead. The two lines wheeled in succession and passed the royal yacht close on either side. The cruiser line went to starboard, then the destroyer line to port. On each big ship, guards and bands were paraded and the massed ships' companies gave three cheers as they rocketed by the royal yacht.

Elizabeth had just emerged on deck from morning church and was greeted by the sight of virtually the whole Mediterranean Fleet thundering towards her at over 21kts. They ran up *Britannia*'s side at distance abeam of only 100 yards with ships having to use up to 25 degrees of wheel to stay on station and on course, due to the turbulent wake of the ship ahead. On board *Britannia*, the Queen was also buffeted by the wash of her perilously close and fast escorts.

Once the port column of nine ships had completed their pass up the yacht's side, HMS *Eagle* executed her own steam past to starboard before taking station one mile ahead of *Britannia*. Finally, *Glasgow* transferred

Admiral Mountbatten by jackstay to join Queen Elizabeth, and with her
escort all around her, the Queen headed into Grand Harbour, Malta, and
a tumultuous welcome. The Royal Navy had just shown its monarch that
it could still put on a show worthy of its Edwardian forebears.

Nevertheless, the frequency of fleet reviews was much reduced post-war.
But two smaller ones took place in 1957 and 1965, both against the background of continued cuts in naval budgets and resources. The Suez Crisis of
1956, and the subsequent debacle of withdrawal, was a diplomatic disaster
and revealed the poor state of readiness of British forces and the obsoles-
cence of much of their equipment. The rearmament of 1951 had proven to
be financially unviable and had failed to produce effective results. Indeed,
the Anglo-French response to Nasser's nationalisation of the Suez Canal
took three months to organise, largely due to a shortage of available forces.

Defence priorities were thus once more reviewed in Conservative
Defence Minister Duncan Sandys'* White Paper of April 1957. At the
outset, the document stated that 'Britain's influence in the world depends
first and foremost on the health of her internal economy and the success
of her export trade. Without these, military power cannot in the long run
be supported. It is therefore in the true interests of defence that the claims
of military expenditure should be considered in conjunction with the
need to maintain the country's financial and economic strength.'[7] The
Edwardian and Victorian paradigms had been broken – no longer would
the armed forces be strengthened to permit trade but only as a result of it.

The Sandys review placed great emphasis on nuclear deterrence as the
mainstay of Britain's defence policy. It also recommended the abolition of
national service, the need for European allies to take up more of the
conventional burden within NATO, reducing overseas garrisons, a significant reduction in RAF Fighter Command and placed the naval emphasis
on aircraft carriers as an effective means of bringing power rapidly to bear
in peacetime emergencies or limited hostilities. Nonetheless the navy
suffered cuts. Manpower was to be reduced from 121,000 men to 75,000
and most of the reserve fleet was to be scrapped. Smaller, cheaper guided-
missile destroyers replaced the large missile cruisers that the Admiralty had
hoped for, and the last remaining battleship, *Vanguard*, pride of the
Coronation Review, was to go for scrap in 1960.

———⊱⊰———

On 27 May 1957, the royal yacht *Britannia* was sailing towards the coast of
Scotland, escorted by HMS *Duchess*, *Diamond* (both *Daring*-class
destroyers) and the 'Battle'-class destroyer *Corunna*. On board were Queen
Elizabeth II and the Duke of Edinburgh, returning from a state visit to
Denmark where they had, *inter alia*, met with Professor Niels Bohr and
visited the Carlsberg Breweries. In Invergordon, elements of the Home

* Winston
Churchill's
son-in-law.

Fleet were putting out to welcome her back, under the command of C-in-C Home Fleet Admiral Sir John Arthur Symons Eccles, with his flag in the *Abdiel*-class fast minelayer *Apollo*.

Out in the Moray Firth the ships formed into two columns; Rear-Admiral J David Luce, Flag Officer Flotillas and with his flag in the 6in-gunned cruiser *Superb*, led the port column followed by *Agincourt*, *Alamein* and *Barossa* (all 'Battle'-class destroyers), while the starboard line was comprised of three aircraft carriers, *Ark Royal*, *Albion* and *Ocean*. When the distance between the royal yacht was down to two and a half miles, all ships fired a 21-gun salute and increased speed to 21kts, the two columns wheeling outwards, and passing *Britannia* at no more than 100 yards. The royal couple were clearly visible on the bridge and each ship's crew gave the customary three cheers as they sped past.

It was no doubt a proud day for many of the sailors present and a fine demonstration of the Royal Navy's skill at sea. But the Sandys review had already done for Luce's flagship. Immediately before she led the fleet out of Invergordon, plans for her modernisation had been abandoned. In fact, no more cruiser modernisations were to be approved and new guided missile ships took precedence. *Superb* was decommissioned that year and broken up three years later. Her admiral would also become a victim of cuts. Luce became First Sea Lord in 1963 (the first specialist submariner to hold the post) but on 15 March 1966 resigned from his post (together with Navy Minister Christopher Mayhew), and from the Royal Navy, in protest over the decision by the Labour government's Secretary of State for Defence, Denis Healey, to cancel the CVA-01 aircraft carrier programme.*

But the Healey review lay in the future. Despite Suez, throughout the late 1950s and early 1960s government intent was still an attempt to maintain the world role and the Sandys review had largely focused on the implementation of existing policy.

But the world of all navies had been changed irrevocably on the commissioning of the USS *Nautilus* in 1954, the first nuclear-powered submarine. With nuclear power, the endurance of a vessel at sea was limited only by the endurance of the crew. Britain's first such vessel was HMS *Dreadnought*, recycling the name of another game-changer, launched by Queen Elizabeth II on Trafalgar Day 1960 and commissioned into service with the Royal Navy in April 1963. She used American technology as a result of the 1958 US – UK Mutual Defence Agreement which allowed the sale to the UK of one complete nuclear submarine propulsion plant, plus ten years' supply of enriched uranium to fuel it.

Dreadnought was the centrepiece of the next Royal Fleet Review on 10 August 1965, where the queen was to review the Home Fleet on the

* Together with the Type 82 destroyer class that was intended to protect the carriers.

Clyde prior to a five-day family cruise around the Scottish coast. Seventy-two ships were assembled to pay their respects as the royal yacht *Britannia* brought the queen to her fleet. The usual gunnery salutes were fired and the Queen boarded the guided-missile destroyer HMS *Kent* (laid down in 1960 as part of the Sandys plan), the submarine depot ship *Maidstone* and talked to some of the senior ratings of both vessels before proceeding to *Dreadnought*. Here a large royal entourage embarked on the submarine, including the Duke of Edinburgh, Admiral Lord Mountbatten of Burma, Prince Charles and Princess Anne, the First Sea Lord and the C-in-C Home Fleet and various other flag officers. The Queen first called at the wardroom and then the royal party were given a conducted tour of the vessel.

In the evening, Admiral Sir John Frewen, Commander-in-Chief Home Fleet, welcomed the queen to dinner on his flagship. The following day, the royal party departed on their cruise, escorted by the frigate HMS *Salisbury*.

1969, NATO and Colours

In 1964 the Labour Party government of Prime Minister Harold Wilson had come to power in the United Kingdom. They opposed nuclear weapons, preferring to focus on conventional armaments, and thus wished to reverse the emphasis of the Sandys plan. However, the UK had already committed to the American Polaris missile system, delivered by nuclear-powered submarines, and four Polaris vessels had been ordered, the first of them, *Resolution*, commissioned in 1967 and operational by 1968. The political left has opposed them and their successors ever since.

A new Defence Review was issued in 1965 by Defence Secretary Denis Healey and amended in 1967 and 1968. This stated that 'the present government has inherited defence forces which are seriously over-stretched and, in some respects, dangerously under-equipped … .there has been no real attempt to match political commitments to military resources, still less to relate the resources made available for defence to the economic circumstances of the nation'.[8] In other words, there still wasn't enough money.

This situation was made worse by the financial crisis* which enveloped the government, leading to the devaluation of Sterling by 14 per cent on 18 November 1967. This was accompanied by a series of austerity measures, including a further cut in defence budgets. As far as the navy was concerned these cuts included the cancellation of further aircraft carrier construction. Britain withdrew from Aden, Singapore, Malaysia and the Persian Gulf. As Dr David Owen, Under Secretary at the Ministry of Defence told the House of Commons on 10 March 1969

the future shape of the navy is now clear. Aircraft carriers will phase out when the military withdrawals from the Far East and the Persian Gulf

* There were probably four main causes of the financial crisis; 'a dockers' strike which held up UK exports leaving the country, worsening the monthly trade balance figures; financial flows out of sterling following weak trade data and waning confidence in the fixed exchange rate holding; the Bank of England running low on foreign currency reserves and international creditors … less willing to lend the UK the substantial amounts needed to prop up the pound; and the June 1967 Six-Day Arab-Israeli War which resulted in the closure of the Suez canal disrupting trade flows and a sell off of sterling assets by Arab countries' (House of Commons Library, *Pound in Your Pocket Devaluation*, 17 November 2017).

have been completed. The strategic Polaris force, apart from the nuclear-powered fleet submarines building up, will then provide the main striking power of the navy. Work is going ahead on the three classes which will form the main surface fleet: the frigates to succeed the *Leanders*, the destroyers to carry the Sea Dart surface-to-air missile system, and the cruisers to follow the converted *Tiger* class.[9]

Moreover, the review included a commitment that Britain would 'not undertake major operations of war except in co-operation with allies'.[10] In other words, Britain would rely on NATO.

Indeed, as historian Glen O'Hara has observed, 'by the late 1960s, no more would the Royal Navy attempt to be the world's policeman, or even the chief lieutenant to the real maritime power, the USA. Instead she would concentrate on her contribution to NATO operations in the Atlantic and the Mediterranean and perhaps amphibious operations in those theatres, along with NATO's flank in Norway.'[11]

So it was perhaps no surprise that in 1969 the Queen was invited to review an assembly comprised of NATO country vessels, a Royal Fleet Review to mark the twentieth anniversary of that organisation's formal foundation. The review was held at Spithead on Friday 16 May; but it was not a Royal Navy review, despite the presence of the monarch. It was a NATO and not a national ceremonial, as was made clear by Defence Secretary Denis Healey in the House of Commons. In response to the question 'Why had he not informed Parliament of a fleet review which is taking place at Spithead', he replied 'This is a NATO Naval Review – not a national one – and a press release was issued on 17th February last by the Secretary General of NATO stating that it would take place at Portsmouth on 16th May as part of the international commemoration of the twentieth anniversary of the signing of the North Atlantic Treaty'.[12]

Twelve NATO countries participated, Belgium, Britain, Canada, Denmark, Germany, Greece, Italy, Netherlands, Norway, Portugal, Turkey and the USA. The largest ship present was the aircraft carrier USS *Wasp* which arrived the day before the review as the flagship of the eleven-ship* USN delegation, Task Force 87. She was carrying helicopters and Grumman Tracker and Hawkeye aircraft, and operating as an Anti-Submarine Warfare platform. The largest Royal Navy warship present, flying the flag of Rear-Admiral Michael F Fell, was HMS *Blake*, ex-*Tiger*, an anti-submarine helicopter cruiser, originally laid down in 1942 and converted to her present role in between 1965 and 1969.

Of the sixty-four ships assembled only fifteen were British (thirteen warships, another in the Standing Naval Force Atlantic group, and an RFA). There were none of the real capital ships of the day, the nuclear SSBN[†] submarines, kept secreted away from prying eyes. The fleet was

* Plus another in the Standing Naval Force Atlantic grouping.

† A submarine capable of deploying submarine launched ballistic missiles (SLBMs) with nuclear warheads.

USS *Wasp* (CVS-18) under way in the Atlantic in 1969. She was the flagship of US representation at the NATO review. *(US Naval History and Heritage Command USN 1151477)*

predominantly comprised of smaller vessels; there were seventeen destroyers, eighteen frigates and fifteen minesweepers present.

HMY *Britannia* awaited the Queen alongside the Portsmouth South Railway Jetty, flying the NATO flag. But first the Queen had to receive the keys to the Fortress from the Lord Lieutenant of Hampshire and the lord mayor at the railway station. The royal party, which included Prince Philip and Princess Anne, then travelled by car to the dockyard. On their arrival, Queen Elizabeth was greeted by Admiral Sir John Frewen, now C-in-C Portsmouth, and Admiral Lord Mountbatten. She inspected a NATO Royal Guard, made up of men drawn from the ships of the Standing Naval Force, and boarded *Britannia*, which was also home for the day to an assembly of NATO's great and good. In some ways, Elizabeth might have thought that a shame, for it was the first time that she had carried out a review from *Britannia* at Spithead, the traditional home of Royal Naval Reviews.

At 1230 Queen Elizabeth entertained the NATO top brass to lunch on board and at 1500, the royal yacht commenced the inspection, escorted by the frigate HMS *Wakeful** and the Belgian support ship *Zinnia*. She proceeded west on the north side of the fleet, turning to return along the Isle of Wight side of the ships, which had been arranged in three loose lines. By 1700 it was all over and both Queen Elizabeth and Prince Philip quickly departed, to separate destinations and appointments.

Unlike previous reviews, there were no merchant ships present except for a few ferries and passenger vessels carrying spectators. Nor was there a souvenir programme produced, although the *Portsmouth News* printed a local special edition. But at the conclusion of the formal review, twenty-eight of the ships on show berthed in Portsmouth Harbour and, on the Saturday and Sunday, twenty-one of them were opened to the public.

But there was no comparison with the mighty Spithead displays of the late Victorian and Edwardian navies. No thunder of gunfire, no dashing manoeuvres, no night-time illumination. It was a fairly tame affair.

* Originally launched as a destroyer in 1943, *Wakeful* was converted to an anti-submarine frigate between 1951 and 1953. She had been present at Queen Elizabeth's Coronation Review in her new guise.

There was a greater opportunity for old-fashioned power and glory two months later. On 28 and 29 July, Torbay saw a Royal Fleet Review of a type which would have been recognised by an observer from prelapsarian times. The occasion was the presentation of Colours to the Western Fleet, when thirty-nine warships and auxiliaries anchored for an inspection by the queen and other members of the royal family. And it was peak holiday time, with the area full of vacationers; there were numerous pleasure boats taking them out into the bay to view the fleet at close quarters.

The Western Fleet had been formed in 1967 from the old Home Fleet, as a result of the disbandment of the Mediterranean Fleet, a casualty of Britain's withdrawal from a world role. Its responsibilities included United Kingdom home waters, the North and South Atlantic and the Mediterranean, together with all Royal Navy operations 'West of Suez'. In a change from past tradition it was not headquartered at one of the great south coast ports but at Northwood in Middlesex, many miles from the sea.

Commander-in-Chief for the review was Admiral Sir John Fitzroy Duyland Bush, doubled-hatted with the NATO responsibility of Commander-in-Chief Allied Command Channel and Eastern Atlantic, with his flag in the largest ship in the Royal Navy, the strike carrier HMS *Eagle*, carrying Buccaneers, Gannets, Sea Vixens and Wessex helicopters.

The fleet had been in the bay from 26 July and had gathered a host of spectators on shore, for whom the ships were illuminated that night. On the Sunday, twenty vessels were opened to the public and the upper works of the vessels were again lit up from 2130 that evening.

At 0700 on Monday 28th *Britannia* arrived and anchored off Torquay, and at 1020 the royal barge took the Queen, the Duke of Edinburgh, Prince Charles and Princess Anne to board her. When the Royal Standard broke out at her foremast, the fleet fired a 21-gun salute, reverberating around the bay. As it was July in England, the weather was poor and the fleet was shrouded in rain and mist; nonetheless, the ships were assembled in five columns when, at 1035, *Britannia* entered the lines, preceded as always by a Trinity House vessel, *Patricia*, sailing first south and then east through the assembled warships. As was long-established tradition, all ships were dressed overall. The transit through the fleet took 25 minutes at which point the royal yacht anchored next to the flagship.

There then followed a series of royal visits to ships, broken by lunch on board *Britannia*. The Queen and Duke of Edinburgh visited the air-defence destroyer HMS *Hampshire* and the nuclear-powered (but not armed) submarine *Valiant*. Anne called upon the anti-submarine frigate *Eastbourne* and the deep ocean survey vessel *Hecate* while Charles visited RFA *Resource* and the general-purpose frigate *Phoebe*.

Just before 1500, the royal suite boarded HMS *Blake* for tea with the chief petty officers of the fleet. Regaining *Britannia*, Elizabeth hosted a

reception for senior officers and that evening dined on board *Eagle*, afterwards attending a concert party given by members of the ship's company. Once again, the fleet was illuminated until one minute to midnight. The weather had steadily deteriorated throughout the day and became so bad that boat traffic had to cease and some 3,000 liberty men were stranded ashore at Torquay. This no doubt caused much confusion (but possibly pleased the publicans).

The following day the weather was fair but very windy. The presentation of new Colours was to take place on HMS *Eagle* at 1000. It happened exactly 381 years after Sir Francis Drake fought the last battle of the Armada; and to recall that victory, a replica of the famous Drake's Drum was loaned by HMS *Drake* (Her Majesty's Naval Base, Devonport) for the event.

There were 1,500 men assembled on *Eagle*'s flight deck, together with a WRNS detachment from Northwood. Two royal guards of ninety-six men each were drawn up for inspection, after which the old Colour was trooped off while massed bands played *Auld Lang Syne*. A drum party then piled up a heap of drums, on top of which was placed Drake's, to await the Queen placing the new Colour atop of them. Admiral Bush invited representatives of the Anglican, Catholic and Scottish churches to consecrate the new Colour, whereupon the Queen passed the new device to the Colour Officer and the National Anthem was played.

As soon as the presentation concluded, there was a fly-past of eighty-nine Fleet Air Arm aircraft. First came thirty-one Wessex helicopters, just 400ft above the fleet. Then nine Fairey Gannet anti-submarine planes, followed by twenty of the magnificent Blackburn Buccaneers, at 800ft and 360kts, demonstrating their low-level penetration abilities. Next were twenty de Havilland Sea Vixens, air-defence fighters, travelling at the same speed, and finally the navy's latest aircraft, of which it was extremely proud, nine McDonnell Douglas F-4 Phantoms.

Now followed another ceremony which would have been approved of by the Queen's father, grandfather and great-grandfather. At 1230, *Britannia* headed the fleet in two columns out to sea. Once more, the Lord High Admiral of England led her ships to claim her rightful sovereignty of the oceans. Around 1400, 10 miles off Torquay, the royal yacht slowed her speed and the fleet, all ships manned and cheering, steamed past while Queen Elizabeth II took the royal salute. This exercise was not without alarm, for the frigate HMS *Keppel* (1954) had engine failure and came to an abrupt halt as the ships dispersed; a little earlier and it would have caused some difficulty.

As the ships melted away, the Queen signalled from *Britannia* 'I have been glad to present the new Colour to the Western Fleet and I was impressed by the excellent ceremonial at the presentation. My family and I have enjoyed visiting ships and meeting officers and ratings … I am delighted to find you in good heart. The appearance of ships and companies during today's steam past was especially good … Splice the mainbrace!'

When the fleet had departed, *Britannia*, escorted by the anti-submarine frigate HMS *Duncan*, returned to port; the royal suite disembarked at 1630 and the spectacle was done. For the first time in 16 years, there had been a Royal Fleet Review which respected the once-established traditions.

HMS *Eagle*, seen here berthed at Portsmouth's South Railway Jetty. In July 1969 Queen Elizabeth II presented new Colours to the Western Fleet aboard her. *(Photo; Royal Navy/MOD)*

'Take my drum to England, hang it by the shore,
Strike it when your powder's runnin' low;
If the Dons sight Devon, I'll quit the port o' Heaven,
An' drum them up the Channel as we drummed them long ago'.*

1977, The Silver Jubilee of Queen Elizabeth II

British maritime (and indeed defence) policy continued to be dictated by money, or rather the lack of it. Writing in 1972, the political journalist Patrick Cosgrave noted that 'the stark truth is that the strength of the Royal Navy has fallen below the safety level required to protect the home islands, to guard the ocean trade routes for the world-employed British mercantile marine (still the largest in the world), to protect the vast commercial and financial interests overseas, and to meet NATO, ANZUK and other treaty commitments'.[13] This state of affairs was blamed, amongst other things, on two key factors; 'the wholly inadequate, and unnecessarily complicated, system of naval procurement in existence in Britain, though, to be fair, naval – like all other military – programmes were severely dislocated by the disastrous shift and inconsistencies of the last Labour government'.[14] Cosgrave then excoriated the 'subconscious wish that still dominates the Admiralty Board to build ships for a fleet of the line, rather than for specific tasks of trade protection and local – usually combined – operations. Ships initially designed as light, and for specific tasks, became heavier and multi-purpose, as time goes by their completion is delayed, and their cost increased.'[15] In other words, admirals still wanted the glory of the capital ship rather the utility of the destroyer, frigate, sloop or corvette.

The coming and going of governments around this time and the parlous economic situation did not help matters. The Labour government was unseated in June 1970 when its share of the vote fell to its lowest level since 1935. It was replaced by Edward Heath's lacklustre regime which itself ended in 1974 to bring Harold Wilson's Labour Party back to power.[†] This was the signal for yet another Defence Review in 1974 and 1975, led by Roy Mason.

The Mason review was pre-empted and determined by a government decision that defence spending should be reduced from approximately 5 per cent of GDP to around 4.5 per cent over ten years, justified as moving towards the NATO average but in reality precipitated by the economic situation of the United Kingdom.[‡] As with the Healey reviews, the Mason scheme was driven by financial needs as opposed to foreign policy ones or national necessity.

Mason decreed that four major commitments were essential: the UK's contribution to NATO front-line troops in Germany, anti-submarine forces in the eastern Atlantic, home defence and the nuclear deterrent. The Army's strategic reserve division was disbanded, the RAF's transport fleet

* Henry Newbolt, 'Drake's Drum', from *Admirals All* (1897).

† Wilson resigned in 1976 and was replaced by Jim Callaghan.

‡ Oil prices had rocketed due to the Yom Kippur War which had doubled the cost of crude oil; this drove British inflation to unprecedented levels. As a result, there were industrial unrest and unsustainable wage awards and the country became mired in stagflation. Unemployment soared and worst of all Denis Healey, now Chancellor of the Exchequer, had to go cap in hand to the IMF for a bail out loan in 1976.

cut by half and amphibious forces reduced. Airborne capability was also significantly lessened. It virtually eliminated Britain's ability to project force out of the local area of Europe and was in stark fact a realisation that the UK was not and could not afford to be a world military power.

It was against this sorry background that, in 1977, Queen Elizabeth celebrated her 25th year on the throne, her Silver Jubilee. Needful of the economic situation, the Queen did not want a lavish celebration of the event, but a 'bread and circuses' philosophy seemed to overtake the government and in fact the year was commemorated widely. Elizabeth made a tour of thirty-six countries and many UK town and cities. There was a church service at St Paul's on 7 June followed by lunch at the Guildhall and a procession to Buckingham Palace with an estimated one million spectators lining the route. All over Britain there were some 4,000 celebratory street parties. On 9 June, the Queen made a royal progress by boat down the River Thames from Greenwich to Lambeth, as Charles II had done in 1662. In the evening, she presided over a firework display and was then taken in a procession of lighted carriages to Buckingham Palace.

On Tuesday 28 June there was a Silver Jubilee Royal Fleet Review. The ships began to assemble on Friday 24th. Ninety-eight HMS vessels converged on Spithead where Admiral Sir Henry Leach raised his flag in *Ark Royal*, now the navy's sole aircraft carrier. This was a far cry from the 183 at the 1953 Coronation review; but actually, the decline was steeper than it first appeared for the 1977 numbers were boosted by the presence of twenty-nine mine countermeasures vessels and eleven survey ships. Fifty-three units of the Merchant Navy and Royal Fleet Auxiliary were also in attendance.

As in previous reviews, there were also foreign warships present. Much internal debate had taken place in the Department of Defence as to which foreign countries should be invited. Norway and Sweden were placed on the invitee list because their kings were honorary admirals in the Royal Navy. And it was deemed appropriate to extend invitations to NATO, Commonwealth, European Community and CENTO* partners.

Other nations were given signs of disapproval, however. The Soviet Union had been represented at the 1953 Coronation Review, but it was now thought that other countries might object given that she posed a clear and present danger to the Western World. Spain was considered 'a European Monarchy whose movement towards democracy we wish to encourage but which has not achieved sufficient movement to justify an invitation',[16] while Finland was to be excluded for reasons which were not specified. One W J A Wilberforce concluded that a ceiling of twenty-five foreign vessels should be imposed, and that the Queen should approve the final list. In the end only twenty foreign naval vessels were present. These alien attendees helped pad out the numbers.

* Central Treaty Organization (CENTO), originally known as the Baghdad Pact, was a military alliance of the Cold War. It was formed in 1955 by Iran, Iraq, Pakistan, Turkey and the United Kingdom and ended in 1979.

The Royal Navy of 1953 could boast 302 ships; that of 1977 only 178. Manpower was 75,150 men as opposed to 146,600 of 24 years earlier.[17] There were no longer any battleships, only one aircraft carrier, and just nine destroyers, down from forty-five (see also Appendix 7). As Captain John Moore, editor of *Jane's Fighting Ships* remarked 'the navy is ... considerably down in numbers and firmly in the second division, alongside France'.[18]

Moreover, it was a defensive navy. Most warships were anti-something; anti-aircraft, anti-submarine, anti-mine. Admiral Sir Terence Lewin blamed this on the Healey cuts. The abandonment of aircraft carrier construction in 1966 'was imposed on us by economic necessity' he told *Navy International* 'and the loss of our primary striking power forced us to carry out a major reappraisal of our operational concepts'.[19] Now, 'nuclear submarines are the capital ship for anti-ship and anti-surface roles' he added. This latter statement was evidenced by the Royal Review being the first of the Royal Navy at Spithead in which there was no battleship or line-of-battle ship present. Instead there were four nuclear-powered submarines, *Superb*, *Valiant*, *Churchill* and *Dreadnought*, with *Superb* wearing the flag of Rear-Admiral John D E Fieldhouse,* Flag Officer Submarines. But Britain's pride and joy were missing, her four Polaris submarines – *Resolution*, *Revenge*, *Renown* and *Repulse* – which, according to the *New York Times*, 'are seldom seen by the public'.[20] There was also a visiting nuclear-powered surface vessel, the USS *California* (1971), a guided-missile cruiser with an array of weaponry – guns, missiles and anti-submarine – which were designed to combat all threats. She was capable of over 30kts and had an indefinite range.

Apart from *Ark Royal*, the RN had only a handful of large ships present. *Hermes* had been converted to an anti-submarine helicopter carrier the year previously and carried Wessex 5s and Sea Kings. *Fearless* was an assault ship, capable of transporting an assault group; and *Tiger* and *Blake* were helicopter cruisers carrying four Sea Kings each and originally laid down as conventional cruisers in 1941 and 1942 respectively. In fact, the second largest vessel at the review was the Australian navy's aircraft carrier *Melbourne* (1945). The newest vessel was the Greek *Lieutenant Troupakis*, a missile-armed fast attack craft, built in France and not yet actually commissioned. The largest civilian craft was the British Petroleum super tanker, the *British Respect*, at 270,000 deadweight tons the biggest ship in the review. Only one ship which had been present at the 1953 Coronation Review had returned to be present at this one, *Reclaim* (1948), a deep diving and submarine rescue vessel.[†]

The pattern of the review largely followed tradition. On the Saturday there were rehearsals, and the fleet was illuminated at night. On Sunday there was a Jubilee thanksgiving service on board *Ark Royal* and that evening Admiral Leach gave a reception in his flagship for Commonwealth

* Later to be commander of Task Force 317 and given responsibility for Operation 'Corporate', the mission to recover the Falkland Islands in 1982.

† She was decommissioned two years later.

and foreign officers. Here he received mariners from countries as varied as Brunei, Iran, and India. The fleet was again lit up from 2200. Monday morning was once more devoted to rehearsals. Then at 1740, the Queen arrived at Portsmouth railway station to be welcomed by, amongst others, Admiral Sir David Williams, C-in-C Naval Home Command and the Earl of Malmesbury, William James Harris, Lord Lieutenant of Hampshire. Transferring to the South Railway Jetty, Queen Elizabeth boarded *Britannia*; as she stepped aboard and the Royal Standard broke at the mast head, the Naval Saluting Battery fired the 21-gun salute. The fleet was again illuminated that evening.

On Tuesday 28 June, the weather was unhelpful; cold, windy and wet. Nevertheless, at 0800 all ships in the review lines, seven columns in all, dressed overall. Special guests at the review came by train from Waterloo in reserved carriages, arriving at Portsmouth Harbour Station by 0927. From there they were escorted to the destroyer HMS *Birmingham*, acting as yacht for the Board of Admiralty and illustrious visitors. These included Sir Herman Bondi, mathematics professor and chief scientific advisor to the MOD, and Fred Mulley, Secretary of State for Defence, with his wife.

At 1100, *Britannia*, with the Queen and royal family embarked, departed harbour; she was led out by the Trinity House vessel *Patricia* and followed by HMS *Birmingham*. Bringing up the rear came the helicopter support ship RFA *Engadine* with 200 reporters on board. They were joined from Southampton by the RFAs *Lyness*, *Sir Geraint* and *Sir Tristram* carrying

USS *California* (CGN 36) represented her country at the 1977 Silver Jubilee Review. In background is USS *Nimitz* (CVN-68) with RH-53 helicopters on her deck. *(US Naval History and Heritage Command USN 1178473)*

'County'-class destroyers HMS *Fife* (foreground) and HMS *Glamorgan* (left) at Spithead for the Silver Jubilee Fleet Review. *(photo: Alamy PJRCNY)*

lesser official guests, Members of Parliament, naval holders of the VC and GC, and other invitees.

As the royal procession passed HMS *Vernon* and *Dolphin* there was a royal salute from guards and bands assembled there; and as *Britannia* transited the Spit Refuge Buoy the guns of *Ark Royal*, *Hermes*, *Fearless*, *Tiger* and the 'County'-class guided-missile destroyers *Glamorgan*, *Fife* and *Kent*, together with selected foreign ships, fired off their homage to the monarch.

The royal yacht anchored at the head of the lines at 1130 and the Admiralty Board and flag officers of the fleet came aboard for lunch. And at 1430, *Britannia*, with her attendant vessels astern, entered the lines of the queen's navy, the ships' signal pennants popping in a stiff breeze. As the royal yacht moved past, Queen Elizabeth observed the scene through binoculars from the afterdeck as the sailors lining the ships' rails with their arms linked together snapped to attention.

All the while there were yachts and pleasure boats, together with small passenger steamers full of sightseers, circling the review area. The former included quondam prime minister Edward Heath at the helm of a yawl. Spectators ashore also braved the elements, while the Queen made the two-hour, 15-mile circuit of her fleet.

Cheering and saluting greeted the monarch as her vessel moved through the columns until *Britannia* regained her anchoring point at the head of the lines. From here she was meant to observe a fly-past by 150 Fleet Air Arm aircraft in three waves, led by the single Wessex of Rear-Admiral John O Roberts, Flag Officer Naval Air Command. However, weather conditions were so poor that it was cancelled and replaced by a fly-past of 110 helicopters.

Now came the festivities. At 1745 there was a reception on board *Britannia* for 200 ratings of the fleet. An hour later, Royal Marines gave a display on Southsea Common. At 2015 Queen Elizabeth and Prince

Philip, with other family members, dined on board the flagship in the upper hanger, surrounded by the monarch's admirals and captains, and at 2205 there was a firework display on Southsea Common. It was organised by Portsmouth Council but, in a sign of the times, had now to receive sponsorship; Schroeder's Life Group obliged. The fleet was illuminated for the last time as the final rocket flared out.

The following morning, *Britannia* returned to harbour, receiving another 21-gun salute as she departed, and the queen prepared herself for a royal visit to the City of Portsmouth itself. The second Silver Jubilee Royal Naval Review was at an end.

———

But this was not quite the Royal Navy's last involvement in the celebration of the Queen's 25 years on the throne. On Thursday 30 June there was a Royal Review of Reserve and Cadet Forces at Wembley Stadium as part of a musical pageant of over 2,000 musicians from seventy-five bands. Pipes and drums, bugles and corps of drums of all three services marched and counter-marched in celebration of the Silver Jubilee.

Preceding the 'Services' Musical Pageant', the Queen reviewed a parade of 2,000 men and women from the three services, together with the Royal Observer Corps, Territorial Army and Cadet Forces, all with their guidons, colours and banners.

Sub-Lieutenant Bob Horner RNR was second-in-command of the naval component and remembered that they had to rehearse on the lawns of the Inns of Court, near to HMS *President*. They had no band and wheeling on the grass was very difficult. Sailors don't really like marching but on the day the men marched in sixes behind Sub-Lieutenant Horner and his commander in something like good order. Bob received a Silver Jubilee Medal for his efforts.

———

The festivities were over but the arguments continued. Prior to the review, Admiral Leach had previously quoted Walter Raleigh, stating that 'the nation's wealth, prosperity and peace chiefly depend on the navy and said that the navy was up to its task'.[21] Captain Moore of *Jane's Fighting Ships* begged to differ. He argued in an interview 'that Britain, at great cost, had built "the wrong kind of first-class fleet" – a fleet he considers too highly sophisticated for the sort of mundane jobs it must face'. Moore also claimed that 'we need smaller, more flexible ships. We have tried to maintain a standard higher than we could afford.'[22] *Ark Royal*, Admiral Leach's flagship, 'will head for the breaker's yard next year, and she will not be replaced. Too expensive, the Government decided, for a country in economic straits.'[23]* There would not be another Royal Naval Review for 16 years.

* *Ark Royal* was actually decommissioned in February 1979.

Chapter 16

... and Fall, 1993–2005

IN THE YEARS following the Silver Jubilee Royal Naval Review, the armed forces suffered further cuts to their budgets and Britain entrenched even more firmly into NATO. Secretary of State for Defence John Nott took up his role in January 1981 and immediately set to work on a defence review which was intended to bring expenditure on equipment and procurement into line with the resources allocated.

He concluded that Britain had a choice between either making a land or maritime contribution to NATO and decided on the former, except that his review, widely criticised by service chiefs, committed to the renewal of the nuclear deterrent and emphasised the UK's reliance on its nuclear capability to counter the Soviet threat. It effectively surmised that the UK would only act as part of the NATO alliance in any other expeditionary operations.

The navy was to take the main impact of the proposed cuts, being designated to lose approximately one-fifth of its destroyers and frigates, one aircraft carrier and two amphibious ships, thereby further reducing the UK's expeditionary capability. Even the naval ice patrol ship, HMS *Endurance* was also to be withdrawn from the Southern Atlantic. In total the Royal Navy suffered 57 per cent of the planned cuts in expenditure.

Argentina took these cuts and the reduction in out-of-NATO-area capabilities as a sign that Britain could not, and would not, resist an invasion of the Falkland Islands and in April 1982 did just that. Operation 'Corporate', a brilliantly improvised largely navy-led counterstroke, showed the British ability to snatch victory from the jaws of defeat. But as Professor Sir Lawrence Freedman has written, given that it was fought well out of the NATO area and with the Royal Navy as the lead service, 'it was precisely the war for which Britain was planning least'.[1]

The Falklands campaign won, the services faced yet more pain in the 'Options for Change' White Paper of 1990, which was concomitant with the collapse of the Soviet Union and the Warsaw Pact in 1989.

The objective of the review was to establish a smaller, more flexible force structure within the confines of NATO and its main conclusions involved a decrease in manpower across all three services of some 18 per cent (56,000) by the mid-1990s. The navy would be reduced to a manning level of only 60,000.* The Royal Naval Auxiliary Service was to be scrapped (it was finally disbanded in 1994) and the Royal Naval Reserve reduced by a quarter. The review also called for a downsizing of the Royal Navy fleet from forty-eight destroyers and frigates to forty (similar to Nott's original proposals) and a 15 per cent reduction in Nimrod maritime patrol aircraft. But it once again stressed the importance of retaining a strategic nuclear deterrent, although quite who it was going to be used against seems unclear. It was thus an ever-declining Royal Navy that involved itself in the next Royal Fleet Review, that of 1993.

1993, Battle of the Atlantic Fifty Years Commemoration (BA50)

Between 25 and 30 May, a commemoration of the Battle of the Atlantic – BA50 – was held in the general area of the City of Liverpool. It is difficulty now to see this event as anything other than a moneymaking opportunity, for the emphasis seemed firmly on Mammon rather than the many men who lost their lives in the fight to keep Britain supplied with food and raw materials.

During the Second World War, German U-boats very nearly succeeded in bringing the county to its knees through interdiction of the nation's food and *materiel* supplies. The lessons of the Great War, when the same disaster nearly befell Britain, had been either forgotten or, in the case of the politicians who so wantonly neglected Britain's defences in the inter-war years, ignored.

So the Battle of the Atlantic was crucial to Britain's survival. But it hardly ended in May 1943; yes, Dönitz withdrew his U-boats to the Azores on 24 May in the face of heavy losses. But men continued to die. The first merchant ship to be lost in the Western Approaches was SS *Athenia*, on the opening evening of the war; and 17,000 merchant seafarers would die in the North Atlantic before the war ended. Men died after 1943; nineteen merchant ships were sunk in the Western Approaches in January–May 1945 and thirty-one the year before (see also Appendix 8). So the chosen date of Bank Holiday week May 1993 was somewhat arbitrary, although 1943 can certainly be seen as the turning of the tide.

The celebration centred on Liverpool, a region of Britain desperately trying to regenerate at the time. The event was paid for by over fifty-three corporate sponsors, even including the Metropolitan Borough of Wirral, and brought thousands of tourists to the city. In fact, it was so commercially successful that it was repeated in 2013.†

There was a comprehensive souvenir programme (price £2.50) and a

* The Royal Navy's lowest manpower level since the 58,000 of 1885.

† When, according to the *Liverpool Echo* of 16 May 2013, 'all of Liverpool's 5,400 hotel beds have sold out on Saturday May 25 and most are also booked for the following Sunday night. It is expected that the five-day event will bring in around £5m to the city's economy.'

range of tawdry knick-knacks for sale. There were also special first-day postal covers. Amongst the attractions promised were the Wigan Jazz Youth Orchestra, several wartime themed dances, an ENSA* concert and a Glen Miller musical.

Some forty ships were involved, but only twelve from the UK (see Appendix 9). Thirty-four of them moored up in Liverpool docks for the duration, as did *Britannia*, so the public could view them. HMS *Ark Royal* (1981) was meant to have been amongst them, but she was required on active duty in the Adriatic instead.

As for the Royal Review itself, it took place on 26 May, off Moelfre, Anglesey. Thirty-four warships, together with eight commercial vessels, from sixteen countries, led by HMS *Cornwall* (flagship of Rear-Admiral Michael C Boyce) were intended to participate. The Royal Navy was to be represented by only eight warships together with six blue-ensign support ships. There were to be eight Merchant Navy vessels present and twenty ships from foreign nations. All were to assemble in six lines for inspection, not by the Queen but by HRH the Duke of Edinburgh accompanied by King Harald V of Norway.†

But once more the weather took its toll. Force eight winds sprang up the evening before and the vessels fought all night to maintain their positions at anchor. The American mine countermeasures vessel USS *Devastator* lost power and was dragged from her anchorage. Eventually she manged to regain some propulsion and departed for Liverpool, accompanied by her sister-ship, USS *Scout*. A number of smaller naval units had to pull out because of the battering they were taking from the elements and the conditions prevented the cable-laying ship MV *Iris* from joining up.

In the end, twenty-six warships and seven merchantmen survived in formation, battered but unbowed, to greet the royal yacht. As always, a Trinity House vessel, *Mermaid*, led the way. Behind *Britannia* came the hydrographic survey vessel HMS *Bulldog*, the Type 21 frigate HMS *Active*,‡ the excursion ship MV *Balmoral* (of 1949 vintage) and the ferry MV *Stena Cambria*: both motor vessels were carrying veterans and their families, who were reliving not just the danger but also the capricious elements often encountered during their merchant sailing days.

When it was all over, *Britannia* departed the scene and Prince Philip sent a signal to the naval command; 'Weather conditions could hardly have been worse but they had no effect on the smartness and turnout of the aircraft and ships companies taking part in the review. The presence of so many representatives of the wartime allies was a worthy tribute to the service and sacrifice of those who fought and won the battle of the Atlantic fifty years ago. Splice the mainbrace!'[2]

Many of the ships then sailed back to the Mersey. There was a march-past on 29 May of over 2,000 veterans and service personnel, including

* Entertainments National Service Association.

† An avid sailor, he represented Norway in the yachting events of the Summer Olympics in Tokyo in 1964, Mexico City in 1968 and Munich in 1972.

‡ *Active* would be sold to Pakistan the following year.

men from HMS *Liverpool* and HMS *Birmingham* together with four Royal Marine bands. The route was lined by members of the Sea Cadet Corps.

That same day there was an air display over the river which featured five Royal Navy Sea Harriers, a helicopter formation and displays and closed with a salute from a pair of Second World War Fairey Swordfish biplanes. But all together it seemed a rather muted affair, a royal review without the monarch, a fleet with a minority Royal Navy presence, a week tinged by pecuniary gain and with none of the grandeur of pre-war times.

1994, D-Day 50th Anniversary

The presumed end of the Cold War led to the Defence Costs Study of 1994 and talk of a 'peace dividend' across Europe, at a time of general economic slump. Defence once more became the target of the Treasury's axe. The stated goal was to achieve further cost savings without reductions in the front line. Total armed forces personnel were slashed by 18,700, to be achieved within six years; of these, for the Royal Navy and Royal Marines, a further 1,900 service positions were to go. Already, by 1 April 1994, the navy had 6,400 men less than at the beginning of the decade.[3]

In contrast to the shrinking size of the British naval forces in the 1990s, on 6 June 1944, the largest amphibious invasion fleet ever assembled had set sail for France and started the process of liberating northern Europe from the German yoke. The transit of such a fleet would not have been possible without the command of the sea, held primarily by the Royal Navy, and the mastery of the air above it controlled by the RAF and USAAF.

It was a savagely-fought battle. By the end of the first day, 4,000 British and Canadian troops, together with 6,000 Americans were either killed or wounded. By September, there were 210,000 Allied casualties of whom 37,000 were dead.[4] But their sacrifice changed the course of history and would directly lead to the end of the war. And again, the Royal Navy maintained sovereignty of the seas throughout the operation, with the 10th Destroyer Flotilla guarding the supply chain across the Channel from German surface forces based in Biscay while fifty-five escort destroyers, sloops and frigates from the RN and RCN mounted anti-submarine patrols between Ushant and Ireland.

Fifty years later, it was right and proper that the success of Operation 'Overlord' (as it was code-named) and the men who took part and oft-time died, should be commemorated. Planning began the previous year, and in early 1994 Prime Minister John Major announced the programme at the Imperial War Museum in London. Not everyone was pleased. The build-up to the events of June were marked by both excitement and a little criticism. Some veterans' groups complained that the schedule contained a little too much celebration and not enough commemoration. Certainly, there were the usual tacky souvenirs rushed into production. But come the day, the ceremonies were largely considered to be appropriate.

The main official events took place at Portsmouth and on the Normandy beaches. On 4 June, a garden party was held five miles north of Portsmouth at Southwick House (in the grounds of the 'stone frigate' HMS *Dryad*) the headquarters from which General Eisenhower issued the order to launch the invasion. That same day, massed bands performed beating the retreat at HMS *Excellent*, on Whale Island, and in the evening there was a banquet for 500 people at Portsmouth Guildhall. The attendees included representatives of all the nations which took part in D-Day itself and those organisations who contributed to the invasion operations.

Veterans groups from Britain, Canada and the USA were prominent in the commemorations which followed over the next two days. The Royal British Legion chartered the cruise ship SS *Canberra* to take Normandy veterans and their families across to France. In France, on the 5th, thirty-eight American D-Day paratrooper survivors, called by the French *papys sauteurs*,* parachuted once again over Sainte-Mère-Eglise. One 70-year-old ex-GI's parachute failed to open and he had to use his reserve.

Heads of state from thirteen countries participated. These did not include Chancellor Helmut Kohl of Germany, who asked not to be invited. The French anyway refused to have Germans present at the D-Day beaches. This may have seemed a little hypocritical as France was represented by President Mitterrand, who had worked for the Vichy regime in the first part of the war. America was embodied in the person of President Clinton, who many believe had fled abroad to avoid Vietnam 'and who once said publicly how much he hated the military'.[5]

Nevertheless, on 5 June Clinton and Major joined President Lech Walesa of Poland, Paul Keating, Prime Minister of Australia, Presidents Havel and Kovac of the Czech and Slovak republics and Commonwealth leaders on board *Britannia* where they met Queen Elizabeth, the Duke of Edinburgh, the Queen Mother, the Princess Royal and Princess Margaret. On shore on Southsea Common, a drumhead service was held in front of the naval memorial; and off shore lay an international flotilla of thirty-one ships which included the largest aircraft carrier in the world, the USS *George Washington*, and the Royal Navy's somewhat smaller vessel HMS *Illustrious* (1978), a light carrier with a ski-jump take-off ramp and flying the flag of the Commander-in-Chief Fleet, Admiral Sir Hugo Moresby White.

Other notable craft lined up in the Solent that day were an original American Liberty Ship *Jeremiah O'Brien*, which had made eleven crossings in support of the D-Day invasion and was under the command of a veteran of the operation, Captain George John; and the motor launch *ML-293* (a Fairmile B-type launched in 1941), the first bowed vessel into

* Jumping grandpas.

1994 D-Day Fleet
Review. *Britannia*,
with the Queen and
President Clinton
on board, sails
through the fleet.
*(photo: Alamy
HFFK3Y)*

Boulogne harbour during the liberation of France, and which nearly fell
victim to army sharpshooters exploding mines close to her stern.
Restored, she was serving as a training vessel for sea cadets.

Britannia sailed past the naval memorial, and the salutes of the men gathered there, towards the twin lines of the assembled ships. As the queen's
vessel prepared to enter the lines, *Illustrious* fired a 42-gun salute. The royal
yacht initially sailed west along the lee side of the first column, then east
back along the more southerly line. As always, she was preceded by a
Trinity House vessel, *Patricia*. As escort, *Britannia* had the Type 21 frigate
HMS *Avenger*, on almost her last duty before being sold out of the navy.
And immediately astern of her came the ocean-going survey vessel HMS
Hecla, which carried the press. Within three years she too would be sold.
As the royal yacht transited the lines, there was a fly-past led by two
ancient Swordfish, followed by both modern and older warplanes,
including a Lancaster, Spitfire and Hurricane, and a formation of Hawk
trainers, which spelled out '50'.

On completion of the circuit of the international flotilla, *Britannia* and
Avenger picked up speed and set off for the French coast, followed by
Canberra, Cunard's *Queen Elizabeth II* and other vessels, carrying both
veterans and spectators.

In mid-Channel, at a point known in 1944 as 'Piccadilly Circus', they
rendezvoused with two lines of warships, named Formation Ramsey in
honour of the British naval commander of Operation 'Overlord'; one

column was headed by the Type 42 destroyer HMS *Edinburgh*, wearing the flag of Vice-Admiral Michael Boyce, and one by the French frigate FS *Duguay Trouin*. *Canberra* and *QE2* took position on the wings of the lines and *Britannia* sailed through the middle of them. As she passed each pair of ships, instead of the customary cheering, wreaths were cast into the sea. And overhead, an Avro Lancaster bomber dropped 850,000 poppies over SS *Canberra* and her contingent of ex-servicemen. It was a most poignant moment.

In the early afternoon of the next day, 6 June, Queen Elizabeth and other heads of state joined together at Omaha Beach for an international ceremony. There was the traditional D-Day march-past at Arromanches. And the conclusion of the ceremonial was marked by another 42-gun salute from the offshore naval vessels and a fly-past by aircraft from the Battle of Britain Memorial Flight and the Royal Naval Historic Flight.

The commemoration was over. The Royal Navy had again been in a Royal Review, albeit of a very different type to convention, and in company with many other nations. But there had also been many similarities with reviews of times past. And as for the merchandising and souvenirs, 'never before was so much effort spent designing commemorative chinaware that was produced by so many and enjoyed by so few'.[6]

—————

The year 1995 was another *annus horribilis* for the Royal Navy, and indeed the 1990s in total represented a dark decade. Between the time of the D-Day celebrations and April 1995, nearly 5,000 ratings and 400 officers were chopped out of the naval service. Operating strength in ships was also badly hit. Five fleet submarines were lost versus 1994, leaving just twelve. Two frigates were cut, together with two patrol ships and two squadrons of helicopters. And the long-term trend left little doubt where the navy was headed. The Strategic Defence Reviews of 1998 and 2002 imposed further pain. Comparing 1999 with 1990, manpower fell by 20,000. The number of submarines was cut by eighteen to just fifteen. There were twenty-one less mine countermeasures vessels. Two destroyers went as did twelve frigates and ten patrol ships; and there were five fewer helicopters squadrons.[7] The cuts are detailed in Appendix 10; over the decade the Royal Navy's fighting strength declined by nearly 40 per cent. There was hardly any navy left for the Queen to review.

To make matters worse, in 1994 the Conservative government announced, almost immediately after the D-Day review, that *Britannia* would be decommissioned in 1997. It had been estimated that she required a £17 million refit which would only prolong her working life by five years. 'The queen and royal family were saddened at the decision ... they were aware that public opinion would probably not countenance a new yacht from the state purse.'[8] It should be recalled that this decade was one of growing anti-royalist sentiment, following the divorces of the Prince of Wales and the Duke of York in 1996 and the death of Princess Diana in 1997. *Britannia* paid off on 11 December that same year.

It is thus small wonder that, unlike Victoria, Elizabeth did not receive the tribute of a Royal Naval Review to celebrate 50 years on the throne in 2002. A tentative plan to hold one was scotched by Tony Blair's Labour government on the grounds of cost. As the *Daily Telegraph* put it, 'there was a review for her Silver Jubilee in 1977, following the tradition of marking such events throughout the century, but that custom ended in 2002 when it was decided not to hold one to mark Queen Elizabeth II's Golden Jubilee'.* The newspaper went on to allude to Britain's diminished world status by adding 'that in itself proved again why the fleet review is such an eloquent marker of Britain's place in the world, because the decision was taken on broadly financial grounds'.[9] So the next time that the Queen met her navy was a lower-key affair in 2003.

2003, New Colours for Old

On 23 July 2003, the monarch presented new Colours to the Royal Navy in a ceremony off the coast of Plymouth. This was only the third presentation of Colours, and Queen Elizabeth's second, since 1926 and represents another example of 'instant tradition'. It is perhaps useful to note how the custom developed.

Originally, Colours were called ensigns, which came into use on the ships of Queen Elizabeth I reign in the 1570s. They were similar to regimental flags, which at that time were also called ensigns. Until the early 1600s each ship had its own individual ensign (Colour) that was different to the ensign of any other ship. By this time the flags on land were being called Colours, and distinguished one regiment from another. The equivalent naval flags retained the name ensign, and it became the habit for all the ships in a squadron to have a flag of the same design.

There things lay until 1807, when an Admiralty Board Minute proposed that a White Ensign paraded by a naval guard would be considered a Colour. By 1920 there were regulations regarding the use of the White Ensign by landing parties ashore. However, although these flags were reduced in length to make then appropriate for use in a parade, they were no different in design to any other White Ensign.

This caused a problem when, at a ceremony, there were both naval and military guards of honour. The naval guard saluted their military equivalent as a mark of respect for the King's Colour of the regiment providing the guard, but not *vice-versa*, as there was no Colour to salute. Following an incident at the Royal Tournament of 1923, King George V was asked to approve the use of Colours by the Royal Navy, which would correspond to the King's Colours carried by military forces. On 5 March 1924, the king approved a Colour which consisted of a silk White Ensign, 36in by 45in, with red, white and blue cord and gold tassels, carried on a staff, capped with a crown and a three-faced shield bearing the Admiralty fouled anchor. A Colour with the addition of a crown and royal cypher superimposed in the centre was approved as a King's Colour on the 12 May 1925;[10] it was these Colours which George V gave to the navy in 1926 (*vide supra* Chapter 13). The Queen had presented new Colours in 1969 (*vide supra* Chapter 15). Now she was to do so again, although according to the *Daily Telegraph* newspaper 'the navy said there was no particular significance in the timing of yesterday's presentation other than that the old Colour had become "a bit tatty and was looking jaded"'.[11] Two months earlier, on 17 May, the Prince of Wales, in his rank as Vice-Admiral of the Royal Navy, had presented new Sovereign's Colours to the Royal Naval Reserve. Now the Queen herself would undertake the same office for the Royal Navy.

The ceremony took place on HMS *Ocean* (1995), flying the flag of Admiral Sir Jonathon Band, Commander-in-Chief Fleet. *Ocean*, a helicopter carrier designed to provide amphibious assault capabilities and the navy's largest ship, had just returned from a deployment in the Iraq war. The event followed many of the now-established traditions, excepting that there was no longer a royal yacht to carry the monarch and dignitaries around the fleet. But then there was only a small fleet. Just nineteen RN and RFA vessels assembled in the Sound to greet their monarch. As Queen Elizabeth boarded *Ocean*, the Type 23 frigate *Norfolk* fired a 21-gun salute. On board the flagship, the Queen inspected a parade of 300 Royal Navy

HMS *Ocean*, flagship at the Colours presentation of 2003, seen here off the coast of Norway. *(Photo: LAPhot Bernie Henesy/ MOD)*

personnel drawn up on the flight deck and told them that she wanted to express 'her sympathy to the families and friends of those who recently gave their lives in active service. As a daughter, wife and mother of naval officers I want to pay tribute to families for the support they give to those who serve far from home.'[12]

Being with her navy, of which she was still Lord High Admiral, and in Plymouth, home to the legendary Sir Francis Drake, she added 'it is most appropriate that I should be presenting this Colour in Plymouth Sound with its long association with the service and on the 415th anniversary of the defeat of the Spanish Armada'.[13] The new Colour was received from the Queen on bended knee by Lieutenant Steven Berry, the Colours officer, on behalf of Admiral Band. And after the presentation the queen watched a sail-past, a sort of milksop Royal Review, and a fly-past of modern and historic aircraft, the latter another 'instant tradition' dating from 1912.

Despite the weather, which was once again windy, wet and miserable, thousands of people packed Plymouth Hoe to watch the proceedings; a new innovation was the provision for them of two giant screens to relay the events at sea. Royalty may have been through a rough patch in the 1990s and the navy had shrunk significantly but there was still clearly a considerable appetite among the populace for such pomp and circumstance. And to extract maximum value from the trip to the West Country, the Queen also formally named the city's latest lifeboat, the *Sybil Mullen Glover*.

2005, Trafalgar 200 and the Commercialisation of the Navy

When the Royal Navy defeated the combined French and Spanish fleets off Trafalgar on 21 October 1805 it created four conditions, all of which have been reflected in the Royal Fleet Reviews described in this book. First, it established the Nelsonian tradition, which by the middle of the nineteenth century had become a dead hand on some areas of naval thinking. Secondly, it removed Spain from the list of Britain's long-term enemies for good. Thirdly, it marked the beginning of the end for French hegemony in Europe. Finally, the victory reasserted Britain's sovereignty of the seas, allowing free trade, the expansion of Empire and making the Royal Navy the protector of Imperial commerce for the next 150 years.

The Nelson legend became part of Britain's culture. Pubs, street names, music, books and art were all inspired by his glory and his name joined the pantheon of naval heroes that included Drake, Raleigh, Grenville, Blake, Rodney, Howe, St Vincent and Hawke. Trafalgar too became a watchword for British maritime supremacy, alongside the destruction of the Spanish Armada.

It was thus considered appropriate, and possibly politically expedient, that a festival be built around the 200th anniversary of such national success. In days past, as has been noted, the Royal Navy used Royal Fleet Reviews as both a form of advertising for funds and justification of expenditure, together with a glorification of naval strength and a warning to potential enemies. The latter function had long since been made untenable and the *soi-disant* 'Trafalgar 200' festivities were overtly positioned as of commercial intent, a puff for Britain and for international collaboration and trade. The Minister of State at the Ministry of Defence in Prime Minister Blair's Labour government, Adam Ingram, made this clear beyond doubt in a written ministerial statement of 21 June. 'The Royal Navy's Trafalgar 200 programme forms part of the Trafalgar festival which is at the heart of the "SeaBritain 2005" initiative sponsored by the Department of Culture, Media and Sport. '"SeaBritain 2005" aims to raise the profile of the United Kingdom's maritime interests.' He then added 'the Trafalgar 200 programme of events will also strengthen the Royal Navy's maritime partnerships, help develop interoperability and build on multinational maritime cooperation … Trafalgar 200 … provides a major vehicle for the Ministry of Defence to promote public awareness and support for defence in 2005'. As if this were not enough, the festival was to be funded 'through a combination of public funding and commercial sponsorship and revenue'.[14] It was, in fact, a sort of floating Blairite 'Cool Britannia'.

The official brochure reflected this, and the shrivelled size of the navy compared to past glories, by making a benefit out of a necessity, stating that the event was 'less formal than those of the last century. Rather than being primarily combat power on display … [it] sought to link with the past by the inclusion of many tall ships and to link to the future with 1,200 schoolchildren and naval cadets embarked in the fleet'.[15] This rectitude may have had something to do with the fact that a year earlier, on 21 July 2004, the MoD announced that twelve ships (three Type 42s, three Type 23s and six mine countermeasures vessels) were to be paid off within the next two years. Additionally, Royal Navy personnel was to be reduced by 1,500 to 36,000 and the upcoming Type 45 order cut from twelve to first eight and then six. The First Sea Lord at the time, Lord West, stated that the changes would leave the navy better organised and equipped for the future, which seemed at best dissembling.

Nonetheless, the plan was to hold a Royal Fleet Review in June 2005 with a sequence of other experiences, including an International Festival of the Sea, followed in October by events in Britain and Gibraltar themed around Nelson and the battle. Not everyone was enamoured of the commerciality of the events. The *Independent* newspaper accused the navy of 'cheapening the monarchy by offering invitations to a reception with the Queen and the Duke of Edinburgh … at the Royal Naval Museum in Portsmouth'. It asserted that 'corporate sponsors and wealthy individuals

HMS *Invincible*, flagship for the Trafalgar 200 event, pictured at the review with her sides manned. A few weeks later she was laid up. *(Photo: Geoff Parselle/MOD)*

are being charged up to £25,000 to have dinner on HMS *Victory* with senior Naval officers … however, the official price tag hanging on a dinner with the queen on Trafalgar Day itself is relatively cheap. The Royal Navy is asking just £500 for the privilege of enjoying what it promises will be "a truly atmospheric, historic atmosphere and once in a lifetime opportunity'". Such venality was necessary because, according to the newspaper, 'the Ministry of Defence has been forced to raise funds to help cover the costs of a lavish series of public celebrations to honour Lord Nelson, Britain's greatest naval hero'.[16] And the Conservative opposition's Defence Spokesman Andrew Robathan sought to score political points with a comment that 'it is totally inappropriate and disgusting that the queen should be hired in this way'.[17] *O tempora o mores!*

Nevertheless, on 28 June 2005, some 170 ships were drawn up in the Solent to greet Queen Elizabeth II. The Royal Navy claimed sixty-five of them; but this was to mislead. There were only thirty-one RN surface combatants present in the review lines, with another seven vessels on sentinel duty. Twenty-seven of those RN ships painted grey were not in fact warships (see also Appendix 11). Thirty-five other nations provided fifty-eight vessels whilst eight countries sent twenty-three tall ships (sailing ships). Of the enemies at Trafalgar 200 years previously, the French had seven naval representatives, including the nuclear-powered aircraft carrier, FS *Charles de Gaulle*, and Spain two. The world's largest navy was represented by two vessels, the USS *Saipan*, an amphibious assault ship, and the USCGC *Eagle*.* And from Italy came the naval square-rigger *Amerigo Vespucci*, a sail training ship of 1931 vintage which had also been present at the 1953 Coronation Review. Additionally, there were representative vessels from all sectors of the marine industry from around the world.

Flagship for the occasion was the aircraft carrier *Invincible*. However, she

* The only square rigger still in US government service, she was previously the German sail training ship *Horst Wessel*, launched in 1936 and taken as war reparations at the end of the Second World War.

was already doomed to extinction, for on 6 June the Ministry of Defence had announced that she would become inactive and the carrier was decommissioned immediately after the Royal Review.

Royal yachts were now, of course, a distant memory; instead Queen Elizabeth and the Duke of Edinburgh sailed in HMS *Endurance* (1991), a diesel-powered, Norwegian-built Antarctic Patrol Vessel and ice-breaker, where they were joined by First Sea Lord Admiral Sir Alan West and Defence Secretary John Reid. A special viewing platform had been built for the royals atop the bridge and a Royal Marine band was positioned on the forward working deck. The royal couple reviewed a joint Royal Navy and Royal Marines guard of honour in front of *Victory* and met the families of the crew of *Endurance* before embarking, which took place to the echoes of a 21-gun salute from the Type 22 frigate HMS *Chatham*. Although entitled to, the Queen did not wear a naval uniform, instead sporting a light blue coat and hat covering a blue floral print dress.

The review pursued the customary pattern. *Endurance*, led towards the lines of ships by the Trinity House vessel *Patricia*, was followed by the *Chatham*, as royal escort, the survey ships *Scott* (with the Prince of Wales on board in the uniform of a vice-admiral, together with the Duchess of Cornwall) and *Enterprise* (carrying the Duke of York), RFA *Sir Bedivere*

Sailors of the USS *Saipan* salute Queen Elizabeth II as HMS *Endurance* passes along the lines at the Trafalgar 200 Royal Fleet Review. *(Photo: US Navy)*

(with the Princess Royal) and MY *Leander*,* with the tall ship *Grand Turk* bringing up the rear. It had been intended that the press would be hosted on board HMS *Scott* but, in the end, they were allocated across two of the P2000 *Archer*-class fast training boats.

As the makeshift royal yacht made its way west through the assembled ships, the skies began to darken and by the time *Endurance* had moored at the head of the assembly, for the steam past and overflight, the weather had closed and the heavens opened with thunder and torrential rain. Queen Elizabeth seemed to have no luck with weather at Royal Reviews, unlike her great-great-grandmother Victoria, who usually enjoyed what was known as 'Queen's Weather', with the sun unexpectedly appearing.

Ashore and in a flotilla of private yachts, an estimated 250,000 people watched the procession and braved the elements for the two hours that it took for the ice-breaker to sail up and down the lines of ships, while the Queen inspected them from her lofty perch and was given the traditional three cheers from each vessel she passed. But not only was the review condemned for its commercialism, it seemed that its relevance of the event and the navy had failed to leave a mark on much of the audience.

> Many of the … spectators on the beaches and seafront enjoying the largest international fleet review of its kind, admitted that they were embarrassed about their knowledge of the naval battles that shaped the modern world … At times it seemed that the spectacle unfolding before them was a source of curiosity rather than national pride. The atmosphere was strangely subdued.[18]

* At the time, owned by Sir Donald Gosling, a great supporter of the RN and a member of the Royal Yacht Squadron at Cowes. Sir Donald was an honorary captain in the RNR (and later an honorary vice-admiral) and President of the White Ensign Association. *Leander* was a 245ft yacht with nine double guest state rooms and two suites, and carried a crew of twenty-two.

In an attempt to bring more movement to the review, a new feature was a sail-past of warships through the anchored lines. Led by HMS *Cumberland*, and including HMAS *Anzac*, and HMCS *Montreal*, the frigates undertook the manoeuvre at 17kts, with impeccable station-keeping both necessary and achieved. At the rear of the line came *MTB-102* (1937), a survivor of the 1939 Royal Fleet Review by Queen Elizabeth's father and now owned and operated by a trust. She kept perfect station just 50 yards from the stern of HMS *Grafton*. Undeterred by the atrocious weather, a planned flying display went ahead; and with the arrival of the Red Arrows at 1730 the clouds began to clear, after which, and in keeping with the historic antecedents of a Royal Review, the Queen boarded the flagship for a reception with flag officers and captains.

There was also an 'all ranks' reception held on board HM *Illustrious*, which gained royal kudos from the attendance of the Duchess of Gloucester and the Duke of York, a dinner at Southsea Castle, in the company of Princess Anne, the Princess Royal, accompanied by her husband Rear-Admiral Timothy Laurence, and another dinner aboard

HMS *Invincible*, graced by the Duchess of Gloucester, Prince and Princess Michael of Kent, the Duke of York, Queen Elizabeth and the Duke of Edinburgh.

At 1900, a *son et lumière* Battle of Trafalgar was re-enacted by seventeen tall ships from five nations, with blazing cannon broadsides, gun smoke and state-of-the-art pyrotechnics. This tableau began when an actor playing the part of Nelson sailed from shore in a small cutter to board the tall ship *Grand Turk*, a replica nineteenth-century frigate. This ship played the part of Nelson's flagship *Victory* during the fight, billed as between a blue and a red team, rather than Britain versus France, a decision that upset some who saw it as unnecessarily politically correct. This category certainly included the on-shore narrator who represented the event throughout as the British beating the French. Patriotism was largely absent from the blaring musical accompaniment too. *Rule Britannia* was noticeably omitted and Holst's *Jupiter*, otherwise the hymn *I Vow to Thee My Country*, provided the closest encounter with national pride. Finally, at 2130 there was a spectacular firework display over the ships, 'one of the most spectacular ever staged in the UK'.[19] It utilised 10,000 individual fireworks fired from thirty-five pontoons and six barges. The fleet was then illuminated for the remainder of the evening.

It had been quite a show. But the BBC could only find 30 minutes or so of broadcast time in its schedules to cover such a celebration of victory and might. Criticism of the BBC's well-known antipathy to Britain's imperial heritage soon followed. Frank Johnson, writing in the *Daily Telegraph*, imagined the scene in the BBC offices; 'a half an hour or so. This has doubtless provoked a crisis for the director-general, Mark Thompson, and the corporation's higher ranks. Half an hour? Too much!'[20] But the *Portsmouth News* made the most of the opportunity, producing a commemorative glossy 48-page magazine and giving extensive in-paper coverage to the events. Their reporter Simon Coughlin also joined in the spirit of the day when he was told by the organisers that he could only cover the sea battle re-enactment if he dressed as an eighteenth-century powder monkey.

The costs had been significant; these included a massive security operation costing £1.7million and involving more than 400 naval personnel and scores of police officers, which had been laid on to protect the public, the royal family and the navy during the event. Just over a week later came the 7/7 London bombings.

It was the end of the last Royal Fleet Review up to the time of writing. A magnificent spectacle to be sure, but the Royal Navy was now a shadow of its former glory and its combatant fleet a poor shadow of its quondam prowess.

But it is not quite the end of the Trafalgar 200 story. The following day there was a drumhead service on Southsea Common, attended by some 10,000 people including veterans and schoolchildren. And a day later, Portsmouth played host to its third International Festival of the Sea. And then …

The Trafalgar Night Dinner 2005

On the morning of 21 October 2005, a service was held on board HMS *Victory* to commemorate Trafalgar and Nelson's death. In blustery wet weather, wreaths were laid and at noon bells were rung on Royal Navy warships around the world to mark the moment Nelson and his fleet went into battle off southern Spain on 21 October 1805. Prior to the service, Nelson's famous signal to his ships, 'England expects that every man will do his duty', was hoisted on board *Victory*.

The First Sea Lord, Admiral Sir Alan West, attended the hoisting of the signal at Portsmouth before returning to London to lay a wreath at the tomb of Nelson in St Paul's cathedral. And in Cadiz, crew members from frigate HMS *Chatham* represented the Royal Navy in commemorative religious services and a military parade. She then sailed in company with the Spanish aircraft carrier *Principe De Asturias* and the French frigate *Montcalm* towards Cape Trafalgar where another wreath-laying service was held.

That evening, Queen Elizabeth attended a special Trafalgar Night dinner on board HMS *Victory*. This dinner always follows a traditional format. Beef is the main course and prior to serving it, a baron of beef is paraded by personnel dressed in early nineteenth-century naval attire. They carry the joint at shoulder height around the mess and are accompanied by a drummer. Next, 'ships of the line' are paraded. These are mini-replicas of galleons and are made of chocolate. They are displayed in a manner to signify the battle of Trafalgar – the galleons having lit sparklers protruding which, when the lights are dimmed, give the effect of galleons firing broadsides. On completion, the little ships are filled with petit fours which are served during coffee (the full menu for the evening can be seen at Appendix 12).

The three protagonists in the battle of Trafalgar are represented in the menu. The English from the beef, the French and Spanish in the choice of wines. During the dinner, two toasts are given. Firstly, the First Sea Lord proposes the Loyal Toast to Her Majesty the Queen. All diners remain seated as per naval tradition. The second toast is made to the 'Immortal Memory'.*

On this special occasion, Queen Elizabeth made a short speech and proposed the 'Immortal Memory' toast to Nelson herself. As a part of the evening's festivities she lit a 'Trafalgar Weekend National Beacon', the first of 1,000 to be lit around the country, and witnessed a special beating of

* 'To the immortal memory of Horatio, Lord Nelson, and to all those who fell with him.'

the retreat by the band of the Royal Marines, together with the firing of a 52-gun nighttime broadside from *Victory* herself.

In pageantry, if in nothing else, the Royal Navy still held 'Sovereignty of the Seas'.

Postscript

Although the story told in this book ends in 2005, there was still worse to come for the Royal Navy. On entering office in May 2010, one of the first actions of David Cameron's new coalition government was to establish a National Security Council and announce the implementation of a Strategic Defence and Security Review (SDSR).

The SDSR produced recommendations leading to several changes in the configuration of each of the three services. As far as the Royal Navy was concerned these included: the intention to decommission the UK's current aircraft carriers and Harrier aircraft, thereby creating a ten-year gap in carrier strike capability; to continue with the procurement of the *Queen Elizabeth*-class aircraft carriers and procure the carrier-variant of the Joint Strike Fighter from 2020, immediately to cancel the Nimrod MRA4 maritime patrol aircraft project and a further reduction in the surface fleet to nineteen frigates and destroyers, down four from twenty-three. There was also a further cut in naval personnel.

This was followed by SDSR 2015 whose headline decisions included the long called-for reinstatement of a maritime patrol aircraft capability and two classes rather than one of new frigates. But these naval benefits were contingent upon the MOD and the services making efficiency savings in existing programmes to provide funds for new commitments – an outcome many considered unlikely. The SDSR also pledged to hold a debate in Parliament on the principle of the Continuous at Sea Deterrent and the plans for succession. That vote was held in July 2016 with the Commons approving the decision to maintain the UK's nuclear deterrent beyond the early 2030s.

Importantly from a naval perspective, the SDSR made no mention of the defence of merchant shipping nor the potential threat of terrorist or otherwise mining of important UK ports. This omission seems strange from the government of an island nation which depends on the sea for much of its commerce and fisheries within a UK Economic Exclusion Zone.

But the navy continued to waste away. In July 2018, Peter Hitchens in the *Daily Mail* noted that 'many of our shrunken navy's ships are stuck immobilised at the quayside because they won't work in warm water. And it [the RN] has just been forced to sell one of its most important and powerful vessels, HMS *Ocean*, to the Brazilian Navy for a song.' Hitchens also drew attention to the cost and potential usefulness of the SSBN submarines. 'There's our ridiculous cold war superpower Trident deterrent, which no British premier would dare to use, whatever they say, and which will utterly cripple our economy and the rest of our defences unless we swap it soon for something much more modest. We only look as if we are an important, advanced country – and the illusion only works if you are a great distance away.'[21]

There was merit in his argument, for a nuclear response would hardly be launched by any of the current breed of politicians; and in any case, as experience in two world wars has shown, there is no need to attack Britain with nuclear weapons – an enemy merely needs to cut her supply chain by sinking incoming merchant vessels. The Royal Navy has so few anti-submarine and anti-surface assets now that it could hardly prevent such a blockade.

On 3 March 2019, the *Sun* newspaper reported that 'the shrunken Royal Navy now has more admirals than warships', claiming that 'official documents reveal there are thirty-four senior fleet commanders but, after years of cuts, the number of operational vessels with offensive capability is down to nineteen'. The report went on to state that the Royal Navy comprised only seventy-five ships, of which only twenty were classed as major surface combatants.

There were six guided-missile destroyers, thirteen frigates and one aircraft carrier, HMS *Queen Elizabeth*, which would not be in service until 2020. The *Sun* went on to note that 'the Royal Navy said there were thirty-four serving admirals, vice admirals and rear admirals and seventy-five ships'. The Admiralty was clearly guilty here, as it had been in 2005, for example, of claiming something was a warship if it was painted grey, irrespective of it being a patrol craft, used to train university students and patrol inland waters, a tanker or a survey ship used for mapping.

Nonetheless there are some recent positives to be taken. Many brave and dedicated men and women still serve in the Royal Navy. Two major aircraft carriers have been ordered and are being commissioned and worked up at the time of writing; and new frigate contracts have also been laid. At some time in the future Britain may well see a navy which has the *Queen Elizabeth*-class aircraft carriers, *Dreadnought*-class ballistic missile submarines, Type 26 'City'-class and Type 31 frigates, the F–35B fifth-generation strike fighter and the P–8A maritime patrol aircraft.

But the carriers are for offensive purposes, to take the fight to the enemy, and in any event could not be protected without the assistance of other NATO members; and the North Sea, the English Channel and the Atlantic remain vulnerable and open to interdiction. As Max Hastings wrote in *The Times* in May 2019, 'the navy needs a substantial number of cheap and cheerful warships, rather than carriers that are merely yachts for admirals'.[22]

This charge has some justification. The 2015 Strategic Defence and

Security Review called for the development and construction of the Type 31 frigate, intended to be a more cost-effective class of vessel that did not have the hi-tech specifications of the navy's fleet of Type 26 frigates.* The idea was that these cheaper, more versatile ships would be better suited to everyday naval policing operations, such as interdicting smugglers and combating piracy on the high seas, which do not require the deployment of a state-of-the-art warship (although, again, this does not address the issue of protecting Britain's home waters). Nonetheless, such vessels would allow the Royal Navy to increase the numbers of ships at its disposal while boosting export opportunities. But defence commentator Con Coughlin avers that, 'four years after the idea was first proposed, the navy has still been unable to agree on a design for the new ship, prompting suspicions in Whitehall that it has no real interest in developing a cheaper alternative'.[23]

According to the *New York Times*, the American perspective is that 'budget cuts have led to sharp reductions in troops, equipment and investment, and analysts warn that Britain is no longer capable of defending its homeland by itself'. The *NYT* added that while 'Britain remains a nuclear power and a member of the United Nations Security Council … Britain's role as a military power will be vital to its self-image, its geopolitical clout and its relationship with the United States'.

However, this relationship is under threat for 'budget cutbacks have contributed to growing doubts in Washington about whether Britain remains capable of fighting a war alongside the American military. The British House of Commons Library assessed that in real terms, between 2010 and 2015, Britain's defence budget fell by eight billion pounds … a cut of eighteen percent compared with the 2009–10 budget. The budget has stabilised since then, but has not grown significantly.'

Moreover, and a worrying blow to British prestige, the *New York Times* believed that 'France is gradually supplanting Britain as the leading European military ally of the United States, further weakening the "special relationship" between Britain and America'.[24]

In September 2019, Admiral Lord West of Spithead (First Sea Lord 2002–6), in a letter to the *Spectator* venting at the capture by Iranian National Guards of British-flagged oil tankers and the governments seeming inability or unwillingness to do anything about it, noted that 'we have ignored a real threat to UK ships and crews. The desperate shortage of frigates in the navy is a problem. For such a great maritime nation as ours to have only thirteen frigates is a national disgrace.'[25]

* The *Daily Telegraph* of 23 July 2019 reported that eight Type 26 frigates were under construction at BAE's Govan yard, but will not enter service until the mid-2020s. And in November 2019, Babcock signed contracts to build five Type 31 vessels to be in service by 2028.

Chapter 17

The Royal Yacht

ROYAL YACHTS were an essential part of any Royal Fleet Review until the decommissioning of *Britannia* in 1997, the end of a long line as the eighty-third such vessel since King Charles II acceded to the throne in 1660. Charles fully indulged his passion for yachts and ran his fleet of them as a private navy; but he was careful to make them available for naval purposes in times of emergency, thus ensuring that much of the costs were not incurred by the Privy Purse. Twenty-four yachts were built for royal purposes between 1660 and 1688. Charles used eleven of them as his principal private yachts and another nine smaller ones as what we might now call 'despatch vessels'.

James II had eighteen yachts available to him on his succession; he built no new ones and disposed of four during his reign. William III inherited fourteen royal yachts of which eight were designated for his regular transportation. By the time of Queen Anne, the number of royal yachts was down to nine. By now all such vessels had been changed from the single-masted rig of the Stuarts to ketch- or ship-rig. George I came to a throne that boasted nine principal, five secondary and two small yachts; they were not all for his own usage as the smaller ones were allocated to officers of

HMY *Victoria and Albert III* at Portsmouth from a painting by WM Atkins. *(Author's collection)*

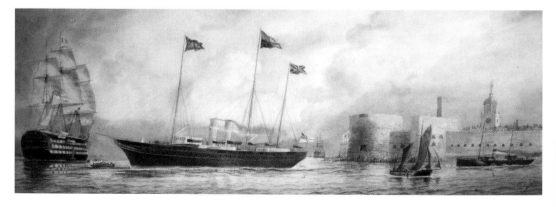

272

HMY *Osborne*,
commissioned in
1874. *(US Naval
History and Heritage
Command
NH 57570)*

the crown. Four of the larger vessels dated from Charles II's reign and were decidedly aged. George II inherited six principal yachts as did George III. His main vessel was *Royal Caroline II* (1749) which he renamed *Royal Charlotte*.

At the beginning of the nineteenth century, the royal yachts were nine strong and all now appeared on the Navy List. The most recent of them was *Princess Augusta*, built in 1771 at Deptford. But George ordered new vessels to be commissioned and his brother as Regent gained *Royal Sovereign* (1804) supported by *William and Mary III* (1807); he soon lost the latter which was allocated to the Lord Lieutenant of Ireland in 1813. William IV had access to five large yachts together with three smaller vessels for the benefit of officers of state.

When Queen Victoria ascended to the throne in 1837, she did not immediately make any use of the royal yachts. It was not until 1842 that she embarked on *Royal George* (1817) for a journey to Scotland. Owing to the weather, the ship had to be towed by two steamships, much to the Queen's distaste. Moreover, when finally under way it made very slow progress and the motion made her violently seasick. The voyage took three days to cover 404 miles at an average speed of 6kts; Victoria was not amused and let Prime Minister Robert Peel know it. On 22 September 1842, Peel wrote to his monarch that he had urged on the Admiralty the necessity of providing her with a steam vessel and that 'the Admiralty is now building a large vessel to be worked by steam power' for her use.[1] This was a slight exaggeration for the keel was not laid until 9 November and it was this vessel that became *Victoria and Albert I.*

Victoria's reign was the high point of the royal yacht. Three principal yachts were built during her monarchy, each named *Victoria and Albert*; in addition, there were a number of smaller vessels with clearly delineated duties. *Victoria and Albert I* was a much larger ship than *Royal George* and it soon became apparent that she could not visit minor ports. Accordingly, *Fairy* was laid down in 1844 as a screw-driven iron yacht, capable of matching the larger ship's 11kts and serving as a tender to it. She was followed by *Elfin*, a paddle-wheel steam yacht of 1848, used to ferry the Queen and others from Portsmouth to the Isle of Wight or other short journeys.

By the early 1850s, the growing size of the royal family, and Victoria's evident liking for regal cruising, led to a replacement for her maiden yacht. *Victoria and Albert II* was, anachronistically, another steam-paddle ship, laid down in 1854. With two funnels and three masts she was 100ft longer than her predecessor. The old yacht was renamed *Osborne* and continued in use as a secondary royal vessel until paid off in 1859.

Victoria liked the tender *Fairy*, thinking it 'a beautiful little steamer and charmingly arranged and filled up, with a drawing room, a nice little bedroom for us, dressing room for Albert, and several small berths for ladies & maids'.[2] but by 1863 the Queen was spending considerable time at Osborne, and it was clear that a smaller vessel than *V&A II*, and more comfortable than *Fairy*, was necessary to act as tender. This led to the commissioning of the paddle-wheel steamer *Alberta* at the end of the year.

In 1868 construction of the wooden steam paddle yacht *Osborne II* commenced, a slightly smaller vessel than *V&A II* and the last of the paddle-

Osborne depicted at the inaugural for the Kiel canal in 1895 during a visit by the Duke York. The Kaiser had invited the Prince of Wales, his uncle, but it clashed with Ascot week so the future Edward VII sent his son. *(Author's collection)*

wheel royal yachts. She was a comfortable sea boat and used extensively for cruising by the Prince and Princess of Wales, Edward and Alexandra.

The twin-screw schooner *Victoria and Albert III* (1899) had been launched in Victoria's lifetime but she never set foot on her. Instead she became the yacht of choice for Edward VII. A smaller yacht was still necessary and in 1908 the *Alexandra* was commissioned, replacing *Osborne II*.

George V gained both *V&A III* and *Alexandra* on his accession, together with *Alberta* and the racing yacht *Britannia*. By the time George VI came to the throne, there was only *Victoria and Albert III*. In the last year of peace, on 22 July the king, with his family and Lord Louis Mountbatten, embarked on her for a cruise to the West Country. Their first call was to the Royal Naval College, Dartmouth, where Mountbatten's 18-year-old nephew, Prince Philip of Greece, was a cadet. Philip met the 13-year-old Princess Elizabeth who seemed struck with him; only Mountbatten and Elizabeth's governess seemed to note the impression that Philip had made. And as the royal yacht departed, accompanied by a collection of sailing, rowing and motor boats, the last to obey the signal to turn back was a young solitary rower – Prince Philip.

Laid up during the war and used as an accommodation ship, *V&A III* was unfit for service after the war. Her eventual replacement was *Britannia*, commissioned in 1954 and the first royal yacht specifically designed for oceanic travel; her 12,000 horsepower could drive the ship at a maximum 22.5kts. She was also given the ability to be converted into a hospital ship in time of war. In the early years of the *Britannia*'s life the ship was also home to the Queen's Rolls-Royce Phantom V which was hoisted and lowered from a special garage compartment once in port. The space was slightly too small and the car's bumpers had to be removed in order to get it into the garage. Ultimately Elizabeth used cars provided at her destination instead and the garage was converted into a storage area for beer! *Britannia* served until 1997, covering over 1.1 million miles: and then the era of the royal yacht was no more.

Service in the Royal Yacht

By Victorian times, the royal yachts were all on the Navy List and commanded by a senior Royal Navy officer, usually a commodore or rear admiral. It was a job that required a lot of patience, tact and the ability to mix with royalty and their acolytes; royal connections helped too.

The 25-year royal yacht career of Lord Adolphus Fitzclarence, of illegitimate but royal birth, has already been noted (*vide supra* Chapter 7). Captain His Serene Highness Prince Ernst Leopold Leiningen was the son of Queen Victoria's maternal half-brother and commanded the royal yacht before being advanced to rear admiral in 1876. Admiral Sir John Reginald Thomas Fullerton was another who commanded the royal flotilla for a considerable period, serving for 16 years. On retirement in 1901, he was awarded Knight Grand Cross in the Royal Victorian Order on 1 February and by the end of the month was appointed an Honorary Naval Aide-de-Camp to King Edward VII.

The Hon Hedworth Meux, already met in this book and the son of the Earl of Durham, held the position for the first years of Edward VII's reign. He was an expert on racehorses (and ran a stud when he retired), a passion of the King's as well. Meux was followed by Sir Archibald Berkley Milne. Milne was the son of an admiral and baronet, who had been First Naval Lord under both Gladstone and Disraeli, and grandson of another admiral. In appearance, Milne was affected, sporting a non-regulation stiff turned-down collar and bow tie, a white, trimmed beard and luxuriant black moustache. He was a snob of the worst kind. Once his sleeve was brushed by a passing seaman; Milne took out his handkerchief, flicked some imagined dirt from his sleeve with it and threw the contaminated linen over the side.

After service in the Zulu War as an ADC to Lord Chelmsford, and escaping the massacre at Isandlwana, Milne, as a captain RN, accepted the post of captain of *Osborne*, an appointment usually held by a commander, reasoning that exposure to royalty offered him better hopes of promotion. Milne loved the ceremony and obsessive spit and polish of service and became good friends with King Edward VII and, especially, Queen Alexandra who nicknamed him 'Arky-Barky', an appellation which soon got around the fleet with risible effect. A fellow officer asserted that Milne's hobbies were 'collecting rare orchids and entertaining royal ladies'.[3] Milne commanded *Victoria and Albert III* at the 1905 review.*

He was succeeded by Rear-Admiral Colin Richard Keppel. Keppel was related to Admiral Augustus Keppel (*vide supra* Chapter 5) and the son of a distinguished sailor, Admiral the Hon Sir Henry Keppel, who had held the office of Groom-in-Waiting to Queen Victoria between 1859 and 1860, was awarded the Order of Merit and made an Admiral of the Fleet. Colin Keppel too was well connected with royalty. Whilst serving as a commander in charge of Kitchener's naval forces in the Sudan during the 1887–98 Mahdist war, his forces were engaged in the battle for Omdurman and Khartoum. *The Times* reported that 'the bombardment by Commander Keppel's gunboats was a complete success. All the forts on the east bank have been destroyed or captured. The Omdurman forts fired incessantly at the gunboats but did no damage.'[4] Keppel's royal connections were such that when Queen Victoria heard of the victory she telegraphed his wife from Balmoral 'the queen wishes you to know that telegram just received Kitchener arrived Omdurman in cool weather … Keppel and gunboats have demolished forts on right bank and Tati Island and taken guns'.[5]

Another admiral of the royal yachts with impeccable credentials was Henry Tritton Buller, who commanded them from 1922 to 1931. He had

* Milne's career ended when he played a key role (together with Churchill) in allowing the German battle-cruiser *Goeben* to escape to Turkey at the start of the First World War, an event instrumental in bringing Turkey into the war on the German side.

The steam paddler
royal yacht *Victoria
and Albert* II, laid
down in 1854.
(author's collection)

been flag lieutenant to Sir John ('Jackie') Fisher, and was the son of Admiral Sir Alexander Buller, the ex-C-in-C of the China Station in 1895 and whose family had owned estates around Morval in Cornwall since the fifteenth century. Henry, born in 1873, had a family lineage which included several admirals and was married to Hermione, the daughter of the 17th Earl of Moray, Morton Gray Stuart, who claimed descent from King James V of Scotland. In 1932 he became Groom-in-Waiting to the King and in this position, he was to serve no less than four monarchs, George V, Edward VIII, George VI and Elizabeth II until his death at the age of 87 in 1960.

Buller was succeeded by Admiral the Hon Sir Herbert Meade-Fetherstonhaugh, son of the 4th Earl of Clanwilliam, himself an admiral and a former Commander in Chief at Portsmouth and later an Admiral of the Fleet. Sir Herbert inherited Uppark* in Sussex, built for the Earl of Tankerville in 1690, which he and his wife restored, and from 1939 to 1946 was Sergeant-at-Arms of the House of Lords.

As a final example, the admiral commanding from 1934 up to the Second World War was Vice-Admiral Sir Dudley Burton Napier North. He struck his flag on 18 September 1939 to take up the post of Flag Officer North Atlantic Station, from which position he was (unfairly) fired by Churchill for his action (or lack of action) over the Dakar affair. But at King George VI's express wish he was reappointed to the royal yacht command in August 1945 and until his retirement in 1947 he was tasked with putting together a skeleton staff to ensure the preservation of royal yacht 'knowledge'. There was then no incumbent until 1953.

* Now owned by
the National Trust.

Selection to serve in the royal yachts initially depended much on family connections. William Edmund Goodenough (later to become an admiral and command a cruiser squadron at Jutland) recalled being posted to the *Victoria and Albert*;

> I had just time to buy the gold laced trousers and laced mess jacket that traditions enjoined … It was, of course, an appointment of patronage. I went as my father's son* (his mother was Queen Victoria's godchild). There was some tradition … to give early promotion to someone who had done good service … but I don't know how far this was observed in reality.[6]

In 1893, 21-year-old Sub-Lieutenant Roger Keyes joined *Victoria and Albert*. He recalled that the royal yachts at this time were all paddlers; apart from *Victoria and Albert*, there were *Osborne* (*Victoria and Albert I*), *Alberta* and *Elfin*, described as a despatch vessel. *Alberta*, at 370 tons, was considerably smaller than the main yacht (at 2,470 tons) and was small enough to berth at Cowes pier. *Victoria and Albert* would remain in the Cowes Roads with a guard ship and *Alberta* was used to ferry passengers to and from the Isle of Wight and the larger royal yacht.

Nevertheless, the royal yachtsmen took pride in their slightly antiquated flotilla. When Kaiser Wilhelm arrived for the Cowes Regatta in his brand new royal yacht *Hohenzollern (II)*, Keyes observed that it 'looked overwhelming beside our ancient paddler but on board gave one the impression of being rather like a flashy modern hotel alongside a quietly dignified private house'.[7] It was the *arriviste* versus old money.

New officers were presented to the Queen on arrival; Roger Keyes thought her 'a most alarming old lady'.[8] The subbies would go to Osborne House each day for orders and generally lunched with the royal household. Often, they were sent with the royal children in a barge on little excursions; these always ended 'in an enormous tea on board the *Victoria and Albert*'.[9]

Life on board the royal yacht was dominated by spit and polish, ceremony and social calls and punctilious adherence to protocol and orders. It did not always appeal to the martial spirit but there were benefits. By convention, after two years' service and upon a new posting, a one-step advancement in rank was guaranteed. And proximity to royalty could bring unexpected rewards. Punctilious, always immaculately turned out and something of a ladies' man, Lieutenant Christopher 'Kit' Cradock was assigned to *Victoria and Albert* in 1894. Two years later, on 5 February 1896, he acted as a pallbearer at the funeral on the Isle of Wight of Prince Henry of Battenberg, husband of Queen Victoria's fifth daughter Princess Beatrice, who had died off the coast of West Africa of malaria whilst on

* His father had been killed by natives while serving as commodore on the Australian Station in 1875.

active service in the Ashanti War. For this service, Cradock was honoured by the Queen.

George V ended the system of patronage; instead he asked the Admiralty to submit a list of suitable officers from whom he would select his wardroom. Lieutenant Commander Augustus Agar VC joined the royal yacht in this way in 1924. 'This was the more surprising to me,' he later wrote, 'because it was usual in the navy to select officers for the yacht from those who had family influence, either in the service or outside, and I had neither.'[10]

During Agar's service there were three lieutenant commanders aboard, two of whom, Agar and Victor Crutchley, were holders of the Victoria Cross and another, Frederick Dalrymple-Hamilton, would play a key part in the sinking of the *Bismarck* as captain of HMS *Rodney*. But they did not consider the royal service in any way demanding. 'Service in the royal yachts could not in any stretch of the imagination be called arduous,' thought Agar. 'The few weeks when the royal yacht was put into service, exclusive of Cowes week, could be counted on the fingers of one hand.'[11]

Under George V, two or three officers were invited to dinner in the Royal Saloon (of *V&A III*) every evening; one sat next to the King and the other by Queen Mary. Agar remembered such an occasion in 1926 when 'through the window of the dining saloon … we could see the hand of O'Donnell the bandmaster conducting the Royal Marine Orchestra in light music, usually Strauss and other Viennese waltzes which Queen Mary adored. Afterwards, we sat around on the upper deck in small groups before the king and queen retired to their apartments about 2200.'[12]

The provision of high-quality food on board the royal yachts was a given. After all, monarchs and their guests need to be fed in a manner appropriate to their station. Queen Victoria was an enthusiastic, if rapid, eater. Edward VII was a dedicated trencherman who enjoyed the richest dishes and George V was no slouch at the table either. Although the navy crewed the yachts, the cuisine was the responsibility of the monarch's household. The 'chefs loathed working in a cramped galley',[13] and supply issues meant that under Victoria livestock was sometimes carried on board. The Queen loved animals and would often prevent them from serving their proper purpose of being slaughtered to provide her dinner. Nonetheless, the chefs were able to turn out some interesting dishes. As an example of the fare provided, consider the menu when Edward VII entertained the Shah of Persia, Mozaffar ad-Din Shah Qajar, on 20 August immediately after the 1902 Coronation Review. For luncheon alone the menu featured a bisque with a fish mayonnaise, lamb cutlets, chicken in tarragon, roast grouse, dressed crab, jellied cold meats, various salads, cauliflower puree, Portuguese rice cakes and a greengage compote. Despite this lavish spread, the Shah departed a disappointed man; he had set his heart

The beautiful and elaborate binnacle on *Osborne*. (author's collection)

HMY *Fairy* depicted in 1865 in a painting by George Mears. *(Author's collection)*

on receiving the Order of the Garter but had to settle for a jewelled portrait of Edward, who had cavilled at giving the Garter to a Muslim.

Engagement in sport did not stint the appetite either. On 3 August 1935, King George V was racing his yacht *Britannia* at Cowes. Lunch on board that day included poulet mascotte (chicken breasts with artichoke and truffle), petit pains a la mayonnaise with ox tongue, ham, Derby beef (pickled silverside), pigeon pie, four different vegetable dishes, mashed potatoes, tomato and green salads and cherry tart.

Once aboard the royal yacht, visitors were generally struck by the almost total absence of noise. Orders were given by signs or flags, ratings walked about instead of at the double as on other RN ships, and pumps were worn instead of boots when royalty was present. Seamen's dress was also different to a regular warship. By order of Edward VII, royal yachtsmen wore the pre-1906 cloth trousers with the waistband up over the frock. Their badges were of gold and the cap ribbons were of watered silk with the words 'Royal Yacht' separated by the crown in gold and red. In 1904, King Edward had decreed that sub-lieutenants serving in the yachts should wear gold-laced trousers with 'full' and 'mess' dress, instead of the plain ones worn by others of that rank. And the last royal yacht, *Britannia*, was also the last ship in the Royal Navy where the crew members slept in hammocks, a practice maintained until 1973.

Overall it can be seen, that in almost every way, service in the yachts was akin to that in a royal palace. Kings and queens were thought different from other people and were treated by the navy as such.

Chapter 18

———⊶⊷———

Conclusions

The Reasons for Naval Decline

Of course, the reason the Royal Navy existed, and the need for it to be both strong and large, was a direct result of Britain's island status, its dependence on trade and its possession of an empire. Britain was built on international commerce, as has been demonstrated in the early chapters of this work. The need to police and keep open trade routes led directly to a blue-water navy. This navy had to have foreign bases, and later coaling and oiling stations, which meant that territory had to be gained, purchased or appropriated to fulfil that necessity. Historian Paul Kennedy described British eighteenth and nineteenth-century pre-eminence as a three-sided, self-reinforcing, equation.

> An adequate, not to say overwhelming, naval force which utilised a whole host of bases and protected an ever growing global trade: an expanding formal empire which offered harbour facilities for the navy … [and] which provided essential raw materials and markets for the British economy: [and] an industrial revolution which poured out products into the rest of the world, drew large overseas territories into its commercial and financial orbit, encouraged an enormous merchant marine and provided the material strength to support great fleets. It was an outstandingly strong framework for national and world power.[1]

The requirement to open new markets for trade, to make them tied 'customers' and 'suppliers' to British commerce was the causation of the somewhat unplanned acquisition of territory around the globe – land which then itself had to be policed and defended by the Royal Navy. As Niall Ferguson has written, the British Empire may have begun in a 'maelstrom of seaborne violence and theft' but it had been transformed into the world's most powerful polity through 'globalisation by gunboats'.[2]

The jewel in the crown of this empire was seen as India, and the need to protect the routes to and from it, and to keep potential impingement away from India's borders, animated much of British strategic thinking in the eighteenth, nineteenth and early twentieth centuries. Lord Curzon thought that 'as long as we rule India, we are the greatest power in the world. If we lose it, we shall drop straight away to a third-rate power.'[3] Furthermore, politicians such as Joseph Chamberlain believed that the possession of an empire brought an opportunity for a world-dominating trading block to be established, based on the British Empire.

But the empire proved to be more burden than boon. As early as 1883, Sir John Seeley noted that 'it can be fairly questioned whether our possession of India does or ever can increase our power and security, while there is no doubt that it vastly increases our dangers and responsibilities'.[4] The onus of protecting these far-flung commitments fell upon the Royal Navy, and the costs accrued to the Treasury.

The self-governing Dominions welcomed the protection that the navy provided. Indeed, as Australian Prime Minister Billy Hughes remarked at the 1921 Imperial Conference 'the Dominions would not exist if it were not for the British navy'. But they would not pay for it. In 1907-08, naval expenditure totalled £35.14 million; the Dominions contributed only 2.95 per cent of the total. Per hundred pounds of trade, naval expenditure represented £3.00 for Britain; the highest Dominion was New Zealand at £0.27 (see also Appendix 13). In 1909 the Admiralty's bid for an Imperial Navy, including the Dominions and able to access funding from them, was thrown out at the Imperial Conference of that year by precisely those entities which sought Admiralty protection.

After the First World War, the situation had not changed. In 1925-6, Commonwealth expenditure on defence for Britain was 51s 1d per head per annum; Canada was 5s 10d, South Africa 2s 2d, Australia 25s, NZ 12s 11d. And in 1937, First Lord of the Admiralty Samuel Hoare noted that 'a great proportion of the expenditure of naval defence is required to meet our imperial as distinct from United Kingdom, obligations. The question must occur to all of us whether this little island can continue to shoulder the financial strain involved.'[5]

As has been seen, naval costs became a bitter political battle and this was reflected post-Great War in the gradual 'make-do-and-mend' nature of naval reviews, as the Royal Navy was progressively starved of funds. The fig leaf behind which this disinvestment took place was that of world disarmament and appeasement. Thanks to the teachings of religion and the credos of the Victorian public schools, both of which induced a sympathy for failure and the underdog and a corresponding suspicion of ability and success, 'appeasement had become a conditioned reflex of the British middle and upper class'.[6] Many such people came to believe that Germany had been unfairly treated by the Treaty of Versailles.

Appeasement had, in fairness to those involved, considerable public support. The Great War had left such horrible memories that the nation could claim to have good cause to shutting its eyes to the prospect of another match with Germany. Hitler was also considered by many to be a potential barrier against the spread westwards of communism, while Prime Minster Stanley Baldwin was uninterested in foreign affairs and believed in Count Douhet's dictum that 'the bomber will always get through', to the point where he thought expenditure on defence wasteful.

Moreover, the Labour Party of the 1930s was 'entranced by pacifistic illusions, [and] doggedly opposed British rearmament until it was too late'.[7] In 1934, for example, Clement Atlee,* leading a debate for the Labour Party opposing the acquisition of new aeroplanes for the RAF, 'denied that there was such a thing as defence against air attack and reaffirmed his party's commitment to total disarmament and the pooling of national air forces into one international police force'.[8] Even King George V supported the appeasers; 'I will not have another war; I will not,' he shouted at Lloyd George.[9]

A few stood against this trend, mavericks such as that perpetual stormy petrel Winston Churchill. Commenting on the abandonment of Czechoslovakia in 1938, he raged that

> for five years … I have watched this famous island descending incontinently, fecklessly, the stairway which leads to a dark gulf. It is a fine broad stairway at the beginning, but after a bit the carpet ends. A little further on there are only flagstones, and a little further on still these break beneath your feet … now the victors are the vanquished and those who threw down their arms in the field and sued for an armistice are striding on to world mastery.[10]

The Royal Navy nonetheless acquitted itself well through the Second World War; but from then on it fell into long-term decline and the character and content of the Royal Fleet Reviews that took place under Queen Elizabeth II reflected the threadbare and declining state of the navy, a sort of distant great uncle fallen on hard times, living in an old house with peeling paintwork and no heating, reminiscing of the good old days long since gone.

Britain's relationship with the United States of America was another important factor in the decline of the Royal Navy and the country's position in the world. Britain and the United States were at odds throughout the 1920s and 1930s. At the heart of American antipathy there were two issues. Firstly, according to historian Kathleen Burk, 'Britain's intention to maintain the Royal Navy's abilities to enforce belligerent rights versus the American desire to maintain neutral trading rights in time of war'.[11] The

* At that time, Deputy Leader of the Labour Party.

Royal Navy had stopped all manner of neutral ships in the First World War and Britain refused to bow to American pressure to give up that right. Even in 1916, Jellicoe was looking over his shoulder at a potential American naval threat given their strongly-expressed objection to 'stop and search' as part of the British blockade of Germany, and in the 1920s many in America thought that the next war would be with Britain.

This was because of the second reason for mutual distrust. America was jealous of Britain's commercial and naval reach. There was a systematic attempt by American policy makers to reduce Britain's standing and wealth, especially during wartime. As early as July 1917, US President Wilson was recorded as saying that England and France would soon be 'financially in our hands' and that the beauty of having financial leverage over Britain and France was that 'when the war is over, we can force them to our way of thinking'.[12]

The Washington and London Treaties can be seen in the same context. As First Lord of the Admiralty Lord Selborne said in 1901, 'Great Britain's credit and its navy are the two main pillars on which the strength of this country rests, and each is essential to the other. Unless our financial position is strong, the navy cannot be maintained. And unless the navy is fully adequate for any call which may be made upon it, our national credit must stand in jeopardy.'[13] By forcing reductions in the Royal Navy on a not altogether reluctant British government, especially in cruisers, vital for trade protection, these concords made Selborne's insight come true.

Moreover, relations between Britain and the USA deteriorated further during the 1930s because 'the US wanted to be a great power with the attendant respect and deference but declined to take on the responsibilities of the position'.[14] A broken Britain and its navy was still expected to act as the world's policeman.

During the period 1942–5, Lend-Lease was used by the US Treasury to bring Britain to 'a state of such financial weakness that the British would not ... be able to obstruct its plan to eliminate the Sterling Area, imperial preference and discrimination against dollar priced imports'.[15] As historian Corelli Barnett has written 'Lend-Lease gradually consummated the process Churchill had begun of transforming England into an American satellite warrior-state dependent for its existence on the flow of supplies across the Atlantic'.[16]

But in 1947, the United States realised that, with the rise of the USSR as an enemy, Britain and its empire was an important strategic ally with assets around the world. However, the damage had already been done for by then the British Empire was crumbling away. After the war, America tried to assist Britain through the injection of Marshall Aid, primarily so that Britain could continue to maintain an army of occupation in Germany and help the US defend the Free World. But the Suez crisis of

1956 proved the USA to be only concerned with its own interest. America engineered a run on the pound and cut Britain off from oil supplies in order to force her to abandon the attempt to retake the Canal, which was strategically key to Britain for communication and trade with India, Australia and New Zealand as well as for oil supply. From that moment, Britain was a second-rate power and subordinate to the USA.

After Suez, the US looked to the NATO Alliance rather than Britain, and the Labour governments of Harold Wilson and his Defence Secretary Dennis Healey began a swingeing programme of cuts to all three services which precipitated the final decline of the Royal Navy, whilst the remaining colonies were abandoned with alacrity. Britain's navy was a function of its need for (and eventual dominance of) maritime trade. If in the future, Britain will want to trade with a wider world outside of the EEC, would this trigger a renewed interest in matters naval? Probably not.

The understanding between the nation and the Royal Navy no longer seems to hold. From the seventeenth century, the Royal Navy was seen as Britain's first and last line of defence. Britain was protected from conti-nental despotism by geography and this made a large (and expensive) standing army unnecessary. The periodic naval agitation which perturbed British *sangfroid* in the nineteenth century, especially that of 1888 (discussed in Chapter 9), heralded a wave of naval enthusiasm which lasted until the First World War and produced the fleetingly influential Navy League. But after the Great War, the League had to search for both rele-vance and members, in the face of the anti-militarism of the time; it attempted to broaden its message from one of naval power to an emphasis on the Merchant Navy, shipbuilders, and fishing industries – Britain's whole maritime community – all without any noticeable success. Indeed, the only lasting memorial to the Navy League's efforts was the Sea Cadet movement. Eventually, the League was wound up, and lives on only through the Sea Cadet Association.

But in a nuclear, fast jet, ICBM* world, Britain's island security is threat-ened. Many believe, as once did Baldwin, MacDonald and Neville Chamberlain, that the bomber will always get through and death will rain down from the skies, irrespective of the size of the navy. This is an illog-ical standpoint. The necessity of protecting the sea lanes, and the trade that traverses them, remains, as does the requirement to protect Britain's supply chain. Reliance on NATO is possibly self-deceiving, for NATO is dependent on American funding and this largesse is increasingly resented in some parts of the United States body politic. As former German Foreign Minister Joschka Fisher wrote in December 2016, 'Europe is far too weak and divided to stand in for the US strategically; and without the US lead-ership the West cannot survive'.[17] And during his presidential election campaign, Donald Trump stated that 'NATO had become obsolete'. As

* Inter-Continental Ballistic Missile.

president, at his first NATO summit, 'Trump did not endorse the commitment of the twenty-nine alliance countries to come to the defence of any member that is attacked. The president has frequently complained that too many NATO members, particularly Germany, don't spend enough money on mutual defence.'[18]

Nonetheless, the need to defend Britain's seaways, or at least to deny them to an enemy, is largely ignored by modern politicians and the public. Voters are unconvinced by the argument and would rather have increased social spending than see resources spent on defence.

The Story of Fleet Reviews

As can be seen, the story of Royal Fleet Reviews is a history of the Royal Navy and of the United Kingdom in miniature – a somewhat random beginning, a high point from George III to George V and a steady decline thereafter. It is also a stage for the theatre of culture and politics, represented in naval form.

Early fleet reviews, from (say) the seventeenth century to the 1840s, were extensions of the behaviour of an admiral on taking over a new command. Such a commander would have gone ship by ship around his new responsibilities, checking muster books, weapons and the like. George III's reviews followed this template; he boarded ships, inspected them, moved on.

By Queen Victoria's reign, the format settled into a standard ritual, a review not an inspection. The Golden Jubilee Review of 1887 saw a whole set of 'invented traditions'; illumination, manning of ships,* saluting, the Trinity House yacht as a harbinger of the monarch, a balletic progress around the fleet and a reception for senior officers. This became a pattern which, with minor variation, was carried on until the last Royal Fleet Review in 2005. Indeed, 1887 was the first review for which the Admiralty required the officers in charge of organisation of the event to document their plans, for future reference and use.

Fireworks featured from 1842. Parliament had become a part of this tradition in 1853, illumination of the fleet since 1856 (although there was a proto-illumination in 1773), searchlights since 1887, the celebration of a coronation from 1902. 'Invented tradition' gave a spurious sense of history and tied the ritual back to Britain's legends and Britannia's foundations.

Royal Reviews may have started as a celebration of sovereignty of the seas but by late Victorian times they had evolved into a complex display of might, fixated only on self-advertisement and deterrence. With regard to the former function, ensuring that the navy gained its 'fair share' of Treasury funds, Captain F C Doveton Sturdee, Assistant Director of Naval Intelligence, opined in 1902 that 'I believe it may be generally accepted that public opinion has been largely responsible for all the great

* Manning ship developed from the tradition of entering a foreign port, when it was customary to man ship. Men drawn up on the side of the ship facing outboard, or in the rigging of a sailing ship, in a single rank and holding hands means that they can't fire the guns.

increases in our fleet'.[19] As to the latter role, First Sea Lord Admiral Sir John 'Jackie' Fisher wrote in February 1905 that 'if you rub it in both at home and abroad that you are ready for instant war with every unit of your strength in the first line … people will keep clear of you',[20] and *The Times* noted in 1909 that fleet reviews were an 'exhibition aimed at potential enemies'.[21] In this regard, quantity was often seen as better than quality, as has been highlighted in the preceding chapters. The naval historian Nicholas Lambert has noted that 'statesmen thought of navies and sea power in terms of deterrence and prestige rather than fighting capability; this was just as true in 1914 as in 1880. From this perspective, numbers of warships (and their costs) were more important than combat effectiveness.'[22]

There was also an element of 'bread and circuses' apparent in the late nineteenth and early twentieth centuries. 'The striking development of seapower as public entertainment after 1890 reflected the need to keep an ever-expanding electorate engaged with the message, despite the competing attractions of tax cuts, old-age pensions and welfare provision.'[23]

From the end of the Great War onwards, successive fleet reviews showed that the Royal Navy had lost none of its ability to stage a spectacular show, but the theatre became increasingly threadbare and eventually reliant on other navies to bring its cast of characters up to the levels needed to produce an award-winning performance.

However, the rituals on display still harked back to the illustrious traditions of the Victorian and Edwardian Royal Navy. The navy that made Britain great, the navy that helped Britain rule the waves and the empire, the navy that produced so many great (and not-so-great) ships and men, some of which and whom have been noted herein.

It was a fighting force which made the country proud, which stirred British hearts and minds and which kept the *pax Britannia* for over a hundred years. Royal Naval Reviews gave the nation the ability to wallow in reflected glory and delight in the golden-hued charm of those prelapsarian times. For as the 'Articles of War', codified under King Charles II (and subsequently ordered to be read out to each ship's crew as they commissioned) state, it is 'the navy whereon, under the providence of God, the wealth, safety and strength of the kingdom chiefly depend'. It was a sign of the times when, in 1956, 'chiefly' was replaced by 'so much'.

In the Easter terms of 1893 and 1894 the then Regius Professor of Modern History at Oxford, James Anthony Froude, gave a series of lectures on the theme of *English Seamen of the Sixteenth Century*. In his introduction to them he identified what – in his view – was the source of British late Victorian greatness and also her vulnerability. 'Take away her merchant fleet, take away the navy that guards them; her empire will come to an end; her colonies will fall off like leaves from a withered tree; and Britain will become once more an insignificant island in the North Sea.'

He has been proved correct. For it appears that sovereignty of the seas and national self-defence have been abandoned and with them, it would seem, the marvellous Royal Fleet Reviews of yesteryear. *The Power and the Glory* is their memorial.

Envoi

THE ROYAL YACHT SQUADRON* at Cowes and the Cowes Week of yacht racing have both been a backdrop to many Royal Fleet Reviews. Formed in 1815, it welcomed the Prince Regent as a member in 1817. Three years later, when the Regent became George IV, it was entitled the Royal Yacht Club. The club organised yacht racing as part of its annual regatta, which eventually became known as 'Cowes Week'. And in 1833, William IV renamed the club the Royal Yacht Squadron. The Squadron has hosted royal visitors of many nations over the years and has always maintained strong links with the British monarchy and Royal Navy.

It was perhaps no surprise, therefore, that the Royal Navy played a lead role in helping the RYS celebrate its 200th anniversary. So it was that on 9 June 2015, the Type 23 frigate HMS *Northumberland* (1992) provided a backdrop for four days of festivities at the Royal Yacht Squadron, together with the patrol and training vessels HMS *Ranger* and *Smiter* (both *Archer* class of 1988) which hosted members of the royal family. Off Cowes, the Duke of Edinburgh, Admiral of the Royal Yacht Squadron, accompanied by First Sea Lord, Admiral Sir George Zambellas, conducted a 90-minute review of 200 civilian vessels owned by Squadron members from *Ranger*. Close behind, *Smiter* accommodated Prince Michael of Kent and Second Sea Lord Vice-Admiral Sir Jonathon Woodcock. As in days of yore, foreign royalty was present, including King Harald of Norway, Juan Carlos, the former King of Spain, and Prince Henrik of Denmark.

Northumberland gave a demonstration of her wartime capabilities and Vice-Admiral Woodcock hosted a formal reception on board the frigate. Students from Sussex University Royal Naval Unit (to which *Ranger* was attached) had the chance to meet the duke and exchange a few words during the review. And in the evening of Friday 12th, the band of Her Majesty's Royal Marines, *Collingwood*, performed a beating the retreat ceremony near to the RYS, watched by hundreds of spectators, with the Duke of Edinburgh taking the salute.

It was a like a Royal Fleet Review in miniature.

* Members' yachts are given the suffix RYS to their names and permitted to fly the White Ensign of the Royal Navy rather than the Red Ensign flown by the majority of other UK registered vessels.

List of Royal Fleet Reviews from 1346 to 2005

Edward III (one)

1346: Portsmouth, invasion of France

Henry V (one)

1415: Southampton, invasion of France

Charles II (two)

1662: Portsmouth and London, marriage to Catherine of Braganza
1672: Thames, after the battle of Sole Bay

William III (three)

1691: Limerick, Treaty of Limerick
1693: Spithead, after the battles of Barfleur and La Hougue
1698: Spithead, Peter the Great

George III (five)

1773: Spithead, Official Birthday
1778: Spithead, Admiral Keppel's fleet
1789: Plymouth, the King's recovery from madness
1794: Spithead, after the Glorious First of June
1814 (Prince Regent): Spithead, defeat of Napoleon and the French

Victoria (sixteen)

1842: Portsmouth, Grand Fleet Review
1844: Spithead, King Louis Philippe of France
1845 (two): Spithead, the Experimental Squadron (twice, in June and July)
1853: Spithead, a show of strength
1854: Spithead, Admiral Napier and the Baltic Squadron
1856: Spithead, the Crimean Fleet returns
1865: Spithead, another show of strength
1867: Spithead, the Sultan of Turkey
1873: Spithead, the Shah of Persia

1878: Spithead, the Reserve Squadron
1887: Spithead, Golden Jubilee
1889: Spithead, Kaiser Wilhelm II
1891: Spithead, visit of the French Fleet
1896: Spithead, Li Hung Chang
1897: Spithead, Diamond Jubilee

Edward VII (five)

1902: Spithead, Coronation
1905: Spithead, visit of the French Fleet
1907: Spithead, *Dreadnought*
1909 (two): Spithead, battlecruisers and the visit of the Tsar

George V (seven)

1911: Spithead, Coronation
1912: Torbay, the dawn of airpower
1912: Spithead, for the Houses of Parliament
1914: Spithead, test mobilisation
1922: Portland and Torbay, Atlantic Fleet
1924: Spithead, the Reserve Fleet
1935: Spithead, Silver Jubilee

Edward VIII (one)

1936: Weymouth and Portland

George VI (three)

1937: Spithead, Coronation
1938: Weymouth and Portland
1939: Portland, the Reserve Fleet

Elizabeth II (ten)

1953: Spithead, Coronation
1957: Moray Firth, return of the Queen from Denmark
1965: The Clyde
1969 (two): Spithead, NATO: and Torbay, new Colours
1977: Spithead, Silver Jubilee
1993: Off Anglesey, Battle of the Atlantic Commemoration (BA50)
1994: Portsmouth and Normandy, D-Day 50-year anniversary
2003: Plymouth Sound, New Colours
2005: Spithead, Trafalgar 200

Appendix 1

Ships' Rates, Seventeenth to Nineteenth Century

First Rate

First Rate ships were the largest of the fleet with their gun batteries carried on three decks. They were often used as flagships and fought in the centre of the line of battle. They were armed with a minimum of 100 heavy cannon, had a crew of about 850 and were over 2,000 tons Builder's Measure.

Second Rate

The Second Rate ships of the line were also three-deckers but smaller and cheaper. They carried between 90 and 98 guns and like the First Rates fought in the centre of the line of battle. Around the 2,000-ton mark, they had a crew of about 750. Unlike the First Rates, which were too valuable to risk in distant stations, the Second Rates often served overseas as flag-ships. They had a reputation for poor handling and slow sailing.

Third Rate

The most numerous line-of-battle ships were the two-decker Third Rates with 64–80 guns. The most effective and numerous of these was the 74-gun ship, in many ways the ideal compromise of economy, fighting power and sailing performance. They carried a crew of about 650 men and were the backbone of the battle fleet.

Fourth Rate

Two-decker ships of 50–60 guns were no longer 'fit to stand in the line of battle' by the end of the eighteenth century. With two decks, their extra accommodation made them suitable flagships for minor overseas stations, while their relatively shallow draught made them useful as headquarters ships for operations in the North Sea and the English Channel. They were also useful as convoy escorts and troopships. In normal service they had a crew of 350 and measured around 1,000 tons.

Fifth Rate

These were the frigates. With their main armament on a single gundeck, they were the fast scouts of the battle fleet, when not operating in an independent cruising role, searching out enemy merchant ships, privateers or enemy fleets. They mounted a variety of armaments and gun arrangements from 32–40 guns. Captured enemy frigates were also used in service, and many of the best British-built ships were copied or adapted from French designs. Their tonnage ranged from 700 to 1450 tons, with crews of about 300 men.

Sixth Rate

The Sixth Rates were smaller and more lightly-armed frigates, with between 22 and 28 guns, a crew of about 150, and measured 450 to 550 tons.

(With grateful acknowledgement to the National Maritime Museum, Greenwich.)

—◦—

Appendix 2

Queen Victoria's Navy, 1837

Type of Ship	Active	Harbour Service	In Ordinary	Totals
First Rate	1	5	12	18
Second Rate	4	0	10	14
Third Rate	12	0	44	56
Fourth Rate	6	0	19	25
Fifth Rate	9	1	51	61
Sixth Rate	18	0	6	24
Ship–Sloops	19	0	1	20
Brig–Sloops	40	2	8	50
Steam Vessels	15	3	6	24
Totals	124	11	157	292

Excludes ships and frigates relegated to harbour. They were employed as hulks on such duties as depots, barracks, hospitals *et al* and had no wartime role.

(Source: Navy List of 20 December 1837 and Naval-History.net)

Appendix 3

The Royal Navy Fleet in 1897

Class	In Commission	In Reserve	Under Construction	Total
Battleship 1c	21	8	5	34
Battleships 2c	7	5	0	12
Battleships 3c	2	9	0	11
Coast Defence Ships	4	11	0	15
Armoured Cruisers	10	8	0	18
Cruisers 1c	9	5	7	21
Cruisers 2c	22	34	0	56
Cruisers 3c	34	19	0	53
Sloops	11	6	0	17
Gun Vessels 1c	2	0	0	2
Gun Vessels 2c	2	0	0	2
Gun Boats 1c	37	14	0	51
Gun Boats 2c	5	0	0	5
Gun Boats 3c	19	21	0	40
TB Destroyers	19	13	52 (25 on trials)	84
Special Service Vessels	3	1	0	4
Special Torpedo Vessels	3	1	0	4
Despatch Vessels	2	0	0	2
Totals	212	155	64	431

1c = First Class, 2c = Second Class, 3c = Third Class

For some reason, the official list excluded torpedo boats

The number of RN personnel borne, at 92,322, was the highest since the end of the Napoleonic Wars and the Naval Estimates for 1897, in excess of £22 million, had never previously been equalled.

(Source: *Abstract of the Ships and Vessels constituting the Fighting Division of the British Navy, on January 1897* and naval-history.net)

Appendix 4
Foreign Navy Ships at the 1897 Diamond Jubilee Review

Inter alia

Country	Ship	Type
USA	*Brooklyn*	Cruiser
Germany	*König Wilhelm*	Old battleship
France	*Pothuau*	Cruiser
Spain	*Vizcaya*	Armoured cruiser
Russia	*Rossiya*	Cruiser
Austria	*Wien*	Small battleship
Japan	*Fuji*	British built battleship
Sweden	*Freja*	Cruiser
Siam	*Maha Chakrkri*	Small cruiser

Appendix 5
Foreign Navy Ships at the 1911 Coronation Review

Inter alia

Country	Ship	Type
Denmark	*Olfert Fischer*	Coastal defence monitor
France	*Danton*	Battleship
Germany	*Von der Tann*	Battlecruiser
Greece	*Georgios Averof*	Cruiser
Japan	*Kurama*	Battleship
,,	*Tone*	Protected cruiser
Russia	*Rossia*	Armoured cruiser
USA	*Delaware*	Battleship

Appendix 6

Foreign Navy Ships at the 1953 Coronation Review

Country	Ship	Type
Belgium	*Luitenant Ter Zee Victor Billet*	Frigate
Brazil	*Almirante Barroso*	Cruiser
Denmark	*Holger Danske*	Frigate
Dominican Republic	*Trujillo*	Destroyer
France	*Montcalm*	Cruiser
Greece	*Navarinon*	Destroyer
Italy	*Amerigo Vespucci*	Sail training ship
Netherlands	*Tromp*	Cruiser
Norway	*Narvik*	Destroyer
Portugal	*Bartolomeu Dias*	Frigate
Spain	*Miguel de Cervantes*	Light cruiser
Sweden	*Gota Lejon*	Cruiser
Thailand	*Posamton*	Minesweeper
Turkey	*Demir Hisar*	Destroyer
USSR	*Sverdlov*	Cruiser
USA	*Baltimore*	Cruiser

Appendix 7

Comparison of Royal Navy Fleets, 1953 vs 1977

	1953	1977
In reserve or in refit	49	44
On operations	70	36
At review	183	98
Total	302	178
Of which		
Battleships	1	0
Aircraft carriers	12	1
Destroyers	45	9
Frigates	63	60
Cruisers	14	3
Total manpower	146,600	75,150
Number of C-in-Cs	9	2

(Source: DEFE 69/6005, NA)

Appendix 8

Allied Merchant Shipping Losses (all causes) in the North Atlantic, 1939–1945

1939:	47
1940:	349
1941:	496
1942:	1,006
1943:	284
1944:	31
1945:	19
Total:	2,232

Appendix 9

Main Warships at the BA50 1993 Commemoration

Country	Ship	Type
Britain	HMS *Cornwall*	Type 22 frigate
	Liverpool	Type 42 destroyer
	Beaver	Type 22 frigate
	Birmingham	Type 42 destroyer
	Oracle	*Oberon*-class submarine
	Charger	*Archer*-class fast training boat
	Biter	,,
	Puncher	,,
	Humber	'River'-class minesweeper
	Middleton	'Hunt'-class mine countermeasures vessel
	Chiddingford	,,
	Quorn	,,
Canada	HMCS *Algonquin*	'Tribal'-class destroyer
New Zealand	HMNZS *Canterbury*	Frigate
	Endeavour	Oil tanker
Italy	ITNS *Danaide*	Corvette
USA	USS *Moosbrugger*	*Spruance*-class destroyer
	Devastator	Mine countermeasures vessel
	Scout	,,
	Gallatin	Coast Guard cutter
Iceland	*Aegir*	Coast Guard vessel
Belgium	BMS *Westdiep*	*Wielingen*-class frigate
France	FS *Aconit*	Destroyer
Denmark	HDMS *Niels Juel*	Corvette
Norway	HNoMS *Trondheim*	*Oslo*-class frigate
	Horten	Training ship
Germany	FGS *Bremen*	*Bremen*-class frigate
	S174	206-class submarine
Brazil	BNS *Defensora*	Anti-submarine frigate
Netherlands	HNLMS *Witte de With*	*Heemskerck*-class frigate
	Poolster	Support ship
Greece	HNS *Nearchos*	Destroyer, ex-USN
Russia	*Gremyashchy*	Destroyer
South Africa	SAS *Drakensberg*	Fleet replenishment ship

Appendix 10

The Decline of the Royal Navy in the 1990s

Type of unit	1990	1999
Manpower	63,200	43,200
Submarines	33	15
Of which Trident/Polaris	4	3
Carriers	3	3
Assault ships	2	3
Cruisers	0	0
Destroyers	14	12
Frigates	35	23
Mine countermeasures	41	20
Patrol and other	34	24
Total vessels	162	100
Fixed wing aircraft (squadrons)	3	3
Helicopters (squadrons)	17	12
Other vessels		
Support ships	8	0
Survey ships	8	6
Ice Patrol ships	1	1
Tankers	13	9
Fleet replenishment ships	4	4
Aviation training ships	0	1
Landing ships	5	5
Forward repair ships	1	1
Total other vessels	40	27

(Source: House of Commons Library Research Paper 99/112.

Appendix 11

Numbers of Vessels at the 2005 'Trafalgar 200' Fleet Review

Number	Type	Notes
Royal Navy		
Aircraft carriers	2	*Invincible, Illustrious*
Amphibious assault ships	3	*Ocean, Bulwark, Albion*
Antarctic patrol vessel	1	*Endurance* acting as royal yacht
Type 22 frigates	2	
SSN	3	No SSBN
Destroyers	5	
Type 23 frigates	7	
Mine countermeasures vessels	9	
Additional RN craft at review (non-warship)		
Survey ships	4	
Fishery protection vessel	1	
Training craft	9	
Total RN ships at review	**46**	Of which 15 were not warships
RN ships on sentry duty	**7**	
Royal Fleet Auxiliary	**12**	
Total British naval forces	**65**	Of which 27 were not warships
Ships of foreign navies	**58**	France sent 7, Spain 2
Sailing ships		
British	11	
Foreign	12	
Miscellaneous non-military vessels	26	Including Cunard's *QE2*, 2 lifeboats and the Northern Lighthouse Board
Total Vessels	**172**	

Navies represented at the review: Algeria, Australia, Canada, Belgium, Brazil, Colombia, Denmark, Estonia, Finland, France, Germany, Greece, India, Indonesia, Ireland, Italy, Japan, Latvia, Lithuania, Morocco, Netherlands, Nigeria, Oman, Pakistan, Poland, Portugal, Romania, Russia, Serbia, South Africa, South Korea, Spain, Turkey, Uruguay, United States (Navy and Coastguard). Thirty-five countries in total.

    Tall ships at the review: Britain (11), Bulgaria (1), France (3), Ireland (1), Netherlands (3), Poland (2), USA (1) and Russia (1).

Appendix 12

21 October 2005 Trafalgar Night Dinner Menu

Starter: 'Leviathan's Prize from the Deep'. Smoked Salmon Tartare
  bound with an Aged Dill Sauce and mixed with Caviar Cream
Main Course: 'Fighting Temeraire'. Rare Roast Slices of Prime Norfolk
  Fillet of Beef served on a bed of Sautéed Savoy Cabbage with a
  Vintage Port and Merlot Jus
Dauphinoise Potatoes
Roasted Shallots and Trimmed Baby Carrots
Dessert: 'Lady Hamilton's Delight'
Warm Chocolate Soufflé with Spiced Poached Pears served with Cream
  and a Warm Chocolate Sauce
Red Wine
Marques de Murrieta Gran Reserva 1997
White Wine
Maison de Bourgogne Montagny Cuvée 1993

Taylors Port Vintage 1963
Pellegrino 'Victory' Marsala (35 years old)

Author's Note: Marsala was served at this bicentennial dinner, rather than
Madeira as was traditional, as Nelson had popularised this wine in the
Royal Navy. In March 1800, following his return from victory at the
battle of the Nile (1799), he ordered 500 pipes of Marsala (equivalent to
348,000 bottles) to furnish the British Fleet off Malta. As for the vintage
offered, it was not quite as ancient as it seems, for Marsala uses the *in
perpetuum* system, similar to *solera* for sherry.

(The primary source for this information is a MOD press release of 20 October 2005.)

Appendix 13

Ratio of Naval Expenditure to Foreign Trade in the United Kingdom, Self-governing Dominions and India 1907–1908

Prepared for the Imperial Conference on Naval and Military Defence 1908

Country	Exports (£m)	Imports (£m)	Total Foreign Trade (£m)	Naval Expenditure (£m)	Naval Expenditure per £100 of Trade (£)
UK	520.14	649.61	1196.75	35.14	3.00
Canada	57.56	76.21	133.76	0.10	0.07
Australia	72.82	51.81	124.63	0.27	0.22
New Zealand	20.07	17.30	37.37	0.10	0.27
South Africa	45.21	25.36	70.74	0.09	0.12
India	125.96	124.17	250.13	0.48	0.19

(Source: A Offer, *The Economic History Review*, New Series vol 46, no 2, May 1993, p 231.)

Author's Note

I HOPE THAT YOU, the reader, have enjoyed this book. It came about as the result of a conversation with my publisher, Julian Mannering. I thank Julian for commissioning it, for the writing of the book has taken me to areas of naval history that I have previously not explored.

The book is a threnody – for a lost navy, a lost empire and a lost country. But it is also a celebration of remarkable feats, ships, men and women, and of the Royal Navy itself, once our strong and sure shield.

We ignore the fact that we are an island at our peril. The seas made Britain, but they can unmake her too. If we continue to disregard the lessons learned from the past, regarding the absolute necessity of retaining command of the sea and the freedom to transit the oceans, as we seem determined to do, then we risk the loss of our security, our economy and our supply chain.* Politicians please take note.

I owe a huge debt of gratitude to the trustees and staff of the excellent archives that we have in Britain, but in particular to the National Maritime Museum in Greenwich whose picture library has been invaluable in the making of this book. As always, the National Archives at Kew, the Churchill Archive at Churchill College, Cambridge, the National Museum of the Royal Navy at Portsmouth and the Imperial War Museum in London have proved happy hunting grounds. Contemporary newspaper accounts have been very useful and I particularly offer my hand in thanks to the *Spectator* magazine, whose archive is a treasure trove of nineteenth-century information. The decision by the Royal Archives to place Queen Victoria's journals on-line is a boon to all historians.

American picture archives are both extensive and more generous than British ones; many images are provided free of charge, a boon not granted by any British picture repository and more's the pity. I offer heartfelt thanks to the Library of Congress in Washington DC and the US Naval History and Heritage Command at the Washington Navy Yard for their munificence in this respect. Their imagery adds much to the comprehensiveness of this book.

I must thank Lieutenant Commander Bob Horner RD RNR (rtd) for his recollections. From Boston, USA, Tony Lovell helped clarify a gunnery and rangefinding issue. Historian of Southampton Russell Masters was kind enough to share his local knowledge. Andrew Choong kindly read

---

* In 2017 the UK imported 50 per cent of the food it consumed (National Statistics; Agriculture in the United Kingdom, 2017).

the manuscript and made helpful comments. Peter Wilkinson drew the map with his usual skill. And Dave Cradduck produced another invaluable index.

My friends in both Britain and France support me in my peculiar fascination for the Royal Navy, without necessarily understanding it. And to Vivienne I offer, as always, my undying thanks for the help, support and belief in me and my books which makes them possible.

Most books contain errors of commission or omission. If there are errors or solecisms in this volume the fault is mine and I should like to hear of them; to err is human.

Steve R Dunn
Worcestershire

Notes

The following abbreviations will be used for brevity.

Institutions

CAC   Churchill Archive, Churchill College, Cambridge

HCL   House of Commons Library

IWM   Imperial War Museum, London

LHMA   Liddell-Hart Military Archives, King's College, London

NA   National Archives, Kew

NMRN   National Museum of the Royal Navy, Portsmouth

Other

QV Journal;   Queen Victoria's Journal

It is the convention that page numbers be given for citations. This is not always possible in the modern world. Some digitised documents lack page numbering and some archives hold unnumbered single or multiple sheets in bundles under one reference or none at all. Thus, page numbers will be given where possible but the reader will understand that they are not always available or, indeed, necessary.

Preface

1. Book title, Margerison, see Bibliography.

Chapter 1

1. O'Hara, *Britain and the Sea*, p 37.
2. Fayle, *Seaborne Trade*, vol III, p 469.
3. Quoted in O'Hara, *Britain and the Sea*, p 111.
4. Daniel Defoe, *A tour thro' the whole island of Great Britain, divided into circuits or journies,* Letter 1, Pt 3.
5. Shakespeare, *King Lear*, Act IV, Scene iv.
6. Savage, *Anglo-Saxon Chronicles*, p 288.
7. Cannadine, *Victorious Century*, p 75.

Chapter 3

1. Rose in *Oxford Illustrated History*, p 10.
2. Mortimer, *The Perfect King*, p 222.
3. Stephen Cooper Blog; *Did Henry V found the Royal Navy?*.
4. Friel, *Henry V's Navy*, p 106.
5. Mortimer, *1415*, p 325.
6. Gates, *The Portsmouth That Has Passed*, p 18.
7. Holinshed (Chron. 1587, iii 1330) cited in *Archaeologia Cantiana*, vol 6 (1866), pp 43ff, quoting Visits to Rochester and Chatham made by royal, noble, and distinguished personages, English and foreign, from the year 1300 to 1783, by William Brenchley Eye, esq.

Chapter 4

1. Pepys' diary, 15 May 1662.
2. Wright, *The Story of the 'Domus Dei' of Portsmouth*, p 21.
3. Gates, *The Portsmouth That Has Passed*, p 37.
4. Ibid.
5. Ibid.
6. Pepys' diary, 23 August 1662.
7. Davies, *Kings of the Sea*, p 80.
8. Ibid, p 82.
9. At the time of writing, these include, *inter alia*, Wikipedia, the National Museum of the Royal Navy and a plethora of other sites. The author has written to the NMRN with a full listing of reviews.
10. Silver Jubilee Review Official Souvenir Programme (1977), p 12.
11. Massie, *Peter the Great*, p 214.

Chapter 5

1. Rodger, *The Insatiable Earl*, p 200.
2. Willis, *The Struggle for Sea Power*, p 190.
3. Ibid, p 198.
4. Ibid, p 217.
5. *Oxford Illustrated History*, p 105.
6. Mahan, *The Influence of Sea Power upon History*, p 534.
7. Dalton, *British Royal Yachts*, p 92.
8. Burke, *Annual Register*, vol 31, p 264.
9. Ibid.
10. Ibid, p 265.

11. Ibid.
12. Cannadine, *Victorious Century*, p 65.
13. Hibbert, *George IV*, p 410.
14. Ibid.
15. O'Hara, *Britain and the Sea*, p 107.
16. Cannadine, *Victorious Century*, pp 101–2.
17. Percy Bysshe Shelley, *England in 1819*, in *The Poetical Works of Percy Bysshe Shelley*.
18. *The European Magazine and London Review*, vol 80, p 63.
19. Ibid.
20. *The Times*, 15 July 1830.
21. Percy Bysshe Shelley, *England in 1819*, in *The Poetical Works of Percy Bysshe Shelley*.

Chapter 6
1. *Spectator*, 5 March 1842.
2. Ibid.
3. Ibid.
4. Ibid.
5. Troubetzkoy, *The Crimean War*, p 54.
6. *Punch* VI 1843, p 124.
7. Troubetzkoy, *The Crimean War*, p 11.
8. *Encyclopaedia Britannica 1911*, Nicholas I.
9. Troubetzkoy, *The Crimean War*, p 6.
10. For example, the National Museum of the Royal Navy.
11. *Spectator*, 14 September 1844.
12. Ibid, 12 October 1844.
13. Ibid, 19 October 1844.
14. Ibid, 19 July 1845.
15. *The Times*, 23 June 1845.
16. QV Journal, 21 June 1845, vol 19, p 244.
17. *The Times*, 23 June 1845.
18. Ibid.
19. Ibid.
20. Ibid.
21. Ibid.
22. *Spectator*, 19 July 1845.
23. Ibid.
24. Ibid.
25. Ibid.

Chapter 7
1. Cannadine, *Victorious Century*, p 202.
2. Wilson, *Empire of the Deep*, p 485.
3. Dixon, *Ships of the Victorian Navy*, p 46.
4. *Spectator*, 13 August 1853.
5. Ibid.
6. Ibid.
7. *The Times*, 9 August 1853.
8. *Spectator*, 13 August 1853.
9. *The Times*, 12 August 1853.
10. Ibid.
11. *Spectator*, 13 August 1853.

12. *The Times*, 15 August 1853.
13. Ibid, 11 August 1853.
14. Cannadine, *Victorious Century*, p 304.
15. Troubetzkoy, *The Crimean War*, p 7.
16. Ibid, p 161.
17. Ibid, p 192.
18. *Encyclopaedia Britannica 1911*.
19. *Spectator*, 18 March 1854.
20. Ibid.
21. QV Journal 11 March 1854, vol 37 p 112.
22. *Spectator*, 18 March 1854.
23. Ibid.
24. *The Times*, 24 April 1856.
25. *Spectator*, 26 April 1856.
26. *News of the World*, 27 April 1856.
27. Ibid.
28. *Spectator*, 26 April 1856.
29. Ibid.
30. Ibid.
31. Ibid.
32. Ibid.

Chapter 8
1. Hibbert, *Queen Victoria*, p 337.
2. Navy List, 20 June 1861.
3. Fisher, *Memories*, p 149.
4. *Queanbeyan Age and General Advertiser*, 30 November 1865.
5. Ibid.
6. Ibid.
7. *Spectator*, 2 September 1865.
8. Ibid.
9. *Illustrated London News*, 16 September 1865.
10. Ibid.
11. *Spectator*, 2 September 1865.
12. Ibid.
13. Hibbert, *Queen Victoria*, p 346.
14. *Spectator*, 20 July 1867.
15. Ibid.
16. Ibid.
17. Dixon, *Ships of the Victorian Navy*, p 74.
18. *Spectator*, 20 July 1867.
19. Ibid.
20. Ibid.
21. Ibid.
22. QV Journals 17 July 1867, vol 56, p 183.
23. McMeekin, *Ottoman Endgame*, p 137.
24. Hibbert, *Queen Victoria*, p 347.
25. Ibid.
26. *Wellington Independent*, 27 September 1873.
27. Ibid.
28. Dixon, *Ships of the Victorian Navy*, p 38.
29. *Wellington Independent*, 27 September 1873.
30. Ibid.
31. Ibid.

32. Ibid.
33. Redhouse, *Diary of H M The Shah of Persia*, p 36.
34. *Wellington Independent*, 27 September 1873.
35. Fisher, *Memories*, pp 142–3.
36. *Wellington Independent*, 27 September 1873.
37. Redhouse, *Diary of H M The Shah of Persia*, pp 56–7.
38. Ibid, p 57.
39. Ibid, p 58.
40. *Wellington Independent*, 27 September 1873.
41. Hibbert, *Queen Victoria*, p 364.
42. Ibid.
43. QV Journals 13 August 1878, vol 69, p 57.
44. Ibid.
45. Ibid.
46. Banbury, *Shipbuilders of the Thames and Medway*, p 280.
47. *The Times*, 14 June 1878.

Chapter 9

1. Hibbert, *Queen Victoria*, p 379.
2. Dixon, *Ships of the Victorian Navy*, p 100.
3. Ibid.
4. QV Journal 22 July 1887, vol 86, p 22.
5. Ibid, 23 July 1887, vol 86, p 25.
6. *Spectator*, 30 July 1887.
7. QV Journal 23 July 1887, vol 86, p 25.
8. Ibid, p 26.
9. *The Times*, 25 July 1887.
10. Kane report, ADM 231/10, NA.
11. Bennett, *Charlie B*, p 140.
12. *Spectator*, 30 July 1887.
13. QV Journal 23 July 1887, vol 86, p 26.
14. *Spectator*, 30 July 1887.
15. Ibid.
16. Hibbert, *Queen Victoria*, p 383.
17. Roberts, *Salisbury*, p 539.
18. Ibid.
19. Ibid, p 540.
20. Ibid.
21. Ibid.
22. Ridley, *Bertie*, p 260.
23. Ibid, p 261.
24. QV Journal 5 August 1889, vol 90, p 35.
25. *Spectator*, 10 August 1889.
26. Penrose-Fitzgerald, *From Sail to Steam*, p 172.
27. *Spectator*, 10 August 1889.
28. Ibid.
29. Ross, *Admiral Sir Francis Bridgeman*, p 84.
30. Bacon, *A Naval Scrapbook*, p 174.
31. Speech to the House of Commons 1 March 1848.
32. *Spectator*, 22 August 1891.
33. Ibid.
34. Ibid.
35. Ibid.
36. QV Journal 20 August 1891, vol 94, p 72.
37. Ibid, p 73.

38. *London Echo*, 22 August 1891.
39. Ibid.
40. QV Journal 21 August 1891, vol 94, p 96.
41. Ibid, p 77.
42. *Spectator*, 29 August 1891.
43. Hansard HC Deb 20 July 1896, vol 43 c141.
44. QV Journal 4 August 1896, vol 104, p 42.
45. Ibid, 5 August 1896, vol 104, p 44.

Chapter 10

1. *Freeman's Journal and Daily Commercial Advertiser*, 23 June 1897.
2. QV Journal 21 June 1897, vol 105, p 207.
3. Bull 2/14, CAC.
4. *Spectator*, 3 July 1897.
5. Ibid.
6. *Guide to the Naval Review*, June 1897, p 2.
7. Ibid, p 3.
8. QV Journal 26 June 1897, vol 105, p 226.
9. Smith, *A Yellow Admiral*, p 126.
10. Ibid.
11. *The Times*, 28 June 1897.
12. Smith, *A Yellow Admiral*, p 126.
13. ADM 116/113, NA.
14. *Spectator*, 3 July 1897.
15. Ibid.
16. Ibid.
17. Ibid.
18. *Spectator*, 11 November 1899.
19. Ibid.
20. *Daily Mail*, 20 November 1899.
21. Ibid.
22. Kennedy, *The Samoan Tangle*, p 242.
23. Rose, *King George V*, p 75.

Chapter 11

1. Wilson, *Empire of the Deep*, p 508.
2. Ibid.
3. Scott, *Fifty Years in the Royal Navy*, p 60.
4. Ibid, p 61.
5. Ibid, p 198.
6. Cannadine, *Victorious Century*, p 446.
7. ADM 176/56, NA.
8. Scott, *Fifty Years in the Navy*, p 169.
9. *Walsall Advertiser*, 23 August 1902.
10. *Daily Express*, 15 August 1902.
11. ADM 1/7579, NA.
12. ADM 1/7956, NA.
13. *Walsall Advertiser*, 23 August 1902.
14. Ibid.
15. *Spectator*, 23 August 1902.
16. *Sydney Morning Herald*, 18 August 1902.
17. Bull 3/6, CAC.
18. *Spectator*, 23 August 1902.
19. ADM 136/132, NA.

20. ADM 116/113, NA.
21. Ridley, *Bertie*, p 376.
22. Ibid, p 380.
23. *Spectator*, 15 July 1905.
24. *Register*, 8 August 1905.
25. Ibid.
26. *Spectator*, 12 August 1905.
27. Ibid.
28. ADM 178/58, NA.
29. *Queenslander*, 28 October 1905.
30. 26 February 1904 memo to Cabinet, quoted in Burk, *The Lion and the Eagle*, p 363.
31. A Lambert, *Admirals*, p 312.
32. Scott, *Fifty Years in the Royal Navy*, p 203.
33. *The Singapore Free Press and Mercantile Advertiser*, 5 August 1907.
34. Hattersley, *The Edwardians*, p 473.
35. Ibid, p 471.
36. *Argus*, Melbourne, 6 August 1907.
37. *The Times*, 5 August 1907.
38. HC Deb 31 July 1907, vol 179 c947.
39. Fisher, *Memories*, pp 1–2.
40. Rose, *George V*, p 72.
41. HC Deb 29 July 1909, vol 8 cc1356–8.
42. Ridley, *Bertie*, p 438.
43. ADM 179/57, NA.
44. Ibid.
45. Quoted in Massey, *Nicholas and Alexandra*, p 174.
46. BGGF 1/60, CAC.
47. Fisher, *Memories*, p 12.
48. Ibid, p 14.

Chapter 12
1. Rose, *George V*, p 7.
2. Ibid, p 189.
3. Ibid, p 112.
4. Ibid, p 160.
5. *Spectator*, 1 July 1911.
6. Ibid.
7. Ibid.
8. ADM 116/1158, NA.
9. Rose, *George V*, p 165.
10. *Adelaide Advertiser*, 14 March 1912.
11. Ibid.
12. 15 June 1912, T1/11642, NA.
13. *New York Herald*, 10 May 1912.
14. *Morning Post*, 9 May 1912.
15. *Daily Chronicle*, 9 May 1912.
16. *Daily Mail*, 9 May 1912.
17. 2 July 1914, ADM 116/1372, NA.
18. ADM 116/1372.
19. Diary 16 July 1914, Docs 11336, IWM.
20. H Grant, *My War at Sea*, p 7.
21. Agar, *Footprints in the Sea*, p 53.
22. Quoted in Ruger, *Heligoland*, p 124.

23. Agar, *Footprints in the Sea*, p 53.
24. Rose, *George V*, p 168.
25. Quoted in Broome, *Make a Signal*, p 166.

Chapter 13
1. Churchill, *World Crisis*, vol 1, p 929.
2. Jane, *Fighting Ships of WW1*, p 36.
3. Barnett, *The Collapse of British Power*, p 248.
4. Bonar Law to Geddes, 23 Nov 1918, ADM116/1809, NA.
5. 22 November 1918, ADM 116/1605, NA.
6. Hansard HC Deb 16 March 1922, vol 151 cc2409-57.
7. Ibid,
8. Taylor, *The End of Glory*, p 20,
9. Roskill, *Hankey, Man of Secrets*, vol 2, p 348.
10. Ibid.
11. Marquand, *Ramsay MacDonald*, p 250.
12. *New York Times*, 27 July 1924.
13. *Argus*, Melbourne, 28 July 1924.
14. *The Times*, 28 July 1924.
15. *Argus*, Melbourne, 28 July 1924.
16. Talbot-Booth, *All the World's Fighting Ships*, p 266.
17. 28 November 1929, ADM 116/2689, NA.
18. Barnett, *The Collapse of British Power*, p 290.
19. Hore, *Henry Harwood*, p 35.
20. Barnett, *The Collapse of British Power*, p 297.
21. Rose, *George V*, p 395.
22. ADM 116/3011, NA.
23. *Daily Telegraph*, 17 July 1935.
24. *The Times*, 17 July 1935.
25. *Daily Telegraph*, 17 July 1935.
26. Roskill, *Naval Policy*, vol 2, p 352.
27. Talbot-Booth, *All the World's Fighting Fleets*, p 270.
28. Ibid, p 269.
29. Diary 16 July 1935, NMRN.
30. Cunningham, *A Sailor's Odyssey*, p 172.
31. *Daily Telegraph*, 18 July 1935.

Chapter 14
1. *Sydney Morning Herald*, 14 November 1936.
2. Ziegler, *King Edward VIII*, p 297.
3. *New York Times*, 21 May 1937.
4. Keystone View Company stereographic image in private collection.
5. Howarth, *Cambridge Between Two Wars*, p 256.
6. *Sydney Morning Herald*, 10 August 1939.
7. Quoted in Bradford, *King George VI*, p 302.
8. CHAR 20/136, CAC.

Chapter 15
1. Hore, *Henry Harwood*, p 137.
2. *Spectator*, 12 June 1953.
3. Ibid.
4. *The Advertiser*, Adelaide, 15 June 1953.

5. *Spectator*, 12 June 1953.
6. Ibid.
7. Quoted in HCL Briefing paper no 07313, 9 July 2018.
8. Ibid.
9. Hansard HC Deb 10 March 1969, vol 779 cc991-1120.
10. HCL Briefing paper no 07313, 9 July 2018.
11. O'Hara, *Britain and the Sea*, p 205.
12. Hansard HC Deb 16 May 1969, vol 783 cc277-8W.
13. *Spectator*, 5 August 1972.
14. Ibid.
15. Ibid.
16. DEFE 24/1170, NA.
17. DEFE 69/6005, NA.
18. *Sunday Mirror*, 3 June 1977.
19. *Navy International*, June 1977, p 12.
20. *New York Times*, 29 June 1977.
21. Ibid.
22. Ibid.
23. Ibid.

Chapter 16

1. Freedman, *The Politics of British Defence 1979-1998*, p 83.
2. Original signal flimsy in private collection.
3. HCL, Research Paper 99/112.
4. D-Day 50th Anniversary Souvenir Brochure, p 46.
5. Paul Johnston in *Spectator*, 4 June 1994.
6. www.dday.center.
7. HCL research paper 99/112.
8. Dalton, *British Royal Yachts*, p 288.
9. *Daily Telegraph*, 25 June 2005.
10. The author is grateful to an on-line article by David Prothero on the website 'Flags of the World' for some of these details.
11. *Daily Telegraph*, 24 July 2003.
12. Ibid.
13. Ibid.
14. Hansard 21 June 2005, columns 31 and 32WS.
15. Trafalgar 200 Official Brochure, p 6.
16. *Independent*, 14 August 2005.
17. Ibid.
18. *Daily Telegraph*, 29 June 2005.
19. *The Times*, 29 June 2005.
20. *Daily Telegraph*, 2 July 2005.
21. *Daily Mail*, 1 July 2018.
22. *The Times*, 3 May 2019.

23. *Daily Telegraph*, 21 May 2019.
24. *New York Times* on line. 27 April 2019.
25. *Spectator*, 14 September 2019.

Chapter 17

1. Dalton, *British Royal Yachts*, p 134.
2. QV Journal 15 July 1845, vol 20, p 18.
3. McLaughlin, *The Escape of the Goeben*, p 25.
4. *The Times*, 5 September 1898.
5. 3 September 1898, Balmoral to 82 Eaton Place, Keppel Scrapbook #1, LHMA, KCL.
6. Goodenough, *A Rough Record*, p 30.
7. Aspinall-Oglander, *Roger Keyes*, p 22.
8. Keyes, *Adventures Ashore and Afloat*, p 109.
9. Ibid, p 112.
10. Agar, *Footprints in the Sea*, p 160.
11. Ibid, p 166.
12. Ibid.
13. Gray, *The Greedy Queen*, p 228.

Chapter 18

1. Kennedy, *The Rise and Fall of British Naval Mastery*, p 157.
2. Ferguson, *Empire*, pp 1 & 17.
3. Barnett, *The Collapse of British Power*, p 76.
4. Sir John Seeley, *The Expansion of England*, p 13.
5. CAB 32/118, NA.
6. Barnett, *The Collapse of British Power*, p 63.
7. Ibid, p 19.
8. Bouverie, *Appeasing Hitler*, p 31.
9. Rose, *King George V*, p 387.
10. Hansard HC Deb 24 March 1938, vol 333 col 1454.
11. Burk, *The Lion and the Eagle*, p 386.
12. Ferguson, *The Pity of War*, pp 327 & 329.
13. Burk, *The Lion and the Eagle*, p 381.
14. Ibid, p 390.
15. Ibid, p 401.
16. Barnett, *The Collapse of British Power*, p 592.
17. Quoted in Hawes, *The Shortest History of Germany*, p vii.
18. *USA Today* online, 2 April 2019.
19. ADM 1/7596, NA.
20. Marder, *Fear God and Dread Nought*, vol 2, p 51.
21. *The Times*, 1 June 1909.
22. N Lambert, *Sir John Fisher's Naval Revolution*, p 15.
23. A Lambert, *Seapower States*, p 300.

Bibliography

The following resources have been cited in the text.

Primary Sources

Private papers of V J Robinson, docs 11336, Imperial War Museum, London.

Private papers of W J Bull, BULL 2/14 and 3/6, Churchill Archive Centre, Churchill College, Cambridge.

Private papers of B Godfrey Faussett, BGGF 1/60, Churchill Archive Centre.

Papers of Sir Winston Churchill in the CHAR series, Churchill Archive Centre.

Diary, Dudley Davenport, 1986/431(5), National Museum of the Royal Navy, Portsmouth.

Keppel Scrapbook #1, Liddell-Hart Military Archives, King's College, London.

Various files in the ADM, T and DEFE series, The National Archives, Kew.

Secondary Sources

Books

The place of publication is London unless otherwise stated.

Ackroyd, P, *Dominion* (Macmillan 2018).

Agar, A, *Footprints in the Sea* (Evans Brothers Ltd, 1959).

Aspinall-Oglander, C, *Roger Keyes* (Hogarth Press, 1951).

Bacon, R, *A Naval Scrapbook* (Hutchison and Co, 1925).

Banbury, P, *Shipbuilders of the Thames and Medway* (Newton Abbot: David & Charles, 1971).

Barnett, C, *The Collapse of British Power* (Eyre Methuen, 1972).

Bennett, G, *Charlie B* (Peter Dawnay Ltd, 1968).

Bouverie, T, *Appeasing Hitler* (Vintage, 2019).

Bradford, S, *King George VI* (Weidenfeld and Nicolson, 1989).

Broome, J, *Make a Signal* (Sussex: Douglas-Boyd Books, 1994, originally Putnam 1955).

Burk, K, *The Lion and The Eagle* (Bloomsbury, 2018).

Burke, E, *Annual Register for the Year 1789*, vol 31 (J Dodsley, 1792).

Cannadine, D, *Victorious Century* (Penguin Books, 2018).

Churchill, W, *The World Crisis* vol 1 (Thornton Butterworth, 1923).

Dalton T, *British Royal Yachts* (Tiverton: Halsgrove, 2002).

Davies, J D, *Kings of the Sea* (Barnsley: Seaforth Publishing, 2017).

Defoe, D, *A tour thro' the whole island of Great Britain, divided into circuits or journies* (1724).

Dixon, C, *Ships of the Victorian Navy* (Southampton: Ashford Press Publishing, 1987).

Fayle, C, *Seaborne Trade*, vol III (John Murray, 1924; republished Sussex: Naval and Military Press, undated).

Ferguson, N, *The Pity of War* (Penguin, 1999).

_____, *Empire* (Penguin, 2004).

Fisher, J, *Memories* (Hodder and Stoughton, 1919).

Freedman, L, *The Politics of British Defence 1979-1998* (Macmillan Press, 1999).

Friel, I, *Henry V's Navy* (History Press, 2015).

Gambier, J, *Links in my life on land and sea* (Fisher Unwin, 1906).

Gates, W, ed Peake, N, *The Portsmouth That Has Passed* (Portsmouth: Milestone Publications, 1987).

Goodenough, W, *A Rough Record* (Hutchinson & Co, 1943).

Gordon, A, *The Rules of the Game* (John Murray, 1996).

Gray, A, *The Greedy Queen* (Profile Books, 2018).

Hattersley, R, *The Edwardians* (Little Brown, 2004).

Hawes, J, *The Shortest History of Germany* (Devon: Old Street Publishing, 2018).

Howarth, T, *Cambridge Between Two Wars* (Collins, 1978).

Hibbert, C, *George IV* (Penguin, 1976).

Hibbert, C, *Queen Victoria* (Harper Collins, 2000).

Hill, J, ed, *The Oxford Illustrated History of the Royal Navy* (Oxford: OUP, 1995).

Hore, P, *Henry Harwood* (Barnsley: Seaforth Publishing, 2018).

Jane, F, *Fighting Ships of World War 1* (Jane Publishing Company, 1919).

Kennedy, P, *The Samoan Tangle* (New York: Barnes and Noble, 1974).

_____, *The Rise and Fall of British Naval Mastery* (Allen Lane, 1976).

Keyes, R, *Adventures Ashore and Afloat* (George G Harrap and Co, 1939).

Lambert, A, *Admirals* (Faber and Faber Ltd, 2009).

_____, *Seapower States* (New Haven: Yale University Press, 2018).

Lambert, N, *Sir John Fisher's Naval Revolution* (Columbia: University of South Carolina Press, 2002).

Mahan, A T, *The Influence of Sea Power upon History 1660 – 1783* (Boston: Little Brown, 1890).

Marder, A, *Fear God and Dread Nought*, vol 2 (Jonathan Cape, 1956).

Margerison, J, *Our Wonderful Navy; the story of the sure shield in peace and war* (Cassell and Co, 1919).

Marquand, D, *Ramsay MacDonald* (Jonathan Cape, 1977).

Massie, R, *Nicholas and Alexandra* (World Books, 1968).

_____, *Peter the Great* (Head of Zeus, 1980; republished 2016).

McLaughlin, R, *The Escape of the Goeben* (Seeley Service, 1974).

McMeekin, S, *The Ottoman Endgame* (Penguin, 2016).

Mortimer, I, *The Perfect King* (Jonathan Cape, 2006).

_____, *1415: Henry V's Year of Glory* (The Bodley Head, 2009).

O'Hara, G, *Britain and the Sea since 1600* (Palgrave Macmillan, 2010).

Penrose-Fitzgerald, C, *From Sail to Steam* (Edward Arnold, 1916).

Redhouse, J, *Diary of H M the Shah of Persia, tour through Europe in AD 1873* (Harrison and Sons, 1874).

Ridley, J, *Bertie* (Chatto & Windus, 2012).

Roberts, A, *Salisbury, Victorian Titan* (Weidenfeld and Nicolson, 1999).

Rodger, N, *The Insatiable Earl* (W W Norton and Co, 1993).

Rose, K, *King George V* (Macmillan, 1984).

Roskill, S, *Hankey, Man of Secrets* vol 2 (Collins, 1972).

_____, *Naval Policy Between the Wars*, vol 2 (Collins, 1976).

Ross, S, *Admiral Sir Francis Bridgeman* (Cambridge: Baily's, 1998).

Ruger, J, *Heligoland* (Oxford: OUP, 2017).

Savage, A, *Anglo-Saxon Chronicles* (Papermac, 1988).

Scott, P, *Fifty Years in the Royal Navy* (John Murray, 1919).

Seeley, J, *The Expansion of England* (Macmillan, 1883).

Shelley, P, *The Poetical Works of Percy Bysshe Shelley* (Edward Moxon, 1839).

Smith, H, *A Yellow Admiral Remembers* (Edward Arnold and Co, 1932).

Talbot-Booth, E, *All the World's Fighting Fleets* (Sampson, Low, Marston and Co, 1943).

Taylor, B, *The End of Glory* (Barnsley: Seaforth Publishing, 2012).

Troubetzkoy, A, *A Brief History of the Crimean War* (New York: Carroll and Graf, 2006).

Willis, S, *The Struggle for Sea Power* (Atlantic Books, 2018).

Wilson, B, *Empire of the Deep* (W&N, 2014).

Wright, H, *The Story of the 'Domus Dei' of Portsmouth* (James Parker & Co, 1873).

Ziegler, P, *King Edward VIII* (Harper Press, 2012; originally published 1990).

Shakespeare's Plays
King Lear.
King Richard II.

Newspapers and Magazines

Adelaide Advertiser.
Argus (Melbourne).
Daily Chronicle.
Daily Mail.
Daily Telegraph.
Freeman's Journal and Daily Commercial Advertiser (Dublin).
Liverpool Echo.
London Echo.
London Gazette.
Morning Post.
Navy International.
New York Herald.
News of the World.
Punch.
Queanbeyan Age and General Advertiser (New South Wales).

Queenslander (Brisbane).
Sunday Mirror.
Sydney Morning Herald.
The European Magazine and London Review, Volume 80, James Asperne (1821).
The Independent.
The Register (Adelaide).
The Singapore Free Press and Mercantile Advertiser.
The Spectator.
The Sun.
The Times.
USA Today.
Walsall Advertiser.
Wellington Independent (NZ).

On Line Resources

Stephen Cooper Blog 9 June 2015, *Did Henry V found the Royal Navy*; http://www.agincourt600.com/2015/06/09/did-henry-v-found-the-royal-navy/
Samuel Pepys' Diary; https://www.pepysdiary.com/
Encyclopaedia Britannica, 1911, Cambridge University Press.
Grant H, ed Tanner M, *My War at Sea*, Warletters.net (2014, originally 1924).
Queen Victoria's Journal, Royal Archives, on line
www.dday.center
www.fotw.info

Other

The Navy List, various dates.
Archaeologia Cantiana, Vol 6 (1866).
Guide to the Naval Review, June 1897.
D-Day 50th Anniversary Souvenir Brochure (Tri-Service Publications Ltd, 1994).
Trafalgar 200 Official Brochure, June 2005.
House of Commons Library Briefing paper no 07313, 9 July 2018.
House of Commons Library, Research Paper 99/112, 1999.
House of Commons Library, *Olympic Britain, Social and economic change since the 1908 and 1948 London Games*, 2012.
The Economic History Review, New Series vol 46, no 2, May 1993.

Index

Page numbers in *italic* indicate illustrations and/or their captions.

Index of Reviews and their Ports

1346 Review 8
1415 Review 8
1662 Review 32–3
1672 Review 35, 36
1691 Review 37–8
1693 Review 38
1698 Review 40
1773 Review 42–3, *43*
1778 Review 44–5
1789 Review 47–50
1794 Review 52–3
1814 Review 53–4, *55*
1842 Review 59–61
1844 Review 63–7
1845 June Review 68–70
1845 July Review 70–2
1853 Review *75*, 76–8
1854 Review 80–2
1856 Review 84–8
1865 Review 92–4
1867 Review 95–8
1873 Review 102–04
1878 Review 105–07
1887 Review 109–16
1889 Review 119–22
1891 Review 124–5
1896 Review 127–8
1897 Review 130–41
1902 Review 149–55
1905 Review 159–60
1907 Review 166–7
1909 first Review 169–72, *170, 173*
1909 second Review, for Tsar's visit 172–3
1911 Review 178–82, *178, 179, 181*
1912 first Review, Torbay 183, 184–5, *185*

1912 second Review, Spithead 183, 185–6, *186*
1914 Review 186–90, *188*
1922 Review 197–9
1924 Review 200–03
1935 Review 205–09
1936 Review 210–11
1937 Review 211, *212, 213–20, 213, 214–15, 218–19, 220*
1938 Review 222
1939 Review 223–4
1953 Review 229–38, *229, 230, 235, 236–7*
1957 Review 239
1965 Review 239, 240–1
1969 Spithead Review, NATO 242–3
1969 Torbay Review, new Colours 244–6, *245*
1977 Review 248–52, *250–1*
1993 Review 254, 255–6
1994 Review 257–9, *258*
2003 Review 261–2, *261*
2005 Review 263–9, *264–5*

Limerick 37–8
London 32–3

Plymouth 47–50
Portland 197–8, 210, 222–4
Portsmouth 8, 32, 59–60, 257–8

Southampton 8
Spithead 38, 40, 42, 44, 52, 54, 66, 68–72, 76–8, 80–2, 84–8, 92–3, 95–8, 102–04, 106–07, 110–16, 119–21, 124–5, 127–8, 130–41, 150–5, 159–60, 166–7, 169–73, 178–82, 185–90, 201–03, 205–09, 211, 213–20, *214–15, 218, 220,* 229–38,

236–7, 242–3, 248–52, *251,* 263–9, *265*

Torbay 183, 184–5, *185,* 244–6

Weymouth 210–11, 222

Index of Ships

Achilles, HMS 97
Aconit, FS 298
Active, HMS 255
Admiral Graf Spee 216, *216*
Admiral Makarov 173
Adriatic 172
Aegir 298
Africa, HMS 184
Agamemnon, HMS 74, 76, *173*
Agincourt, HMS 101, 102, 103, 109, 136, 240
Ajax, HMS 67, 109
Alamein, HMS 240
Albemarle, HMS *159*
Alberta, HMY 109, 110, 119, 124, 127, 137, 144, *144,* 159, 169, 171, 274, 275, 278
Albion, HMS 68, 69, 240
Alecto 67
Alexandra, HMS 135–6, *138,* 146
Alexandra, HMY 169, 171, 180, 189, 197, 275
Algonquin, HMCS 298
Almirante 202n
Almirante Barroso 296
Amerigo Vespucci 264, 296
Amphion, HMS 54
Amsterdam 39
Andromache 54
Anne *35*
Anson, HMS 124
Ant, HMS 160
Anzac, HMAS 266

Apollo, HMS 239–40
Aquilon 52
Arethusa, HMS 66n, 226
Argus, HMS 199, *199*
Ark Royal, HMS 218, 240, 249, 251, 252
Armadale Castle, RMS 160, 185
Assistance, HMS 192
Association 40
Athenia, SS 254
Auguste Victoria, SS 153
Aurora, HMS 124
Austerlitz 80
Australia, HMS 142
Avenger, HMS 258
Azuma 152

Baden, SMS 119, *119*
Balmoral, MV 255
Baltimore, USS 296
Barfleur, HMS 41
Barham, HMS 193, *195,* 197, 205, *219*
Barossa, HMS 240
Bartolomeu Dias 296
Battleaxe, HMS 233
Beagle, HMS 56
Beaver, HMS 298
Belfast, HMS 226
Belle Poule 54, 66
Berengaria, RMS 208–09, *208*
Berlin 177
Birmingham, HMS 250, 256, 298
Bismarck 198, 279
Biter, HMS 298
Black Eagle, HMS *59,* 62, 68, 70, *70,* 76, 81, 87
Black Prince, HMS 97, 101, 109, 136
Blake, HMS 242, 244, 249
Blenheim, HMS 127–8, *128*
Blonde, HMS 103–04, 128, *see also* Shah, HMS

Boscawen, HMS 82
Bremen, FGS 298
Brielle 37
Britannia, HMS 38, *39*
Britannia, HMY 23, 232,
    238, 239–40, 243, 244–5,
    245, 246, 250, 251–2,
    255, 257, *258*, 259–60,
    272, 275, 280
British Respect 249
Broadsword, HMS *233*
Brooklyn, USS 131–2, *132*,
    139, 295
Brunswick, HMS 51
Buffalo, HMS 153
Bulldog (paddle sloop) 77
Bulldog, HMS 255
Bustard, HMS 112n

Caiman 66
Cairo, HMS 211
California, USS 249, *250*
Calliope, HMS 152
Cambrian, HMS 142
Cameronia, SS 218
Campania 137, 140
Camperdown, HMS 124, 152
Canberra, SS 257, 258, 259
Canopus, HMS 68
Canterbury, HMNZS 298
Canterbury, HMS 41
Captain, HMS 100
Cardiff, HMS 223
Carnatic 49
Carthage 137, 153
Centurion, HMS 201
Cerberus 61
Charger, HMS 298
Charles de Gaulle, FS 264
Charlotte, SMS *116*, 117
Chatham, HMS 265, 268
Chiddingford, HMS 298
Childers, HMS 50
Churchill, HMS 249
Cleopatre, HMS 54
Cleveland 35
Cobra, HMS 138
Cog Thomas 26
Collingwood, HMS 113–14,
    142, 190, 289
Columbus, SS 209
Comet 66, 186
Comte d'Eu 91
Conqueror, HMS *193*
Coquette, HMS 166

Cornwall, HMS 255, 298
Corunna, HMS 239–40
Courageous, HMS 211, 218,
    220–1, 224, 231
Crescent, HMS 176
Cressy, HMS 82
Crocodile 110–11
Crossbow, HMS 233
Cumberland, HMS 49, 82,
    188, 266
Cyclops 61

Dainty, HMS *234*
Danaide, ITNS 298
Danton 179, 295
Danube 137
Daring, HMS 151
Defence, HMS 51
Defensora, BNS 298
Delaware, USS *179*, 295
Demir Hisar 296
Devastation, HMS 100–01,
    102, 109, 152
Devastator, USS 298
Diamond, HMS 239–40
Dolphin, HMS 251
Dongola, SS 181
Dragon, HMS 81
Drake, HMS *170*, 245
Drakensberg, SAS 298
Dreadnought, HMS 90–1,
    100, *163*, 164–6, 172,
    177, 181, 240–1, 249
Dryad, HMS 257
Du Chayla 85
Duchess, HMS 239–40
Duchess of Fife, SS 154
Duguay Trouin, FS 259
Duke of Wellington, HMS
    74, *74*, *75*, 76, 77, 80, 82,
    84, 92, 96
Duncan, HMS 246
Dunkerque 216, *217*, *219*

Eagle, HMS 38, 202, 229,
    233, 238, 244, 245, *246*
Eagle, USCGC 264
Eastbourne, HMS 244
Edinburgh, HMS 126, 259
Effingham, HMS 224
Elan, L' 65
Eldorado 137
Elephant, HMS 96, *see also*
    Minotaur, HMS
Elfin, HMY 77, 81, 110,

    124, 137, 274, 278
Emerald 60n, 67
Empress Queen 161
Enchantress, HMS 112, 124,
    137, 154, 159, 171, 180,
    188, 189, 201, 218
Endeavour 298
Endurance, HMS 265, *265*
Enterprise, HMS 265
Erin, HMS *193*, 194
Euryalus, HMS 82, 180
Excellent, HMS 60, 160,
    176, 257
Exmouth, HMS 156, 189,
    224

Fairy, HMY 71, 76, 77, 81,
    274, *280*
Farringford 232
Favourite 66
Fearless, HMS 249, 251
Ferret, HMS 151, *151*
Fife, HMS 251, *251*
Fire Queen (paddle yacht)
    81, 91, 137
Firebrand 70, *see also Black*
    Eagle, HMS
Firequeen, HMS 171, 180
Fleetwood, HMS 235
Flying Cloud 218
Formidable, HMS *59*
Freja 295
Fuji 295
Furious, HMS 192–3, *194*,
    218
Fury, HMS 211

Galetea, HMS 54
Gallatin, USS 298
Gefion 77
George Washington, USS 257
Georgios Averof 179, *180*,
    295
Glamorgan, HMS 251, *251*
Glasgow, HMS 67, 229,
    238–9
Glatton, HMS 84
Glorie, La 90
Glorious, HMS 218, 231
Gloucester, HMS 182
Goeben 276n
Gomer 64, 66, *66*
Gorgon 77
Gota Lejon 296

Gothic, SS 238
Grafton, HMS 266
Grand Turk 266, 267
Gremyashchy 298
Guardian, HMS 211

Hamburg 156
Hampshire, HMS 244
Harlequin, RFA 172, 185,
    201
Havock, HMS 151
Hecate, HMS 244
Hecla, HMS 124, 258
Hector, HMS 101
Helmsdale, HMS 235
Henry, HMS 31
Hercules, HMS 101, 106,
    186
Hermes, HMS 202, *202*,
    249, 251
Hero, HMS *111*
Hibernia, HMS 71, 184,
    184, 190
Himalaya, HMS 83–4, *83*,
    87
Hohenzollern I, SMY 119
Hohenzollern II, SMY 142,
    142, 143, 278
Holger Danske 296
Holigost 28–9
Hood, HMS 197–8, *198*,
    205, 216
Horten 298
Howe, HMS 119, 120–1,
    121, 124, 142
Humber 40
Humber, HMS 298

Illinois, USS 187
Illustrious, HMS 229, 257,
    258, 266
Immortalité, HMS 124
Imperator 208n, *see also*
    Berengaria, RMS
Implacable, HMS 229
Impregnable, HMS 48, 50,
    53, *55*
Indefatigable, HMS 229–30
India, SS 153
Indomitable, HMS *170*, 171,
    177, 229–30
Inflexible (French warship)
    66
Inflexible, HMS 113, 115,
    120, 135–6, 171, 177

Insolent, HMS 160

Invincible, HMS 171, 177,
  264–5, *264*, 267

Irene, THV 137, 171, 180

Iris, MV 255

Iron Duke, HMS 187, *188*,
  207, 216, 223, 224, 229

Jauréguiberry 157

Jeremiah O'Brien 257

Jumna 110–11

Juno, HMS 142, *152*, 153

Katherine 34

Kelvin, HMS 226n

Kent, HMS 241, 251

Keppel, HMS 246

King Edward, TS 138

King George V, HMS *193*,
  194

Kingfisher, HMS *108*

Kite, HMS 112–13

Koh-i-Noor 131

König Wilhelm SMS 132,
  295

Kurama 295

Lancashire Witch 112

Lancastria, RMS 209

Laurentic, SS 218

Leander, HMS *206*, 211

Leander, MY 266

Leopard, *HMS* 81

Leyden 37

Liberty, HMS *108*

Lieutenant Troupakis 249

Lightning 63

Lightning, HMS 106–07,
  106

Lion, HMS 189, 194, 231

Liverpool, HMS 256, 298

London, HMS 76, 88, 148,
  212, 213

Lord Nelson, HMS 187, *189*

Lowestoft, HMS 48

Luitenant Ter Zee Victor Billet
  296

Lusitania, RMS 171, 186

Lyness, RFA 250–1

Lynx 48

M-1, HMS 202

Magicienne, HMS 54, 77

Magnificent, HMCS 229

Magnificent, HMS 47

Maha Chakrkri 130, 295

Maidstone, HMS 241

Maine, RFA 209

Majestic, HMS 126–7, 138

Malabar 110–11, *112*

Malaya, HMS 193

Manxman, HMS *237*

Marceau 123

Marceaux 124

Marlborough, HMS 51

Mars, HMS *137*

Martin, HMS *108*

Mary 37, 39

Masséna 157, *158*

Mastodon, HMS 225

Mauretania, RMS 186

Melampus, HMS 176

Melbourne 249

Merassie 61

Mermaid, THV 255

Meteor, HMS 84,

Meteor, 190

Middleton, HMS 298

Miguel de Cervantes 296

Minerva, HMS 142

Minotaur, HMS 96–7, *96*,
  102, 136

Missouri, USS 187

ML-293 257–8

Monarch, HMS 82, 100,
  101, *193*, 194

Monarch, SS 64

Monck 37

Montagne 50

Montcalm 268, 296

Montreal, HMCS 266

Moosbrugger, USS 298

Moreno 216–17, *217*

MTB-102 266

Myrtle, HMS 224

Narvik 296

Narwhal, HMS 211

Nautilus (Nordenfelt
  submarine) 113

Nautilus, USS 240

Navarinon 296

Nearchos, HNS 298

Nelson. HMS 205–06, 213,
  213–15, 216, 225, 229

Neptune, HMS 82, 209, 211

Newcastle, HMS 213

Niels Juel, HDMS 298

Nile, HMS 124, *125*

Nimble, RFA 201

Nimitz, USS *250*

Nord 65

Norfolk, HMS 261–2, *261*

Northampton, HMS 136

Northumberland, HMS 101,
  289

Nubia, SS 153

Ocean, HMS 240, 261

Olfert Fischer 295

Ophir, RMS 152–3, *153*

Oracle, HMS 298

Orion, HMS *193*, 194, 211

Orontes, HMS *110*

Osborne (previously *V&A I*)
  87, 92, 96, 274, *274*, 278,
  279

Osborne II, HMY *107*, 110,
  119, 137, 159, *273*,
  274–5

Osprey, HMS 211

Otway, HMS 224

Pallas, HMS 124

Panther SMS 177

Patricia, THV 201, 234, 244,
  250, 258, 265

Pegasus, HMS 218

Perseus, HMS 229, 230–1

Perseverance, HMS 87

Philomel, SS 131

Phoebe, RFA 244

Pilot, HMS *108*

Poolster 298

Portsdown, SS 218

Posamton 296

Pothuau 132, *132*, 295

Powerful, HMS 133, *133*

President, HMS 252

Prince George, HMS 45

Prince of Wales, HMS 52

Prince Regent, HMS 76, 82

Princess Alice 61, 71

Princess Augusta 41, 44

Princess Augusta, HMY 273

Princess Margaret 201

Princess Margaret, HMS
  199

Principe De Asturias 268

Pucher, HMS 298

Queen, HMS 51, *59*, 60, 67,
  68, 71, 76

Queen Charlotte, HMS 51,
  51, 52

Queen Elizabeth, HMS
  (aircraft carrier) 270

Queen Elizabeth, HMS
  (battleship) 193, *193*,
  195, *195*, 197, 201, *201*,
  202, 205, 216

Queen Elizabeth II (QE2)
  258, 259

Quorn, HMS 298

Ramillies, HMS 205, *219*,
  223, 224, 225, 229

Ranger, HMS 289

Rapide 104

Rattler 67

Reclaim, HMS 249

Redpole, HMS 232, 234

Regent 30

Reine Hortense 91, 92, 95

Renown, HMS 131, *134*,
  137, 205, 249

Repulse, HMS 197–8, 213,
  213, 249

Resadiye 194, *see also* Erin,
  HMS

Resolution, HMS 205, 249

Resource, RFA 244

Revenge, HMS 194, 205,
  223, 224, 229, 249

Rewa, SS 181

Ripon 96, 98

Roberts, HMS 225

Rodney, HMS 68, 71, 88,
  124, 205–06, 216, *218*,
  225, 229, 279

Romney 39

Ronald Reagan, USS 23

Roslin Castle, SS 201

Rossia 295

Rossiya 295

Royal Alfred, HMS 90

Royal Caroline II, HMY
  273

Royal Charles 34

Royal Charlotte, HMY 273

Royal Frederick, HMS 60

Royal George, HMS 82, 84,
  85

Royal George, HMY 51, 72,
  273–4

Royal Oak, HMS 194, 211

Royal Sovereign, HMS 91,
  94, 97, 100, 150–1, *150*,
  194, 205, 209, 211

Royal Sovereign, HMY 273

Royal Transport 39–40
Royal William 40
Rurik 173

S174 298
St Patrick, SS 235, *235*
St Vincent, HMS 60, 68, 69, 96
Saipan, USS 264, *265*
Salisbury, HMS 241
Sans Pareil, HMS 142–3
Sapphire, HMS 156
Saudadoes 34
Schleswig-Holstein, SMS 224
Scorpion, HMS 233
Scott, HMS 265, 266
Scout, USS 255, 298
Scylla, HMS 225
Seaflower, HMS *108*
Seahorse, HMS 172
Sealark, HMS *108*
Serapis 110–11
Shah, HMS *103*, 104
Shannon, HMS *170*
Sheffield, HMS 222
Sir Bedivere, RFA 265–6
Sir Geraint, RFA 250–1
Sir Tristram, RFA 250–1
Smiter, HMS 289
Soleil Royal 38
Solferino 91, 92, *92*
Southampton HMS 47, 48–9, *48*
Southampton, HMS 213
Sovereign 30
Sprightly 78
St George, HMS 142
Standart 173
Starling, HMS 235
Stena Cambria, MV 255
Strathmore, SS 218
Stromboli 76–7
Sultan, HMS 98, 101, 103
Superb, HMS 68, 240, 249
Surcouf 125
Surprise, HMS *231*, 232, 234, 235
Sverdlov 233–4, 296
Swift, HMS 180–1
Sybil Mullen Glover 262
Syria 96, 98
Tagus 71
Takasago *148*, 152
Tanjore 96
Temeraire, HMS *173*, 231

Terpsichore, HMS 54
Terrible, HMS 67, 133, *136*, 149
Teutonic, RMS 120, *120*
Theseus, HMS 229, 232–3
Thrush, HMS 176
Thunder, HMS 84
Thunderer, HMS 100, 114, *193*, 194
Tiger, HMS 194, 249, 251, see also *Blake*, HMS
Tone 295
Trafalgar, HMS 60n, 67, 68, 69, 142
Transit, HMS 87
Trinity Royal 28–9
Tromp 296
Trondheim, HNoMS 298
Trujillo 296
Trusty HMS 84
Turbinia 137–8, *139*

Valiant, HMS 193, 205, 244, 249
Valorous, HMS 81
Vandyck, SS 218
Vanguard, HMS 68, 229, *230*, 231, 235, 239
Vengeur 51
Vernon, HMS 106, 251
Vesuvius, HMS 106
Victoria, HMS 152
Victoria, SS 110
Victoria and Albert I, HMY 22, 64, 66, 68, 70, 71, 72, 76, 77, 83, 274, see also *Osborne* (previously V&A I)
Victoria and Albert II, HMY 22, 86–8, *86*, 97–8, *98*, *101*, 102, *102*, 103, 106, 110, 111, *111*, 124, 128, 137, 144, 274, *277*, 278
Victoria and Albert III, HMY 22, 137n, 149, 150, 154–5, 158–9, 169, 171, 172, 173, 180, 181, *181*, 184–5, 189, 197, 201, 207, 208, 211, 219, 222, 231, *272*, 275, 276, 279
Victory, HMS 40, 60n, 61, 64, 67, 68, 92, 96, 143, 165, 180, 265, 268, 269
Vigilant 100, 101
Ville de Paris, HMS 54

Viper, HMS 138
Vivid, HMS 77, 87
Vizcaya 295
Volta 224
Von der Tann SMS 295
Vulture 77

Wakeful, HMS 243
Warrior, HMS 90, 97, 106
Warspite, HMS 225
Warwick, HMS 223
Wasp, USS *243*
Westdiep, BMS 298
Whippingham, SS 218
Wien 295
Wildfire, HMS 150
William and Mary III, HMY 273
Windsor Castle, HMY 87, see also *Victoria and Albert II*, HMY
Witte de With, HNLMS 298

Yorke 39

Zinnia 243

Index of Royal Persons, Admirals and Politicians

Abdülaziz, Sultan of Turkey 94–6, 97–8, *98*
Aberdeen, George Hamilton-Gordon, 4th Earl of 63, 75, 80, 84, 111
Albert, Prince Consort 17–18, 59–60, 62, 63, 64, 65, 68, 71, 82, 85, 89
Albert Edward, Prince of Wales see Edward VII (and Prince of Wales)
Albert Frederick Arthur George, Prince see George VI (and Prince Albert)
Albert Victor, Duke of Clarence and Avondale, Prince 'Eddy' 176
Albert William Henry of Prussia 132, 189–90
Alexander I of Russia 53–4
Alexandra of Denmark 105, 106, 110, 111, 149, 150, 155, 166, 275, 276

Alexis of Russia 174
Alfonso XIII of Spain 169
Alfred, Duke of Saxe-Coburg and Gotha, and Duke of Edinburgh 19, 63, 101, 109
Alfred 'the Great' 16
Alice, Duchess of Gloucester, Princess 266, 267
Amery, Leo 196, 199
Andrew, Duke of York, Prince 19, 260, 265–7
Anjou, Francis, Duke of 30
Anne, Princess Royal 241, 243, 244, 257, 266
Anne, Queen 40
Anson, George 42, 44
Argyll, George Campbell, 8th Duke of 79
Arthur, Duke of Connaught and Strathearn, Prince 97, *98*, 105, 143, 169
Arthur, Prince Arthur of Connaught 169
Asquith, Herbert Henry 167, 173, 177, 178, 185
Atlee, Clement 283

Backhouse, Sir Roger Roland Charles 213, 223
Baldwin, Stanley 211, 283, 285
Balfour, Arthur James 143, 184
Band, Sir Jonathon 261
Bayly, Lewis 36, 188
Beatrice, Princess 97, *98*, 105, 128
Beatty, David 152
Bedford, John of Lancaster, 1st Duke of 29
Beresford, Lady Charles, née Ellen Jeromina Gardner 111–12
Beresford, Lord Charles 111–13, 117, 135–6, 147, 162–5, *162*, 167
Berkeley, Maurice Frederick FitzHardinge, 1st Baron FitzHardinge 76
Bickerton, Sir Richard 48, 54

Bismarck, Otto von 63, 118, 122

Bowles, William 66

Boyce, Michael C 255, 259

Bridgeman, Sir Francis 121, 166, 179

Buller, Sir Alexander 277

Buller, Henry Tritton 276–7

Buller, Hermione Moray Stuart 277

Bülow, Bernhard von 143

Bush, Sir John Fitzroy Duyland 244

Caillard, Leonce Albert 156–7, 159, 160

Callaghan, Sir George 186

Camilla, Duchess of Cornwall 265

Campbell-Bannerman, Henry 166

Caroline of Brunswick 55–6

Catherine of Braganza 31–3

Cecil, Robert Arthur Talbot Gascoyne see Salisbury, Robert Arthur Talbot Gascoyne-Cecil, 3rd Marquess of

Chamberlain, Joseph 129, 130, 282

Chamberlain, Neville 205, 222, 223, 231, 285

Charles I 17

Charles II 8, 17, 19, 20, 22, 31–4, 36, 272, 287

Charles IV of France 24

Charles VI 27

Charles, Prince of Wales 19, 241, 244, 260, 261, 265

Charlotte of Mecklenburg-Strelitz, Queen Consort 45, 49, 52

Charlotte of Wales, Princess 56, 70

Chasseloup-Laubat, Justin Napoleon Samuel Prosper de, 4th Marquis of Chasseloup-Laubat 91, 92, 93

Chatfield, Sir Ernle 210

Chatham, John Pitt, 2nd Earl of 47, 49, 52

Chesterfield, Philip Stanhope, 5th Earl of 47

Chulalongkorn, Somdetch Phra Paramindr Maha of Siam 130

Churchill, Winston 168, 178, 183, 184, 188, 189, 190, 191, 194, 203, 204, 225, 226, 234, 277, 283

Clinton, Bill 257

Cochrane, Sir Thomas 76, 81

Cockburn, Sir George 66

Codrington, Edward 67

Colville, Stanley 174

Commerell, Sir John Edmund 120–1

Cooper, Duff 223

Corry, Armar Lowry 76, 82

Cowan, Sir Walter 148, 197, 218

Cradock, Christopher 'Kit' 121, 278–9

Creasy, Sir George E 229

Culme-Seymour, Sir Michael 124

Cunningham, Andrew Browne 208, 218, 226

Curzon, George, 1st Marquess Curzon of Kedleston 99–100, 282

Daladier, Édouard 223

Dalton, Hugh 228

Darlan, Jean Louis Xavier François 224

Dawes, Charles G 200

Derby, Edward Smith-Stanley, 14th Earl of 95

Derby, Edward Stanley, 15th Earl of 105

Diana, Princess 260

Disraeli, Benjamin 12, 104, 105

Domvile, Compton 121

Dorset, Thomas Beaufort, Earl of 28

Drake, Sir Francis 12, 14, 262

Dupetit-Thouars, Abel Aubert du 63

Eccles, Sir John Arthur Symons 240

Edelstan, Sir John Hereward 234

Edgar, King 16

Edinburgh, Duke of see Philip, Duke of Edinburgh, Prince

Edward III 8, 18, 21, 24–7, 29, 95n

Edward VII (and Prince of Wales) 8, 19, 95, 97, 98, 98, 99, 101, 105, 106, 108, 110, 111, 118–20, 137, 139, 144, 147–50, 154–6, 158–60, 165, 166, 167, 169, 172–3, 178, 275, 276, 279, 280

Edward VIII 174, 207, 210–11

Eisenhower, Dwight D 225, 226

Elizabeth I 17, 30

Elizabeth II 23, 219, 229, 232, 234–5, 238–9, 240, 241, 242, 243, 244–6, 248, 250–2, 257, 259–60, 261–2, 264, 265–7, 268, 275

Elizabeth Angela Marguerite Bowes-Lyon, Queen and Queen Mother 180, 182, 219, 221–2, 234, 257

Ernst Leopold, 4th Prince of Leiningen 275

Ewart, Charles Joseph Frederick 69n

Eyres-Monsell, Bolton 209

Fanshawe, Sir Arthur 171

Fell, Michael F 242

Field, Sir Frederick 204

Fieldhouse, John D E 249

Fisher, Sir John Arbuthnot 'Jackie' 19, 47, 90–1, 102–03, 106, 152, 161–4, 162, 167, 171, 174, 176–7, 183, 193–4, 198, 287

Fisher, Joschka 285

Fitzclarence, Adolphus 68, 87n

Fitzroy, Edward Algernon 205

Franz Ferdinand, Archduke 186

Frederick, Duke of York and Albany 56

Frederick, Prince of Wales 17

Frederick Augustus II of Saxony 61

Frederick William III of Prussia 53–4

Fremantle, Sir Edmund 161

Fremantle, Sir Sydney 201

Frewen, Sir John 241, 243

Friedrich of Prussia, Empress (Victoria Adelaide) 137

Frobisher, Sir Martin 12

Fullerton, Sir John Reginald Thomas 275–6

Gage, Sir William Hall 68

Geddes, Eric 196

George I 41, 272

George II 41, 42, 273

George III 41–3, 44–5, 47–50, 52–3, 273

George IV 53–6, 289

George V (and Prince of Wales) 8, 19, 21, 121, 149–50, 153, 166, 171, 176–8, 181–4, 186, 188–90, 192, 197–201, 205, 207–09, 260–1, 275, 279–80

George VI (and Prince Albert) 19, 22, 174, 184, 211, 213, 219, 220, 221–2, 224, 225–6, 229, 231, 275, 277

George, Duke of Cambridge, Prince 70–1, 95, 97, 98, 102

George, Duke of Kent, Prince 19, 207, 219, 222

Gervais, Alfred Albert 122

Giffard, Hardinge, 1st Earl of Halsbury 160

Gladstone, William Ewart 98, 99

Glyndŵr, Owain 27

Goodenough, William Edmund 278

Göring, Hermann 212

Goschen, George 127

Graham, Sir James 82

Granville, George Leveson-Gower, 2nd Earl 101

Graves, Sir Thomas 46
Gravière, Edmond Jurien
  de la 85, 86, 88
Grenville, Sir Richard 262
Greville, Daisy, Countess of
  Warwick 167
Grey, Sir Edward 173
Guizot, François Pierre
  Guillaume 64

Haddington, Thomas
  Hamilton, 9th Earl of
  59, 68, 69, 72
Halsbury, Hardinge Giffard,
  1st Earl of 160
Hamilton, Lord George
  Francis 111, 118
Hamilton, Thomas *see*
  Haddington, Thomas
  Hamilton, 9th Earl of
Hankey, Sir Maurice 209
Harald V of Norway 255,
  289
Hardwick, Charles Philip
  Yorke, Earl of 62
Harwood, Henry 230
Havel, Václav 257
Hawke, Edward 14, 41, 262
Healey, Denis 240, 241, 285
Heath, Edward 251
Hebeler, Chevalier 63
Heneage, Algernon Charles
  Fieschi 'Pompo' 146
Henrik of Denmark, Prince
  289
Henry, Prince Albert
  William Henry of
  Prussia 132, 189–90
Henry of Battenberg,
  Prince 128, 278–9
Henry V 8, 18, 21, 27–9
Henry VII 18
Henry VIII 18, 29–30
Henry of Prussia, Prince
  119
Herbert, Arnold 172
Herbert, Arthur 36, 37
Hewett, Sir William Nathan
  Wrighte 113
Hitler, Adolf 204, 205, 212,
  221–3, 283
Hoare, Sir Samuel 210, 282
Hood, Horace 12, 198
Hornby, Sir Geoffrey
  Thomas Phipps 100,

102–05, 111, 117
Horton, Max 36, 223
Hotham, Sir Charles
  Frederick 150–1, 154
Howe, Richard, Ist Earl
  51–3, *51*, 262
Hughes, Billy 282

Ingram, Adam 263
Isabella of France 24
Ismail Pasha 95, 96

James I 17
James II (and Duke of York)
  8, 18, 31, 33, 36, 272
Jellicoe, Sir John 47, 82–3,
  121, 167, 179, 186, 284
Jervis, John 12
Joinville, François
  d'Orléans, prince de 63
Juan Carlos 289

Keating, Paul 257
Kennedy-Purvis, Charles
  213
Keppel, Augustus 44, 45–6
Keppel, Colin Richard 276
Keppel, Sir Henry 276
Kerr, Lord Walter Talbot
  127, 131, 150
Key, Sir Astley Cooper
  105–06
Keyes, Roger 223
King, W L Mackenzie 218
Kitchener, Herbert 148,
  150
Kohl, Helmut 257
Kováč, Michal 257

La Suisse, Baron 66
Lambton, Hedworth
  133–5, 276
Laurence, Timothy 266
Law, Andrew Bonar 196
Leach, Sir Henry 248,
  249–50, 252
Lee, Arthur 161
Lennox, Charles, 3rd Duke
  of Richmond 48
Leopold I of Belgium 70
Leopold, Duke of Albany,
  Prince 97, *98*
Leveson-Gower, Granville
  George, 2nd Earl
  Granville 101

Lewin, Sir Terence 249
Li Hung Chang/Li
  Hongzhang 126–7, 128
Liverpool, Robert Banks
  Jenkinson, 2nd Earl of 54
Lloyd George, David 167,
  168, 173, 177–8, 197,
  283
Louis of Battenberg, Prince
  182, 190
Louis XIV 38
Louis XV 14
Louis XVI 50
Louis of Hesse, Prince 97,
  98
Louis Philippe I 63–5, 73
Louise-Marie, Louise of
  Orléans 70
Louise Margaret of Prussia,
  Duchess of Connaught
  169
Lowry-Corry, Henry
  Thomas 66
Lowther, James William 160
Luce, J David 240
Lytton, Robert Bulwer-
  Lytton, 1st Earl of 104

MacDonald, Ramsay 200,
  203, 205, 218, 285
Madden, Sir Charles 195,
  197, 204
Major, John 256
Margaret, Princess 219,
  234, 257
Maria Amalia, Queen 65
Maria Nikolayevna,
  Princess 76
Marina, Duchess of Kent,
  Princess 219
Mary of Modena, Queen
  of England 36, 37
Mary of Teck 153, 169,
  177, 279
Mason, Roy 247–8
Massey, William 199
May, Sir William Henry
  106, 172
Mayhew, Christopher 240
McClintock, Leopold 100
McKenna, Reginald 168,
  172, 173, 178, 183
Meade-Fetherstonhaugh,
  Sir Herbert 277
Mennes, Sir John 31

Metternich, Prince
  Klemens von 53
Meux, Hedworth 133–5,
  276
Meux, Sir Henry Bruce,
  3rd Baronet 134, 276
Meux, Valerie, Lady 133–4
Michael of Kent, Prince
  267, 289
Michael of Kent, Princess
  267
Milne, Sir Alexander 109
Milne, Sir Archibald
  Berkley 276
Mitchell, Sir David 39
Mitterrand, François 257
Montagu, Edward, 1st Earl
  of Sandwich 31
Montagu, John, 4th Earl of
  Sandwich 42, 44, 46
Montague, Sir Charles 39
Moore, Arthur William 179
Moray, Morton Gray
  Stuart, Earl of 277
Mountbatten, Louis, 1st
  Earl Mountbatten of
  Burma 229, 238, 239,
  241, 275
Mozaffar ad-Din Shah
  Qajar, Shah of Persia
  279–80
Mulley, Fred 250
Mussolini, Benito 205, 221

Nakhimov, Pavel 78
Napier, Sir Charles ('Black
  Charlie') 79, 80–3, 84
Napoleon III 73, 75, 78, 91
Naser al-Din Shah Qajar,
  Shah of Persia 99–104
Nelson, Horatio 12, 18, 53,
  161, 262, 269
Nicholas I of Russia 61–3,
  75, 78
Nicholas II of Russia 127,
  172–3
North, Lord 44
North, Sir Dudley Burton
  Napier 277

Olga Nikolayevna, Princess
  76
Owen, David 241–2
Owen, Sir Edward William
  Campbell Rich 60, 68

Page, Walter 187
Palliser, Sir Hugh 45–6
Palmerston, Henry John
    Temple, 3rd Viscount 66,
    86, 91, 122
Parker, Sir Hyde 65, 68, 69
Patricia of Connaught,
    Princess 169
Peel, Sir Robert 59, 72,
    273–4
Peel, William 62
Peter the Great 38–40
Petty-Fitzmaurice, Henry,
    5th Marquess of
    Lansdowne 99
Philip VI of France 24
Philip, Duke of Edinburgh,
    Prince 19, 233, 234, 239,
    243, 244, 251–2, 255,
    257, 265, 267, 275, 289
Philippe, Count of Paris,
    Prince 73
Pitt, John, 2nd Earl of
    Chatham 47, 49, 52
Pitt, William the Younger
    47
Pound, Sir Dudley 213–16,
    224

Raleigh, Sir Walter 12, 13,
    14, 252, 262
Ramsey, Bertram 225, 226
Reed, Edward James 109
Reid, John 265
Robathan, Andrew 264
Robeck, Sir John de 201
Roberts, John O 251
Robertson, Edmund 167
Rodman, Hugh 217

Rodney, George Brydges
    12, 14, 46, 262
Rooke, Sir George 38
Rowley, Sir Charles 61, 65,
    68
Rupert of the Rhine,
    Prince 33
Russell, Sir Edward 38

Salisbury, Robert Arthur
    Talbot Gascoyne-Cecil,
    3rd Marquess of 109n,
    117–19, 127
Salmon, Sir Nowell 130–1
Sandwich, Edward
    Montagu, 1st Earl of 31
Sandwich, John Montagu,
    4th Earl of 42, 44, 46
Sandys, Duncan 239
Saxe-Coburg and Gotha,
    Prince Albert of see
    Albert, Prince Consort
Saxe-Coburg and Gotha,
    Alfred, Duke of 63
Saxe-Coburg and Gotha,
    Prince August of 59
Saxe-Coburg and Gotha,
    Ernest I, Duke of 59
Saxe-Coburg and Gotha,
    Prince Leopold of 59
Scott, Percy 19n, 146, 149,
    165
Selborne, William
    Waldegrave Palmer, 2nd
    Earl of 164, 284
Seymour, Edward, 12th
    Duke of Somerset 92
Seymour, Sir George 84,
    88

Sheffield, Sir Berkeley 167
Simmons, Sir Lintorn 104
Smith-Stanley, Edward
    George Geoffrey 95
Sophia, Princess 63
Stanhope, James, 7th Earl
    224
Stanhope, Philip, 5th Earl
    of Chesterfield 47
Stanley, Edward Henry,
    15th Earl of Derby 105
Stanley, Victor Albert 201
Stuart, Morton Gray, Earl
    of Moray 277

Tirpitz, Alfred von 164
Truman, Harry S 228
Trump, Donald 285–6
Tryon, George 152

Van Stabel, Pierre Jean 50
Vernon, Edward ('Old
    Grog') 17, 41
Vian, Philip 225
Victoria, Queen 8, 12,
    17–18, 20, 58–60, 62,
    64–72, 76–8, 81–83,
    85–9, 94–8, 98, 99, 102,
    105–111, 113, 115–19,
    122–4, 126–30, 136,
    143–4, 273–4, 276, 278,
    279
Victoria Adelaide, Empress
    Friedrich of Prussia 137
Victoria Eugenie of
    Battenberg, Queen of
    Spain 169
Villaret-Joyeuse, Louis
    Thomas 50

Villaumez, Bouet 91

Wałęsa, Lech 257
Washington, George 46
Wellington, Arthur
    Wellesley, 1st Duke of
    59, 63
West, Sir Alan 263, 265,
    268, 271
White, Sir Hugo Moresby
    257
Wilhelm, Crown Prince of
    Prussia 63
Wilhelm II 109, 116–17,
    118–20, 122, 141–2,
    156, 182, 278
William III (William of
    Orange) 16, 36–8, 39
William IV (and Duke of
    Clarence) 18, 19, 53, 56,
    108, 289
Williams, Sir David 250
Wilson, Sir Arthur Knyvet
    156, 178
Wilson, Harold 241, 285
Wilson, Stanley 172
Wilson, Thomas Woodrow
    284
Wolseley, Sir Garnet 104
Woodcock, Sir Jonathon
    289
Wyndham, George 168n

Yorke, Charles Philip, Earl
    of Hardwick 62

Zambellas, Sir George 289

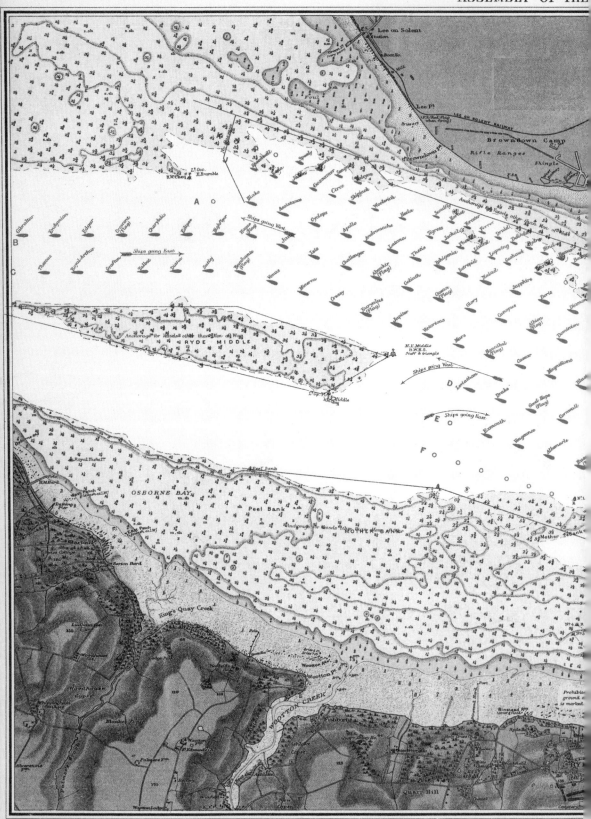

Cables 10   5   0

London. Published at the Admiralty, 6th July 1914,
Sold by J.D.Potter,